Kabbalah and Literature

Comparative Jewish Literatures

Bloomsbury's **Comparative Jewish Literatures** series creates a new venue for scholarship and debate both in Jewish Studies and Comparative Literature as it showcases the diversity of a nascent field with unique interdisciplinary footprints. It offers both a new way of looking at Jewish writing as well as insights into how Jewish literature is looked at by scholars indifferent to or sympathetic with these texts. Through its focus on the diversity of these groups' perspectives, the series suggests that disciplinary location informs how comparative Jewish literatures are understood theoretically, and it establishes new sectors that abut and intersect with the field in the twenty-first century.

Series Editor
Kitty Millet, San Francisco State University, USA

Advisory Board
Sarah Phillips Casteel, Carleton University, Canada
Bryan Cheyette, University of Reading, UK
Wlad Godzich, University of California Santa Cruz, USA
Nan Goodman, University of Colorado at Boulder, USA
Vivian Liska, University of Antwerp, Belgium
Orly Lubin, Tel Aviv University, Israel
Susan McReynolds, Northwestern University, USA
Paul Mendes-Flohr, University of Chicago, USA
Anna Parkinson, Northwestern University, USA
Na'ama Rokem, University of Chicago, USA
Maurice Samuels, Yale University, USA
Axel Stähler, University of Bern, Switzerland
Ilan Stavans, Amherst College, USA

Volumes in the Series:
Jewish Imaginaries of the Spanish Civil War: In Search of Poetic Justice, edited by Cynthia Gabbay
Derrida's Marrano Passover: Exile, Survival, Betrayal, and the Metaphysics of Non-Identity, by Agata Bielik-Robson
Holocaust Literature and Representation: Their Lives, Our Words, edited by Phyllis Lassner and Judith Tydor Baumel-Schwartz
Poesis in Extremis: Literature Witnessing the Holocaust, by Daniel Feldman and Efraim Sicher
Kabbalah and Literature, by Kitty Millet

Kabbalah and Literature

Kitty Millet

BLOOMSBURY ACADEMIC
NEW YORK • LONDON • OXFORD • NEW DELHI • SYDNEY

BLOOMSBURY ACADEMIC
Bloomsbury Publishing Inc, 1359 Broadway, New York, NY 10018, USA
Bloomsbury Publishing Plc, 50 Bedford Square, London, WC1B 3DP, UK
Bloomsbury Publishing Ireland, 29 Earlsfort Terrace, Dublin 2, D02 AY28, Ireland

BLOOMSBURY, BLOOMSBURY ACADEMIC and the Diana logo are
trademarks of Bloomsbury Publishing Plc

First published in the United States of America 2024
Paperback published in year 2025

Copyright © Kitty Millet, 2024

For legal purposes the Acknowledgments on p. vi constitute
an extension of this copyright page.

Series design: Eleanor Rose
Cover image: "Lost Communities" (2007)
by Romy Achituv at the Ghetto Fighters' Museum in Israel

All rights reserved. No part of this publication may be: i) reproduced or transmitted in any form, electronic or mechanical, including photocopying, recording or by means of any information storage or retrieval system without prior permission in writing from the publishers; or ii) used or reproduced in any way for the training, development or operation of artificial intelligence (AI) technologies, including generative AI technologies. The rights holders expressly reserve this publication from the text and data mining exception as per Article 4(3) of the Digital Single Market Directive (EU) 2019/790.

Bloomsbury Publishing Inc does not have any control over, or responsibility for, any third-party websites referred to or in this book. All internet addresses given in this book were correct at the time of going to press. The author and publisher regret any inconvenience caused if addresses have changed or sites have ceased to exist, but can accept no responsibility for any such changes.

Library of Congress Cataloging-in-Publication Data
Names: Millet, Kitty, author.
Title: Kabbalah and literature / Kitty Millet.
Description: New York : Bloomsbury Academic, 2024. |
Series: Comparative Jewish literatures | Includes bibliographical references and index. |
Summary: "Focuses on a range of Jewish and non-Jewish writers in Europe
and the Americas to examine the intersection of Kabbalah, the Jewish
mystical tradition, and secular Jewish literatures"– Provided by publisher.
Identifiers: LCCN 2023030914 (print) | LCCN 2023030915 (ebook) |
ISBN 9781501359682 (hardback) | ISBN 9781501379611 (paperback) |
ISBN 9781501359699 (epub) | ISBN 9781501359705 (pdf) | ISBN 9781501359712
Subjects: LCSH: Cabala in literature.
Classification: LCC PN56.C313 M55 2024 (print) |
LCC PN56.C313 (ebook) | DDC 296.1/6–dc23/eng/20230926
LC record available at https://lccn.loc.gov/2023030914
LC ebook record available at https://lccn.loc.gov/2023030915

ISBN: HB: 978-1-5013-5968-2
PB: 978-1-5013-7961-1
ePDF: 978-1-5013-5970-5
eBook: 978-1-5013-5969-9

Series: Comparative Jewish Literatures

Typeset by Integra Software Services Pvt. Ltd.

For product safety related questions contact productsafety@bloomsbury.com.

To find out more about our authors and books visit www.bloomsbury.com
and sign up for our newsletters.

Contents

Acknowledgments	vi
Introduction: Preliminary Remarks	1
Kabbalah in Fiction	3
Literature, Mimesis, Fictional Genealogies	6
Scholem's "Metaphysics" of Kabbalah and Literature	10
Parsing the Kabbalah in Modern Fiction	14

Part 1 The Other's Path and the Redemption of Aher

1	Jacob Frank, "Heretic of Kabbalah"	25
2	Heretics and Heresies of Innovation	39
3	Heinrich Heine, Poet/Prophet of the "Innovated Text"	53
4	Kafka, Prophet of Failure	71
5	Being and Nothingness: The Matter of Golems	91

Part 2 Letter Phenomenologies of Modernist Kabbalahs

6	Golems of Text and Bruno Schulz's "Interminable *Aggadot*"	113
7	The "Absolute Object" in Argentino's Basement	129
8	Lost Letters	141
9	"There Must Be Other Songs beyond Mankind"	151

Conclusion: Literature's Messianic Moments	167
Notes	176
Bibliography	239
Index	252

Acknowledgments

This book was written with the assistance of my college's Marcus Transformative Research Award. As its inaugural recipient, the award provided necessary support for the project. I am grateful to my former dean, Andrew T. Harris, whose promotion of faculty research fostered an environment that elicited the Marcuses' support. I also thank AVP Carleen Mandolfo, an unexpected interlocutor always willing to discuss "the book." I thank my colleagues on the College of Liberal and Creative Arts Professional Development Committee who recognized the project's merits and nominated me for the award.

I extend my sincere thanks to Isabel Gil, rector of the Universidade Catholica Portuguese. Her generous invitations to speak in Lisbon enabled me to test its claims with a global cohort of scholars. I also want to thank WIPHA collective for their encouragement. Their belief in the project's merits motivated me, especially when the pandemic's challenges threatened its completion. I am especially grateful to Agata Bielik-Robson and her insights on Derrida and Polish Frankism, Romy Achituv, Noam Rachmilevitch, and the Ghetto Fighters' Museum in Israel for their generous approval to use stills from Achituv's "Lost Communities." Thanks also to SFSU colleagues, Venise Wagner, and Julietta Hua, who read and commented on the manuscript.

Haaris Naqvi, a gracious, tireless editor, encouraged my imagination of the manuscript in relation to its series, *Comparative Jewish Literatures*. Likewise, Amy Martin has been integral throughout the process. Her thoughtful nudges enabled me to "think out loud" about the text and the series. Special thanks are due to Bloomsbury's copyeditors for their patience. Despite the pandemic's foreclosure of research facilities, campus library staff, Jesse Ataide and Jamie Lamberti, worked tirelessly to get access to books from around the world.

Special thanks to former and current students, whose revelations over the years prompted and challenged my thinking about kabbalah and literature: Yulia Paluy, Matthew Dillon, Shawna Vesco, Anthony Abuan, Epiphany Rae Martin, Viviana Zettina, Yadira Arreola, Samantha Goss, Emily McMullen, Mikey Pagan. Of course, all errors of this study are mine alone.

Introduction: Preliminary Remarks

Within the study of literature, several scholars suggest that kabbalah intersects with narrative and they locate the clues to understanding that intersection within the work of Gershom Scholem. I have followed their arguments' "breadcrumbs," discovering, among their counterparts within Jewish Studies, scholars who have likewise puzzled over kabbalah's unique migration from *halakhic* or Judaic religious content into secular thought.[1] Thus I trace a literary project of kabbalah, a secular kabbalah, the footprint of which seems to vanish just as it appears.[2] My work maps these elusive traces, pulsating within our global literary traditions.

This book has required me to step away from Holocaust Studies in order to pursue a project that some might presume is a minor, if not a heretical, trajectory of Jewish aesthetics. Its focus is explicitly neither the mimetic representations of Jews' lived and historical experiences, nor their religious practices, but rather the imagined universes produced by their texts at both *halakhah*'s margins and modernity's center. This book incorporates traditions both within and beyond the borders of the English-speaking world.[3] As a result, I work from the initial premise that kabbalah and literature have reciprocally changed each other.

Their transformations occur because of where they meet. If as Joseph Dan observes, "mysticism is a phenomenon" that finds its final expression as an object in religion, it entails a specific kind of exhibition (*Darstellung*).[4] In that construction, mysticism signals its kinship to an aesthetic experience in religion. Thus if kabbalistic narratives behave as aesthetic phenomena in religion, does their exhibition in literature, the work of art, occur without effect or does it change the nature of aesthetic experience? Do kabbalah's constitutive elements impact literature, in both the reading and writing of secular texts, texts that are neither religious objects, nor do they elicit religious response? Quite simply, is the relation between sacred phenomena and profane objects a one-way street, in which the sacred animates the profane, causing it to mimetically represent a holy core?

In a world of pandemic and social injustice, I have struggled with the merit of answering these questions, proposing a work about literature, in which the heretic's transcendence, the redemption of failure, the transformation of transgression, and the liberation of Hebrew letters from *logocentric* thought are not only primary concerns, but also displace human existential crises. How can such a project talk to peoples whose lived experiences demand not only their representation, but also a path forward from the political limitations of that lived experience? How could a text about the esoteric and imagined worlds of Jews, representing something beyond their lived experience in literature, speak to the hopeless whose phenomenal experience has been so often eclipsed by privilege, political oppression, violence, and injustice?

These issues haunt this project because they were and are the same questions that Jews have asked for centuries. The desire to enter history as subjects has not only punctuated human experience but it is echoed in every Judaic sacred text, and buried in every petition made in prayer. Whether as a secular writer, a Frankist messiah, a Hasid, a *donmeh,* a *marrano,* or an isolated, alienated subject, Jews have asked why their persecution exists and what they must do to end it? Their questions intimate that perhaps "there are some truths that elude the capacity of reason, maybe not everything can be contained within the Scriptures, maybe a new entry needs to be created" to address the abject, the forgotten.[5]

In this way, the book rethinks transcendence in its reduction either to Faustian bargain—no matter the cost in human life—or to the province of the privileged—scholars in ivory towers pondering sublimity while the world around them burns.[6] Perhaps its "paraphrase" can enable us to intuit stories that give us new predicates for the ways we imagine ourselves and our failures. Perhaps read through the lens of a secular kabbalah, these narratives can help us move beyond legacies of persecution.

Thus I propose a kabbalistic aesthetics in secular texts that re-valences the mistake by restoring to us in our particularities an-"other" way to read subject positions of difference. I have embarked on an analysis of how discrete kabbalistic principles underpin the development of modern literature and its relationship to Jews, who imagine themselves as modern subjects after centuries of subaltern existence, and sometimes, much less than that status. This book aims then at these imagined worlds of books and letters, the inevitable "pleasures" of the text, in both reading and writing, in order to assert the necessity of such pleasure now.

I have written a book for modern readers, for Jews both within and without Jewish social institutions, for those readers who do not possess the common signifiers of a post-Holocaust, collective American Jewish experience, who are also reducible to neither their nationality nor their ethnicity, and for all peoples who likewise struggle with the hopelessness and despair of this historical moment. It is a text for "Isaac Deutscher's…. 'non-Jewish Jews,' or George Steiner's 'meta-rabbis', i.e. Jewish intellectuals striving against their particularistic background in order to achieve a universal validity and those Jewish thinkers who are fully content to write nothing but, to use Rosenzweig's chagrined formulation, 'Jewish books.'"[7] It freights these characteristics to suggest a subjective experience of "shared" liberations.

In this way, I have written a book for disaffected, alienated, subjects, like myself, whose navigation of a modernity fraught with the horrors of ruins, ashes, war, torture, the collective memories of shackles, isolation, pandemics, incomprehensible shootings, and climate change, never ends in a safe harbor, or even a promised land. As Harold Bloom notes, "normative Judaism" has never spoken to my "many students," while "Kafka, Freud, Scholem" resonate with them. Therefore, if "Jewish high culture, intellectually speaking, is now an amalgam of imaginative literature, psychoanalysis, and a kind of kabbalah," then literature is the key site of this transformation. In this way, my project encompasses both the hopeful and the hopeless, the "thought-full" and the "thought-less."[8]

Finally, this book does not encompass the entirety of the kabbalah, but rather it concerns small intersections where discrete kabbalistic principles, letter phenomenology, and Jewish messianism have adhered to literature in order to produce a modern text.[9] Although the specificity of my focus has required me to ignore many texts that incorporate kabbalah explicitly, it also allows me to make legible literature's ontological transformation because of its absorption of kabbalistic material. With this work, I discern a strata of kabbalistic thought that is both a conscious and unconscious archive from which modern writers draw.

Kabbalah in Fiction

The scope of the book's topic demands the literary scholar take seriously worlds lacking perceptible phenomena, excluded from the senses, heaven and hell, in relation to a world exclusively constructed by the senses and made intelligible to us through perception, earth. In other words, the very underpinnings of traditional aesthetic experience, the exhibition of the work of art, are undermined by kabbalistic phenomena because these phenomena cannot materialize their hiddenness for the human faculties.[10] I have had not only to recognize the disjunction between these two ontologies, but also to trace sudden suture points, ruptures whereby written sacred utterance expresses itself haltingly in the coordinates of human existence, time, and space.

Thus, the text speaks in a register slightly beyond the expected, from a literature professor who has "no authority to speak prescriptively for Judaism."[11] As a result, I ground modern Jewish literary interventions in relation to the "received tradition" of kabbalah whose outlines are often never recognized, but that still punctuate Jewish and non-Jewish modernities so that something of the kabbalah's capacity to reveal "the highest summits," and a path that "leads directly to the Mystical Garden," becomes available to the apostates, the failures, the unredeemable, those who identify themselves as the Talmud's "simpletons."[12] In this respect, the concepts of transgression, failure, and redemption gain new valences when inflected by kabbalah. Moreover, literature too receives a new dimension, a depth that extends into another world: it no longer reduces to mimetic representations of phenomena.

Kabbalah and Literature reflects on literature's outline of an aesthetic project, in writers as disparate as Heine, Borges, Kafka, Schulz, Benjamin, Auerbach, Atlan, Celan, Tokarczuk, and Mulisch. Through this diverse literary landscape, I explore the initial experiments of eighteenth- and nineteenth-century writers who adapt a handful of kabbalistic concepts, as corollaries for aesthetic principles. It is a code, an implication, sometimes buried within aesthetic experience, that points to something else altogether. By the twentieth century, the introduction of such content expands literary representation so that parsing the kabbalah in literature requires not only access to an ever-evolving archive of content, but it also assumes that readers remember how literature operates without kabbalah in order to imagine why its appearance in literature matters.

To that end, this introduction frames kabbalah and literature in relation to three concerns: 1) the implications of a link between kabbalah and literature generally; 2) the identification of how literature acts historically in relation to the concept of mimesis; and 3) the impact of Gershom Scholem's construction of kabbalah as a "metaphysics" in modernity so that the book's nine chapters map two main trends, Jewish messianism, and letter phenomenology, in their transformation of literary ontology.[13]

Of the many questions I hope to raise with readers, several have preoccupied me right from the beginning. How is kabbalah depicted in secular literature?[14] What are its signals? Is there any difference between a Jewish and non-Jewish writer's use of kabbalah? Is there anything significantly different between the use of kabbalistic signifiers, its themes, and other figures of speech in relation to non-kabbalistic signifiers, themes, and figures of speech? Are kabbalistic signifiers reducible to how they express a character's desires or an author's intentions? Can such signifiers exceed their intended usage and what happens if they can? Should kabbalah's use in literature be constrained by religious accuracy or legislated by it? Should kabbalah behave mimetically in order to be a part of literature? In these questions, kabbalah's engagement with literary ontologies implies either kabbalah's pertinence to another register external to literature or its absorption by literature without consequence; that is, it exists as both alien and indigenous to literature.

Moreover, in both of the above perspectives, kabbalistic elements are identified as signifiers, whose importance is circumscribed by the ways readers already analyze fiction. Limiting kabbalistic content to literal meaning within a referential or lexical system, readers ignore its particularities as a Jewish tradition in order to treat its content like any other linguistic or figural element. If everybody knows about golems, Metatron, and Lilith, kabbalah's aesthetic principles become unimportant in their modern uses. There are movies, TV shows, graphic novels, and any number of popular cultural memes that depict kabbalistic characters.[15] Inherently, kabbalistic signifiers have become so prevalent in Western culture that readers' ability to read them as signs occludes the principles that underpin their specificity to Jewish tradition. If understood as a system of signifiers, accessible to readers using familiar literary strategies, discrete signifiers function interchangeably with any number of other signifiers that a reader perceives to be related to them. They can be perceived through literature's mimesis; they don't need to be linked to anything Jewish at all.

For Jewish Studies' scholars, kabbalah is a spiritual renewal within Judaism, its "renaissance .... on a new plane"; they do not often examine it in relation to secular literature.[16] In the larger field of Religious Studies, scholars have folded kabbalah historically into the category of mysticism, subsuming it under Christian mysticism.[17] Within this category, scholars apply to kabbalah "an analogy similar to Christian phenomena."[18] Secular literature with its representations of the lived, imagined experiences of fictional characters remains a field outside of their purview too, unless its content illustrates religious tenets or struggles.[19]

Likewise, the literary scholar whose preoccupation concerns those imagined experiences of characters is not particularly interested in how these experiences reflect on or engage with specific Judaic religious ideas.[20] The nature of disciplinary knowledge encourages this kind of categorical separation: each of these disciplines maintains its own rules in relation to its own objects. Assigned to each discipline's category, objects obey the concepts that define them. Since we expect to find kabbalah in Jewish Studies, its appearance in another discipline suggests that it does not function in its original sense within that unexpected location. It is either an epistemological mistake—a matter of misplacing an object—or it loses its particularity in its reproduction, becoming something altogether different from its original identity.

In fact, for many scholars, kabbalah in literature loses the particularity of its Judaic root precisely because of its recuperation within secular texts, because kabbalistic content has appeared in a non-Judaic category. Kabbalah not only stops signifying Jewish particularity—its pertinence historically for kabbalists—but it also loses its mystical dynamism because of its use either in non-*halakhic*, non-Judaic representations or severed from the specificity of remembered Jewish life "in the ghetto." In this way, kabbalah becomes a literary object without Judaic or Jewish valences.

A handful of literature professors, philosophers, and kabbalah scholars have been drawn to the principles of kabbalah though as indices for the modern condition. For example, Robert Alter writes the definitive introduction to Gershom Scholem's classic *Major Trends of Jewish Mysticism*; Scholem's influence is visible in Alter's subsequent *Necessary Angels* with its analysis of Kafka and Benjamin.[21] Of Harold Bloom's many texts, several focus on how kabbalah's tenets might inform aesthetics, philosophy, and psychoanalysis, reaching deep into intellectual projects where "being Jewish" has been reframed as aesthetic intervention. Bloom not only grounds his readings of Kafka, Freud, and Emerson, in Isaac Luria's kabbalistic aesthetics, but also rethinks the notion of "genius" for the West through kabbalah's *sferot*.[22]

Likewise, Jacques Derrida uses "kabbalist symbols to elucidate central tenets of deconstruction."[23] Moreover, for Derrida, Gershom Scholem remains a key figure in understanding writing as a drive that exceeds lexical meaning.[24] Helene Cixous reiterates the link between Derridean thought and kabbalah in her identification of the philosopher as a "Jewish saint."[25] Agata Bielik-Robson identifies Derrida's perspective on literature, notably his reading of Joyce, as engaging particularly with Marrano and Sabbatian kabbalistic registers in order to think through a new project of redemption for modern subjects, trapped by modernity's recuperation of humans as objects.[26] She implies Derrida's Marranism to be intuitable through literature particularly.

In this spirit, I posit that literature's ontology has been transformed due to the introduction of kabbalistic content. Following Scholem's observation that part of "an ontological kabbalah" is "concerned with 'structures of beings,'" I explore how kabbalah changes what literature expresses in its predicates, how literature offers "novel intuitions" for readers willing to examine new "structures of beings."[27] Essentially, I follow Scholem's hint that kabbalah not only underpins, but also transforms, key themes, principles, and values, in modern literature so that Scholem becomes a prophet of another "new kabbalah."[28] This new kabbalah must represent, then, its intersections with literature through conceptual, imaginable, ideational, and affective registers. Consequently, how literature without kabbalah appears as a field and how its tenets structure human expectations are key parts of this introduction and underscore the stakes of Scholem's project.

Literature, Mimesis, Fictional Genealogies

Literature has historically been understood as the fictive representation of the world around us; its stories reflect our realities, aspirations, sympathies, even our fantasies. In this way, of literature's many possible genealogies, its first one is grounded in the accuracy of its mimetic depictions of phenomena. Our capacity to believe in, to identify with its characters, to accept its answers to moral and social questions, all occur because of a text's capacity for mimesis and its role in fostering identification between reader, character, and writer. A broad category, mimesis offers us a "*conditio humana* .... responsible for variations among human beings .... including the act of resembling, of presenting the self, ... mimcry, *imitation,* representation, and non-sensuous similarity."[29] The human condition embraces mimesis as the basis for representing existence.

The Epic of Gilgamesh, our earliest narrative, chronicles Gilgamesh's quest for immortality or transcendence, his exploits against capricious gods, and its conveyance of the *pathos* of human mortality when Gilgamesh fails.[30] When he meets Utanapishtim in the Netherworld and recognizes him to be "just like him," it establishes that his identification occurs because Utanapishtim bears a mimetic likeness to humans generally. Mimesis not only underwrites the validity of his identification, but at the very beginning of the literary tradition, it is introduced with identification and transcendence, as a pillar of literature's foundations.

The Bible both depicts the ancient history of the Jews and represents mimetically the religious values shaping their ancient culture. The patriarchs, prophets, present templates of behavior so that the Bible provides Jews the Law, anchored to stories illustrating its application. In this way, the text's narratives are expected to confirm the revelation's moral benefits for the ancient Hebrews through narrative depictions of lived experience.[31] Its mimetic representations elicit readers' identification.

Although Plato sees literary reflection or *mimesis* as misleading because it substitutes the imagination's representation for historical experience—"trading in mere images of particulars rather than universal truths"—Aristotle identifies literature's mimetic capacity as its underlying strength.[32] He argues that mimesis' capacity to furnish "universal truths in a readily graspable form," in literature, supersedes "history, which deals merely with particular facts."[33] Mimesis offers universal and timeless truths through its literary images. Moreover, he posits that audiences identify with characters because of their likenesses exhibited before them. In their likenesses, in the verisimilitude of phenomena, represented as literary objects, humans confirm the validity of their lived experiences. It enables them to imagine belonging to a larger society.

In the ancient world, literature's testimony is imagined and debated, then, in terms of its mimetic accuracy, an aspect that leads to the promotion of moral and social improvement, sutured to identification. Ancient audiences ascribe importance to literature because they imagine its mimetic representations are true and beneficial to them. They glean truth about their lives from literature's representations.

When the West approaches Enlightenment, philosophers continue to promote literature's mimesis and its relationship to "self-improvement"; it is conceived as a "particular vehicle for the expression of important truths," and a way to repair social injury.[34] As Benedict Anderson reminds modern readers, these aspects of literary representation enable subjects to "imagine communities" to which they not only belong, but which also confirm the validity of their judgments about the world around them.[35] Steeped in identification, readers have historically expected literature to present characters with whom they can identify. In fact, Robert Alter observes, "[V]ery few people will take the trouble to read a novel or story unless they can somehow 'identify' with the characters, live with them inwardly as if they were real at least for the duration of the reading."[36]

Since literature has historically been invested in mimesis, readers take as a given that literature represents their lived experiences. For victims of persecution, literature preserves them as subjects who have been persecuted rather than objects who have been victimized in or excluded from the historical narrative.[37] Ariel Dorfman notes that the absence of victims' stories—the *desaparecidos* absent from Chile's national narrative—prompts the rise of the *testimonio* or testimonial narrative in his country.[38] In the absence of history, literature's capacity for mimesis is foundational to their political liberation.[39]

In Brazil, Elisa Lispector deploys mimesis to preserve the memory of Brazilian Jewish life during the twentieth century. In her novel, *No Exilio*, she focuses on the lived experiences of Yiddish-speaking Jews who arrive in Brazil from the Pale of Settlement.[40] Likewise, Veza Canetti's literary project of social justice for Europe's working poor during the 1930s utilizes mimesis to elicit her readers' identification with these forgotten laborers.[41] These two writers are emblematic of a group of twentieth-century Jewish writers aiming at social oppression and injustice.

In this way, modern critiques of the Western canon point necessarily to the exclusion of those perspectives marginal to the hegemony of Western societies. The absences of the lived experiences of people of color, indigenous communities, queer peoples, and Jews have pointed to mimesis as both the evidence of the other's exclusion and demands for its inclusion in culture and society. In all of these instances, mimesis is foundational to literary representation.

The prevalence of mimesis as a literary critical tool leads Erich Auerbach to posit it as part of literature's ontology. In "Odysseus' Scar," the introductory essay in his definitive *Mimesis, the Representation of Reality in Western Literature,* Auerbach presents a dialectic at the heart of Western literature which he identifies as the Greek and Hebrew perspectives on the concept of mimetic representation.[42] Coming from the Greek tradition, mimesis reveals truth clearly. Exemplified by the scene of Eurykleia's footwashing of a disguised Odysseus in Homer's *The Odyssey,* Auerbach juxtaposes the clarity of Eurykleia's revelation to the "Akedah," the biblical *aggadah* known as the "Binding of Isaac" story.[43] The *aggadah's* representations point to a shadow and compel mimesis to trace the absence of any *pleroma*.[44] In these two traditions of mimesis, literature indicates, furthermore, both a human desire to progress into the future, full of the revelation, a master of one's destiny, equal to the gods themselves, and the apodeictic judgment that humans exist necessarily with only a fraction of illumination.[45]

For Auerbach, these two forces or perspectives exist in a relative *stasis* and that *stasis* is their strength. Neither supersedes the other.[46] They form an unresolvable, but necessary, tension, whose interplay reflects the pathos and depth of human existence. As readers, subjects are always torn between the possible possession of the clarity, empowerment, of transcendence and the realization that they must instead accept the "partial," a phenomenological "shadow." They cannot be "like divine beings."[47]

In the Greek model, transcendence and revelation occur simultaneously. Eurykleia experiences the revelation of Odysseus' identity and remembers her relationship to him; she recognizes immediately the revelation of the scar's significance.[48] It communicates its meaning literally. In Auerbach's description of Eurykleia, Aristotle's conceptual scaffolding of *mimesis*, recognition, and identification shapes the entire experience. The upshot of the scene ascribes to Eurykleia, the possession of revelation as a personal experience.[49] While her fate is fully determined and imbricated with Odysseus, her possession of revelation transforms her from an unknowing participant in a ritual of hospitality to the one who knows the truth—a subject of the revelation. Transcendence in this model equates to "she knows as the gods know." Implicitly, she knows how to read Odysseus' scar. It is a part of her memory and organizes her consciousness.

For the Hebrew model, Abraham remains a human agent without the grasp of Divine knowledge. He acts, but his actions reinscribe that he can never be "like divine beings."[50] His view of the world around him is partial and must remain so if he is to intuit "the Hidden God" whose voice comes from the "shadow."[51] The representation depicts an Abraham whose fate is undecided, who struggles with the commandment's burden—the sacrifice of a son—and its inherent prohibition on questioning the God who would impose such a demand.

Abraham can trace the outline of the shadow in his thought, but he can never know the mind of God. There remains a gap between his human ontology and Divine Being. He knows its margins, though, and that revelation enables his agency as a patriarch. He can paraphrase transcendence's margins expressed in shadows, but he can neither possess nor conceptualize them. He can only know the absence of God. Biblical narrative does not resolve the tension between shadow and *pleroma* because its internal logic affirms only that Abraham's faculties cannot understand God's thought.[52] Auerbach maps the eternal "lacunae" or gap between humans and God.[53]

Abraham's revelation underscores for Auerbach that the patriarch does not share in Divine ontology; he does not have access to Divine thought. He must obey the commandment given to him, participate in the ritual, without the knowledge that God may provide an alternative to its burden. This is almost a set piece in Judaic literature: it expresses a theme running throughout Judaic sacred texts from Torah to Talmud, as well as the ancillary *midrash*, in which the human agent's partial knowledge of the revelation offers him proximity to God, but not full transcendence, not to be "like divine beings."⁵⁴ The agent can walk with, but can never substitute for God.⁵⁵ Abraham realizes that even in proximity to God, his human ontology is neither transformed, nor dissolved into *ha-Shem,* into "The Name." Human ontology never evolves into Divine Being; in this impasse, an unbridgeable abyss between God and humankind produces the intuition of a shadow. It haunts a Hebrew tradition of mimesis. It suggests redemption, like transcendence, remains the power of a hidden God. Mimesis can only capture the outline of its absence among humans.

However, the depths of the Divine—what humans cannot know—act also as Abraham's shelter. The limitations of mimesis reinforce that the "God who speaks from the shadows" protects Abraham from having to fulfill the commandment of killing his son, Isaac, by offering him finally its alternative.⁵⁶ God shelters Abraham from the consequences of the commandment by hiding Himself in the shadows and excluding the patriarch from Divine thought. Thus, He is merciful; he enables Abraham to intuit only "shadow," to seek solace in a partial revelation experienced among the phenomena of human existence, and to be alleviated from his burden because of it. If Abraham were to experience transcendence fully, he would become aware of his fallen state, plunging the human mind into chaos and despair. Life would be an unending torment.⁵⁷

In this way, Auerbach suggests literature's second genealogy in which mimesis functions as a suture point, the instance of an unresolvable originary conflict at the heart of the literary text as it is imagined in modernity: the revelations of scar and shadow. Literature absorbs these "worlds"—both the Greek model of full revelation and the Hebrew Bible's insistence on the intuition of "shadows," intuitive fragments, disclosures where hidden being flashes just beyond cognition, between the lines of *aggadot.* Literature is the vehicle both for the full revelation of transcendence and the recognition of representation's failure to capture the "Hidden God" in the shadows.⁵⁸

Although both models offer divergent perspectives on transcendence, they still insist that transcendence is a critical component of literature's mission and mimesis is bound up with that aim. Neither of these projects changes literature's ontology since mimesis accommodates the immediate, full, belated, and partial. Moreover, these two alternating methods of reading mimesis, suspended in literature, insist that readers tack between them every time they pick up a book.

Therefore, the two theories produce literature's ontology in a very human key. These two ancient world models of literature suggest that transcendence is not only mimesis' effect, but that it also produces a conflicted text, caught between full and partial revelation, between clarity and shadow. Exhibiting the Hebrew and Greek perspectives of mimesis as its internal tension, literary ontology entertains a central conflict naturally between the mimesis of the *pleroma,* the fullness, and the mimesis of the shadow, the partial, or perhaps even the *kenoma.* In other words, literature "is a representational art" whose "objects of literary representation belong to a wide range of heterogeneous categories, material, conceptual, emotional, relational, personal, and collective."⁵⁹

Literature's mimetic function emphasizes its capacity for a broad range of representations and readers expect literature to represent not only characters' lived experiences, but also their internal conflicts.[60] Thus, literature's value has always been in the depth of the human experience it exhibits. Mimesis represents not only the world's phenomena as intuitable objects that readers can imagine, but also diverse human experiences with which they can identify.

While many Jewish writers endeavor to reflect a lived and an imagined experience in their fiction as any number of their non-Jewish counterparts do, writers informed by kabbalah have never been concerned with the imitation of such reality. In fact, the *mimesis* that kabbalists historically have hoped to attain requires an object without an underlying phenomenon or a world of objects without *mimetic* footprints in human existence. It must be inimitable. Such entities are, to quote Joseph Dan, "signifiers without signifieds."[61] Gershom Scholem associates them with Abraham Abulafia's "absolute objects," objects "capable of stimulating the soul's deeper life because they are freed from ordinary and sensual perceptions."[62]

The stakes of introducing such a project into literature change what literature does, and what literature is fundamentally because it liberates text from a human register that demands a mimetic function tied to the phenomenal world. When kabbalistic patterns and processes substitute for mimesis' phenomenal registers, literature exhibits wholly new objects, suggests texts, words, letters, as phenomena without phenomenal footprints in the faculties, and produces "new creation."[63] In this way, the mystical mimesis inherent in the kabbalah adheres to bits of text in order to express a meaning we cannot know. Auerbach's thesis dovetails then with Scholem's project of a metaphysical kabbalah. We can imagine new "beings" in secular texts because of Scholem's "thoughtful" desire to produce a "metaphysics" of the kabbalah rather than a mimetic representation of its history.

Scholem's "Metaphysics" of Kabbalah and Literature

Scholem constructs the scholarly field of kabbalah around a "philosophical perspective."[64] Its conceptual scaffolding juxtaposes the "living context of Jewish history" to a static, even "dogmatic" system, the representation of Jewish lived experience.[65] This "dogmatic" system reflects the attitudes of scholars organized around the nineteenth-century *Wissenschaft des Judentums* project.[66] From his "philosophical" foundation, Scholem juxtaposes an aesthetic experience active within kabbalah, standing in relief against Judaism's epistemology.[67] Thus he underpins my analysis of kabbalah and literature because he locates the foundations of kabbalah in relation to a modernity, teased into existence by aesthetic experience.

In other words, Scholem sees a dialectic, a tension between the "unclassifiable" and the "classifiable," at the heart of his scholarly project which he maps self-consciously on to an historicist development of the kabbalah.[68] Consequently, through his depiction of the underlying principles that motivate Jewish mystical thought, Scholem not only creates a scholarly history for kabbalah, but also identifies the philosophical conditions for its aesthetic experience.[69]

Writing about kabbalah as a religious and historical tradition, Scholem notes in *Major Trends of Jewish Mysticism* that although Jewish Studies' scholars, associated with the nineteenth-century *Wissenschaft des Judentums* project, disavow kabbalah as a "strange and repellent" phenomenon, it persists in popularity among Jews.[70] As he ponders its enthusiasm among the masses, he posits the "metaphysics" behind his "new kabbalah" and points to its real stakes in modernity. He explains that the kabbalah, and he phrases his English in precise German terms, to hammer the point home, emerges historically whenever Jews seek to transform Judaism from an "object of dogmatic knowledge (*aus einem Objekt des Wissens und der Dogmatik*) into a novel intuition that they can make a living experience (*zu einer neuen und lebendigen Erfahrung zu machen*)."[71] It enables the transformation of an intuitive encounter with an unknowable phenomenon, into an expression of vivid, vital experience. It does not reinforce past lived experience, but instead illustrates something new and "living" that meets the modern Jew "where he, she, they stand."[72]

Scholem's language proposes kabbalah to have been historically, a sanctioned, Judaic aesthetic experience and part of Judaism's received revelation.[73] Its cyclical resurgence among Jews is a fundamental part of Judaism, not a marginal or minor tradition of a few in centuries past. In this way, his phrasing identifies kabbalah as part of the fabric of not only Jews in the *Wissensschaft* era, but also implicitly of all Jews.[74] Its tenets, principles, stories, and signifiers saturate their histories, practices, and culture because kabbalah's emergence is tied to any historical moment when Jews' lived experience becomes so untenable that it forces them to choose to renew themselves individually as Jews.

In German, the structure of Scholem's phrase mimics a familiar mode of thought for *Wissenschaft* scholars because in placing Judaism, an "object of knowledge," in relation to "a novel," intuitive experience, he demonstrates the tradition's resonance with German aesthetics, the language of Kant.[75] He makes the kabbalah recognizable in philosophical terms so that any exclusion of kabbalah forfeits not only a constitutive experience of the historic Judaic subject, but also the constitutive experience of becoming a modern Jewish subject.[76] Implicitly Scholem's language hints that kabbalah could lead Jews to discover a new path to redemption, a new literary kabbalah in which they become subjects "outside the ghetto," finding their redemption in modernity.[77]

Without kabbalah's intervention, Jews remain Judaic objects under the authority of their rabbis, subalterns under the authority of empire, indeterminate and interchangeable objects of a nation-state, signifying exactly the image of the "dark" era that characterizes Jewish history in the discourse of the *Wissenschaft des Judentums* scholar. Hence Scholem's secular, Jewish subject in modernity has a stake in the kabbalah and its transformation of culture because it preserves Jewish particularity as a characteristic of modern "living experience."[78] In other words, kabbalah informs the *Bildung* or intellectual perspective of Scholem's Jewish world intimately.[79] The embrace of Jewish Enlightenment, and its civil, political reforms, echoes the kabbalists in their rejection of Judaism's "dogmatic object of knowledge," in favor of a "living intuition."[80]

Thus Scholem declares the yearning for kabbalah is the "quest for the hidden life of the transcendent element …. one of the most important preoccupations of the human mind."[81] Scholem does not limit the desire for transcendence to religious aims: he extends it to encompass an existential condition.[82] Boldly, he traces the "quest" back through centuries of Jewish texts, to argue that Jews have always sought to "paraphrase …. transcendence."[83] In these writings, kabbalah becomes visible as an historical practice of subjective renewal. The individual practitioner imagines a community to which he (always he) has belonged in contrast to the dogmatic, parochial, and fallen, world in which Jews have been either forced to live or compelled to construct.

Finally, the phrase in German, "the object of dogmatic knowledge" (*aus einem Objekt des Wissens und der Dogmatik*) resonates with the tension he posits at the heart of Judaism between the "object of knowledge" or *halakhah*—how one knows to be a Jew—and "the object of creation" or *aggadah*—how one imagines being Jewish—both of which constitute the Torah.[84] The *halakhah* preserves the particularity of Jews by identifying the boundaries they are prohibited from crossing. The *aggadah* illustrates a new imagination of those boundaries so that story is bound to renewing the Law's relevance in Judaism.

However, since stories are bound in the Torah, they are within the Divine work of creation. In fact, the *Zohar* describes creation as an effect of God reading His Torah, His "work of art."[85] God reads his own writing to produce creation, His "work of art." The "work" is called into being by reading's stimulation of writing. The stories bear within themselves the trace of a hidden writing, enabling the Torah to transcend its static and earthly representation. If creation occurs and continues because of the stimulus of reading and writing, the kabbalistic command to "write one's own Torah" implies that human "works of art" are imbricated in the work of creation too.[86] Thus Torah's stories extend creation through the combined processes of reading and writing: these processes inscribe creation into human cognition.[87]

The *Zohar* adds that God hides His Light within the pages of the Torah so that the Torah exceeds its words and sentences; the "Light" and the "work of art" appear to be more than the meaning of the words on its pages.[88] The Hebrew letters emanate creation. They represent a continuous unfolding of revelation that compels Divine Being to return through them into time and space. We find ourselves with Auerbach at a crossroads: do we elevate the *logos* as the revelation—the scar or the word—or do we elevate the mysteries—the shadows—of its "background" (*Hintergrundlichkeit*) that increasingly resonate with the command we bear within ourselves to "write something new?"[89]

Scholem's "novel intuition of a living experience" versus the "dogmatic object of knowledge" recognizes that kabbalah has offered Jews historically an aesthetic experience through the Torah's stories. Although he draws on a German philosophical tradition, his emphasis relies on an unarticulated, necessary *aggadah,* a hidden writing within creation.[90] Although kabbalistic aesthetic experience offers new access points to Judaic epistemology, meant to preserve the tradition, not to destroy it, its migration into literature, culminating with Kafka, creates the coordinates for a modern Jewish subject beyond *halakhah's* boundaries, and intuitively within reach of the Divine. To produce this path, *aggadah* must mimic literature. Scholem posits this other path as a consequence of the heretical kabbalah's first eruption in modernity, exemplified by Sabbatianism, and its messiah, Shabbatai Zvi.

Scholem considers Sabbatianism to be "the first serious revolt in Judaism since the Middle Ages" because it leads "directly to the disintegration of orthodox Judaism by 'the believers.'"[91] It not only undermines the kabbalah's original purpose, the renewal of Jews in Judaism, but it also introduces Jews without Judaism as its aim.[92] The heretical kabbalah's founding rupture is its sanctification of apostasy. Thus an internal tension emerges within modern Jewish life, between a kabbalistic aesthetic experience previously reinvigorating Judaic epistemology and a lingering desire to dispense with the epistemology altogether, an aesthetic liberated from all constraint, moving farther away from any epistemological and rabbinic authority.[93]

Sabbatianism produces "an outburst of more or less veiled nihilistic tendencies .... a mood of religious anarchism on a mystical basis" so that even after their messiah's death, his followers continue in secret to espouse the beginning of a messianic age. In the next century, the second heretical messianic movement, Frankism, adopts Zvi's "anarchism," but its apostasy clings to and coincides with the "moral and intellectual" reforms of the Jewish Enlightenment.[94] Pointing to the *Haskalah* as a signifier of the messianic age, Frankism's messiah, Jacob Frank, affirms apostasy as an act of redemption. Frankism innovates the kabbalistic theory of exile, Isaac Luria's theory of "praxis," to suggest that the messiah materializes in the body of Jacob Frank, but materialization demands the forfeiture of a Judaic world for the darkness outside the ghetto.

In the transformation of "orthodox" kabbalah, into its heretical cousin, a secret tradition is "put into praxis." Consequently, these Jews imagine becoming subjects in time and space. They "enter into history"; it shifts the object of their contemplation away from Judaism, revealing another world around them, expressed by new discursive signs.[95] It is a world of redemptive transgression coupled to *Haskalah's* religious, social, and political reforms, and it inaugurates an "ethnically Jewish historical experience."[96]

Scholem's construction of the field's metaphysics rests, furthermore, on the centrality of the heretical kabbalah's messianic pretensions for modernity. Frank presents himself as the messiah: he not only sees through the Law, but he also has crossed over to its "other side" so that it no longer applies to him. Frank's heretical kabbalah depicts *halakhah* in ruins, and Judaism's rabbinic gatekeepers transformed into the servants of the penal colony.[97] Thus "the culmination of the tradition" is its materialization of the messianic age on earth, i.e., putting "theory into practice."[98] Accounts of Frank's innovations of kabbalistic redemption circulate as new *aggadot*, juxtaposed to the artifacts of a previous oppression, Torah and Talmud's *aggadot*. These new narratives are the *Sayings and Teachings of the Lord*, the hagiographies and legends about Jacob Frank.[99]

With rabbinic leadership designating Sabbatianism, and then, Frankism as banned practices, "the believers" migrate to spaces where their ideas can flourish, where their innovations instead of being condemned as transgressions and heresies are recognized as new revelations.[100] The heretics of kabbalah target art, philosophy, literature, as well as political revolution, to promote transgression and "anarchy": new signs of human liberation.[101]

It is a "redemption through sin," a "holiness" that adheres to transgression.[102] By inverting the kabbalist's adherence to Divine Glory, to adhere instead to previously designated sin, sin becomes a sanctified imagined aesthetic experience.[103] Moreover, these "sins" are not reducible to objects of knowledge because they belong to a world of messianic "nothingness," a world uncircumscribed by commandments.[104] These textual worlds are without *halakhah*'s phenomenal footprints and it allows the heretical kabbalah to constitute an "other" path in the experience of redemption or in the recovery of paradise.

More importantly, in these stories about transcendent messiahs and prophets, heroes remain "fallen." In a heretical kabbalah's literary project, the fallen messiah transforms transgression itself: the feeling of lawlessness, an imagined antinomianism, produces "an indefinable .... *euphoria*, which manifests itself in absurd, bizarre, and sacrilegious actions, to the rank of a 'sacred act' in which a sublime reality becomes manifest: the state of the new world of *Tikkun*."[105] An "indefinable" and "euphoric" ecstasy engenders a catharsis through "absurd, bizarre, and sacrilegious actions," until "a sublime reality" materializes. It is an "indefinable," ineffable, and "unclassifiable" ecstasy. Its "sublime reality" reveals the actual "state of the new world." Ecstasy confirms the individual sees through the Law's deception.[106] In this way, the heretical kabbalah proposes the "living experience" of transgression as an apodeictic act defying the "dogmatic object of knowledge." It liberates by aiming "to wipe out all laws, all religions .... to bring life into this world." Moreover, it erases distinctions between transcendence, sublimity, and transgression.

The heretical kabbalah's transgressive *tikkun* or "repair" of its messianic age conflates with transcendence so that transgression is no longer evil if done in transcendence's pursuit. All the impetus is on the individual's awareness of transcendent splendor within reach, demanding one cross the abyss to grasp it. Transcendence becomes the effect of an innovated reading and writing of transgression. In this way, the secular text promises a metamorphosis beyond Jews' wildest dreams.

Modernity's political and social projects produce a cultural intersection in which apostasy, heretical and orthodox kabbalahs, secularism, come into contact not only with each other, but also with non-Jews, as well as Jews who have no purchase in kabbalah and for whom *halakhah* is a faded memory if a memory at all. It is a collision of a "mixed multitude" tacking between modern Europe's margins and center, making visible the stakes of Jews' "novel" and collective move from Judaic epistemology to Jewish aesthetics.[107] While Scholem's metaphysics of kabbalah produces the foundation of Jewish cultures on the cusp of modernity, his metaphysics of the heretical kabbalah makes visible a path through literature for Jews and non-Jews to travel. He gives modernity a new kabbalah with new forms of redemption.

Parsing the Kabbalah in Modern Fiction

By the nineteenth century, literature has been exposed, then, to multiple kabbalahs. Scholem claims there would be no alienated Kafka without Hasids, Sabbatians, and Frankists coming before him, and these movements rely likewise on preceding centuries' kabbalistic ideas.[108] In other words, each kabbalah's pattern is repeated and innovated by the next movement so that the kabbalah's aggregate of "stories" not only produces new conditions in their retelling, but also inscribes new patterns in their articulation of the kabbalah's continuity. A writing that breaks through the phenomenal, each of its narratives form mystical rhizomes, at once multiple and singular, imaginatively encoded with fractal aspects of transcendent being. This writing expresses a multiplicity within beings, as it proceeds along its singular path. Scholem indicates that innovation does not distinguish between legitimate *halakhah* and illegitimate secularism.

Implicitly, in a chain of transmission, kabbalists have always experimented with non-*halakhic* sources: new aspects of the revelation, buried shards of Divine insight that have remained unknown until their discovery at distinct moments in an array of non-*halakhic* texts.[109] In this respect, non-*halakhic* operates as an expansive category, an archive composed of religious, non-sacred writing, philosophical, and even heretical texts, within which their readers search for "missing pieces" of the revelation, buried so long ago.

Migrating into secular literature as phenomena without phenomenal footprints, kabbalah's missing pieces continue then to absorb aesthetics so that its traditions reverberate within the writings of Jews and non-Jews. Aesthetic principles retain the echo of a Jewish mystical register, pulsating within narrative. Hence these mysterious "missing pieces" have enabled literary kabbalah to flourish.[110]

With *Kabbalah and Literature*, I trace these "missing pieces," these patterns of heretical and orthodox mystical aesthetic projects, freighted by Jewish and non-Jewish particularities. Their "exceptionalities" demonstrate both the transformative nature of kabbalah in literature, and the necessity of its "absolute objects" liberated within texts, free to press their innovations into creation.[111] There are risks in such an aesthetic project since readers might wander beyond the path of revelation. They might "slip" into the "void" of nothingness and non-meaning, the "chaos" of an unconscious abyss. They might abandon the path altogether, and try to find another way into paradise. In an attempt to scale the *sefirotic* tree, readers might fall again to their deaths; they might discover themselves, untethered from human existence, following Hebrew letters into the Divine Cosmic Stream.

In nine chapters, this book tells a story about kabbalah's creations, revelations, redemptions, and failures in secular literature, its first movement away from sacred tether toward profane objects. Hence its premise is that secular literature absorbs a kabbalistic core in order to tell stories about modern Jews. This first movement expresses itself in both a messianic materialism—a path informed by the heretical kabbalah in which redemption is materialized on earth—and a letter phenomenology, anchored to Hebrew's sacred ontology, in which the letters themselves are agents of new creation. Whereas messianic materialism posits a paradise in time and space—humans innovate matter to reveal its secret—letter phenomenology finds redemption hidden in writing itself—writing innovates text and stimulates stories of "otherness" into existence. Hence "The Other's Path" and "Letter Phenomenologies of Modernist Kabbalahs" divide the book into two parts and demonstrate how both heretical and orthodox kabbalahs transform and are transformed by literature. In other words, juxtaposed to Jewish writers preserving mimetic images of Jews' lived experiences, kabbalah continues to animate secular writing so that the profane accommodates the esoteric, attracts and seduces Jewish and non-Jewish writers to move into its orbit, to interact with it emanations.

Part 1, The Other's Path and the Redemption of Aher, links the Talmudic *aggadah* "The Four who went to Pardes," to its resonance for modern Jewish subjects steeped in the promises of Shabbatai Zvi's and Jacob Frank's heretical kabbalahs with its popular circulation through Jacob Gordin's revision, "Elisha ben Abuya." In Gordin's narrative, Elisha ben Abuya becomes an emblematic figure with whom modern Jewish subjects identify because he abandons "an incomprehensible Law."[112] He walks away from paradise and into history. A "free-thinker," his rejection of Judaism is in the service of preserving Jews as Jews.[113] His rejection is a commitment to the Jewish people rather than the Judaic Law. Thus his rejection of *halakhah* not only is messianic, but also materializes another path to redemption. While the weight of Talmud falls on Abuya, condemning him to be the unredeemable "Aher (the Other)," his apostasy posits a liberation "beyond the pale," founded on the Law's absence, making visible "the other's path." The five chapters in this section map the heretical kabbalah's illumination of "the other's path," revealing how modern Ahers are redeemed through the innovation of this forgotten path in and out of paradise.

Chapter 1, "Jacob Frank, 'Heretic of the Kabbalah," begins with Olga Tokarczuk's *The Books of Jacob*, an historical novel about Jacob Frank's messianic aspirations, to suggest not only the pervasiveness of kabbalistic content in modern literature, but also to illustrate how Jacob Frank proposes his life story as the ground for new *aggadot*. Tokarczuk's novel narrates Jacob Frank's and his followers' lived experiences. By the end of the text, readers know that Frank embodies the hopes, aspirations, of modern Jews, even though he acts as a charlatan among them. Exhibiting Frank as a product of the era, Tokarczuk observes that with his death, the movement fades away into history. His followers become footnotes. Her novel testifies to his mimetic footprints in history.

In this respect, Tokarczuk points to Frank's hagiographies by reinforcing how the historical tales posit a redemption for Jews as common people. Their will, perseverance, and physical strength can save them if they only throw off the shackles of their oppression, and cross over by using their strength and skill to push through darkness to the other side. As she builds her novel on these hagiographies as well as secondary sources of the kabbalah, in the process she produces a fictional genealogy for modern Europe, in which the Frankists are emblematically European, Polish, Jewish, and modern. In other words, she follows a model, introduced by the Frankists themselves, in which profane stories about Frank substitute for biblical and Talmudic *aggadot*.

Circulating in the eighteenth century, the hagiographies from which she derives her narrative, not only act as alternative *aggadot* for Frank's followers, but also introduce to Jews collectively the notion that sacred stories can take secular forms. To that end, Tokarczuk recovers these narratives mimetically so that her project of historical fiction reflects that "any person who toils over matters of the Messiahs, even failed ones, even just to tell their stories, will be treated just the same as he who studies the eternal mysteries of light."¹¹⁴ To tell the stories of Frankist hagiography, to reproduce them somewhat mimetically, accords the writer with the same blessing as the kabbalist "who studies the eternal mysteries of light."

Implicitly, her reproduction of Frank's hagiographies offers to readers an entrance into the Divine Light promised as an effect of the kabbalah, even though these fictional narratives about the Frankists' lived experiences introduce nothing new. In this respect, Tokarczuk uses literature as an alternative site for her thesis about Poland, Europe, in relation to Frank's failed messianic movement. The failure of his messianism is the realization in her novel that Frankists recede into human history as footnotes, their values absorbed in the greater traditions of Enlightenment Europe.

However, bracketing her fictive account of Jacob Frank, kabbalah's heretic, Tokarczuk tells the story of Yente, a character without any historical footprint in Frankism, whose desperate decision to forestall her death in order to "save" a wedding opens the book as well as my volume. Yente's frame tale introduces readers to a power inherent in the Hebrew letters, to the principle of their innovation, and to their necessary violation in order to atone for Yente's act of choosing human connection because she knows her death will likely prohibit the wedding's occurrence. Practicing a heretical kabbalah, Yente innovates המתנה, the command to wait until a condition favorable to death is present. Her innovation is both transgression and redemption; it transforms her into immanent matter. Implicitly, Yente transgresses because of her desire to be with her family one last time before death; it redeems rather than condemns. Her commitment to being with her people demands that she violates the law.

Thus Tokarczuk juxtaposes Jacob Frank, the heretic of kabbalah, to Yente's transgressive innovation, her redemption through her sin. The juxtaposition traces a conflict at the heart of Jewish tradition, between Frank's desire for power, autonomy, freedom from persecution, and Yente's longing for family, to be with her people one more time before her demise. Tokarczuk illustrates how the heretical kabbalah motivates both a messianic materialism that would seep into empires, nations, religions, as a legitimate political aim, and an anarchic letter phenomenology, whose forfeiture of human existence, leads eventually to "the eternal mysteries of light."

The novel hews to Frank's own strategy: he replaces *aggadot* with his own hagiographies. Once these substitutions are introduced as practices, his followers posit the profane to be new sites of innovation. Stories of Frank's profane life enable the heretics of kabbalah to imagine themselves as "heretics of innovation." After Frank's death, and grouped under a sign of radical emancipation, the remaining Frankists link innovation to progress, suggesting that the liberation movements of nineteenth-century Europe are evidence of the inauguration of a messianic age. The previous political, religious, social, orders are obsolete. At the precipice of a new world order, Jews need only their will, determination, desire, to cross over to redemption on the other side. They can live freely, no longer bound to oppressive laws. While the first chapter concludes with Offenbach's remnant struggling to keep Frankism alive in Frank's absence, Frank's followers in Prague remain with his narratives and their promises of a messianic age of radical emancipations.

Chapter 2, "**Heretics and Heresies of Innovation**," follows Prague's Frankists in their attempt to discover where the path of Frank's apostasy leads after his death. The leader of the Prague Circle, Jonas Wehle, emerges, with his son-in-law, Hönigsberg, the first to link Frankism to a code which scholars suggest they find in Kant, Mendelsohn, and Hegel.[115] The link enables Wehle and his followers to parse the Kabbalah, even if the heretical Kabbalah, by innovating secular philosophical texts. In this way, Wehle not only posits innovated principles of Frankist liberation, but also suggests his approach to observers as emblematically "Bohemian." While the Circle presents Europe's political upheavals as signs of their innovations writing redemption across multiple registers, proof of the materialization of the messianic age, inaugurated by Frank, the aftereffect of their Frankist project becomes the introduction of new ways to read and write. Their innovated objects signify both a revelation below the surface materializing and an escape from the condemnation of fallenness.

Their principle of innovation in which writing not only inscribes, but also liberates matter by tearing the illusions of oppression asunder, produces in the minds of modern Jews, the belief that their law has brought them to emancipation. It has been fulfilled and the evidence of its fulfillment is in their civil rights. Thus Prague's "heretics of innovation" embed Frankism's teachings, the heretical *aggadot*, within European culture by positing a link between apostasy and Kant. Wehle's innovations encourage a kabbalistic rethinking of German Idealism.[116] The end result shifts away from Frank, kabbalah's heretic, to a modernity, promising Jews and non-Jews, "heresies of innovation and revelations of progress."

Chapter 3, "Heinrich Heine, Poet/Prophet of 'the Innovated Text,'" pivots from Frankism's political and social expectations to Heinrich Heine whose conversion to Christianity often excludes him from being considered a Jewish poet. However, in his last works he illustrates a remarkable transformation, writing on several Jewish themes and figures. This chapter looks at one of his late poems, "Jehudah ben Halevi," and the principle of innovated *poesie*, introduced by the poet as the ground of a Jewish revelation. Heine offers *poesie* as *aggadah*, finally unbound from *halakhah* through the medium of poetry; thus *poesie* restores to the poet a primordial ontology, no longer subject to condemnation. Heine's experiment with kabbalistic innovation allows him to see a hidden writing animating textuality, in which *poesie* transcends "normative Judaism," even though it does not prevent Halevi's martyrdom.

Against the revelation of *poesie* Heine's *Der Doktor Faust* stands with its allusions to Frankism.[117] The play illustrates Faust's attempt to follow an illegitimate path to transcendence, in order to be free of persecution and oppression that is destined to end in the condemnation of apostasy. Together, the two texts indicate a modest attempt by Heine to use the innovation of literature to explore a textual messianism that fails when forced into materialization, but redeems when liberated as writing.

Chapter 4, "Kafka, Prophet of Failure," continues the thread of writing as unmaterialized redemption by linking Kafka's reimagining of "the Four who went to Pardes," in 1911, to his thinking about a "secular kabbalah," in 1922. The link though is mediated by his 1915 short story, "Before the Law." Beginning with his 1911 sketch of Jacob Gordin's "Elishe ben Avuyah," Kafka reproduces Abuyah or Aher the apostate as the signifier of modernity: a "free-thinker" who abandons Judaism because the *halakhah* and its overseers oppress "those who do not study Torah," the phrase that intersects in Yiddish, Hebrew, and Polish. Aher is an individual who chooses to live life, believing in the Law's obsolescence and fortified by the self.

In 1915, Kafka's "man of the country" in "Before the Law" resonates with the above representation of Aher on his "other's" path.[118] Essentially, Kafka rewrites Aher's heresy as Frankism's failed promise: there is never any redemption for the common man. This chapter links my reading of Aher's failure in "Before the Law" to Kafka's diary entry of 1922, where he revises "The Four who went to Pardes" to suggest redemption's possibility for Kafka as a modern Jew resides in writing.

Chapter 5, "Being and Nothingness: The Matter of Golems," presents Bruno Schulz's *Cinnamon Shops* as an illustration of Frankism's heretical kabbalah animating both Father and Son, as well as its influence on Schulz's own view of lived experience. The narrator describes his Father's experimental creations as a heresy in "defense of poetry." Poetry becomes the principle that the Father must extract from chaotic matter in order to create. Father's "works of art" produce then a tension between creation and golem in which the inevitability of receding back into "matter," voiceless, immanent in death, is the shared state of a fallen creation.

Like Jacob Frank, Father battles the Demiurge to carve out a space and time in this world, "according to human taste," but it ends with Father's failure, the possibility of transformation scattered among ruins and "trash." As Father watches the final destruction of his creations, Chapter 5 ends with the realization that the materialization of new creation, Father's revelation of a "Second Book of Genesis" only attests to his failure.[119]

Part 2, "Letter Phenomenologies of Modernist Kabbalahs," returns to the "Four who went to Pardes," and analyzes it in relation to its kabbalistic transformation from celestial palace, earthly paradise, to textual transcendence to propose how this transformation weights a letter phenomenology previously unknown in modern fiction. Each of the included authors, Schulz, Borges, Atlan, Achituv, Mulisch, and Celan, presses letter phenomenologies into the service of a missing revelation whose existence a character intuits.

While the four chapters within this section analyze the implications of letter phenomenologies, they also illustrate how redemption and transcendence become effects of reading and writing. They posit disparate theses about creation, revelation, and redemption, in spite of Jews' entering history, and abandoning Torah. Moreover, by the section's end, we see with Celan, a moment when the permutation of the letters enables that poet to produce a psalm external to human existence, a song that can be heard by those whom he has lost during the Shoah.

Chapter 6, "Golems of Text and Bruno Schulz's 'Interminable *Aggadot*'," concerns Bruno Schulz's explicit kabbalistic aesthetics in *Sanatorium under the Sign of the Hourglass*. In contrast to *Cinnamon Shops*' Frankist Gnosticism, in *Sanatorium*'s short stories, the narrator, Josef, searches for a textual paradise, a textuality that leads to his subjective redemption. He recognizes the pattern of this textuality to emanate from within a missing and mysterious book. While "The Book" sets free within him a "rapturous ecstasy," by the book's end, that ecstasy also threatens to seal him within its pages, returning him to a state of "interminable stories" and absolute isolation from any other human. In its many manifestations, "The Book" is recognizable to Josef, the narrator, as "that burning Book .... the genuine Book of Radiance."[120] Schulz appears to allude to *The Zohar* in order to discuss the repair writing must perform in order to create a personal redemption.

Although Schulz identifies in "Loneliness," the *Book of Creation* or *Sefer Yetsirah*, as the missing book of his childhood, abandoned in his room, he hints nonetheless that both *Yetsirah* and *Zohar* are only fragments of "The Book" that now threatens to seal him into his own creation. In other words, the chapter explores the implications of kabbalistic unsealing and sealing of creation in Schulz to rethink the transformation of the human condition through writing.

Chapter 7, "The 'Absolute Object' in Argentino's Basement," introduces two competing letter phenomenologies in Borges' short story, "The Aleph." Through a contrast between Borges contemplation of a secret "Aleph" in Carlos Argentino Daneri's cellar and Daneri's own heretical machinations to use the letter to his benefit, I map Borges tacking between "orthodox" and "heretical" kabbalistic registers, to tease out its resonance with the kabbalistic theory of Abraham Abulafia's "absolute object."

In this way, Borges exhibits a writing that refuses to be written; his fictional character perceives the Aleph, but cannot translate it to the page without producing a false idol. In particular, the chapter focuses on Borges' assertion that any attempt to anchor writing to the written must result in heresy. The revelation of writing occurs outside of any testimony left behind in time and space, any written text. The chapter ends with an impasse, a postscript added to the story by Borges' fictional narrator to renounce his experience in the cellar. Daneri's *aleph* is "a false aleph" because Daneri has been able to control it, pressing its emanations into his work, that is, materializing it in time and space.[121] Therefore, Borges' capacity to record the experience in written form becomes in and of itself a false witness because "the absolute object" of the *aleph* cannot be made visible in time and space. With this move, Borges undoes any messianic pretensions suggested by the story. The letters cannot save a condemned world. The world of time and space is foreclosed to them.

Chapter 8, "Lost Letters," juxtaposes three aesthetic interventions that suggest letter phenomenology's foreclosure because of the Shoah: "Lost Communities," by Israeli installation artist Romy Achituv, "The Messiahs," by French dramatist, Liliane Atlan, and *The Discovery of Heaven* by the Dutch novelist, Harry Mulisch. In their respective works, they question whether kabbalah can restore a path back to a hidden or absent God since the Hebrew letters are forced to abandon human existence entirely.

Each one takes up both heretical and orthodox kabbalahs in order to demonstrate why the letters must abandon creation. Each one innovates letter phenomenologies to propose different reasons for the letters' exile from earth. With Achituv, the letters untethered from Jewish bodies, recede into the cosmos, no longer visible in time and space. For Atlan, the letters' redemption is a broken promise: its ruin unmoors the Nazis' Jewish victims not only from their loved ones, but also from their messiahs, leaving them to wander the cosmos in isolation. Mulisch innovates a gnostic fantasy whereby Divine Beings give up on the human experiment, removing from it the tablets penned by God, whose writing was to be a blueprint for redemption. The chapter concludes with a modern Jewish echo, voiced first by Kafka that "there is infinite hope, but not for us."[122]

Chapter 9, "There Must Be Other Songs beyond Mankind," rethinks the possibility that the letters might still possess the power to connect the Nazis' victims with their survivors after the Shoah. Primarily thinking through Paul Celan's poetic oeuvre, I analyze how that poet first applies and then rejects the heretical kabbalah's thesis of a materialized redemption, a lyric to represent the loss, in "Death Fugue." Although this rejection has been extensively examined by numerous scholars, they all leap from "Death Fugue" to "No More Sand Art," using both history and Celan's seeming nonsensical phrasing in the later poem to justify that Celan's poetry bears witness to a lack of sense in the world.

Tracking the arc of Celan's transformation, I move though through several transitional poems in order to show where Celan returns to an orthodox kabbalah to project "other songs beyond humankind." For Celan, letter permutation offers the poet the possibility of restoration not only to Jewish writing, but also to the hidden God. Hence his poems are psalms, songs that push themselves back into the void, touching those whom he has lost even if he cannot perceive it and them. Celan's poems become unclassifiable; they propose a writing of inimitability. They are innovations of Celan's very human loss.

"Literature's Messianic Moments" concludes the volume by focusing on the principle of "inimitability," in relation to human connection, as it transforms literary ontology in the twenty-first century. It juxtaposes the transformation of messianism's isolated failures—the redemption of Aher—to the necessity of human connection, both a phenomenological and a phenomenal metamorphosis whose palpable absence pushes readers to search for the missing traces of a hidden writing—the redemption of Celan. Thus *Kabbalah and Literature* ends with how the ontology of literature has been transformed, revealed, and extended by its absorption of kabbalistic "signifiers without signifieds" because it bears the obligation to continue the writing of "incomplete" narratives of existence beyond phenomenality. Literary lacunae bear witness to a path imaginable, yet beyond human perception. This cognitive scaffolding, literature's inner paradox, underpins why kabbalah and literature must matter to modernity.

Part One

The Other's Path and the Redemption of Aher

Just prior to the heretical kabbalah's emergence in Shabbatai Zvi and Jacob Frank, Isaac Luria introduces a kabbalistic theory of messianism, a proposition or obligation that can never be fulfilled, but that warrants still its completion. An impossible command, the theory proposes a Jewish messianism in which redemption is contingent on the performance of a *tikkun*, a repair done for and to God. With its completion, a messianic age is inaugurated, erasing the boundary between God and human. Essentially, Luria posits the existence of a sanctioned path to paradise's restoration, one that requires Jews to perform *tikkun* in exile. He points allusively to the possibility of redeeming the unredeemable, an epithet resonating with the "other" sage who also goes into exile by abandoning the Judaic way to and through "the Pardes."

In the teachings of Kabbalah and Jewish Mysticism, the Talmud's "Four who went to Pardes" serves as evidence of mystical practices during the *Tannaitic* era.[1] It implies that Judaism accommodates mysticism by necessity: it is part of the revelation. The story is fairly simple: Akiva, a *tanna* takes three other *tannaim*, ben Azzai, ben Zoma, and ben Abuya, with him on a journey to the Pardes.

The Talmudic narrative suggests they travel to a celestial place. Akiva warns his companions that on their arrival, they must not draw inferences from their senses. If they mistake sense perceptions for the revelation, they will be condemned for "speaking untruths," preventing them from standing before God. They must refuse any physiological, psychological, and bodily urges: these are consequences of the Fall and the companions' reliance on them is deception.

When they arrive at the Pardes, ben Azzai gazes at the gleaming plates, and drops dead.[2] He "senses" discrete aspects of the Pardes and it so overwhelms him that he dies. The second companion, ben Zoma, also gazes and he is "smitten" with what he sees; the Talmudist links "smitten" to the biblical "If you find honey, eat only what you need, lest surfeiting yourself, you throw it up": his obsession drives him mad.[3]

Surprisingly, of Akiva's three companions, Elisha ben Abuya, later known as Aher or "Other" moves the farthest into the Pardes. As a consequence of his gazing, ben Abuya "cuts the shoots," and he leaves the Pardes, an apostate.[4] As Sandra Valabregue observes, the condemnation of "cutting the shoots" refers to a "dualistic and gnostic" heresy that "fractures" Divine Unity.⁵ Thus Abuya's heresy severs him from the Pardes; Talmud renames him "other" and declares that this Aher can never be redeemed. The Talmudic pericope ends with Akiva who suffers no injury: he descends and ascends "in peace."⁶

For Talmud's readers, the *aggadah* underscores that each of the *tannaim* has a different reaction to the mystical experience of the Pardes: death, madness, apostasy, and peace. However, all of the weight of the *aggadah* falls on the first three companions whose humanness violates some aspect of the experience so that eventually readers focus on Aher. His judgments and inferences about the separation of human and Divine ontologies lead to apostasy. Although Akiva ends the narrative essentially unchanged by proximity to the Divine, readers still think of Aher who abandons Akiva's path.⁷

For the kabbalah, Aher's transgression begins before his arrival at Pardes because he is unprepared mentally for the mystical experience. He abandons the correct path, relying instead on what he knows about "the dogmatic object of knowledge," and what he infers from his senses. Instead of a "novel, intuitive experience," he maps his journey according to knowledge he already possesses so that the mystical Pardes remains allusively intuited, but ultimately foreclosed to him. When he reemerges among Jews, separated by his choices, he becomes a traveler, following his "other's path." His transgressions are signposts along an illegitimate route. A Jew without Judaism, Aher remains within the Jewish community, but he cannot be redeemed. In *halakhah*, the *aggadah* illustrates the dangers of abandoning the Law, becoming "one who does not study"; in kabbalah, Aher's rejection of the secret, the anchor to the Pardes, its fulfillment, condemns him. For a Jewish *Haskalah* modernity, Aher's transgressions become reducible to rational decisions. For post-*Haskalah*'s Yiddish-speaking audiences, Aher's rejection of an "incomprehensible" tradition, its unreasonable demands, resonates with their own experiences.

Since the narrative's emphasis on mystical experience affirms Scholem's claim that the desire for transcendence is "one of the most important preoccupations of the human mind," Jews on the other side of *Haskalah* desire to find Aher's path to another form of redemption.⁸ In this way, the desire to transcend the limitations of Jewish lived experience becomes mapped on to Aher's illegitimate, heretical path. It furnishes Jews with a pattern of messianism that demands transgression to fulfill its aspirations.⁹ It is a "messianism of the other" that in its transcendence of lived experience offers another *Pardes* in literature. Consequently, each of this section's chapters reflects on how the "messianism of the other" suggests Aher's redemption in modernity. Each one proposes to materialize a messianic age, to propel a messianic textuality into the phenomena of time and space.

1

Jacob Frank, "Heretic of Kabbalah"

Olga Tokarczuk's recent novel, *The Books of Jacob*, opens with a quizzical scene.[1] An anonymous character swallows a piece of paper with mysterious Hebrew letters on it. The letters form a word written in "specially prepared ink."[2] As the ink dissolves, the writing "splits in two: substance and essence."[3] The word becomes reducible to its constituent parts. Although the ink dissipates and the letters "lose their shape," their traces remain, adhering to the character's body "since essences always seek carriers in matter—even if this is to be the cause of many misfortunes."[4] For this character, the transgression of forcing the letters to adhere to human matter creates the future's "many misfortunes."

The anonymous character swallowing the letters is Yente; she has traveled to a wedding at a distant relative's home in spite of her age and ill health. On the way to the wedding, she becomes "weak"; she stops eating and barely tastes "a few drops" of water offered to her.[5] The relatives accompanying her suspect her death is imminent. They will be forced to cancel the wedding because of it. By the time they arrive in Rohatyn, at the house of Yente's nephew, Elisha Shorr, the wedding's host, everyone, including Yente, knows she is dying. To be with her family, she has put the wedding in jeopardy because of the possibility of her death.

Her pending death causes Elisha, a Sabbatian, to write an incantation in Hebrew, "Hey-mem-tav-nun-hey. Hamtana: waiting"; while she sleeps, he slips the "amulet on the dying woman's neck" and backs out of the room.[6] The letters are supposed to pause Yente's death, delaying it until after the wedding. When he leaves, she acts in desperation.

> Yente opens her eyes and, with a weakening hand, feels for the amulet. She knows what's written on it. She breaks the strap, opens the carrier, and swallows the amulet like a little pill.[7]

The simple act of swallowing the Hebrew letters transforms the ritual, forcing the letters to adhere to and transform the body, in order to prevent her death. It is no longer a question of delay, but of a "metamorphosis." Hence her transgression fuses a kabbalistic principle, the dynamism of the Hebrew letters, whose origin in God enables creation, to Yente's "metamorphosis" from dying woman to conscious being even though it traps her between planes of existence. The desire to be with her family at the wedding has produced the scene of her transgression: the letters adhere to her human substance rather than their previous discursive bodies. They animate her physically so that she does not die, yet her body remains without the capacity either to move or to communicate.

Hence she gains another level of intuition; she "sees everything from above, and then her gaze goes back to under her eyelids."[8] Tokarczuk describes it as ascending and descending in which Yente sees "the winding line of the [Dniester] river, its filigrees, like the outlines of the letters *gimel* and *resh*."[9] Essentially, exceeding the limitations of her body, in her metamorphosis, Yente has begun to read the world around her, to see the animation of the letters in creation, their inscription in matter. Yente has forfeited human existence, making her akin to a golem in a Talmudic sense.[10] When Yente swallows the letters, Torkaczuk implies that Yente seeks to overcome the limitations of her body. She forfeits her soul, and returns to a golem state. In fact, Yente's story, her metamorphosis, ends with her transformation into a crystal, buried within a cave, a descending into matter that still emanates mysterious power, that still intuits the world around her.[11] The desire to displace death, to remove its inevitability, transforming human existence into an "other," an unembodied consciousness, brackets the story Tokarczuk wants to tell eventually about Jacob Frank. It also suggests Yente's longing to displace death in order to not pollute the wedding is resolved through necessary transgression, the adoption of an illegitimate path. She sacrifices her soul for her family's happiness on earth.

For reviewers of Tokarczuk's novel, *The Books of Jacob* "focuses on a group of mid-eighteenth-century Jews—a loose collection of mystics and Kabbalists—struggling to reconcile their endless tribulations with an all-powerful God."[12] It is simply historical fiction. More specifically, Tokarczuk produces a fabulist narrative about Jacob Frank, the false Jewish messiah in the eighteenth century who leads Jews into apostasy throughout the Habsburg and Ottoman empires.[13] For Jews, Frank's acts continue the work of his seventeenth-century predecessor, Shabbatai Zvi.[14] He is the last of a line of heretical kabbalists. This somewhat scandalous individual in Jewish history, "a shadowy figure who's almost entirely unknown today," Frank becomes an emblematic and enigmatic character who promotes to both Jews and non-Jews a wholly new identity, a Jewishness free of Judaism that can be incorporated into a secular world.[15]

Hence Tokarczuk's Jacob Frank is uniquely a product of kabbalah, a symbol of both Polish and European modernity, and although he is particularly Jewish, he is not Judaically observant. Freighting his popularity within Poland, Germany, and Turkey, Tokarczuk suggests that as a personality, Frank reflects tensions erupting among Jews and Gentiles as they struggle to move beyond a world of parochial and political oppressions. The vehicle for this popularity is in fact Frank's capacity to narrate the world, the cosmos, and God: he is "the best storyteller they have ever heard."[16] Frank's heresy comes to Jews in the alternative *aggadot* he tells them.

In this way, Tokarczuk links both Yente's and Frank's heretical kabbalahs to a historical contingency: they are necessary and inevitable.[17] While these heresies circulate in the form of stories, among the masses, the nobility, and Jewish communities across Central and Eastern Europe as well as the Ottoman Empire, in the novel, they compel Frank's followers to imagine a physical journey "into the darkness because it's only out of the darkness that you see clearly."[18]

When Jacob "the messiah" takes his retinue back to Poland, to the many Hasidic villages across the Dniester river, and bordering the route from "Kamieniec to Lwow," he returns to the Sabbatian families, embedded among hasids and appearing like them, grouped around Elisha Shorr, Yente's relative.[19] At these villages and shtetls, Frank preaches of a Jewish redemption in which Jews must perform not only "strange deeds," the incomprehensible and even nonsensical acts outside of Jewish custom, but also "they .... have to do everything that was once prohibited."[20]

In Torkarczuk's first iteration of Frank's teachings, his follower and companion Nahman describes the violation of *halakhah* as a key feature of Frank's messianic purpose.[21]

> He proclaims a new religion, one accessible exclusively through Esau, meaning Christianity, just as Sabbatai crossed over to Ishmael, meaning the Turkish faith. The progress of salvation depends on extracting from those religions the seeds of revelation and sowing them in one great divine revelation, the Torah of Atzilut: Torah of the World of Emanations.[22]

Taking up "Esau" as the real signifier of Jewish redemption, Nahman suggests that the messiah and his story have been hidden, traveling on the "other's path" since the time of the patriarchs when Jacob goes into exile from the line of Isaac—the Jews—returning to Esau in the land of Edom for redemption.[23] In fact, Frank asserts that he walks the same path as "Abraham, with Sarah, with Sabbatai."[24] Instead of a path that leads through the rabbinate and the earthly Torah given to Moses, Frank imagines he travels an other's path, in darkness, and that this forgotten road begins with the first patriarch and continues through Sabbatai, finally concluding with him.

He underlines for his listeners that his path will return them to a place essentially *before the Law*. His messianic redemption not only displaces rabbinic authority, but by positing a mystical link between himself and Abraham, Frank also conflates his power now as the messiah with the one patriarch whom kabbalists claim to be the author of *Sefer Yetsirah* and who consequently knows the secret of Divine creation, the secret of letter permutations. In this role, he is accompanied by all "the great sages who have broken down the world into just the letters of which it is composed."[25] He cedes to himself the power to control the letters. Declaring himself to be the real Jacob, Abraham's direct descendant, he claims to reestablish the patriarchal line, a consequence of his primordial essence, in order to redeem the Jews.[26] In his being, he erases the boundary between Divine and human ontologies that the Law enacts in order to deny humans the possibility of redemption. He, the messiah, is a heretic of the kabbalah by divine decree.

Within his new "heretical kabbalah," Tokarczuk's Frank traces the boundary between paradise and human existence essentially through his ability to stimulate the letters, liberating them from their bondage to an earthly Torah or the Torah of *Beriah*. Thus Nahman associates Frank's and Zvi's apostasies with the process of "extracting .... the seeds of revelation and sowing them" in order to produce "the Torah of Atzilut."

Atzilut must be freed from the incomprehensible chaos of *Beriah*. Since the *Atzilut* Torah cannot be manifest in the earthly *Beriah*, the messiah in physical exile forces the letters' emanations to reveal themselves in corporeal form. With "Atzilut," or "the Torah of the World of Emanations," Frank's apostasy—the other's path—is manifested as the path of Divine creation, a path that liberates the letters from text, setting them free to adhere to an "other" substance, a substance that is precluded in Talmud—Aher is condemned because he has hoped for just such an experience, just such a transcendence. That *tanna* is decreed unredeemable by God Himself in "The Four who went to Pardes" because he seeks to erase the boundary between God and human.

In this way, the novel's model, Frank's redemption, as an effect of the letters' adherence to human substance, implies the possibility of Aher's redemption. The messiah's entrance into "darkness" becomes a necessary step of refinement or "perfection" along the "other's path." The messiah's abandonment of *pardes* enables him to reunite with the higher Torah, "the Torah of Atzilut" whose seeds are strewn throughout the darkness. Reunification does not come from obedience to the earthly Torah's laws, but rather through a series of physical transgressions.[27] *Atzilut* materializes in the messiah's body because he has immersed himself in sin.

While Tokarczuk's fictional Jacob repeats many of the doctrines associated with Frankism, in the novel, Frank's narrative aims at Jews reimagining their liberation from persecution through the adoption of an identity that enables them to obscure their identities as Jews. Their earthly redemption is contingent on their abilities to mask their real identities. They "will always be Jews, just our own kind."[28] The actual clue to their apostasy resides with Frank's command to follow the path of "Esau" because he valences it as a necessary part of redemption and it is expressed as an absolute effect of diaspora. The Jews must participate in Esau's "fallenness"; they must become part of Esau's world of sin if they are finally to gain redemption.

> "You have to go over to Catholicism," he told the simple people. "Make peace with Esau. You have to go into the darkness. Only in the worst place can the Messianic mission begin. The whole world is the enemy of the true God, don't you know that?
>
> "This is the burden of silence. Masa duma. Words are such a weighty burden that it is as though they carried half the world inside themselves …. you must cast aside your language, and with each nation speak its proper tongue."[29]

In order for Frank's "messianic mission" to establish itself in this world, the Jews are commanded to forfeit their language, Hebrew, and "with each nation speak its proper tongue."[30] The "burden" of their "silence" will be their immersion within "each nation." Quite literally, they will immerse themselves in the languages of the masses, "masa duma." They will be interchangeable to any other within the masses.

Frank's reasoning for the Jews' "silence" accents the "weighty" nature of the "proper tongue" or vernacular of "each nation."[31] These vernaculars are damned to act "as though they carried half the world inside themselves." They bear an incomplete revelation that only Frank and the Frankists can make intelligible and redemptive, only they can supply the missing predicates of Divine Being to these vernaculars.

By immersing themselves within these vernaculars, his followers will liberate "masa duma" from deep within sin itself. They will awaken the *principia individuationis* of language by innovating this forgotten link between Hebrew and the "proper tongue of each nation."

In fact, the Jewish belief in Hebrew as the language of God, composed of dynamic, living letters, is permutated by Frank into the physical presence of Jewish bodies inaugurating a wholly new socius. The stakes of Frank's theory of materialization—because that is essentially what it is—rest on how kabbalah positions the Torah in relation to human existence. In the *Zohar*, God reads his Torah in order to "create His work of Art."[32] In another thirteenth-century kabbalistic text, "the Torah is, from the first to the last pericope, the form of God, great and awesome."[33] Furthermore, if even "one letter be missing or in excess in the Torah Scroll," then "the Scroll of Torah [is] invalidated, because this change in form caused it to lose the form of God."[34] The upshot of this anonymous text concludes with the kabbalist declaring that not only has "God bound each one to write a Torah Scroll for himself," but also that each "one has made God" because he is obligated to write his own Torah.[35] The kabbalist insists that each Jew is required to "make God" by producing one's own written Torah exactly as that Torah has been given to Moses and to Judaism.[36] Here the kabbalist requires the exact reproduction of the Torah in human existence; the human body conforms mimetically to the earthly Torah so that it is also an exact copy of the Torah of *Atzilut* or heavenly Torah. The "orthodox" kabbalah renews Jews in Judaism.

Frank's heretical "innovation" of the kabbalah relies on the repudiation of the earthly Torah or the "Torah of Beriah." It inverts the kabbalistic *mitzvah* or duty to adhere to the written Torah. In fact, Frankist teachings develop this form of innovation so that the legends, hagiographies, tales, "are based on an exegetical principle of tendentious rewriting of traditional Jewish narratives so as to invert established hierarchies, discredit honored symbols, and reevaluate the negative characters of the Jewish tradition."[37] Thus it forms "heretical kabbalah." Its "rewriting of traditional Jewish narratives" is the circulation of Frank's new narratives repudiating established Judaic prohibitions.

Tokarczuk's justification for that repudiation is a new origin story provided by Frank himself. In the novel's "A tale of two tablets," Frank narrates how the "Torah of Beriah" is used by Samael, the king of the demons, dressed "in the guise of an angel," to supplant the "Torah of Atzilut."[38] It begins with the exodus.

> By the time the Jews left Egypt, the world was ready for salvation .... It was unprecedented .... Everything stopped in anticipation of the new Law .... and so it was that God Himself engraved the Law on two stone tablets in such a way that it would be discernible to the human eye and comprehensible to the human mind. This was the Torah of Atzilut.[39]

Frank explains to his listeners that in "anticipation of the new Law," even the world's substance transforms until "everything" stops, appears to cease moving. Time has been undone enabling Jews to step out of human existence. They no longer exist in familial and social groupings.

This moment when "the world was ready for salvation," God writes the "Torah of Atzilut" by inscribing it on "two stone tablets." In this act, God makes Torah "comprehensible." The claim implies that the human senses that kill Azzai, drive Zoma mad, and damn Aher, are then transformed ontologically so that they no longer bear the evidence of their condemnation. Since in Frank's homily the mysterious *Atzilut* Torah and his heretical kabbalah are implicitly paired, his claim to a "new Law" implies that his ontology has been similarly perfected.

Frank's foundational claim—that *Atzilut* has been made "comprehensible"—is directed at the long-standing objection from the beginnings of kabbalah, in which the secrets of revelation are understood as incommunicable and incomprehensible through human language.[40] Humans are at this moment prepared to read the revelation, "the law of liberty."[41] When Moses returns and discovers that the Jews have fallen to "temptation and indulged in sin …. in great despair [he] shattered the tablets …. so that they broke into a thousand pieces and turned to dust."[42] In Moses' absence, they have crossed back into time and space. With the tablets' destruction, earthly substance or matter returns to its fallen state, and appearing as an angel, Samael "dictates" to Moses a set of replacement commandments. Moses unwittingly presents to the Jewish people the "Torah of Beriah" that would "keep God's people enslaved."[43] It is a Law that is "incomprehensible" and its authority is held in place by a rabbinate in the service of Samael's deception.[44] Additionally, to prevent *Atzilut* from being restored to Moses' heirs, Samael flings its shards "around the world and among many different religions." Therefore, the Messiah is tasked with finding and liberating the shards, in order to exhibit *Atzilut* "in its final revelation."[45]

In other words, Frank removes from the earthly Torah any kind of textual immanence: the Jews must "silence themselves," negate the earthly Torah, usurp the Torah of Judaism, the Torah of *Beriah*, in order to make visible the Torah of *Atzilut*, and *Atzilut* must be adorned in the form of the "other."[46] The "other" form not only allows the Torah of *Atzilut* to be recognizable, but also to be materialized on earth. In fact, the earthly Torah has masked such embodiment since it is an imperfect copy, and tied to Samael's deception. Its imperfection is not only in the Jews' inability to see through *Beriah*, but also in their lack of recognition of Frank's revelation manifest before them.

Tokarczuk underscores that the initial reaction to Frank's "strange deeds," his revelation that the Jews must "ford the Nazarene faith, as they would a river, and that Jesus was a shell and a shield for the true Messiah" prompts his Jewish listeners to reject the teaching, but as the hours go by, they begin to imagine the completion of these very acts of *halakhic* violation and how it will change their lives.[47]

> At around noon, the idea seems shameful. By the afternoon, it's up for discussion. By evening it's been assimilated, and late at night it's perfectly obvious that everything's exactly as Jacob says.
>
> Late at night, yet another aspect of the idea, which they hadn't really taken into consideration before, occurs to them—that once they are baptized, they will cease to be Jews, at least as far as anyone can tell. They will become people—Christians.

They will be able to purchase land, open shops in town, send their children to any schools they wish .... Their heads spin with possibilities, for it is as though they have suddenly been given a strange, almost inconceivable gift.[48]

The arc of the transformation begins with Frank's Jewish listeners' realization that he advocates a "shameful" apostasy. After hours of thinking about it, they imagine the benefits that would accrue to them if they perform Frank's commandments. First and foremost, "they will become people"; they will have rights to live on their own land, to do business in the heart of their towns rather than subsisting at its margins or traipsing through the countryside as itinerant peddlers. Their children will attend "any schools they wish." The horror of transgression converts before their very eyes into entitlement: "they will become people" and "people" is synonymous both with the godless and Jews' civil empowerment or the end of their persecution. Apostasy becomes then recuperated as a "strange, almost inconceivable gift." Readers feel the inevitability of their choices. In the novel, Frank's teachings promise Jews a transformation of their lives on earth and "it cannot be otherwise."[49] They have followed his innovation, moving with him mentally into transgression's inversion.

Tokarczuk links Frank's innovation of the "tablets" narrative to its physical expression in the "Lanckoronie Affair," in which the historical experience results in Frank's arrest and imprisonment. Her source, Pawel Maciejko's summary of the historical account, indicates that Lanckoronie is the seminal moment when Frank's materialization of redemption on earth becomes synonymous in the minds of his followers with their persecution by rabbinic authorities.

Toward the end of January 1756, Jacob Frank and a group of other Sabbatians were discovered conducting a secret ritual in the little town of Lanckoronie, near the Moldavian border. The discovery set a process in motion, which led to the emergence of Frankism as a phenomenon distinct from other branches of the wider Sabbatian movement. The ensuing sequence of events included the arrest of the participants in the ritual, a series of unusually harsh punitive measures enacted by Jewish authorities, public clashes between Sabbatian and non-Sabbatian Jews in Podolia, the involvement of Christians in what would seem an internal Jewish affair, public disputations between the representatives of the Frankists and of the rabbinate, and, ultimately, the conversion of Frank and his followers to Roman Catholicism.[50]

Maciejko establishes that the Lanckoronie affair introduces Frankism as "a phenomenon distinct from other branches of the .... Sabbatian movement." Whereas kabbalah and Sabbatianism are expressed as objects of religion, Frankism's "phenomenon" is expressed in the body as an absolute object of redemption. It is not the consequence of sin. In fact, the object of the Frankist phenomenon is the full social, political, subjective, and sensual transformation of Jewish lived experience. Thus the transgressions of the body reveal the hidden revelation obscured by flesh. By contrast, the object of Sabbatian phenomenality is the soul's uniting with the text of Torah. Maciejko's simple phrase belies how serious a transformation has occurred since Frank's project rests on a specific form of embodiment, the aim of which is the transformation of ontology from human to divine while Zvi's project implies a textual redemption that perfects ontology, excluding the body from that redemption.

Through Tokarczuk's fictional account, we realize the profound stakes of Frank's narrative intervention. In her version, "two curious people" discover Frank and his followers in Lanckoronie meeting with Frank's "prophet," Hayah.[51] These "two curious people," Gershon and Naftali, follow the group to Hayah's house where she lives with her husband, Hirsch, the local rabbi.[52] They discover the windows are covered, the door is bolted. They witness Frank's retinue enter the home, but the house is dark as if the group has "gone to sleep."[53] Gershon finds a small slit in the window coverings—a tear in time and space—"[A]nd so he sees—barely, by the light of a single candle—a circle of seated men, and in the middle of the circle," Hayah stands on a stool, "half naked" and "Jacob Frank walks around her in circles, seemingly babbling to himself."[54]

Her "body is perfect, miraculous, as though she were come from another world. Her eyes are half closed, and her mouth is half open …. Hayah …. the only woman amidst the many men."[55] She appears to have transformed from the woman who runs the household, shreds onions, disciplines the children to a being "from another world." Her breasts "glisten" with droplets of sweat: they appear so heavy that Gershon imagines holding them up. Surreptitiously, he watches the ritual unfold.

> Jacob is the first to approach her. He has to stand ever so slightly on tiptoe to reach her breasts with his lips. It looks as though he even holds her nipple for a moment in his mouth, as though he might be swallowing a couple of drops of milk. And then the second breast.[56]

The ritual is repeated by every man present, even Hayah's brother, who "though hurriedly" demonstrates that he too "has been admitted into the great mystery of this faith," the metamorphosis of the female body into the manifestation of the Torah of *Atzilut*.[57] The men feel themselves transformed into "brothers"; they have witnessed that "the Torah itself has entered Hirsch's wife, Hayah; that is what beams out now through her skin." Even more provocatively, Frank has led the men to the Torah's metamorphosis: they have abandoned a lifeless text and embrace its new embodiment in Hayah whose body exhibits the traces of *Atzilut*, its letters. They stimulate these letters within her. Their senses draw from her the emanations of the Torah of *Atzilut*. Tokarczuk's Frank proposes an erotic *tikkun* ritually enacted on Hayah's body, and as his willing participant, she becomes the fulfillment, the aim of the "Torah of Atzilut's" restoration.[58] This aspect of the "heretical kabbalah" points to an erotic *tikkun* that is fulfilled through the senses.[59]

Maciejko contrasts the Lanckoronie rite with both the Judaic practice during Simchat Torah, the celebration of the gift of Torah to Moses, and the Sabbatian practice of mystical "marriage to the Torah." He suggests compellingly that Frank "innovates" rituals familiar from Judaism and Sabbatianism. Citing the conclusion to the Simhat Torah service, Maciejko describes the custom of men "touch[ing] the edge of their prayer shawl" to the Torah scrolls, and then "kissing" these edges of their shawls.[60] He explains that "the person who completes the reading of the Torah is called .... 'bridegroom of the Torah.'"[61] Additionally, the "normative Jewish practice" is reimagined by kabbalists "as a marriage between Israel and the Torah."[62]

The Sabbatian tradition accents Sabbatai the messiah committing himself to the *Atzilut* Torah in spirit. Consequently, the Torah itself under the marriage canopy is neither conflated with a human form nor is it *Atzilut*.

> In 1648, Sabbatai Tsevi, having invited the most prominent rabbis to a banquet, erected a bridal canopy, had a Torah scroll brought in, and performed the marriage ceremony between himself and the Torah .... Sabbatai was severely censured by the rabbis for his performances; still, the concept of mystical marriage of a Jew and the Torah was deeply rooted in the Jewish tradition, and his action only stretched the boundaries of mainstream Judaism.[63]

Acting as "the 'true' messiah," Sabbatai ascends to the status of bridegroom to the "true" Torah—the Torah of *Atzilut*—: the higher Torah cannot pair with Sabbatai as simply a human agent. He must ascend and in that ascension, the soul transcends. Human substance has yet to transform in this model. In fact, Zvi's body is not perfected; it still retains all of its weaknesses. Sabbatianism recognizes then an imperfect, flawed messiah, whose sin is part of the messiah's redemption. As Maciejko points out, Sabbatian heresy "only" expands "the boundaries of mainstream Judaism."

Tokarczuk's representation of the Lanckoronie rite, even bordering as it does on the lurid, illustrates the radical innovation already inherent in Frank's heretical kabbalah. Frank has declared the female body as the vehicle for the revelation; one no longer reads the Torah for revelation, but instead the messiah engages in an erotic permutation or performance, collapsing the boundary between the earthly and Divine worlds. The woman's body becomes the readable higher Torah.[64] Contrasting him with Sabbatai, Maciejko declares "in Frankism the true word of God descended into palpably material female flesh."[65] The explicit nature of the fictional scene underlines for Frank that Torah's liberation occurs through the transcendence of human substance rather than a sacred textual tradition. The body is stimulated by the messiah. Moreover, the role of the woman is the text to be read rather than condemned. Eve or Hayah enables Jacob to reveal, possess, control *Atzilut*.

Frank introduces two principles. The first, deriving from kabbalah, posits the female body as the embodiment of Torah, to whom the messiah is obligated to adhere in order to perform redemption.[66] The second reflects Frank's heretical innovation of the kabbalah in that it displaces reading the Torah through the substitution of Frank's mandated commandment to focus one's *kavvanah* or intention on the messiah's transformation of human substance as he narrates and/or performs a range of acts, the *tikkunim* of apostasy, materialized before his followers. In this respect, Tokarczuk reproduces Frankist principles as they inform the historical hagiographies and mythical tales about Jacob Frank. For Frankists, his heretical kabbalah elevates these tales to sacred writing.

Frankist hagiographies and mythical tales have long been analyzed exclusively for their historical and religious content in the service of Frankist circles as well as discrete elements' eventual structural and formal adaptation by Hasidic *tzaddikim*.[67] However, Frank's hagiographies are early instances of a literature emerging outside *halakhah*. By "innovating" kabbalistic principles, Frank proposes alternative *aggadot*, specifically associated with Jews who have disavowed the Judaic tradition and who live in a secular world.

In these tales, Frank presents himself as the *prostak* or "common man" in Polish whose pedigree locates him simply as "one of them."[68] Moreover, *prostak* signifies in Polish and in its Yiddish translation, a "simpleton." Frank's use of the term ambiguously points to both his public "identification" with the masses he leads and his rejection of *halakhic* or rabbinic authority he displaces.[69] The tales posit a revolt against a rabbinic elite who have "kept Jews in a psychological state of oppression" by valorizing the figure of the other or "the common man" who has been rejected by that authority. Frank associates the rabbinic elite with the objectives of "a monstrous deception in which an evil power bestowed nonsensical and harmful laws upon the people of Israel."[70] Frank promises his followers that redemption comes not from these elites, but from those commoners, the ones who do not study Torah, essentially declaring that their lack of knowledge protects them from the "evil power" and makes them simultaneously entitled to the revelation he embodies. They can understand him literally.

Frank's use of the vernacular Polish evokes both an explicit rejection of the *tannaim*, and an implicit identification with Akiva, prior to his elevation to *tannaitic* status, when he does not study *halakhah*.[71] Before his elevation to sage status, Akiva describes himself as an *am ha'aretz* or "simpleton."[72] After Akiva studies Torah, he is no longer *am ha'aretz*. Implicitly, the *prostak* identifies with the simpleton and rejects the sage as a false prophet. Frank's innovation hinges on the sage's implied forfeit of the other path Frank now travels.

Frank also has in mind the Yiddish term, *amhoretz*, in which one is a "simpleton," incapable of judgments that distinguish between law and common sense. Consequently, the *amhoretz* is "ignorant" of the Law and Torah. Frank "innovates" the Yiddish term to indicate that as the "real Jacob," he is a patriarch "before the law," and specifically, before the "Torah of Beriah." Frank transforms "simpleton" to a desirable state: someone liberated from the Law.

These linguistic valences underpin the stakes of the Lanckoronie rite, historically, so that when Frank declares in the tales that he is a *prostak*, he locates that same Adamic position not only in the secular world around him, but he also suggests that the "common man" has crossed an abyss at which not only Akiva, but also the entire Jewish people after Jacob have stopped. As redemption materializes, the implication is clear: Frank has bridged the gap that compels Aher's apostasy and the abandonment of Pardes. He has discovered the path that Aher sought. In other words, Frank's revision of *am ha'aretz/prostak/amhoretz* suggests that Talmud testifies to the perennial failure of Judaism. Its rabbis have refused Frank's redemption in favor of an epistemological and premature "withdrawal" from total liberation.

Strikingly, Frank's tales focus the reader's attention away from the received *halakhah* in order to embrace the Frankist transmission of a new revelation, a revelation that implicitly suggests Aher's redemption. Rather than an *aggadah* illustrating how to obey the Law, the mimetic representation of Frank's life testifies instead to the messiah's appearance on earth. As Harris Lenowitz notes, Frank is the hero whose "theft .... of the treasure .... kept away from mankind by a jealous Creator, a cruel or errant demiurge" underscores how he, the messiah, is an adversary of an unjust ruler against whom the violation of received law materializes a cosmic repair.[73] He must defeat "a jealous Creator" in order to bring about human redemption; he opposes a demiurge who maintains the status quo of Jewish oppression.[74] Frank's alleged innate qualities of "resolute, fearless action and physical strength" enable him to act "using determination, courage, and strength as his only tools."[75] He no longer needs mystical power; he redeems by using human skills. He performs the *tikkun* of the world's repair by acting on his own initiative and thereby rescuing the world from "a jealous Creator" because it is good for the self.

In one example, and as part of "The Call" narratives, Frank continues this theme representing himself as a simple traveler who overcomes a narrative of defeat and passivity.

> 36. Having come to the river Totorozh, I found there 150 wagons, standing on the shore, afraid to go further because of the high water. Without saying anything, I took off my robe, put it and my bundles on my head, and despite the most terrible danger, I swam across the river with my horse. From the other shore, people shouted at me, what was I doing? For God's sake why was I taking such a risk? Listening to none of it, I swam across and that same day I managed 6 miles to Roman. Those people had to wait there 11 days, after which when they got there, they asked about me and were surprised at seeing me alive. And my prostak-ness did this.[76]

Essentially, the tale uplifts Frank's lack of pedigree to a holy state and in the process, proposes that he unites in himself "uncommon abilities" because he is guided "by his vision."[77] These "uncommon abilities" enable him to see beyond the Jews' lived experience, his own lived experience, to imagine a life "on the other side." If his "listeners" can imagine his successful crossing of the abyss, if they can identify with him, they too can go beyond their everyday lives, their "common behavior in the Jewish world."[78] They can go to all the places where they have been denied. In other words, his "*prostak-ness*" enables him to go beyond social rank, to challenge physical obstacles, to exist successfully outside the ghetto. He can forego waiting for redemption to occur because he embodies it already. He already has the skills, the tools, the power, to redeem himself. Frank espouses that Jews can choose either to live a life of persecution, eternally waiting for their salvation, or they can recognize the innate "uncommon" qualities they share in common as the basis for their liberation.[79]

In subsequent tales, Frank underscores that he comes to Poland "to wipe out all laws, all religions .... to bring life into this world."[80] Like Maciejko's thinking about the phenomenon of Frankism, Lenowitz observes that in this moment, Frank introduces "something so new" that the innovation itself goes far beyond the heretical precursors of Sabbatianism and Luriannic kabbalah.[81]

> Frank's theology constitutes something so new that it alters the substance of the Kabbalah itself to the same degree that Luria's put a new face on the Zohar. Frank's lacks the fineness of Luria's because his access to the resources of the literature is so limited; but while it is crude, it is striking, going beyond Shabbateanism, particularly in Frank's celebration of his own sturdy character.[82]

Lenowitz points to the realization that Frank's narratives and teachings shift the object of revelation from Torah, and the "old kabbalah" to Frank's personal and human experience and inaugurates a personal "heretical kabbalah," in which lived experience is exalted over decreed law because lived experience materializes the messianic age.[83] The shift encourages, moreover, believers to identify with Frank and to imitate the terms of his redemption.[84] They imagine performing similar acts of self-sufficiency that diverge radically from Sabbatianism in its historical outlines.[85]

Even more pointedly, Lenowitz identifies another aspect that informs Frankism and that would be immediately recognizable to kabbalists.

> Frank refers to this world as that of broken vessels and this tradition he interprets *nefilim* of Genesis 6:4 (elsewhere understood only as giants), through its Hebrew root, as "the fallen." At this point, Frank's new religion, the *das/da'as edom* (the faith/knowledge of Esau, Edom) appears again by name, and Frank laments that if his followers had only shed their attachments to traditional Judaism, its texts and its psychology of submission, they could have reached Esau/Edom.[86]

Frank condemns "traditional Judaism's" investment in the earthly Torah because it has not only prevented Jewish redemption, but it has also encouraged the Jews' "psychology of submission." The ambiguity of Frank's "other path" to paradise underscores the earthly Torah's misrepresentation of "*nefilim*" or "the fallen" as "giants" rather than his realization that the whole of creation takes place in the fallenness of the void.[87] In this way, Esau/Edom become signifiers of a path, submerged within the abyss, an uncanny one perhaps, certainly familiar but unknown. It is a cognitive path imprinted within the unconscious. As a result, to be human is to be imprinted with sin as the actual path to redemption, even if unremembered.[88] To put it another way, the memory of "fallenness" is a trace to a forgotten path.

Hence the casual substitution of *nefilim* for "the fallen" associates it with the locus of the "broken vessels." Frank's heretical kabbalah conflates Luria's realm of the *kelipot* with human existence. If "the fallen" occupy the same terrain as the *kelipot*, then, human existence takes place in the abyss. We live among "broken vessels." The only *tikkun* that could repair this condition requires then the discovery of a path out of or across the abyss and onto the "other side" of "fallenness." Moreover, the path to the other side can only be traveled by a "giant" among men whose ontology resonates with the patriarchs rather than the rabbinate.[89] With Frank, redemption through "fallenness" becomes synonymous with a displacement of "traditional Judaism, its texts" in order for the new representation to purge itself of weakness, to purge a "psychology of submission" from its "structures of beings."[90]

Thus Frank's hagiographies posit key themes of a new heretical kabbalah, concentrated primarily on the emergence of a human messiah who comes from "among the people," without social pedigree, but whose innate and superior qualities are revealed through narrative tales. This messiah's violation of propriety, custom, or *halakhah*, is exhibited as a personal entitlement that enables an individual to accrue wealth, esteem, and power. Frank founds a messianic materialism available to humans.

Describing these tales, Lenowitz states provocatively that they "have the power to repair by being told."[91] However, the repair envisioned is tied to the messiah's gain. He alone benefits from the *tikkun*; his repair benefits himself. The realization reflects Frank's own self-promotion and he juxtaposes it to Jewish suffering as a consequence of their rejection of his messianic materialism. Although in the hagiographies, Frank is an historical agent around whom the events unfold, in the narrative tales that emerge about him, identification is elicited through a fictional character, a subject who exists in "another world .... known to be fantastic."[92] Quite simply, Frank innovates his own biographical narratives in order to tell the Jews a different story of how he is Jewish and Tokarczuk traces this strategy to reveal how Frank's materialized messianism freights a mimesis of lived experience that ends in obscurity.

After Frank, the heretic of the kabbalah, dies, his followers, mapped between Offenbach—his court—Warsaw—where the majority live—and Prague, the Circle organized around Jonas Wehle, begin the work of preserving his teachings and tales. However, they first have to determine how to read his revelation, how to discover "the other's path" in his absence so that an heretical kabbalah could be discovered and recognizable to subsequent generations.

2

Heretics and Heresies of Innovation

The obligation to read and interpret Jacob Frank's tales about "the other's path" falls primarily on an eighteenth-century group of Prague Frankists, called "the Prague Circle," organized initially around Jonas Beer Wehle and his son-in-law, Low Enoch von Hönigsberg, known familiarly as Hönig.[1] Tasked with the dissemination of the Frankist legacy after Jacob Frank's death in 1791, the Prague Circle includes "[s]ome of the most prominent Prague Jewish families, such as the Porgeses, the Mauthners, and the Zerkowitzes."[2] It becomes a prominent benefactor of the Frankist court in Offenbach, where Frank's daughter, Eva, leads a remnant of Frank's followers.

Although Wehle visits Offenbach, accompanied by Hönig, the Circle's importance to Frankism doesn't derive from their presence there: the two men in Prague craft a literary or aesthetic code in which philosophical texts become imbued with mystical significance that only "the believers" can intuit.[3] The project introduces the innovation of philosophical principles to reveal an "heretical kabbalah" translated into a metaphysics of redemptive apostasy. Frank's messianic materialism is reframed by the Circle as part and parcel of Enlightenment philosophy. Hence the metaphysics hints that Wehle's perspective is not aberrant to German-speaking cultures. By extension, it suggests Wehle the Frankist is emblematic rather than alien to Czech culture.

To that end, Vaclav Žáček 's report on the history of Frankism in Prague offers insight into how Wehle is perceived by Prague's citizens, as well as the Jewish community. He declares Wehle, "the modern Bohemian," because his tastes reflect a cultural aristocracy.[4] Since Wehle's home in Prague serves as the meeting place where Frankists read their "religious books .... almost every day," Žáček implies a cognitive link between "the modern Bohemian" and Central European Frankists.[5] Wehle's Circle is recognized as the second most important center of Frankism after Offenbach, so that Frankist pilgrims' "first path" from the Frankist court leads directly to Wehle's door.[6] Likewise, "[T]he vacuum left" by the departure of the Polish Frankists from the court after Frank's death is "immediately filled by new arrivals from Prague."[7] Žáček 's interest is though not in where they go from Prague, but rather who they are to Central Europe. He identifies that Wehle remains within the Jewish community, although he no longer adheres to traditional Judaism, practicing Sabbatianism and Frankism covertly.[8] Much like Frank, Wehle's apostasy eventually leads to open, continuous, conflicts with Prague's rabbinate and the orthodox Jewish community.[9]

When Jakob Frank emerges as the messiah, the Sabbatian communities of Poland, Salonika, and Central Europe consolidate around the idea that a new revelation has emerged for Jews outside of *halakhah* and that Frank fulfills a messianic project, begun by Zvi. However, in Prague, for Žáček, this project turns "the Bohemian countries" into "the scene of a persistent and bitter struggle between rabbinical orthodoxy" and "Jewish mystics and messianists, addicted to innovation."[10] Rather than the promotion of Jacob Frank as the messiah, the conflict appears to Žáček to be over how to read the Kabbalah, and other Jewish sacred texts, as well as how to write Jewish messianism.

The Circle's promotion of textual heresies is linked to the kabbalah also in the minds of those who witness the "struggle." "Addicted to innovation" is the defining principle of the Prague Circle because in the heretical kabbalah, there is no boundary between sacred and profane. Every text becomes the bearer of *sod*, a secret revelation.

Žáček notes that due to the geographical centrality of "Bohemia and Moravia .... in the middle between the European west and east," populations have always been "swayed" by intellectual currents "from both directions."[11] Both Jews and non-Jews have "willingly accepted or fought, processed and redesigned" these trends so that they follow "their own inclinations and interests."[12] This casual aside underscores Žáček's characterization of Wehle as an exemplar of the "modern Bohemian"; the Prague Frankist circle reflects how Bohemians absorb Europe's cultural and intellectual trends, revising them to reflect their own interests. While the Jewish community of the "Bohemian lands" remains historically committed to their "racial and religious exclusivity," Žáček observes that the minority still follows the intellectual trends that pervade the non-Jewish majority. As Stuart Taberner alludes, the symbiotic relationship between the two groups informs then the Prague Circle's involvement with political anarchy and revolt shaping European history in the eighteenth and nineteenth centuries.[13] Thus Žáček concludes that although the Jews continue to be an "intellectually unified people," any charismatic leader, and every "religious fluctuation .... shakes" their entire Jewish world.[14]

Žáček's elevation, then, of a dispute between Judaism's gatekeepers—the rabbinate—and what Jewish Studies scholars, like "Graetz, Zunz, Steinschneider" consider a minor sect within the Jewish community—the Jewish false messianic movement of Jacob Frank—to the status of a controversy preoccupying all of Bohemia, implies that the Prague conflict is public knowledge.[15] He takes as a given, furthermore, the pervasiveness of kabbalistic ideas circulating within a larger social milieu beyond the control of Judaic authority. Žáček implies that Jewish mystical content saturates Czech culture. Since Žáček only reproduces the language "of his sources," he designates these ideas, their "innovations," as part of the kabbalistic practices of Prague's "Jewish mystics and messianists."[16] Hence Žáček's suggestion that Wehle's circle is emblematically Bohemian places these heretics of innovation as key figures in the circulation of kabbalah in German.

Simillarly, Pawel Maciejko identifies that kabbalah—in a Christian variant—is recognizable throughout the German-speaking world and it is a phenomenon of the "eighteenth century," a "paradigm shift," conducted in secret.[17] Although it does not "transform rejection of the Jews .... into acceptance," it does promote among "some circles of .... eighteenth century Christian society .... [a] fascination with the secrets of the Jews."[18] In other words, kabbalistic signifiers and themes are not only well known, but they are reflected in the category of "Taste" during Enlightenment across the German-speaking world in which Prague features prominently.

> Among upper echelons of the society which—in the words of Leibniz—'delighted in getting to know things uncanny', secrecy turned into mystery: the very same qualities that repulsed anti-Jewish theologians of the Reformation often inspired philo-Semites of the Enlightenment .... To be sure, Christian interest in Kabbalah and Jewish esoteric lore can be traced back at least to fifteenth-century Florence. However, early Christian Kabbalah was the province of a small group of erudite scholars; in the eighteenth century it became a fad.[19]

Maciejko connects explicitly popular kabbalistic content in the eighteenth century as elements deriving from the "uncanny." He underlines Leibniz's point that the overt anti-semitism of previous centuries becomes transformed into a "delight in difference" so that Jews themselves conflate with "things uncanny." The Jews become signifiers that disturb, unsettle the status quo. Furthermore, Maciejko identifies it as the "philo-semitism" of modernity that prompts the widespread interest in a Christian Kabbalah. Consequently, kabbalah is "a fad," a trend within non-Jewish culture.[20] In this way, he introduces a link between the recuperation of kabbalah in non-Jewish venues and the significance of a kabbalistic principle of innovation to a theory of the unconscious.

Žáček's use of "innovation," precisely the German word, *Neuerung*, suggests that his Czech narrators not only recognize the term's lexical meaning, but also supply it with a specific kabbalistic practice. Within German-speaking societies, the practice appears to non-Jews as a mysterious mode of reading and interpreting sacred texts.[21] Innovation is a mode that opens up the unconscious world of the sacred and extracts out of it a piece of the revelation. Suddenly, kabbalistic innovation has migrated from the circles of a small elite, trained both in *halakhah*, formal Judaism, and all aspects of Jewish mysticism to "the common man," the epithet that Jakob Frank repeatedly uses to describe himself and that Frankists adopt as the signifier of their freedom.[22]

Kabbalah's practice of "innovation" resonates with several traditions within German-speaking Jewry particularly and all Jews generally. Among the medieval Rhineland Hasids, their leaders, Samuel the Hasid, Jehudah the Hasid, and Eleazar ben Jehudah, all members of the Kalynomous family, and a "natural aristocracy" within the Rhineland, teach "the intensification of prayer," in which the believer focuses his *kavvanah* or intention "on the words of prayer while they are being spoken."[23] As Scholem observes, the Rhineland Hasids discover *kavvanah* "is something to be realized in prayer itself." It is a "mystical meditation" that draws from each familiar prayer a "novel intuition" in the mind of the kabbalist. The Hasid reveals a previously unknown layer of the revelation inherent in the familiar prayer, waiting and intended for that specific Hasid to intuit it. Scholem notes that these "early Hasidim" understood the prayer to be an emanation, transforming itself from a limited human construction, with personal content, specific to one time and space, into a bridge to the "unbound Godhead."[24] In that respect, innovation hints at the Rhineland Hasids' teaching on prayer, a theory expressed in words and letters. The content may even not be known by the one who utters it.[25] Since it is a "novel intuition," it signifies for kabbalists in thirteenth-century Spain, something akin to an "innovation," made popular through the *Zohar*.

They apply "innovation" to the practice of reading Torah, transferring the "realization of *kavvanah*" in prayer to the kabbalist's engagement with sacred text.[26] As Scholem observes, "the *Zohar* is chiefly concerned with the object of meditation."[27] It reflects the kabbalist's desire to "penetrate a new field of contemplation" beyond the visible and he underscores, it "is at the roots of the original impulse of the kabbalah."[28]

In his critical edition of the *Zohar*, Daniel Matt explains that the *Zoharist* approaches the Torah cognizant of each word's capacity for "innovation" and that "every word innovated in Torah by one engaged in Torah fashions one heaven."[29] Creation of new worlds is so intimately associated with kabbalistic innovation that readers of the *Zohar* expect their innovations to produce new spaces, new times, new "structures of beings."[30] Each "innovated word of wisdom" elevates "higher than other new interpretations" so that "one is able to innovate in Torah matters that Moses himself was not permitted to reveal."[31] Implicitly, the *Zoharist* accords to the innovated text, a revelation that not only extends beyond the *pschat* meaning or the literal meaning of the Bible, but also insists that a new agent has emerged. This new agent has been authorized to do what Moses could not, to receive and transmit what Moses is denied from revealing. Innovation appears to be a mode of reading that has awaited a specific set of readers.

> We have learned: The moment a new word of Torah originates from the mouth of a human being, that word ascends and presents herself before the blessed Holy One, who lifts that word, kisses her, and adorns her with seventy crowns—engraved and inscribed. But an innovated word of wisdom ascends and settles on the head of the צדיק (Tsaddik), Righteous One—Vitality of the Worlds. From there, it flies and soars, through 70,000 worlds, ascending to the Ancient of Days.[32]

To distinguish the received revelation of Torah from its transmitted innovation, the *Zoharist* depicts the words spoken by human beings, through prayer and study, "ascending" and "presenting themselves" to the Holy One who "adorns" each word. However, the "innovated word .... ascends" eventually to settle on the *tzaddik* ("צדיק"). The "innovated word" essentially recognizes the ontology of the *tzaddik* and chooses him from among the others praying. Although all prayers "ascend" to God, the prayer attached to the *tzaddik's* petition carries a specific weight and force.

In his footnote to this pericope, Matt explains then the epithet, "Righteous One—Vitality of the Worlds" alludes to *yesod*, one of the ten *sferot*. It "channels the flow of emanation to Shekinah and the worlds below," of which humans constitute one such world. Matt's explanation points though to how late kabbalah freights human agency in the transmission of "new revelations" that do not derive explicitly from Torah. In this way, innovation becomes associated with a "messianic" agent and potentially detached from Torah in its *halakhic* articulation. Moses who initially receives the revelation becomes a transitional figure between the "Ancient of Days" and the *tsaddik* who transmits its innovated meanings. Moreover, the innovation appears to be intended for a *tsaddik* to reveal: it exceeds not only Moses' purview, its original receiver, but also pre-existing interpretations of biblical text.

The *Zoharist* "innovates" the text to reveal another meaning, a "novel intuition," dormant until the kabbalist at that moment retrieves it. Additionally, the *Zoharist's* recognition of the letters' transformation from human instrument to Divine cognition expands the category of sacred text so that it includes every text written in Hebrew letters.[33] Every text written with Hebrew letters has the capacity to be a sacred text simply because we do not know what the letters mean to God.[34]

Neither of these "innovated" projects leads though to heresy. They are focused exclusively on renewing Judaism for its followers through the practice of "innovating" revelation already received. In other words, they engage in the traditional sense of kabbalah as "a received and transmitted tradition."[35] They reaffirm Judaism in its various registers.

Žáček's implications are therefore clear: Wehle and Prague's Frankists practice "innovation" as Jews, whose direct conflict with Judaism leads them to "innovate" content external to the Torah. They have shifted innovation from sacred text to profane narratives not only of Jacob Frank's life, but also of the "grand narratives" of modern Enlightenment. To Žáček, Wehle's theory of "innovation" promotes Frankist heresies, reflecting a part of the fabric of Czech culture and society. To Wehle, his innovations reveal a secret at the heart of German idealism. In this way, Wehle signifies a "heretic of innovation" both for secular Jews and for non-Jews with nothing to do with Judaism.[36] His "heresy" concerns a way of reading culture and text to affirm the "novel" intuitions of the kabbalah associated with Sabbatianism and Frankism, but expressed in secular philosophies.

According to Žáček, Wehle's transformation from well-known kabbalist to a "heretic of innovation" is reflected in a series of discussions between Wehle and his son-in-law. As their relationship develops, Hönig mentions that among Prague's Jews, Wehle has "a reputation for being a very pious man, a great theologian and a good expert on Kabbalah and all Jewish theological literature."[37] This comment inspires their regular meetings for the purpose of discussing and studying both Wehle's heretical kabbalah and Hönig's philosophical texts. Hönig reads to Wehle, explaining the concepts of the philosophical writings, while Wehle reads to him "the theological writings," explicating Kabbalah and "its many 'puzzling matters.'"[38]

Drawing on Hönig's testimony about his father-in-law, Žáček underscores that Wehle teaches Hönig "the religious and ideological systems of the Jewish sages and the essence of the Jewish religion."[39] As a result, Hönig reaffirms Wehle's "hatred of the rabbis," seeing in them, an "ignorance," an "intellectual poverty," and a "narrowmindedness."[40] At this moment, their Frankism has just innovated the meaning of the *amhoretz* /*am ha'aretz* to be those who continue to practice Judaism. Hönig describes the rabbinate as engaging in "oppression," while Wehle seeks "to apply his higher moral principles …. by proclaiming love for every neighbor and rejecting hatred."[41]

As Žáček describes the intimacy of the two men daily reading aloud their books to one another, the historian freights their need to communicate to each other the meanings of their respective texts: Hönig and Wehle insist on contextualizing for the other how the works' "true" meanings have waited for them particularly.[42] At this moment, their explications abandon the traditional dialectic familiar to the study of *midrash*, opting instead to fuse the kabbalah's aesthetic dimensions to philosophical aspects of Kantian and other philosophical texts.

Maciejko describes their exchanges' focus on "quotations, paraphrases, and references to major personalities of the European Enlightenment .... Leibniz and Rousseau," and their utilization of "Kantian and Hegelian terminology (*Weltgeist*)."[43] In order for the individual to experience the liberatory impulse of aesthetic experience, the constitutive foundation of the subject in Kant, the individual has to push out from the *Sinnlichkeit* and act independently to free the self from all legislative restraint. This aspect of aesthetic experience aligns with Frankist messianic antinomianism because it reaffirms a Frankist belief that in the liberation of the imagination from all constraints, the interiority of the modern subject articulates a cognitive messianism proving the obsolescence of all laws. For the modern subject to exist, the imagination as the *principia individuationis* must be liberated absolutely.

Žáček's casual reference to this conversation between the two men suggests perhaps the most important moment in the dissemination of Frankist Kabbalah in the German-speaking lands, as well as Central Europe, and even beyond the German worlds. While Sabbatian messianism resonates with contemporary philosophical and political aspirations for freedom, the Offenbach factions materialize these same aspirations with Jacob Frank. Frank introduces a demand to "enter history." By associating the desire for liberation across all social, cultural, and political registers as evidence that Jews and Gentiles have moved imaginatively into a new world, a messianic age together, the Prague Circle introduces the nascent appearance of a "novel" *sensus communis*, based on a subjective liberation.[44]

Their innovation creates the link between the political path to freedom and the modern Jewish subject's imagined liberation. In that moment, cognitive liberation becomes equated with an imagined "paradise"; the imagination is "unsealed" from the regimes of reason and understanding to emerge with a wholly new ontology. "Fallenness" no longer signifies damnation. For a brief moment, the subject awakens to a new Eden of possibilities. Thus even more than his acceptance of Frankist messianism, Wehle proposes an aesthetic project whose literariness serves as the means not only to communicate the revelation, but also to elicit it. Wehle identifies textual patterns within Enlightenment thought to articulate a mental engagement in text that absorbs and exceeds Frankism's political aims.

Žáček's identification of the kabbalistic roots of Wehle's innovations is critical to understanding the significance of Wehle for the modern Jewish subject emerging during the *Haskalah* in German-speaking lands. First, Žáček points to the political necessity and nature of Wehle's social challenges to rabbinic authority. The Prague Circle's project is politically attuned to another way of thinking about Jews' collective identity.[45] By threatening "the hegemony" of the rabbinate "in the previous century," it offers a way for Jews to move beyond Judaism's past, or more precisely, a rabbinic past, and into the *Haskalah's* political liberation in which Jews can be integrated into the Bohemian narrative.[46] This integration aligns with Frankism generally. Wehle wants an imagined narrative of individual redemption to displace the collective revelation of traditional Judaism, whereby Jews do not belong to the secular narrative. They "wait" for their redemption.[47] In this way, it signals a shared political strategy not only in the next generation of Frankists, both in Offenbach and in Prague, but also inherent in elements of an evolving "heretical kabbalah" that has yet to reveal its real aim.

Žáček's curious identification of rabbinic "hegemony" as a seventeenth-century phenomenon suggests moreover that the modern rabbinate he has in mind operates differently in comparison to ancient and medieval antecedents. Žáček repeats Hönig's accusation of rabbinic impropriety: since "the rabbinical orthodoxy" has failed to see the possibility of a modern Jewish secular subject—like Wehle—they are guilty of overreach. They are incapable of recognizing a modern Jewish subject position because they cling to Judaism.

Thus the Prague Circle represents a liberation from an overweening authority; its members are liberated from the constraints imposed on them in the "previous century" and prior to *Haskalah*, when Sabbatians are compelled to practice in secret and are under the threat of *halakhic* ban or *herem*. Essentially, from Žáček's perspective, Wehle's project takes up Frankism and rethinks it, giving it both philosophical and political dimensions, a legitimacy, previously unimagined by Jews. It offers them a political identity, a way to keep Jews "Jewish" but without the *halakhah*, and without having to abandon their communities. For Jews to emerge as political agents, they must be able to throw off the chains of their past.[48]

More intriguingly, though, kabbalah's capacity to renew Jews as Jews in Judaism becomes reimagined by Wehle and the Circle as a secularized way of imagining Jews as Jews outside of Judaism. Žáček's observation then that Wehle has become the emblematic "Bohemian" points as well to Wehle's adoption of secular cultural registers to express his "Jewishness," rather than *halakhic* prescriptions reiterating rabbinic authority and a burdensome form of particularity.

Additionally, Žáček contrasts Wehle and his Czech followers with the Frankist leader, Jacob Frank, and the Polish members of his court. Žáček frames Frank's many excesses in both the Ottoman Empire and the Bohemian countries, to emphasize Wehle's difference from this "charlatan."[49] Previously, "false doctrines" or "the teachings of Sabbatai Zvi and his later followers" are spread by Frank's Polish followers who traverse "the Bohemian countries."[50] Žáček's depiction implies that the heresy of the movement is imported from outside Bohemia and initially by Poles; that is, it is not a Czech phenomenon. To Žáček, Wehle's transformation of these doctrines suggests, though, a social project more attuned to and better tolerated by "Bohemian culture." Thus Wehle's Frankism circulates as a legitimate Central European intellectual project rather than a Polish heresy.

In this way, Frankism exposes a fault line between secular Jews and "the advocates of official Jewish orthodoxy." Frank's extensive influence over the "strong Jewish minority in Poland" causes both the "Christian clergy and the secular authorities of Poland" to be "aware" of his doctrines.[51] Wehle negotiates this fault line in a way that is thoroughly "Bohemian," presumably because he blends it with the philosophical idealism circulating within the German-speaking lands. He uses the language of the

German philosopher to reveal his new kabbalah as a partner in Europe's cultural elevation and transformation. The outcome of Wehle's regular readings of philosophy and kabbalah with Hönig is then the mapping of the heretical kabbalah on to secular aesthetics as an "enlightened innovation," a code the "believers" could use to recognize fellow travelers on the "other path."[52]

Although the Prague Circle is Frankist and Wehle, its leader, pays tribute to Frank, Wehle's "redemption" appears to be the way he has translated Polish Frankism into the German philosophical registers of eighteenth-century Central Europe. The hours spent with Hönig listening to his son-in-law explain Kant to him and his reciprocal analyses of an innovated kabbalah enable Wehle to fuse these two disparate traditions together into an intellectual project that extends the heretical kabbalah to encompass the cataclysmic changes of the eighteenth and nineteenth centuries. They are prophets of a messianic age essentially becoming visible in two registers: politics and aesthetics.

In his claim that Wehle proposes a kabbalah that accommodates both "Mendelssohn and Kant" and that runs directly from Sabbatianism to the *Haskalah*, Scholem implies that Wehle displaces the "heretic of kabbalah" to shift to a "heresy of innovation."[53] Wehle's association of Kant with the heretical kabbalah underscores, furthermore, Scholem's belief that the kabbalah is an aesthetic drive within Jewish history.

Once kabbalah is intuited by Wehle as akin to Kantian aesthetic experience, the effect of transcendence becomes part of an intuitable, non-*halakhic* experience, a revelation available to Jews and non-Jews. Allusively, the Prague Circle's intervention in Frankism suggests that the aesthetic resolution to Kant's theory of the conflict of the faculties mirrors a similar experience of cognitive liberation in their heretical kabbalah.

A basic tenet of Sabbatianism and Frankism is that with the messianic age's beginning, liberation is finally available to the individual Jewish subject; therefore, the law no longer applies. It has been fulfilled and Jews are free to violate *halakhah* as is the rest of the world. Frank espouses that his messianism is aimed at destroying "all religions"; it is an antinominian project and Frank has political and social aims. Implicitly, Wehle repositions this teaching to include the cognitive liberation of the subject. In other words, the human faculties have been liberated from the law. Humans are obligated to violate the Law in order to experience the full cognitive redemption of the subject. Transcendence appears in this model as the violation of the faculties' control by reason. Its sign is ecstasy.

Liberation also suggests that the faculties can be safely "unsealed" now as a consequence of violation. According to the thirteenth-century kabbalist, Abraham Abulafia, the "sealing" of the mind occurs because of the Fall. Incapable of tolerating the eternal consequences of the act of sin, the fallen human faculties must be closed off from their original state. Thus God "seals" the faculties by imposing the categories of time and space on cognition. Even thought has been transformed because of it. First and foremost though desire is severed from its object.

The implications of "unsealing" are previously only known by an elite cohort of kabbalists, but now with Wehle's implicit "innovation" of Kantianism, "unsealing" is sutured to the experience of sublimity. Transcendence becomes possible for Jews, unmoored from any religious tradition, and explicitly through the reading and writing of secular texts. It is an effect of being a subject. Furthermore, such transcendence enables the individual enter *pardes* cognitively, to imagine fulfilling human desire. For the common person, paradise has materialized on earth.

In this radical modern moment, the Prague Circle's version of Frankism proposes the possibility of redemption for Aher, the unredeemable figure from the "Four who went to Pardes." Through its promotion of another way to read philosophical writing, a new structure of the narrative tale emerges about a human subject who reads, a "freethinker" who can be the self's messiah. The project invites readers to innovate the secular texts of Western Enlightenment in order to redeem themselves.

In Kant, the faculties in conflict are resolved either through the experiences of the Beautiful in which they harmonize or of the Sublime in which they disharmonize in order to produce a new subjective experience. Both experiences resolve themselves though eventually with the faculties aligning or harmonizing in peace. Thus the faculties' liberation from conflict must occur in order to begin their resolution, the unity of the subject in transcendence. This liberation begins with the imagination. Kant's theory of the faculties in conflict, resolved by the imagination's liberation, resonates with a modern Sabbatian notion of liberation. Of the Frankist groups persisting after Frank's death, the Prague Circle is not alone in this assumption.[54]

To Scholem, Wehle's teachings suggest the heretical antinomianism with which Sabbatians are historically associated, that is, a failed messianic project. However, philosophically, Scholem suggests that in Wehle's thinking about Kant, a heretical kabbalistic metaphysics becomes intuitable. If the messianic age has begun, then, the division between "subject and object"—mind and body—has been repaired. The catastrophe of creation has received its *tikkun* in the revelation of its emancipation. Consequently, the faculties are no longer in conflict with each other; the subject has been restored to a primordial ontology in which there is no conflict between substance and intellect, subject and object, mind and body. This identity is neither reducible to the practice of Judaism, nor to rabbinic approval, but in fact, for Wehle, the modern Jewish subject is an effect and evidence of the messianic age already occurring. It is a testimony to the "unified subject."[55]

Thus when Wehle and Hönigsberg describe their lives, their adoption of the language of German idealism to posit a subjective experience characterizes their choices as imaginative, necessary acts which they as subjects are compelled to do. They associate their subjective transformation, furthermore, as an essential expression of political and social reform, the shared aim of *Wissenschaft des Judentums*' scholars, like Zunz.[56] Their "heresies of innovation" carry then the force of the continuation of revelation moving away from the ghetto and into cultural, political, and social arenas.

From the daring jump of Frankist heretics to innovative "philosophers" of a Jewish liberation, Wehle and his Circle contribute to Bohemian visibility during the nineteenth century.[57] Žáček grounds this visibility in Wehle's "innovations" of Enlightenment-era political, philosophical, and social trends, even though they force the Prague leader into public confrontations with a "stubborn rabbinate" who have transformed the

Talmud into "the most harmful and poisonous book."[58] Responsible for promoting "heresies of innovation," Wehle sutures his heretical kabbalah to modern social and political reform as those reforms are expressed philosophically, so that Hönig joins him in positing a redemptive value in "voluntary apostasy."[59]

In other words, the group's keen investment in connecting the foundational principles of Western aesthetics to Sabbatian beliefs and Frankist narrative tales continues in spite of the failure of the Frankists' overall political machinations to materialize messianism. This failure has already begun with Frank's death, but it becomes more pronounced with the successive revolutions occurring across Europe and culminating in 1848 when Wehle's descendants along with other Frankists immigrate to America. From Frank's death to that immigration, the rabbinate in Prague becomes particularly active in persecuting the Wehle family and the remaining members of the Prague Circle. When Jonas Wehle dies in 1823, Jews are incited by the leading rabbi, Eleazar Fleckeles, to attack the funeral procession and profane Wehle's body.[60] These events lead to a dispersal of the Prague Frankists. They join the diaspora of Jews who move to the New World.

Their emphasis on a subjective liberation translates though into its objective expression: they have become citizens of the new world. In fact, Wehle's nephew, Gottfried, the patriarch of the Wehle family in the United States, declares in his will that their glorious tradition is associated with emancipation and freedom from rabbinic authority. As proud bearers of Sabbatianism/Frankism to the United States, they have become signifiers of the true American spirit.

He explains that his family's American trajectory occurs because of the significant persecution his family suffers in Prague. With the persecution of Jonas Wehle in the background of his thinking, he describes his decisions in his will.

> I decided to leave the Continent, the country and the town where I and also you were born; where my ancestors throughout the centuries lived an honorable life agreeable to God; where they suffered innocently and so greatly for their belief and their nationality.[61]

Gottfried Wehle is clear that the individuals he holds responsible for his family's persecution are "the other Jews" who "hated and despised them and accused them of all kinds of terrible things and crimes."[62] He underscores for his family members that they should proudly remember their heritage as Frankists, the legacy of the Prague Circle, even though he never mentions Jacob Frank. While he describes the extraordinary innocence of his family—they wanted their freedom from Judaism, and to remain as Jews—Wehle emphasizes only the subjective choices of the family's patriarch and the Prague Frankists; that is, as Scholem points out, he erases many of the political and social interventions associated with the second generation of Frankists both in Offenbach and in Prague.[63]

What is though the critical implication of these "heretics of innovation?" Quite simply, by introducing an aesthetic register to read the new narrative tales introduced by Frankism, the Prague Circle identifies secular texts as the objects of their innovations, newly innovated "objects of contemplation." Scholem hints at this when he notes that Adam Mickiewicz in Poland and even the minor poet, Thomas von Schoenfeld in Germany, insert their poems into cultural venues and they do so by using national and Christian signifiers as vehicles for their heretical kabbalistic codes.⁶⁴ This poetic and philosophical intervention as a secret vehicle for Frankist revelation coincides with a last strategy out of Offenbach as the movement begins to dissipate.

That last strategy involves the Red Letters sent to all "Eastern and Central European Jewish communities," warning Jews "to heed Frank's calls in the Częstochowa letters," that "terrible catastrophes [were] about to befall the Jews and …. that the 'the faith of Edom' would soon become the only refuge for the Jewish people."⁶⁵ Historians emphasize the desperation behind the strategy; Maciejko points to the lack of nuance in "Edom," the lack of "the specialized meaning that it had acquired in Frank's Dicta," reducing it essentially to a general term for Christianity.

However, for Frankists, "Edom" circulates as a necessary "darkness," a place of authorized transgression, and a place of redemption. The "Red Letters" tie "Edom" to a political and social act in which Jews are to convert, be baptized, and integrate into the people. When the political and social aspirations of the Frankists collapse, "Edom" becomes the sign of that failure. For historians, that failure portends the end of the movement. They look no further than the demise of Frankism's public figures. Implicitly, Prague's Frankism dies out with its "emblematic Bohemian" whose descendants become a minor footnote in American history.

This realization brings me to another implication though regarding Edom, Frankism, and the "heresies of innovation." I have argued elsewhere that literature becomes the site for Sabbatian aspirations and that claim remains true for the Frankists. As the physical movement is eclipsed by the very *Haskalah* values it hoped to usurp, the subjective experience of the Frankist begins to merge Edom with literature. The Frankists must travel into *poesie's* darkness, literature's darkness, in order to rediscover the other's path, a subjective liberation that remains available still in text. Literature is the repository for Frankist revelations.

If Jewish writers without any kind of kabbalistic allegiance, without Frankist leanings, without *halakhic* orientation as well, invest in the various registers of literature to write newly imagined expressions of the secular Jewish subject, then, the heretical kabbalah constitutes a part of their cognitive orientation. For a scholar, like Scholem, Wehle is a missing link between the "heretical kabbalah's" migration into *Haskalah* culture and the emergence of Kafka's modern fiction in the next century. Implicitly, in its "absorption" of an array of kabbalistic signals, literature produces an aesthetic kabbalah, filled with new transgressions, understood as conditions of rupture whose inflection expresses a new form of Jewish liberation from the Law, rabbinic authority, the "darkness of the ghetto," community ostracization, where the subject can "handle good and evil."⁶⁶ For a writer like Heinrich Heine, it suggests the emergence of a crossroads in modernity, where the pursuit of transcendence can lead to a final condemnation, or to the redemption of *poesie*.⁶⁷

If as Yerushalmi notes, "history becomes …. the faith of 'fallen Jews,'" this "aesthetic kabbalah" liberates literature to become a "messianic space" in which readers "unfold," "unpack," and "excavate," hidden traces of the Divine from within its discursive residue.[68] The inauguration of literature's "heretical kabbalah" obligates readers to journey through Edom in order to reach the other's redemption. It signals to modern Ahers that through literature, their redemption is found in writing.

The Talmudic Aher who cannot be redeemed because he has abandoned Judaism becomes transformed into a precursor for an apostate messiah, and Aher's transgression, a redemptive mental act that affirms rather than condemns the modern Jewish subject.[69] Restoring the transcendence denied to Aher in Talmud, Wehle's project implies redemption awaits the modern Aher in a literary Edom. *Finally*, the apostate's desire can be fulfilled and redemption will be restored because God has decreed it so by sending a messiah of sin. It is a textual liberation to pursue transcendence in spite of its *halakhic* prohibition. These modern Ahers read and write their own Torahs, exposing paths to paradise and redemption and along the way, they imagine the reunification of subject and object so that they can be "like divine beings."[70] They will be restored to a primordial existence before the Fall.

Thus coming out of Wehle's and Frank's interventions in "the heretical kabbalah," and Jewish history, the principle of "innovation" emerges as a key interpretive tool focused on a literary object that is neither *halakhah* nor even sacred *aggadot*. Instead narrative, a liberated *aggadah*, posits new messiahs and new prophets, engaged in a world outside the ghetto. It asserts itself as the modern Jewish subject's revelation.[71] In this way, secular stories exist as "innovated" texts, transforming poets into prophets.[72] Poets write the modern Jewish subject into existence.

The most important implication of Jonas Wehle's innovation of the Frankist heresy is precisely his turn away from established, received tradition because it enables Jewish writers after him to focus on a wholly new literary object, a new transmission of revelation, the story articulated through and by the "common man" or *prostak*. While Frank's hagiographies and narrative tales shift the believers away from Torah to a new "object of contemplation," when coupled to Wehle's "innovation" linking Kant and other philosophical writers to a new kabbalah, the two major changes or "innovations" arising from these heresies posit that the "common man" has been invested with gifts. He not only materializes his control over the elements—he has received—but this "common man" can also "transcend" his circumstances and become a subject. He transmits a new revelation of the profane. The next set of kabbalist prophets will find their "secrets" in profane writing. Their "profane" texts will posit the existence of another, previously unimaginable, path to redemption. In this way, the Prague Circle extends a heretical kabbalah into literature and well beyond any of its leaders. Synthesized by a generation of non-Frankists, non-Sabbatians, it reveals the persistence of a search for a way to innovate the mundane, to force it to exhibit a secret world of imagined liberation.

By the nineteenth century, Frankism is in ruins, but remnants of its messianism still adhere to modern ideas of enlightenment. A messianism already arrived and available through a rejection of legal constraint, the possible elevation of any individual to the level of messiah, the idea of a radical cognitive liberation that could create an enlightened, emancipated, redeemed community capable of living a messianic age for millennia, all of these underpin a belief in the "common man's" entitlement to prosperity, happiness, freedom of thought. Essentially, a transcendence of the mundane and unjust world in which Jews are trapped is held out to this emblematic subject as already available. No longer are these promises the remnants of Frank's apostasy, but rather they are the building blocks of the promise of *Haskalah*.[73] All of Frankism's promises re-emerge in the social institutions of modernity regardless of political orientation. They appear as given entitlements that console every one of us: the individual has only to act for the self to gain this redemption.

The only group of kabbalist Jews who will resist being absorbed in this synthesis of Frankist/Sabbatian "heretical kabbalah," the Hasids, will remain the unlikely and wildly popular memory of the "old kabbalah."[74] For a modern Jewish subject, enveloped in the narrative of progress, whose eyes remain fixed on the future, the continued presence of the uncanny Hasid roaming the streets of Europe's urban centers, elicits, as Scholem observes, condemnation because this "old kabbalah" has successfully eluded the "heretical kabbalah's" end in which heretical ideas are absorbed into the notion of "the common good." However, even the "old kabbalah," like the *Haskalah,* has synthesized elements of the heresy in its development of the hagiographic tale, converting these troubling matters into a sanctioned hasidic mode of literary expression.[75]

On the cusp of modern Jewish experience, then, two competing ideas circulate within Jewish literatures. The first or the secular remnants of the "heretical kabbalah" suggest that on the new path of modernity, Jews will finally have access to a lived experience of a messianic age; the Law will grant them emancipation with all of the rights and entitlements that non-Jews enjoy. This political and social redemption will make them interchangeable with non-Jews. "They will have a king" and they will be free.[76]

The second or Hasidic "old kabbalah" freights Jewish particularity and advocates instead the irrelevance of political, social, cultural freedoms. Jews must accept persecution, pogroms, and only fight to preserve Judaism. Jewish communities are suborned to the Law; only the Law can reveal the hidden light of their redemption. Thus the Hasid must be the "gatekeeper" of the Law's mystical power, its redemptive power.

These two competing theses on redemption suggest an array of possibilities to Jewish writers in the immediate century after Frankism's dissolution. Can the apostate, assimilated, everyman Jew, ever be a redemptive figure for Jews? Is the Hasidic gatekeeper entitled to preserve Judaism and the Law at the expense of ordinary Jews? Is the preservation of the Torah the only reason for Jewish existence? If it is, are Jews obligated then to be uninvolved, disengaged, with any kind of earthly reform? Does God forbid happiness on earth for any reason?

The two movements' perspectives on messianism provide the foundation for a modern Jewish subject looking for another textual path to redemption. Each of these questions resonates with what will become a truly new secular kabbalah. In this way, Frankism's heretics of kabbalah transform into Wehle's heresies of innovation, circulating among Jews and non-Jews as something "inimitable" within writing that the subject in the throes of transcendence stimulates in order to complete the creative act.[77]

3

Heinrich Heine, Poet/Prophet of the "Innovated Text"

There is no indication that Heine ever considers himself a kabbalist, Sabbatian, or Frankist, although he learns of the kabbalah from an uncle, Simon von Geldern.[1] Moreover, in two of his last works, "Jehudah ben Halevi," and *Der Doktor Faust*, Heine uses discrete principles that derive from both "heretical" and "orthodox" kabbalahs so that Halevi and Faust produce a tension between what is constitutive to each character's existence.

For Heine, Halevi embodies *poesie*; its redemptive aesthetic project is constitutive to Jewish life in a secular key. It authorizes and obligates Halevi to leave the ghetto, the enclosure of Jewish existence, to see revelation outside *halakhah*. He recognizes in *poesie*, *aggadah's* necessary liberation. Against this redemptive *poesie*, Heine's Faust emerges, willing to constrain "the sacred language" in order to shape phenomena to his will. He represents the antithesis of Halevi because he demands control of the very elements—the animated text—to which the poet suborns himself. As a result, Faust, who can never be redeemed, "enters history." Reimagining the Faustian dilemma as the "desire to think, act and enjoy life," Faust is not only emblematically human, but also historically oppressed. Hence Halevi and Faust bracket Heine's work.

Although Heine never constructs a "secular kabbalah," in the poem, "Jehudah ben Halevi," included in the *Romanzero*, he claims that the poet can "never sin in prose or verse."[2] Is the claim indicative of Heine's imagination, an example of poetic license, but otherwise inconsequential, or does it reaffirm Heine's relationship to Judaism and Jewishness? Jeffrey L. Sammons suggests it relates to Heine's ambivalence about his personal conversion to Christianity.[3] Part of Heine's overall "spiritualism," the poem reflects his "capitulation to the disaster that had befallen his physical being," and is "not a mystical *Erleuchtung*" or Enlightenment.[4] In Sammons' estimation, Heine's poems bear a mimetic relationship to Heine's lived experience. Aspects of Heine's life inform the poet's aesthetic choices.[5]

He notes that Heine's "spiritualist" tendency is "undogmatic and noninstitutional"; thus it enables him to exist "in the only realm in which [he] was able to subsist, the literary imagination."[6] In his veiled juxtaposition of the poem to a "dogmatic object," Sammons rejects that the *Romanzero's* "Hebrew Melodies" cycle, to which "Jehudah ben Halevi" belongs, attests to Heine's "Jewishness." In other words, Heine's "spiritualism" is not epistemological, is intuitive and it seals him within a textual universe. Attributing the religious, theistic references within the *Romanzero* to Heine's "interest in Swedenborg," Sammons declares Heine uncommitted to Judaism and Jewishness.[7]

At face value, the poetic excerpt from "Jehudah ben Halevi" could be Heine's attempt to absolve himself from accusations of apostasy. However, in this particular text, there is an implication that Heine, like Blake, Goethe, and other writers, is not only acquainted with kabbalah, but also integrates its themes, promises, signifiers, and principles into his work.[8] While readers might ponder whether Heine's kabbalistic themes are "heretical" or "orthodox," in this particular poem, he adopts and adapts fragments or elements of a kabbalistically-infused aesthetic register, emblematically exhibited in the figure, Jehudah ben Halevi.

The poem introduces Jehudah, as a boy who is trained by "his strict father" to read "the book of God, the Torah."[9] The child reads "this volume … whose picturesquely hieroglyphic Old Chaldean squared-off letters are derived out of the childhood of the world"; these letters speak to something in Halevi's unique ontology.[10] The letters, the stories, are not only "derived out of the childhood of the world," but they also resonate with something deep within him. The ancient letters present themselves to him, an archive from which he, the child, draws new pieces of the revelation. Heine suggests that reading these letters transforms him.

With ben Halevi's first "steps" in Judaism, the child engages physically with Hebrew. If read mimetically, Heine references the way Halevi is instructed in Hebrew as a child. However, Heine presents Hebrew, the "Old-Chaldean squared-off letters," as a mode of primordial writing that predates Judaism.[11] It triggers a profound recognition in Halevi, even though he is a child. "[O]ld-Chaldean" locates the Hebrew letters as a part of the world before Torah, before Moses, before Abram's transformation to the patriarch Abraham. Since it elicits an unconscious response in the child, it leads him to a "crooning Tagus" river, where he reads the *aggadic* stories. From this primordial writing, he hears the music of creation in its original occurrence; it sings to him. The "Chaldean" letters not only stimulate creation, but they also unseal something within him. Cryptically, Heine introduces the Hebrew letters stimulating nature to produce the river's song and stimulating him as their agent or prophet.

A Hebrew in existence before the world began, the *aggadic* letters now "in exile" point to the primordial beginnings of human existence when the songs of creation are heard throughout the cosmos.[12] This effect of the letters inspires Halevi mentally so that narrative "*re-minds*" him of that which he "may have never known," but whose trace emanates from within the depths of the unconscious.[13] When Halevi reads these "letters," he becomes a subject: his faculties coalesce around the act of reading revelation as the letters write it.[14] Forming *aggadot*, stories, they are constitutive of his subjectivity.

In other words, for Heine, *aggadah* aims to restore child and poet to the beginning of the world so that they become new predicates to Eden's "unfinished story."[15] Walter Benjamin recognizes this aspect of *aggadah* as its ontology: it is *Lehre*, its "teaching," a form of writing that "transmits" what the received Law cannot say, the ineffable core of the revelation.[16] Even more tellingly, Halevi internalizes the "old Chaldean letters" so that they work on him, permutate him, "innovate" his ontology. Heine implies that Halevi becomes a poet when these primordial Hebrew letters embed themselves in his mind, soul, body, emanating their stories' revelations.[17] They are the source of the poet's "innovation" because they write him into being.

In this way, Heine "illustrates the profound connection of tradition and innovation as different aspects of one and the same … process."[18] Since the poet receives the tradition and transmits its innovation, this "poetic move" introduces a "foundational complex" imbricated in "tradition," and its "transmission in modernity."[19] Heine participates in a kabbalistic tradition by proposing that Halevi receives the *aggadah*, and in his innovation's transmission, he writes a secular kabbalah.

In the contrast between Halevi's "strict" father and the "crooning" Tagus river, Heine emphasizes that the two distinct forces producing Jehudah's unique sensibility exist within Talmud initially.

> Likewise, shining in the Talmud
> Is a double light, divided
> In Halacha and Haggada.
> Fencing school I called the former[20]

The "double light" of Talmud guides him so that although Halevi's revelation begins with *halakhah* and *aggadah* safely within the boundaries of Judaism, *aggadah* exceeds these boundaries.[21] *Halakhah* and *aggadah*, "the sun and the moon," unite within this child who has "come into the world."[22]

Heine's "double light" metaphor resonates with the Zohar as well. In that text, Divine Light is expressed as two sides of the *sefirotic* tree or "Tree of Life." When the *sferot* are in balance, both sides emanate creation. When they are unbalanced, the "other" or "left side" emanates evil.[23] Scholem describes the process as a way "to give a real existence and separate identity to the power of evil."[24] Evil comes into being when the "other side" is constrained by a dominating *halakhah*, essentially enslaving it to reproduce uncompromising and absolute judgment.

The "double light" sets up then Heine's main point: ben Halevi's revelation of an "other" world of "Jewishness" is grounded in depths unknowable within Judaism. If he is only trained in *halakhah*, "that prodigious school of fencing," Halevi remains a "master [of] every art and science of polemic." Heine conjures a world of isolated Jewry, where Judaism's focus on *halakhah*, only one of two Divine "kinds of luster" (*zwei verschiedene Sorten Lichtes*), keeps Jews bound to the ghetto. The boundary of the Law cuts Jews off from the world outside the ghetto. From this beginning, though, the "double light" of Talmud has the force of a commandment for Halevi: he recognizes obligations to both *aggadah* and *halakhah*, or the received revelation and its transmitted tradition.

Heine extends Talmud's other "light," its "Haggada," or stories to be akin to "a fantastic garden … that once bloomed and sprouted also from the soil of Babylonia, Queen Semiramis' great garden, That eighth wonder of the world."[25] While he "also" suggests both lights emerge in Babylon, by placing the "Haggada's" origin there, Heine implies the stories form part of a mythical world before Judaism. Hence *aggadic* stories not only share the same "splendor" of Talmud, but in his identification of their origin with "Semiramis' great garden," they reveal themselves to be traces of a secret writing external to the *halakhah*.

More so than the commandment to bind the mind with duty, practice, and ritual, the "other's light" inspires Halevi's imagined return to the "great garden," another dimension of Jewish existence and one that Heine insists is primordial in nature, hidden away in these stories. An eerie echo of the *Zohar*, in which God hides His Light within the Torah, Halevi, in the articulation of his ontology as both child and poet, sifts the biblical stories in order to liberate this "other" garden from their pages. Implicitly, Heine suggests a role for *aggadah* beyond its mimetic illustration of the Law, of *halakhah*. This role underpins his "innovated" or poetic figure of Halevi.

As a result, Heine articulates another terrain for narrative to which the law does not apply. *Aggadah*'s origins are primordial; narrative bears an aura external to *halakhah*, yet absolutely part of the Jewish revelation.[26] The Jewish story exceeds its *halakhic* twin and in its excess, it reveals itself to be the site of a "fantastic garden … very like another." The intentional ambiguity of "very like another" calls to mind Eden so that Heine effectively permutates Babylon to name Eden. Eden has been hidden away by God in the letters of the *aggadot* too. At this point, Heine signifies that the poet, Halevi, could very well reveal Eden and the world before the Fall through a permutation of letters. With Heine, *aggadah* becomes the repository for so much more than a mimetic representation of how Jews live Judaically, of how to fulfill *halakhah*. In their excess, Jewish stories shift the site of *pardes*—paradise—and *PaRDeS*—the sign of an exegetical kabbalah—to the Babylonian exile's archive of mythical narratives. In this way, the poet has been obligated to move the mythical tradition to a kabbalistically-infused secular register.

The fabled garden of myth and legend becomes both the mystery and origin of Jehudah's story: it is also the "secret" to Heine's poem. Only available textually, the poem's "paradise" evokes a garden that is not foreclosed to humans, either by sin, or by history, and thereby collapses the boundaries between them. Moreover, rooted in Babylon, yet tied to the origins of Talmud, this "garden" emerges in Heine's poem as a necessary stage of Halevi's journey and an absolute part of his faith because it leads him to a lost and hidden textual paradise. It is in fact an "old fire" that sparkles, "[b]ubbling with exuberance."[27] It captivates "the youngster's noble spirit," becoming a "wild and wonderful adventure …. of that blissful secret world, of that mighty revelation which we call *poesie*."[28]

Halevi the poet is obligated to *poesie* or *aggadah* and not the *halakhah*. Readers infer that by fulfilling an obligation to literature or *poesie*, Halevi as poet reveals a new form of redemption, possible because of literature and that triggers sublimity. Heine makes legible the possibility that sublimity, and its subjective renewal of the faculties are necessary factors in a modern Jewish redemption. The ground of Halevi's redemptive aesthetic, sublimity, occurs when that poet as a child follows a "crooning Tagus" out of the ghetto and beyond the terms of a parochial Judaism.²⁹ Heine hints that there must be a Jewishness outside of Judaism that does not necessarily invalidate it.

He rethinks the boy's "faith" as an effect of *poesie* leading the child out of the ghetto, Judaism, and even the Jewish community. Jehudah's "faith" depends on *poesie's* ability not only to elicit his imagination, but also simultaneously to open it up to "that blissful secret world," the field in which imagination finds its liberation. The liberation springs from within the world of Judaism, yet finds its full expression, outside of it, and within a world of Jews and non-Jews.

In this way, Heine underscores that the textual revelation of *poesie*, Talmud's other "luster," redeems Babylon—the world before *halakhah*—for Jews. The implications of this redemption are quite radical since Babylon, the site of Jewish exile, enslavement, and dispossession, signifies with Heine, the necessity and transformation of a formerly depicted "world of sin."³⁰ In such a world, Halevi the poet has flourished; in fact, Heine hints at a power within literature that enables both Halevi the Jewish writer and the child reader to transform Babylon into the original sign of redemption.³¹ *Poesie* transforms the spirit of exile, making it into an "adventure," a journey. The child explores the boundaries of this newly imagined world, experiencing it as letters, text, stories.

By reimagining *aggadot* as a "secular" textual project, Heine identifies in literature, a transcendence that begins within a Judaic space, a ghetto, but encourages its initiates to read beyond that space, to follow the "sparks" of transcendence into a voluntary exile, arriving in a new world.³² With both *Zoharic* and Luriannic allusions, reading becomes a voluntary exile that refines mental experience through the subject's "innovation" of text. It enables the imagination to emanate multiple selves from the text, each one arriving at "another" entrance to redemption. Perhaps an unconscious intention, Heine implies a connection between *aggadot*, stories, to the *partsufim*, the "faces" of the *sferot*.

Poesie calls to the poet to exhibit its transcendent disclosures, to the subject to read the revelation, to "innovate" it, and to make its own "novel" ending. In this way, the revelation has fulfilled its purpose in the ghetto and unfolds, emanates its revelation of Jewish redemption purposely to *worlds* outside the ghetto.³³ Writing's liberation refines human existence so that new forms can finally emerge from behind static and mundane lexical meanings.

Furthermore, in his example of Halevi, Heine suggests that the principles underwriting creation—"the sun's harsh-glaring daylight. And the milder moonlight"— these "[T]wo quite different kinds of luster," express a duality, between being alienated from the world as the site of condemnation and taking pleasure in *poesie's* continuous creation within that world. Within Halevi the poet, the tension is resolved through *poesie's* liberation. Through reading and writing, Halevi produces a "novel" ending to Heine's dialectic of "sun" and "moonlight."

Since ben Halevi's rabbinic counterparts subordinate *aggadah's* "luster" to *halakhah*, they ignore its path and extension beyond Judaism, the ways it extends Jewish and human experience beyond their purview. Thus they miss the path out of the ghetto; they ignore the testimony of their own redemption, a tension building within them.³⁴

They are the "fencing" masters, whose "squabbling over the Halacha" prevents them from recognizing "the other light." For the sake of the Jewish subject, Halevi must leave the ghetto because the poet is obligated to follow *aggadah*'s "unfolding."[35] He must follow it leaving its textual ghetto, the static epistemology that constrains it. In this way, *aggadah* exceeds the boundaries of *halakhah*, so that creation not only continues, but also reveals its poetic core.

Thus, Heine posits a convergence between the idealistic worlds of German *poesie* and Hebrew *aggadah* outside the ghetto, "the youngster's noble spirit .... enraptured ... by that mighty revelation ... *poesie*." The imagined intersection of secular poetry, with Hebrew narrative, proposes that *poesie*, or liberated *aggadah*, articulates the forgotten and hidden part of the revelation. The poet reveals Eden, perhaps Pardes, made available again to the subject through "innovated" experiences of reading and writing.

Imagining a kinship between himself and the medieval poet, Heine posits that in ben Halevi's reading of *aggadah*, the poet recognizes story as the basis not only for the revelation of Judaism, but also for all revelation.[36] Thus transcendence becomes an effect of Jews "being-in-the-world"—and a necessary aspect within *aggadah*. With Heine, we see the necessity of Jews pushing out (*darstellen*) from a phenomenological ghetto, writing themselves into the world, and in so doing, they perceive the revelation of their own narrative "luster."[37]

In his use of "luster" (*die Glühend*), Heine characterizes it an "incandescence" that is compelled to move outward.[38] He implies that within narrative an immanent "splendor" aims at a world including and beyond Judaism. Its emanations have always renewed creation, the promotion of a "novel intuition" in lieu of an "object of dogmatic knowledge."[39] Furthermore, the "luster" appears to emanate from narrative itself. Narrative's core is ontologically driven to produce infinite emanations. In this way, buried within the Torah's words and stories, the "two lusters" are hidden, awaiting Jehudah's arrival. However, only one, *aggadah* demands its liberation from the text.

With Heine's return to Jehudah, the child is always aware of the foreign ground from which Judaic *halakhah* and *aggadah* have emerged: it is an imagined place, "a garden of ... childlike airy fancy."[40] This imagined space of myth and tale offers "the young Talmudic scholar," a refuge from "the noisy squabbling over the Halacha," where continuous "quarrels" prevent the renewal of "the spirit," instead leaving the heart "dry, dusty, and musty."[41] Babylon keeps both "lusters" balanced in relation to each other. They are neither isolated nor segregated from each other although only *aggadah* has the capacity to provide Jehudah with "refuge." In order to "renew" his "spirit," Jehudah sequesters himself away within *poesie*. He removes himself from the *halakhah*.

These stanzas underscore that *poesie* might begin within Judaism's revelation, the core to *halakhic* epistemology, but as it moves necessarily away from it, it imbues literature with its vitality: *poesie* pulsates within it. *Poesie* in exile from *halakhah* awakens to itself. Consequently, literature produces whole new worlds, in which human beings imagine different ways of renewing themselves as they continue on their "journeys."[42] To put it another way, when Judaic epistemology ceases to renew Jehudah's subjective experience, he searches for *poesie* with its "blissful secret world" outside of that epistemology. Jehudah's discovery though demands its liberation. In this way, narrative is freed from a dead, inchoate lexicon. As Sammons observes, Heine believes that *aggadah* "expands the imagination" in order to produce the coordinates of "the poetic mind."[43]

Heine's poet combines *poesie* and *aggadah* to produce transcendent writing. In a pact of mutual obligation, the poet is obligated to exhibit the immanent text before the reader and the reader responds with its innovation. In this way, *poesie* is more than the representation of that "secret world," more than mimetic depiction of a phenomenal place. *Poesie* is imbricated with, bound to, a mysterious phenomenology, articulated as contiguous aspects, refracting, rearranging, and producing continuous emanations at play.

Thus Halevi's *poesie* suggests a kabbalistic principle in whose proximity, narrative is transformed, innovated, from static, inanimate words conveying one story, to an animate, evolving field of stories producing new creation. Text shifts from its mimesis of human existence to radiate, emanate, the act of creation in which the Hebrew letters, those "hieroglyphic Old Chaldean squared-off letters … derived out of the childhood of the world," proceed from the Divine to redeem the world with wholly new predicates of beings. If Heine's *poesie* is read as a kabbalistic principle, then, its expression takes the form of multiplicities, an infinite diversity of singularities, a manifold of "beings" becoming intuitable to poet and reader.

This transformation of text performs three essential actions: first, the transformation of literature's ontology forecloses its use as mimetic instrument; the literary text no longer "imitates life," represents lived experience. In its innovation, it is "living." Second, literature's transformation ostensibly prohibits its recuperation as an "idol." The text as an "idol" of representation and literal meaning is displaced by a textual drive, an endless writing. No longer the golem, writing insists on its own unboundedness, the disruption of *logos*, so that the components of the word become free floating—the letters are liberated.[44] Third, since these texts of letters are no longer static, but shimmer instead with the "luster of the moon," their writing propels an even more dramatic conclusion: emerging at the site of conflict, "the squabbling over halakha," *poesie* harmonizes—provides its resolution of the conflict—when it is separated from the *halakhah's* legislative field.

On the one hand, the "lusters" harmonize in the text; the letters produce "beauty," that is, "the poet's art" that "worked upon his spirit."[45] On the other hand, it reflects the push/pull between epistemology and aesthetic, the dialectic that Scholem identifies and Alter underscores at the heart of Jewish existence.[46] We might formulate it as writing versus written: we struggle to be writing but we are always written. In the human desire to enter history, Jews are resigned to time and space, written into existence. This freights the imagination as the faculty that reaches into that which is not known and retrieves writing, but when represented in time and space, we only see its trace alluded to by the written object. Thus any epistemology shatters this writing, with a view to reassembling it into phenomena that can be categorized as objects in one system. In its attempt to control humans through epistemology, *halakhah* ends up positing an idol, a righteous golden calf, but an idol nonetheless. Heine applies the same formula to Christianity and by implication to all religion.⁴⁷ Epistemology's drive to control meaning collides with writing's liberation. In the moment of their conflict, the poet's path to transcendence emerges.⁴⁸

In pegging ben Halevi as the figure who discovers the path to transcendence, Heine sees the poet not only producing in his poetry a harmony between the written *halakhah* and *aggadah's* writing, but also restoring textual immanence. The poet awakens the letters of the text, and thereby identifies how *poesie* leads to sublimity. Ben Halevi is "not just a scholar, but a master of poetics." He is "a mighty poet, star and beacon for his age, light and lamp among his people"; his "light" illuminates their exile.⁴⁹

> Pillar of poetic fire
> In the vanguard of all Israel's
> Caravan of woe and sorrow
> In the desert waste of exile.⁵⁰

In Heine's innovation of *Exodus*, the biblical "pillar of fire" is resolved in Halevi.⁵¹ He harmonizes the two "lusters" in himself by acting singularly, becoming a "pillar of poetic fire," to lead "all Israel's caravan of woe and sorrow in the desert waste of exile."⁵² Halevi becomes *poesie's* instrument, its prophet, redeeming Jewish suffering in exile. However, rather than invert Moses, the first prophet to whom God reveals Himself, as a "pillar of fire," Heine innovates *poesie*, but not to lead Jews back into Egypt.⁵³

The basis for Halevi's transformation reaches into the earliest strata of Jewish mystical thought. Metatron, formerly the patriarch, Enoch, is transformed into a "pillar of fire" and charged with writing the book of human existence for eternity.⁵⁴ Metatron's transformation is tied to his perfect soul, his righteousness, that enables God "to take him." He never experiences death but is transformed into the archangel Metatron. These first two figural iterations conceive of the poet as an instrument of God. However, God reveals Himself in the pillar of fire, i.e., something humans can see and intuit. By associating Halevi with this trope, Heine appears to link the poet to Divine Being more purposively. Heine suggests that *poesie's* expressions—art, culture, literature, the aesthetic—accompany Jews through "exile," and in the process, they unseal a primordial condition of the mind, an experience of subjective restoration even if only for the fleeting moment of engaging with an innovated text through reading.⁵⁵ Since *poesie* writes through the poet, Heine suggests Halevi to be the poet and prophet of the innovated text.

Ben Halevi's poetic ontology unseals a lexical desert because Halevi's "song" and "soul" share the same substance.⁵⁶

> Pure and truthful, without blemish,
> Was his song-his soul was also.
> On the day his Maker fashioned
> This great soul, He paused contented⁵⁷

Halevi's song "pure and truthful" uncouples his "great soul" from the limitations of human existence. He produces a music akin to the "crooning Tagus." In effect, this union enables a second "pause," in which God rests, "contented" with the poet. The poet's soul and *poesie* are not subject to the Fall because *poesie* proceeds from the primordial condition of *aggadah*. In fact, the "song" like the "soul" is without sin, the "song" is the trace of the blameless soul before the Fall.[58] Thus "his Maker fashions" the poet. Since the poet's soul bears the trace of Divine creation before the Fall; *poesie* continues to create in its textual garden. In his outline of Halevi, the poet, Heine traces how *poesie* repairs a world of idols, death, exile, and destruction.

One of the few times when Heine explores an imagined link between mimesis and phenomenon, the phenomenon is external to the physical world. *Poesie* does not "imitate" the physical world of phenomena, but instead it reaches inside the poet's being to produce an image not only of the interiority of "spirit," but also of the soul before condemnation.[59] Ben Halevi's "soul … without blemish" expresses a perfection shared between "soul" and *poesie* and pushes Heine to imagine God at rest because of it. Heine's implication is striking: poets are evidence of redemption in the world. The condemnation of lived experience is relieved by the divine command of aesthetic experience. If humans are liberated from the Fall through *poesie*, Heine implies it is due to imagination awakening in a reader a textual *sensus communis* in which every reader and writer shares. Thus the "poet's every measure" is "hallowed by this grace and bounty."[60] Implicitly, Heine transfers the sanctioned Judaic experience of kabbalah to Halevi's "songs" in a secular world.

As the modern equivalent of *aggadah*, *poesie* sanctifies then "[b]oth in poetry and life…. he who has this highest good"; the poet "can never sin in prose or verse."[61] Heine argues that the poet's ontology is "measured" by a principle in which he not only cannot "fall," but he also is no longer part of the phenomenal structure of time and space because of the Fall. He can "never sin in prose or verse."[62] In this way, *poesie* is "pure," and this purity has nothing to do with content, nothing to do with specificity, nothing to do with lived experience. Purity is due to the animating principle of the "hieroglyphic Old Chaldean squared-off letters … derived out of the childhood of the world." The poet's writing is liberated from the imprisonment of words. Purity has nothing to do with corruption or particular pollution and everything to do with writing's liberation.

This radical subject position is staked by Heine to be "genius" and because of that "genius," the poet, "any poet" who possesses "[T]his, God's grace," is not only "a Monarch in the realm of thought, he Is responsible to no man."[63] *Poesie* reveals itself as divine mandate beyond the ken of any and all human oversight so that the poet's only obligation is to innovate the written by releasing writing.

> He accounts to God, God only,
> Not the people; both in art
> And in life, the people can
> Kill us but can never judge us.[64]

Both in "life" and "art" the poet signifies a different plane of being. People can condemn; they can persecute, but in the articulation of *poesie,* the poet remains beyond judgment. On the one hand, if Heine writes philosophically, then, he declares the poet and *poesie* liberated from the Beautiful, a relationship Kant posits as the staging for the Sublime to occur. In the poet's sublimity, transgression no longer exists in any meaningful way. On the other hand, Heine's use of a kabbalistic register to describe the poet's ontology connotes that the poet inaugurates a messianic age within his work: the messiahs have come in the form of poets and their texts are authorized to violate, to transgress the Beautiful because of it. Redemption is at stake.

Sammons sees a Christian allusion in the phrase, "kill us, but can never judge us." If the poem bears a mimetic likeness to Heine, Sammons posits a veiled reference to Heine's identification with the Christian messiah. It evokes the heretical kabbalah too with its insistence that the poet is not subject to the Law. Heine's Halevi could be understood to negate Judaism, except that the ending of the poem undoes that assumption: Halevi follows his people into martyrdom. However, if Heine's "mystical Enlightenment" conflates poet, prophet, and messiah, it does not exhibit the poet to be a messiah, but rather *poesie* to be messianic writing.

Heine applies to literature an "innovated" pattern of the Frankist/Sabbatian messiah, and undermines it in order to identify *poesie's* immanence in the poetic text.[65] Moreover, Halevi's revelation is fundamentally Jewish: *poesie* underscores the beauty of Jewish particularity and not the negation of its difference. In this "literary kabbalah," the poet acts as both receiver and transmitter of revelation. *Poesie* transforms the poet into kabbalist.

Heine's radical vision of ben Halevi continues with how a "monarch of thought" could only be revealed outside the ghetto, in Spain.[66] He is "sovereign ruler of the dream world, monarch of the mind and spirit."[67] Thus when he moves into "sirventes," "madrigals," "terzinas, canzonets, and sultry ghazels," he makes visible the "incandescent ardors" of hidden being. Reminiscent of the *romanceros* associated with Sabbatai Zvi and even Jacob Frank, these Spanish and Arabic "songs" create an imagined path between Halevi, the heretical kabbalah of these two figures of Zvi, Frank, and Heine in which the poet is refined by each iteration.[68] Even heresy is undone in poetic writing.

Like Semiramis' garden, the songs are secular sites for revelation. These songs in Christian and Muslim registers become representations of his soul's connections to a hidden realm of "emanations," from an "unfallen" human ontology, and linked through the signifier of Babylon earlier in the poem. Heine implies that he knows these registers' and their heretical or Frankist/Sabbatian genealogies, but their representations do not confirm the supersession of Judaism by Christianity or Islam, but rather express traces of original creation. The clue is in Heine's use of "incandescent" (*weißglühend*) because it requires Halevi to traverse "gallant Christendom" in order to express it: like Jacob Frank in the previous century, Halevi travels the other's path of Christianity because it harbors a shard of the illumination.

> Ah, our gallant Christendom's
> Lovely lands of orange blossoms!
> Ah, how fragrant, shining, plangent
> In the twilight of remembrance![69]

Yet Halevi's exile through Christian Spain does not endorse Christianity. Although Halevi appears to follow Frankism's path, Heine innovates the Frankist journey through Christianity with its "false god of Love," in order to arrive at a place beyond "Christendom," and still uniquely Jewish.[70]

Heine's use of kabbalistic principles comes to its critical juncture: the allure of the sensual, of sexual desire, "the false god of Love," the temptation to become the "troubadour," can lead the poet away from his obligation to *poesie*. Heine traces Halevi's journey to redeem the world through *poesie*, and readers recognize that the poet's redemption is the production of a secular literature, awakened to its ontological capacity to transform subjective experience. However, its transformation results neither in condemnation, nor in deification. It intensifies instead Halevi's imagined relationship to other Jews in their suffering. It renews him as a Jew among Jews.

Changing registers, Heine pulls Jehudah back from falling into a total immersion within the sensual and this shift reflects a fundamental prohibition that Heine comes to in his last work. It is the difference between immersion in the cosmic stream of Being, an engagement with the innovated text, and immersion in substance, a desire to possess transcendence. In fact, the desire to possess transcendence is synonymous in Heine's thinking with magic. Hence Halevi is a prophet/messiah/poet, but not a magician, like Faust. The poet transmits the revelation, but does not control it.

With "Jehudah ben Halevi," Heine posits a subject position, then, in which the poet redeems creation by liberating *poesie* from mimesis, by enlivening texts, awaking them to their immanence. The poet does this by "innovating" stories, forgotten, and untold, but available in the archive of the poet's soul. In his poem, Heine identifies the fragments of a Jewish aesthetics, perhaps a secular kabbalah, in which obligation is synonymous with liberating textual immanence. The threat though to this aesthetic kabbalah causes Heine to engage in one last literary project.

Written just before his death, and under commission for "Mr. Lumley, director of her Majesty's Theater," Heine's *Doktor Faust, A Dance Poem* addresses the need for an aesthetic strategy that is not only faithful to the spirit of the original or past—to its mimesis—but that also compels readers to move into the new spaces or "structures of beings" afforded by the innovated text.[71] He juxtaposes implicitly Faust, the apostate, to Halevi, the poetic "pillar of fire."

Heine calls his *Doktor Faust*, an "innovation" and the designation sutures the kabbalistic project of innovation, its *Neuerung,* to the literary work he names one of his "highest poetic achievements."[72] By using "innovation" in this context, Heine points, both to a liberation of the poem's ontology and to a subjective liberation, a process in which subject and object have been liberated from the epistemological constraints of historical representation, of religious orthodoxy and dogma, and even of an aesthetic mimesis of phenomena.[73] However, Heine's liberation hews between apostasy and redemption, a realization that Heine feels is intimately connected to the Faust legend and the experience of oppression.

Heine's innovated *Faust* compels him to map transcendence both in dynamic property—revelation—and in its detachment from the text—a forbidden aim. In this way, Heine locates his Faust at a similar crossroads as Halevi; both figures leave their communities in pursuit of revelation, coming to an intersection between transcendence and immanence. Faust can either allow the revelation in its immanence to draw him closer to Divine Being or he can attempt to wield transcendence, compelling mystical power to overcome the limitations of his lived experience. While Halevi the poet engages these two elements with a view to liberating *poesie*—liberating the text's immanence—Heine's Faust uses transcendence to liberate his body, to experience everything denied to him.

Thus Heine's Faust manipulates phenomena to reshape the world around him. Heine's "innovation" requires the "novel" meaning of "the older, marginalized sources" Goethe's *Faust* excludes. Heine recognizes that either he can mimic Goethe, or he can liberate Faust.

The *Dance Poem* begins with Faust in his study, surrounded by alchemical and mystical items.[74] He wears the costume of a "sixteenth-century scholar."[75] His gait is unsteady; nevertheless, "his inner struggle of fear and courage" motivates him to unlock "The Power of Hell," a tome "chained," within his bookcase.[76] Compelled by his "courage," he starts his incantation "in the ancient language," an unidentified language, but one that Faust knows to be powerful.[77] Even when "terrible peals of thunder and a monstrous serpent appears," Faust sends the serpent dismissively back to the "fiery abyss" and demands the devil appear in his "most dangerous form."[78] His challenge prompts the emergence of Mephistophela, in the form of a beautiful ballerina.[79]

> Suddenly the darkness is banished by a blaze of light. In place of thunder and lightning the most charming dance music is heard, and a basket of flowers from the chasm in the floor. It breaks apart and a lovely ballerina steps forth ... circling the conjuror in a characteristic *pas de seul*.[80]

The English translation misleads a bit here. Instead of a "blaze of light," in French, and in German, the text's original languages, Heine describes "innumerable lights" that erase the darkness. The nuance offers an intriguing image in which the abyss is represented by the spectacle of "punctiform lights."[81] At the edges of Heine's description, Isaac Luria's kabbalistic "doctrine of the Breaking of the Vessels" and the "primeval space of the *Tsimtsum*" are evoked.[82] Inverting the order of Luria, Heine has the abyss and its terror give way to "innumerable lights," accompanied by "charming dance music." Mephistophela suggests that a divine beauty has not only been summoned, but also that Faust stands at the cusp of creation. Faust recognizes it to be illusion.

The thunder and fear-inducing spectacle has been displaced by the "most dangerous form," rising from within the abyss a "basket of flowers." When it "breaks apart," a ballerina emerges dancing around "the conjuror." The illusion of beauty breaks into its constituent parts, but what emerges from these shards is a being whose "vulgar pirouettes" around Faust offer him sex. The frightening "abyss" illusion of "beauty" metamorphoses into a crude wantonness. Heine's language purposely conflates the representation of beauty with the qualifier's connotations: they are "vulgar" solicitations. The ballerina's desire is base, raw, and without nuance. She lures Faust, but she could lure anyone. Faust as an object of desire is interchangeable with any other being.

Heine both encourages and subverts Mephistophela's materialization into the devil's "most dangerous form" by implying she is a power he controls. She stands before him and he intuits the illusion of her possession. "Impressed by the gracious, smiling apparition," Faust compliments her. He bows before her and the two begin to dance together: as they dance, Mephistophela responds "coquettishly" to the Doktor's advances. The whole scene revolves around Mephistophela's encouragement of Faust's lust for her. In the German and French versions, the scene is explicit: Mephistophela solicits Faust to act on his desires. He imagines he transcends this world and the illusion of the abyss. Heine evokes the narrative of the golem, with Faust acting as the inversion of the Maharal.

With her "magic wand," Mephistophela proceeds "to transform everything within the room."[83] However, the transformation remains incomplete because "the shape of the original object is not entirely extinguished."[84] Its phenomenal footprint remains traceable beneath the image of the illusion.

> The gloomy zodiacal pictures glow with bright inward colors. Exotic birds appear on the brackets which had previously contained dead specimens. Little owls fly around with nosegays in their beaks. The walls begin to flower with golden ornaments, Venetian mirrors, antique friezes and *works of art*.[85]

The whole impression is chaotic, ghostly, and at the same time, exquisitely beautiful, like a "monstrous arabesque."[86]

Mephistophela offers Faust deception: objects come into being at her command, and by extension to please him, but she cannot obscure completely their "dead" forms. Mephistophela has no power to create life; she only has the ability to craft illusion. The promised transformation of Faust's world can never be complete because "the shape of the original object" remains liminally present. Faust shares with all of creation, the same phenomenal being. No illusion can hide this difference: the created is never interchangeable with the creator.

This is the unarticulated crux of her offer. Faust can have the illusion of metamorphosis; he can manifest power over the elements. He can manipulate objects. His desires can materialize, but there remains a gap between the phenomenal world and Divine Being. This gap is never completely erased even though he might appear to cross the boundaries of time and space, and human existence. Heine's innovation reinforces that Faust cannot be "like a divine being."

After the display of new creatures, arising from within the inanimate objects surrounding him, Mephistophela proffers Faust the contract. He rejects it, demanding instead to see the "infernal empire" of hell. To this demand, Mephistophela waves her wand, and the "elite of Hell" appear and just as suddenly, she transforms them into "a troupe of ballerinas." Still Faust resists her. These "metamorphoses" do not elicit the forfeiture of his soul. Faust commits to apostasy because he wants to materialize his desires. He wants to cross a line between created and creator, between object and subject.

When Mephistophela shows him a woman in "a mirror," Faust recognizes her to be a real, living being and tries to seduce her. He prostrates himself before her, but she insults and demeans him. He appears without any enhancements, untransformed and repulsive. Her rejection reiterates that he can never achieve his desires in his present state. Concha Zardaya explains that since the mirror is a "symbol of the imagination or the conscience," its effect is to "reflect the real form of the objective world."[87] Thus the mirror functions for Faust as a mimetic symbol, magically reproduced as the object of his desire while simultaneously it reflects his hideousness back to the woman. The intensity of his desire causes a reconsideration of Mephistophela's offer. He begs for her help and she waves her wand, bringing out of the abyss another creature, a "hideous monkey." She waves her wand again, a "young, handsome ballet-dancer" appears, triggering the woman's explicit "wantonness." If Faust accepts apostasy, he can be transformed, like the "hideous monkey." Apostasy becomes the sign of his desire's fulfillment.

As Faust rages at her rejection of him in favor of the illusion, Mephistophela produces the contract again. If he signs the contract, he can experience a similar metamorphosis, becoming the woman's lover. He signs, "arrays himself in the Devil's borrowed finery," and surrenders himself to Mephistophela.

"Before long her apprentice is dancing a brilliant pas de deux": Faust and Mephistophela cavort before the mirror and the other dancers; they perform a public spectacle of sexual anarchy. When Faust approaches the woman again, she declares her love for him. He continues his sexual dance before her until Mephistophela makes the mirror disappear. Act 1 concludes with Faust's "original state" masked by the image of virility, vitality, vulgarity.

Readers see through Faust's disguise, but we are aware that Faust's lack of hope drives his actions. Heine deems it the allure of antinomianism: if Faust's actions, his transgressions do not change anything, then, nothing is really transgression. Moreover, a transgressive alchemy, masquerading as transcendence, still allows Faust to materialize his desires. Mephistophela promises Faust what has been denied to Aher, even as it repeats the Edenic Fall. The desire to change one's ontology, one's embodiment, provokes a desire to "cover up" that difference by adopting the "borrowed" clothes and adornments of Mephistophela's illusion, a heretical transcendence because he wants to "think, to act, and to enjoy life to its full extent."[88]

At its conclusion, Heine's Faust attempts to abandon his apostasy. He runs away from the witch, the woman in the mirror whom he seduces with Mephistophela's help, and now he stands at the altar in an earthly paradise, with the woman of his dreams. Up until this point, all of his adventures with Mephistophela have taken place among magical beings, practitioners of esoterica, but he has rejected all of it in order to marry and live his life "to its full extent."

Still appearing as a young handsome man, he prepares to marry when his former lover arrives and reveals his deception; he is a "hideous monkey." The earth opens up and swallows Faust screaming into Hell's abyss. Heine ends the poem with condemnation: any attempt to materialize transcendence does not exculpate the sins accrued because of it. Heine's *aggadah* warns of the false promises of a materialized redemption, transcendence justified by any means.

At first reading, the poem imitates the biblical tale of the Fall of Adam and Eve. Faust is aware that he is "naked," an aged, unattractive, "hideous monkey" who appears before the object of his desire. In his moment of rejection, he chooses to cover himself with Mephistophela's help. Faust's choice derives from his desire to possess what has been denied to him: like Eve, he wants to know and experience "like a divine being" the "perfection that destroys." However, Adam and Eve never become apostates. Faust's actions make him though unredeemable, as unredeemable as Aher. Like Aher, he abandons the Pardes and chooses apostasy.

Heine warns his readers: there is no redemption for Faust because Faust not only solicits Satan's help, but he also uses "the ancient language" to materialize his desires. In this way, he taps into the "ancient language's" secret. This language is animate and compels beings from within the abyss to appear. In this way, Heine suggests Faust has used Hebrew crudely to fulfill his desires. He mimics the actions of Aher joining him on the path of apostasy, through its "darkness," to condemnation.

Heine attributes to Goethe's *Faust* a similar strategy. Covering himself with Mephistopheles' help, Goethe's protagonist relies on the justification that his quest for transcendence justifies his actions. He can murder, steal, dispossess, seduce and he bears no responsibility for his actions when they injure others because ultimately, God understands that he engages in a higher purpose, the quest for transcendence. For this reason, Heine accuses Goethe of "failing" the aesthetic, of violating *poesie*, reconstructing the legend's "secret" in the shape of the "puerile."[89] Since Goethe "allows him to enter Paradise triumphantly to the accompaniment of dancing cherubims and heavenly choirs," Faust's "pact with evil, which inspired hair-raising terrors in our fathers, ends like a frivolous farce."[90]

In the moment that Mephistopheles claims Faust for the abyss, Faust cries out for forgiveness and God negates Mephistopheles' judgment. His sins are no longer binding; apostasy has no consequence. Goethe's Faust experiences a "redemption through sin." In this way, Goethe constructs a recognizable figure for his readers, whose Frankist promises of a redemption in spite of sin encourage antinomianism as a necessary act of rebellion and redemption.

Thus Heine presents two perspectives on transcendence. They both hinge on "reading." Goethe's Faust in his study abandons the text to possess transcendence in a material form; although Heine's Faust does something similar, the clue is bound up with Heine's "innovation" of the legend. He introduces new elements—"terror and erotic anarchy"—to expose an unarticulated depth to the legend. The new events and characters reflect a dynamic, vital writing pushing from beneath the legend's surface. While scholars cite Heine's innovations as evidence that he violates the mimesis of the original Faustian legend too, Heine suggests his innovation reveals a forgotten phenomenology emanating within the story, a mystical textuality, as yet unarticulated in the legend, but nonetheless constitutive of it.

Consequently, Goethe's failure is one of intuition: he does not intuit the spirit of the original—what Benjamin would later call the work of art's "aura." Goethe fails because he innovates "according to his own heretical outlook."[91] His heresy not only strips away the tale's "true spirit"—its animation—but it also severs the German people from "piety" because it severs them from their own *poesie*.[92] Heine's allusive kinship between Goethe's Faust and Jacob Frank rests on a heretical kabbalah.

Hence Heine innovates the legend to perform a *tikkun*, a last mystical *tikkun* for Germans and Jews. It is the heart of Heine's aesthetic project because it addresses why his last work, *Doktor Faust,* is not reducible to his despair over his "mattress-grave."[93]

When Heine elevates the legend in itself over any attempt to identify an historical Faust, he does so to demonstrate the necessity of thought because thought challenges the "acceptance of the Church's total authority in matters spiritual and temporal."[94] Readers feel still the sympathy in Heine's words when Faust's "desire to think, act and enjoy life" is thwarted by religious authority so that he "uses the language of the ancients," and embraces "apostasy .... turning to Satan."[95] Religion "keeps the humble charcoal burner on his knees" incapable of questioning why he is persecuted, reviled, marginalized.[96] This is the last piece of the Frankist puzzle, the heretical kabbalah, where in his rebellion against oppression, Faust imagines an enjoyable life.

> Faust began to *think* .... He was not content to tread in dark places .... He demanded to be allowed to think, to act and enjoy life to its full extent, and so .... to use the language of the ancients .... he became an apostate, renounced all hope of heavenly bliss, and turned to Satan ....[97]

An individual who "began to *think*" rebels "against the meek acceptance of his forefathers" to embrace apostasy.[98] Although Heine identifies with "the humble charcoal burner" who imagines leaving "dark places" associated with the religion "of his forefathers," by linking Faust, to the longing for freedom from oppression, the poet forecloses the path from religion, through oppression, to apostasy. Apostasy might signify liberation to Goethe, but Heine's Faust is condemned for it.

In contrast, Heine portrays Jehudah still oppressed, even though he has liberated *poesie* to act according to its own aims. Interacting with its immanence, the poet is always aware of a fundamental difference between revelation and the self. Jehudah's aim unseals the revelation in him; that is, he writes his own Torah. If he experiences transcendence as a result of his actions, Halevi is not preoccupied with it. Transcendence is never his to possess; it is a fleeting intuition of a future redemption. He cannot attempt its materialization. He must accept its transitory flash of enlightenment and adhere to the writing and its immanence. In contrast, Faust posits transcendence as a property to control. He materializes it, to bring himself out of the ghetto and into history. Thus he uses transcendence in order to liberate himself, and it results in his condemnation. As I note earlier, Faust attempts with this act to make transcendence constitutive of the subject, to wrench it from the epiphenomenal, not only reducing it to tangible experience, but also making it akin to power.

Heine grapples with these two positions repeatedly: can innovated *poesie* lead poet and reader to redemption or does it remain a silent object the essence of which—its transcendence—is taken by the subject for the self? Does transcendence detached from text lead to power or is it a simulacrum of redemption, a masquerade that must end in condemnation?

Heine contrasts the heretical kabbalah's messianic apostasy with the poet's secular kabbalah. In "Jehudah ben Halevi," and *Der Doktor Faust,* the persistent question of how redemption relates to Jewish lived experience motivates Heine to tack between transcendence as a constitutive element of the subject, in which the Jewish subject enters history and gains emancipation versus an immanence of the text imposing itself as the underwriting obligation of the poet. With "Jehudah ben Halevi," redemption is vested in the poet who alone knows how to liberate the Jewish subject even though the poet suffers martyrdom too. Lest readers then be tempted to abandon the tradition, follow their desires indiscriminately, *Doktor Faust* emerges, reminding them that transcendence proffered is illusion, a simulacrum that leads them to judgment rather than redemption. Consequently, Heine never has to be a kabbalist; he doesn't even have to identify with Judaism. Like Jehudah, he can follow the path of *poesie* even if he knows the ending of that story. He is called to poesie, the prophet/poet of the innovated text.

4

Kafka, Prophet of Failure

A Descent into Yiddishkeit

On October 28, 1911, Kafka attends the Yiddish production of Jacob Gordin's play, "Elishe ben Avuya," a fictional account of the apostate ben Avuya's life story after his abandonment of Judaism in "The Four who went to Pardes." On October 29, he reproduces in his diary a brief summary of the Talmudic *aggadah*, based on an account by his friend, Isaac Löwy.[1] Löwy's story focuses on four renowned scholars of the Talmud, whose study of the Law affects each one's fate.

> Löwy: Four young friends became great Talmud scholars in their old age. But each had a different fate. One became mad, one died, Rabbi Eliezar became a free-thinker at forty and only the oldest one, Akiva, who had not begun his studies until the age of forty, achieved complete knowledge. The disciple of Rabbi Eliezar was Rabbi Meyer, a pious man whose piety was so great that he was not harmed by what the free-thinker taught him. He ate, as he said, the kernel of the nut, the shell he threw away. Once, on Saturday, Eliezar went for a ride, Rabbi Meyer followed on foot, the Talmud in his hand, of course only for two thousand paces, for you are not permitted to go any farther on Saturday. And from this walk emerged a symbolic demand and the reply to it. Come back to your people, said Rabbi Meyer. Rabbi Eliezar refused with a pun.[2]

Missing from Kafka's brief entry is any mention of kabbalah or Jewish mysticism; in fact, the only way that a reader would recognize its original content is if one already has some familiarity with the story from its Talmudic antecedent, its resonances with *The Zohar*, or its implications for Frankism's heretical kabbalah.[3] In the diary's reproduction, each companion's "fate" is tied to his relationship to Judaism, specifically to the study of *halakhah,* rather than any one individual's behavior within the Pardes.[4] Of the four companions, two of the "friends" experience their "fates" of death and insanity in anonymity. They have dedicated their lives to Talmud, only to be driven to death or insanity by it. The other two, Avuya or Eliezer and Akiva, experience their "fates" as mid-life occurrences in which Avuya becomes an apostate and Akiva achieves "complete knowledge," but as with Talmud, all the weight of Kafka's entry falls on Avuya.

Instead of ben Avuya's apostasy as a mystical event, Löwy follows Gordin's depiction of the apostate as a "free-thinker."[5] Eliezer's "sin" is due to a conflict of conscience over Jewish adherence to an inflexible system—an incomprehensible law—rather than any desire for transcendence. In the play, Gordin's reimagination sets up Avuya's apostasy as ethical necessity: he is committed to thought's liberation. Echoing Heine's innovation of Faust, Elishe's desire "to *think*" triggers his condemnation by the rabbinate, his "people"; he exists as unredeemable to them and they are the "gatekeepers" of tradition. Avuya the "free-thinker" pits himself against them so that his quest for the liberation of thought is juxtaposed to those rabbinic leaders who would insist on its suppression. Thus Elishe is the sign of the modern Jewish subject whose apostasy becomes an effect of modernity. The play depicts his choice to walk away from Judaism because of his commitment to rational thought. In this way, Gordin's Avuya tries to save his people, to redeem them from a "dark" tradition. When he abandons the law, it is a necessary evolution; he recognizes in the Law's incomprehensibility a means for rabbinic control of Jews.

Kafka's short rehearsal of Löwy's account reproduces Avuya/Eliezer as both a potential figure of Jewish messianism, and a "free-thinker." Elishe is not only a cipher for the modern Jewish subject, but also through "the kernel of the nut," Aher's teachings suggest a philosophical, political, and social transformation of the world of Jewish lived experience. The pattern is clearly mimetic.

While scholars approach Jacob Gordin and his oeuvre as representative of the "origin of Yiddish drama," they regularly ignore its relationship to the original *aggadah*, and the ways Gordin repeatedly incorporates the familiar tropes, images, and themes of late kabbalah's Jewish messianism circulating throughout Jewish communities.[6] The play reflects a *Haskalah* sentiment, in which audiences expect a perspective extoling the necessity of embracing a secular world. However, in their legends, hagiographies, and teachings, Jewish and non-Jewish audiences know Jewish messianism's promises and sentiments coming out of the early modern and *Haskalah* eras in their vernacular languages. Consequently, scholarship often overlooks how Elishe's actions reflect the actions of Shabbtai Zvi and Jacob Frank, transforming them from heresy to rational thought.[7]

The historical arc of Jacob Frank's apostasy underpins how Kafka imagines the story of Eliezer. Since Frank makes "heretical clarity" the ground for his revelation and his "persecution,"[8] he declares explicitly that he has come to liberate the Jews and the world from "all religions, and all law." In other words, the patterns that drive Gordin's play resonate with Jewish messianic movements of the seventeenth and eighteenth centuries more than scholars recognize. Although Kafka's entry doesn't include an explicit reference to the heretical messianism of the preceding century, it still implicitly integrates Avuya's transformation, "into the tradition."

In Kafka's diary account, Eliezer's metamorphosis from Talmud scholar to "free-thinker" is understood to be the reason for Meyer's plea to "come back to your people."[9] "Free thinker" implies that Eliezer is one who does not study Torah, Talmud's *am ha'aretz*. He remains a Jew, but without the Law. David Biale recognizes this as the "secular Jew's crisis."[10] In Yiddish, the term translates to *amhoretz* and signifies ignorance—the opposite of the Hebrew's significance. When Gordin's protagonist presents himself as *amhoretz*, ignorance conflates not studying with not knowing. In order to experience the liberation of thought, Elishe must not know the Law. The shift would be familiar to Kafka since part of Prague's Jewish history includes Jonas Wehle's Frankist circle.[11] Their political and social ideas, as I illustrate in Chapter 2, are absorbed into *Haskalah* thought, and their kabbalistic perspectives are integrated into Bohemian Jewish culture as secular ideas.[12]

Like the *halakhic* source-texts, Kafka's diary entry, and Gordin's play, Avuya's student, Rabbi Meyer (Meir), for example, continues to interact with him, suggesting that Avuya's sin—whatever it might be—does not preclude his former student from learning from him.[13] Avuya's teachings retain a value, "the kernel of the nut."[14] Avuya's continued presence among Jews is then hardly surprising since his value to the community remains in his ideas even though he is their scapegoat.[15] If Jews obey "a Law which is neither reasonable nor comprehensible," their obedience leads them to accept their oppression, the social injustices of a world to which their leaders have forbidden them to belong, but within which they nevertheless are punished.

The rabbinate's failure to address the absence of redemption for the modern Jew underwrites the "parable" Gordin's Elishe ben Avuya tells his audience so that the play's significance is anchored to the parable's depiction of rabbinic authority as part of the experience of oppression. It reproduces Gordin's antipathy for both *halakhah* and the rabbinate.

> God and the Torah is exactly like a king who captures a bird and says to his servant, "Keep it and guard it all your life; if you do not, you will pay with your life." The servant does not know what kind of bird this is, or why he should keep it, but he keeps it anyway and guards it for years and years. Do you know why? Because he is a slave, because although he does not live, he fears to die ... I have let the bird go free."[16]

The parable's crux depends on an association Elishe makes between the servant who "keeps it anyway," without knowing "what kind of bird" it is, and why it is important. Gordin implies that Avuya's desire for thought liberates him from "guarding" the Torah. Unlike the servant, he is no longer a gatekeeper. Moreover, the "parable" also creates a connection in the audience's mind of the correlation between the king who enslaves his servants and the God who tolerates his people's enslavement as they seek to fulfill his wishes, expressed in the Law.

In a Frankist echo, the King becomes the "evil Demiurge" who keeps paradise from his servants, and to whom Frank alleges the rabbinate have committed themselves. Thus Avuya's desire to be more than labor, to be a liberated subject so to speak, is juxtaposed to the king's unquestioning servant. The play illustrates the conflict between a *Haskalah* Jewry, intent on assimilation, and an orthodoxy, tethered to an ancient and "dark" tradition, willing to force their constituencies to remain without answers and within oppression. In this way, Gordin produces a Yiddish revision of Talmud's *aggadic* narrative about Avuya, a modern Jewish subject who embarks on a path of his own redemption in the world. He essentially "writes" his own Torah, but he does not *integrate* it into the tradition, even though Meyer values the "kernel of the nut."[17]

This discursus into the play's reception, its fictionalized biography of Elisha ben Avuya, and how these elements intersect with Kafka's thinking brings me to a final aspect of the play's significance for Kafka. In Evelyn Torton Beck's estimation, Elishe rejects "orthodoxy" because "by their stubborn insistence on carrying out every detail of the Law as it was handed down to them, the Jewish people have made themselves responsible for the great suffering and the many tortures and indignities which, as a people, they had to endure throughout history."[18]

However, as I note earlier, Elishe occupies simultaneously the roles of the *amhoretz*, and the *am ha'aretz*: his community sees him as one who does not study Torah, and due to his rejection of their Law, they see him as interchangeable with the Gentiles around them, "men of the country" (*am ha'aretz*). He becomes "ignorant" because of the transgression that he does not know the Law (*amhoretz*). Although Elishe's parable implies the servant acts as the common man, the Yiddish *amhoretz* or "simpleton," the play suggests to Kafka that Elishe chooses to become a common man because he believes in the "possibility" of his redemption, tied to liberation from the Law.

Yiddish audiences identify with Avuya/Aher as a protagonist who reaffirms modernity's promises rather than a Jewish figure who abandons Jewish mystical experience, and adopts apostasy as a result. Moreover, the exclusive focus on Elishe as a cipher for Kafka leads scholars to almost uniform acceptance of an implicit identification between Elishe and Kafka so that his diary entry confirms Kafka's alienation from Judaism.

For Klaus Grözinger, Kafka's 1911 transcription of the Pardes narrative is added proof though of Kafka's knowledge of kabbalah; he "certainly had some knowledge of the mystical tradition of the journey through heaven as well as the gatekeeper tradition connected with it already."[19] Citing it as the "main piece of Talmudic evidence for the mystical journey through heaven and its gatekeeper tradition," Grözinger notes that "all subsequent Jewish mystics" rely on the story as "the original paradigm of the mystical journey through the celestial spheres."[20] He adds that the Talmudic story includes Rashi's commentary in which the four companions "ascended into heaven with the help of one of the Names of God." Hence he concludes that Kafka's familiarity with how they enter the pardes includes the use of "an invocation," and "one of the Names of God."[21] Moreover, he attributes to Kafka this knowledge.

The argument produces an interesting implication because it suggests that in spite of where he learns the story, with his brief descent into *Yiddishkeit*, Kafka dispenses with its plot to focus on an unarticulated connection between the "common man" and Löwy's "free-thinker." To some extent, Löwy's development of Avuya enables Kafka to link the apostate to Frankism's implied promise that the common man can be redeemed on earth.

David Suchoff comes closest to understanding how Kafka "reads" the figure of Elishe in its transmission by highlighting that the Gordin play is "a Gnostic heresy that Kafka saw in Prague."[22] In Suchoff's brief phrase, Prague, Gnosticism, and Jewish heresy are imbricated since Avuya's apostasy circulates among Jews as "common knowledge." It hints at the heretical kabbalah underpinning Scholem, Benjamin, Alter, and so many others in their analyses of Kafka.

Harold Bloom sketches these gnostic underpinnings in order to make visible the implicit stakes of Aher's transformation for Kafka: if Aher represents the modern Jewish subject who seeks another path to paradise, then, the individual should see the "possibility" of a future redemption even though he cannot attain it.

> In Gnosticism, there is an alien, wholly transcendent God, and the adept, after considerable difficulties, can find the way back to presence and fulness. Gnosticism therefore is a religion of salvation, though the most negative of all such saving visions. ... Kafka is not gnostic. ... [He] takes the impossible step beyond gnosticism, by denying that there is any hope for us at all.[23]

In Bloom's "Gnosticism," the "Demiurge," as in Frank's hagiographies, is defeated by the human subject who after "considerable difficulties" is able to "find the way back to presence and fulness." The "wholly and transcendent God" is "alien" to human existence, inhuman, yet "Gnosticism" promises "salvation," a redemption won through struggle. The gnostic fantasy is the belief in a messianic age that the human can materialize or achieve. However, as Bloom declares, "Kafka is not gnostic"; any fantasy of redemption and a messianic age across any plane of existence must fail because Kafka forecloses "any hope for us at all." In this way, Kafka recognizes in Aher the outline of Frank's failure with its false promise that a messianic age has begun for everyone. Even though his diary entry suggests a simple reproduction of Löwy's account, he traces the liminal outline of the heretical kabbalah's pattern of messianism. Finally, he recognizes that he must write another *aggadah*, a story that outlines Aher's error.

When Kafka reimagines the story, he returns it to its Jewish gnostic roots as they are allusively hinted at to underscore its failure. In the metamorphosis that Kafka envisions, Aher's "other" path leads to a backdoor into paradise, but he cannot enter it. Embedded in this "Gnostic heresy" is the sense that modernity has promised "the common man" the redemption previously only known and guarded by Judaism's elite. Moreover, with its allusion to Frankism, an implicit link emerges between Talmud's Elisha and the Yiddish Elishe, who opts to become a "man of the country," rather than be subject to the rabbinate and *halakhah*. The link transforms Aher from apostate into "common man." In this way the heretic becomes the common man who expects redemption as an entitlement of his being.[24]

"Before the Law"

In 1915, Kafka publishes "Before the Law," a short story that Grözinger declares establishes a key connection between the *Pardes* narrative, known to Kafka through Löwy's account, because it connects the story of a journey to paradise with the "gatekeeper" stories, popular among the Hasidim.[25] To Grözinger, "the gatekeeper" punctuates many of Kafka's short stories and novels, and affirms that Kafka regularly has access to a "popularized kabbalah and the Jewish traditions influenced by it."[26]

The short story reappears later, in Kafka's *The Trial*, when a priest tells the condemned Josef K., the novel's protagonist, a parable.[27] The story remains though one of his most enigmatic narratives; it has elicited so much attention that George Steiner remarks it is an experience of "fear and trembling," over a "page and a half."[28] Walter Benjamin insists it overshadows *The Trial* in which it appears.[29] Adorno states bluntly " 'Each sentence says: interpret me.' Adding, immediately after: 'and none will permit it.'"[30] Readers cannot but help to fulfill the story's obligation to interpret and reinterpret, never quite sure of what the story means.

The perpetual compulsion to reinterpret causes many to question how much Judaic knowledge does one need to read "Before the Law," and by extension, Kafka? With its accent on *halakhah*, the question presupposes that Kafka works from a Judaic or religious orientation at times.[31] His work is particular in its use of Judaic signifiers, perhaps even themes; thus readers focus on isolated symbols, identifying their religious significance within the story. The approach requires readers to know basic meanings for Judaic symbols.

Another way of entering Kafka's work asks how much Jewish knowledge does a reader have to know? This question assumes that Kafka's Jewish or ethnic identity is the sole reason he writes using mysterious Jewish signifiers. The simple statement, "Kafka is a Jew," is supplemented with biographical details to explain his aesthetic choices. The approach highlights the role of the law in his stories to suggest his alienation from Judaism: his rejection of Judaism and the Law is a sign of his alienation. Still for others, Kafka's story signifies universal truths, like all of his work, because Kafka speaks to an universal audience and presumably, one doesn't need to supply any Jewish content at all. In this third iteration, Kafka is no longer Jewish or at least it is an inconsequential aspect of his identity as a writer. It doesn't even merit consideration. Those Jewish signifiers that bother the first two sets of readers are cast as universal themes, for instance, a "law of the unconscious" that compels human beings to never achieve their conscious aims.[32] The law signifies here a nihilism that inscribes itself in human existence. Ironically, it resonates with "the man from the country's" desire for entrance to a law about which he knows nothing.

The real question should be though how much kabbalah does a reader need to know to read this particular short story, or any of Kafka's work? Is it enough to identify the mention of kabbalah in his texts?[33] Can the identification of kabbalistic signifiers and excerpts provide insight into Kafka's thinking? In one instance, Grözinger identifies kabbalistic tropes in Kafka and then suggests their mimetic parallel in Hasidic tales. His claim asserts that Kafka's knowledge of "a popular kabbalah" derives from the writer's visits to neighboring Hasidic "wonder rebbes" around the outskirts of his native Prague and in Warsaw.[34] He concludes that Hasidic kabbalistic tales motivate many of Kafka's narratives.

Grözinger follows Iris Bruce in her identification of *gilgul* or Isaac Luria's concept of "transmigration of the souls" as a kabbalistic foundation to many of Kafka's "animal stories." She links Kafka's use of kabbalah to her thesis of "cultural Zionism."[35] David Suchoff connects Kafka's kabbalistic content to his thesis about *The Trial* in which Josef K's visitor, Leni, warns him against "the stereotypic obedience" to the law, of those who would put him to death.[36] Kafka produces a multivalent text that demands readers join his characters in their search for a *pleroma* of meaning. In that moment, Suchoff underscores a tension in Kafka between the followers of the Law—its gatekeepers—and those destined to be its "heretics," the condemned. The nature of the heresy is the translation of "the law into multiple meanings" rather than a "dogmatic object of knowledge."[37] Suchoff's brief comments on "Before the Law" reinforce that a tension ensues because Kafka works from a multivalent tradition of orthodox and heretical kabbalahs.

The "quality of strangeness" that animates Kafka's fiction transforms his work into the 'inimitable, the "unclassifiable."[38] The "accidental product" of a "heretical kabbalah," he is not necessarily a heretic, but walks nevertheless "the razor's edge" of his own "dissolution" because of it.[39] Biale notes that in this way, Scholem and Kafka articulate a "shared sense"; that is, Scholem too is a "product" of the "heretical kabbalah."[40]

Thus several kabbalistic registers appear in Kafka's work. While these kabbalahs might be particularly Hasidic, Sabbatian/Frankist, or Luriannic, they are all part of the tradition, subsumed under its two dominant strains, "orthodox" and "heretical."[41] Their importance for Kafka isn't necessarily reducible to proof that he knows them or even that he espouses any particular belief in the projects; it is, however, as Harold Bloom notes, a "modernist kabbalah."[42] In other words, Kafka's use of kabbalistic material reflects modernity's eclecticism.[43] However, Kafka's "modernist kabbalah" exhibits all of modernity's promises, broken on the shoals of Jewish lived experience.

The plot of "Before the Law" is very simple. When the story opens, "a man from the country" asks for "entrance" to the Law, but a gatekeeper forbids it.[44] The gatekeeper stands before the Law, and restricts access to it.[45] Already Kafka has sent his first kabbalistic signal, "a man from the country." The phrase resonates in multiple registers associated with Jewish traditions.

Many scholars link Kafka's phrase to its Hebrew equivalent, *am-ha'aretz* because "Kafka knew both the Talmudic and the Yiddish usage of the term."[46] Eli Schonfeld cites its biblical meaning, "people from the earth," and its origins, informing readers that it derives from "the *Book of Ezra*" in which "the *am-ha'aretz* is opposed to the *am Yehuda*, the people of Judah."[47] In Schonfeld's description, "the people from the earth" are always implicitly juxtaposed to "the people of Judah."[48] Biblically, *am-ha'aretz* refers literally to "people from the land or country." In *Ezra*, it refers to people living in the land already who see the returning Jewish exiles as their enemies.[49] The term implies a hostile world, whose defining trait is the rejection of the Torah; it is contrasted with "the people of Judah" in whom the Torah is constitutive. Thus the biblical *am ha'aretz* carries with it the connotation of a people 1) challenging the Jews' return to "the land," 2) attempting to subvert the Jews' reconstruction of the temple, and 3) preventing the Jews from the fulfillment of a Divine commandment. This last aspect implies that the biblical "people of the Land" attempt to prohibit the expression of what is constitutive about the Jews, the key difference between the two groups. The "people of the land" are committed to stopping the Jews from the articulation of their difference in the Law.

The phrase is revised in Talmud subsequently to refer to anyone who does not study the law in relation to other Jews. It gains this meaning in several contexts, not least of which is when Akiva, the *tanna*, describes himself as having been at one time, *am-ha-aretz*; he uses the term to contrast his position as a *tanna* with his life before study. It signifies that previously, he belongs to a people whose primary trait is a lack of knowledge of the Law because they do not study it. Hence he is one of many and they are all interchangeable with each other. By placing himself within this group, Akiva identifies himself as previously being a Jew who does not study, but who still remains identifiably Jewish within the terms of Judaism. This lack of study is constitutive of a new group of Jews; therefore, they are "people of the land" in contrast to those who fulfill the commandment of study. Their ignorance of the Law is not synonymous with heresy. He is not "a miscreant or an infidel"; his "disobedience" is not due to a rejection of the Law.[50] He is simply unaware "of what it means to stand before the Law."[51]

Schonfeld connects the next step of the phrase's development to Hillel's teaching that "the *bur*, the ignorant person, and more precisely the person ignorant of the law …. cannot be sin-fearing … cannot be pious."[52] One is incapable of being "sin-fearing" or "pious" because one does not recognize the quality of piety.[53] According to Schonfeld, the Yiddish translation of the Hebrew picks up this signification so that *amhoretz*—the Yiddish term—refers to someone "ignorant in religious matters."[54] By the early twentieth century, the time of Kafka, Heinz Politzer observes the term has not only migrated into "Jewish folklore and Yiddish culture," but Yiddish writers have also made it synonymous with the "simpleton," the "ignoramus," or a "boor."[55] Dan Miron implies that the Yiddish meaning is also inherent in S.Y. Agnon's *Yesteryear*, specifically through the figure of the "*homme moyen sensuel*, a regular and rather unimpressive person."[56] In fact, Asher Zvi Hirsch Ginsberg, later known as Ahad Ha'am, the Israeli writer, changes his name to emphasize that he is "one from the land," a secular Jew living in Israel. In all of the later iterations, Judaism ceases to be a defining factor.

Grözinger adds perhaps the most intriguing aspects of the genealogy in his reading of "Before the Law" because he links how kabbalists "combine" the Talmudic *am ha-aretz* with the kabbalah's "tradition" of "human life as a lifelong journey through the heavenly halls of the Torah."[57] Thus the story's "image of the *am ha-aretz* standing before the gates of the halls of the Torah" is a signifier of "the unsuccessful human life in a Jewish sense." The "man from the country" stands before the law as an inversion of the kabbalist's journey. Grözinger applies, then, Isaac Luria's concept of "transmigration of the soul," or *gilgul*, to Kafka, in order to demonstrate that such an inversion remains an inevitable stage in human experience. Kafka's investment in *gilgul* attests to an inevitable transformation in which the commanded metamorphosis, transformation of the "unsuccessful human life" eventually into "a lifelong journey" through the "halls of the Torah" never actually achieves its aim.[58]

Scholem explains that with Luria, *gilgul* expresses "in a new and forcible way the reality of exile" in which "its function" is "to lift the experience of the Jew in the *Galut*, the exile and migration of the body, to the higher plane of a symbol for the exile of the soul."[59] In this way, Luria connects the Jews' outer experience of exile to an inner alienation since "the inner exile, too, owes its existence to the fall."⁶⁰ Thus *gilgul* describes the process of the soul's metamorphosis, transformation, or "perfection" through its transmigration or *metempsychosis*. It is a process that begins with Adam. Lawrence Fine adds that Luria traces "his own soul and that of his disciples as participating in long chains of transmigrations, reaching back to … the very beginnings of humanity" in Eden.⁶¹ In this way, Luria posits that "Adam's soul originally contained within it all of the future souls of humankind."⁶² As a result, prior to the Fall, all souls are implicit within "Adam's soul." With the fall, in order for the soul to be refined and restored to what it once was, it must travel between bodies; that is, the soul leaves the body in death and transmigrates into another body. With each subsequent reincarnation, the soul is refined until it is "perfected."⁶³

There are though serious implications from Luria's doctrine, as Scholem points out, for if "Adam contained the entire soul of humanity, which is now diffused among the whole genus in innumerable codifications and individual appearances, all transmigrations of souls are in the last resort only migrations of the one soul whose exile atones for its fall."⁶⁴ With Adam as the site for all souls, all human generations reflect the diffusion of the "one soul." As a result, *gilgul* acts "as a law of the universe."⁶⁵ If each person "provides, by his behavior, countless occasions for ever renewed exile," then, this law is in practice infinitely unfulfillable, but it is commanded nonetheless to be the path to redemption. Therefore, "the man from the country" presents himself continuously before the gatekeeper, only to discover that "it is his bad luck" to not merit admission.⁶⁶ He has not been "perfected" although "it is possible."⁶⁷

Grözinger adds that Luria also associates *gilgul* with the mystical exegetical method of PaRDeS so that the way the kabbalist reads also performs aspects of the necessary exile and transformation.

> Know that the person who does not study the Torah does damage to the sefira tiferet [which is at the same time the level of the Written Torah and of the Tree of Life], and to be sure in all four levels, for via the sefira tiferet the Torah is present in all levels of the world. And there are four levels in it, namely PaRDeS [Peshat (literal meaning), Remez (allegorical meaning), Derash (moral meaning), Sod (mystical meaning.)] And the one who succeeds in penetrating profundities of all four meanings has achieved the end of all stages, and about him is written [in the Bible]: "No ear has ever heard, no eye has ever seen any God besides You, Who works for the one who puts his trust in Him."⁶⁸

The reference to the *am-haretz*, "the person who does not study the Torah," in the first sentence, is linked directly to damage of the *sferot* overall, also understood as the "Tree of Life." Specifically, the *sfera tiferet* is a particular point of damage because it is the locus of the "Written Torah," signified by Moses, and the rest of the *sferot*. Luria extends it further, identifying it as a suture point between "the Written Torah" and a mystical exegesis, designated by the acronym, PaRDeS. Through this point of contact, the believer experiences ontological refinement through reading; that is, transmigration of the soul is linked purposively to a mystical exegetical process so that each stage of the PaRDeS requires the reader to move more deeply into the text, until the discovery of its *sod* or secret.

Thus the end of the pericope above declares that "in penetrating profundities of all four meanings," the believer "has achieved the end of all stages" so that his senses and his intention or *kavannah* harmonize because the Torah has become constitutive finally of the believer's entire human existence. The individual can read—innovate—the Torah "in penetrating profundities" and is perfected by the action, transforming "the end of all stages" into the kabbalah, the *sod* finally emerging in the text as its missing piece.[69] The kabbalistic reader has essentially "cleaved" to the text, until it has opened up its "secret." By using the PaRDeS method, the kabbalist reads Torah and changes the phenomenological structure of his subjectivity so that he performs the commanded physical experiences of exile and perfection without ever leaving the kabbalistic experience.

The whole goal of study is the articulation of four stages of reading sacred text and this is something in which the "man from the country" does not participate: he does not bind himself to the Torah. To put it another way, he does not make himself available to the "receiving and transmitting" of the tradition. In other words, as the "man from the country" stands before the gatekeeper and is denied access to the law, he exists as an obvious and profound negation of everything the Law is.

While all of these layers of linguistic analysis give readers a philological genealogy of the Hebrew and Yiddish terms in various Judaic and Jewish registers available to Kafka, they still omit one striking context about the identity of the "man from the country." First and foremost, as a Jew from Prague, Kafka inherits a wealth of orthodox and *heretical* kabbalistic material.[70] From this material, he would know of Frank's "revelation of the *prostak*" or "revelation of the man from the country."[71] In Polish, as in Czech, the terms are synonymous with *amhoretz*.[72] In the Frankist hagiography or "parable," discussed in Chapter 1, Frank proclaims the "revelation of *prostak*" because he has rejected "waiting" for an external force to help him reach the other side of "the river Totorozh." If Jews abandon "waiting" and instead follow his example, they will enter their "promised land."

Frank describes leaving behind a multitude of people, "afraid to go further" because of the river's rising waters, but he leads "his horse across the water." They scream at him for taking the risk; he crosses the river nonetheless and when the river finally recedes, the people who "waited" cross the river, arriving almost two weeks later to the town of Roman where Frank has been all that time. Frank ends the story with "and my *prostakness* did this."[73] *Prostak* is elevated by Frank to be constitutive.

Using *prostak* interchangeably with *amhoretz*, he inverts the idea of the "simpleton," so that *prostak* becomes the sign of the heretical kabbalah's promise of redemption. If all Jews adopt the "revelation of the *prostak*," then they will materialize Frank's "kingdom" on earth. This heretical innovation underpins why Kafka's "man from the country," the *amhoretz/prostak*, believes he is entitled to the Law. He espouses it when after the gatekeeper's rejection he thinks that the Law should "surely be accessible at all times and to everyone."[74]

The last piece of *am ha'aretz/amhoretz* linguistic puzzle concerns the Hasidic innovation of the term. In Martin Buber's *Tales of the Hasidim*, in his introduction to the text, Chaim Potok relates a story about the Baal Shem Tov in which the Baal is asked how "a shoemaker, a wagon driver"—is expected to study, "when one must work day and night."[75] The question implies that one could be forced into the *amhoretz* role because of oppression. The Baal answers that the individual who is forced into such labor can have the burden alleviated by the "splendor" of the Law.[76] Shaul Magid describes it as a "soft antinomianism," popular in some forms of Hasidism, in which study of the Law is displaced temporarily by "fervor and exaltation," the ecstasy of its splendor.[77] The Baal's innovation elevates ecstasy as a substitute for study and this transforms the *amhoretz* from someone who is ignorant and doesn't know to want the study of the Law, to someone who is ignorant, but experiences the Law's "light" anyway. Magid clarifies that in this version of antinomianism "the law is undermined, yet protected .... supplanted, yet not erased."[78]

The paradox produces "twin mediations, halakha for the unenlightened and devekut for the enlightened," in which the "unenlightened" study the law, but "the enlightened" adhere to it in order to prepare "the world for the final fulfilment of the law as an overcoming of the law (this is the Hasidic innovation, part of which it shares with Sabbateanism)."[79] The shock of Magid's statement is that they "by and large" fulfill the law, but they adhere to, "cleave" to its spirit rather than study the *halakhah*.

In this way, the *amhoretz* figure signified by "a man from the country" is a "simpleton," a "heretic," and someone bound to the Law's light, but ignorant nonetheless of what that revelation means. Furthermore, he might be compelled by external circumstances to labor in the "country," to be persecuted by penury, rather than have the privilege of study. He feels entitled to enter into the Law and the nature of his entitlement is grounded in the "shared sense" of his "commonness" with other Jews who are oppressed. The allusion to Frank's promise rests in the premiss that the Law's fulfillment has occurred for everyone and the sign of that fulfillment is the poor shoemaker's liberation from its study. It is a posited *sensus communis*, whose sign is emancipation.

Moreover, when "heretic" and "simpleton" are combined with the Hasidic innovation, "the man from the country" feels entitled to exalt in the splendor of the Law even though he is ignorant of its significance. The force of "*devekut*" in Magid's explanation and in the Baal's response underscores the displacement of "legalism" in favor of "fervor." While readers can't isolate any one of these significations and declare it to be definitive for Kafka's character, readers are still encouraged by *The Trial's* Leni, who instructs Josef K., to avoid the "stereotypical obedience" that constrains meaning to be inflexible and literal.[80]

Therefore, Grözinger's thesis about Kafka's "man from the country" with its connection to Luria's *gilgul* and PaRDeS implies that the man who cannot read the Law glimpses still something of its splendor. In the Hasidic innovation, the common man's repeated coming before the law should enable him to enter into it, but Kafka forecloses its possibility for the Hasid too. The "man of the country" remains ignorant, *amhoretz*. Essentially, he is aware of something desirable of the Law, something withheld from him, but he doesn't really know what that desirable element is. It is indeterminate for him. It avows a purposiveness, the existence of which he intuits by negation. Not only does the "man from the country" inhabit all of these registers simultaneously, but he also recognizes what he lacks in each of them through its absence. Their absence or negation exhibits for him an outline, a shadow, of what he does not have. He is forced to trace its absence, its negation of earthly content until he dies.

In that lingering absence, Kafka implies then the modern trauma of Jewish experience in which Jews bear within their memories a residue of what they lack, and the knowledge that they can never cross that boundary between one dimension and another; they can never go back to what they once were. Scholem calls the awareness of this trace, "the perfection that destroys," or even the "strong light of the canonical—the perfection that breaks" in order to underscore the stakes of Kafka's *aggadah* for the modern Jewish subject.[81] Forced to remember the trace of a revelation that the subject does not know, the image of its negation shatters. In the experience of "breaks," of fragmentation, the modern Jewish subject experiences a fleeting glimpse, "the strong light" of "perfection" as it shatters into an infinity of shards, the image of which is impossible to restore.

This "simpleton," who could be Polish or Jewish—hence the reference to Yiddish—asks for "admittance to the Law" and the gatekeeper's initial response suggests that "at the moment," he cannot admit him, pushing the man to question whether or not, he can expect admission "later." Again, the gatekeeper responds cryptically; "it is possible, but not at the moment."[82] In the brief exchange between the *amhoretz* and the gatekeeper, the reader learns of the theoretical possibility of the individual's admission, but not at this particular moment. Kafka freights particularity so that it signifies a singular moment specific to the "man of the country."

To understand the kabbalistic significance of this "particular" moment Grözinger applies Scholem's perspective on "revelation and tradition" in kabbalah in which the Torah is a personally experienced phenomenon that requires the individual to constitute it as a mental object.

> Scholem says: A widely accepted belief of the later kabbalah states that the Torah reveals to each individual Jew a particular aspect meant for him and understood by him alone. Thus, each Jew actually realizes his own destiny only by perceiving the aspect meant specifically for him and integrating it into tradition.[83]

The excerpt identifies that the kabbalistic revelation of the Torah is personal, and specific to the individual. Only that individual is capable of innovating the Torah to derive that meaning. It becomes the individual's responsibility to apply that particular meaning "for him" and to integrate it "into the tradition." Essentially, the kabbalist constructs a Torah through the lens of these personally innovated meanings.[84] In fact, Grözinger underscores for readers that the obligation encompasses "the mortal life of an individual," that life "is nothing more than a constant penetration into this individual interpretation of the Torah," and it is a mode of making "a lifelong concrete entering into and returning from the heavenly halls of Torah."[85] Essentially, it materializes—"a lifelong concrete entering into"—the journey to and from "the heavenly halls of Torah." It is the revelation of a path between the heavenly Torah, *Atzilut,* and the earth. When added to the respective perspectives of Luria and Scholem, it suggests the materialization of mystical modes of reading and writing that enable the individual to innovate the text, following writing from this world into the world of the Torah, that is, Law.

"Possibility" encourages the "man from the country" to defer admission, to wait for when he merits access or to put it another way, to wait until he is entitled to enter the Law. A "possible" entrance in the future is enough to defer redemption in the present. As he contemplates the gatekeeper's prohibition, he sees his chance to gain a glimpse of the Law's secret: he "stoops" in order to see "through the gateway into the interior."[86] The gate does not offer its secrets at his eye level: the "man from the country" cannot see its contents. He has to contort himself, conform to its entrance in order to see inside the sacred space. Even though he has attempted this conformity, he can see nothing through the gate. It is absence for him. His gesture elicits the gatekeeper's laughter and warning of the obstacles inside the Law should "the man from the country" attempt to enter anyway. He describes for the supplicant not only what these obstacles are, but also what they protect. In the gatekeeper's description, Kafka's second kabbalistic signal, the gatekeeper is an obstacle to the *amhoretz's* redemption.

As the man ponders his options, "the Law, he thinks, should surely be accessible at all times and to everyone," but as he examines the gatekeeper with a "big, sharp nose and long, think black Tartar beard," the stereotypical severity of the figure causes the protagonist to decide to "wait until he gets permission to enter."[87] Although he thinks that this withheld place, essentially the space of the PaRDeS, should be available to "everyone," the gatekeeper's obligation prevents him specifically.[88]

Grözinger describes that Kafka's parable is similar to the genre of Hasidic tales about gatekeepers in which all paths of human existence have one end in that "Man's journey is a path to the Torah."[89] By using the structure of the Hasidic gatekeeper tale to frame the parable, Kafka suggests that even if every path an individual can take is "a path to the Torah," he will not enter. This is the force of *gigul* for the *amhoretz*. Grözinger puts it simply, the *amhoretz* and the gatekeeper "taken together ... both represent the path prescribed for man."[90] In other words, there is a kinship between the *amhoretz* and the gatekeeper.

In *The Trial,* when the priest pronounces the gatekeeper is "simple-minded," he posits that both figures are entangled in the same position, a subtlety, but a necessary one because neither position enters the law: one lacks the capacity, but has the desire, and the other has the capacity, but lacks the desire. Schonfeld notes that the gatekeeper never sees the Law. In fact, he is aware of it, but does not register its "splendor." He does not engage with it beyond enforcing its lack of access. He remains turned away from it, appearing to be charged with simply preventing entrance to "the man from the country."[91] It appears that his whole function is to deny access to this innovated figure of the modern Jewish subject. The system of which he is a part does not accommodate the one to whom it has promised a future redemption, if he will only wait. Moreover, the Law appears to be separated from the protagonist by an abyss that even the gatekeeper dares not cross.

Thus the man "sits and waits for days and years"; eventually the gatekeeper chats with him "about his home and many other things," but every conversation ends with the man from the country's persistent request and its denial, *jetzt aber nicht*, "but not now."[92] The protagonist attempts to bribe the gatekeeper, who takes "everything," declares that he accepts the unsuccessful bribes so that the man can feel confident he has done "everything" possible to gain admission.[93] Finally, as the protagonist nears death, and "his eyesight begins to fail … in his darkness he is now aware of a radiance that streams inextinguishably from the gateway of the law."[94] Just as the world is plunging into darkness around him, when his senses fail, he becomes aware of a light, "a radiance that streams inextinguishably" out of the darkness. The emanation comes "from the law" and has only been intuitable when the illusion of the world around him is exhibited before him on the verge of his collapse.

"Before the Law" ends with the dying man witnessing the "stream" of Eternal Light, emanating from the Law, and in that moment, at the "razor's edge" of creation, and death, "all his experiences in long years" of waiting at the gate, "gather themselves in his head to one point, a question he has not yet asked."[95] Waving the gatekeeper close, he asks, " 'Everyone strives to reach the Law … so how does it happen that for all these many years no one but myself has ever begged for admittance?'" The gatekeeper responds, "No one else could ever be admitted here, since the gate was made only for you. I am now going to shut it."[96] He glimpses a trace of the Law's splendor, its emanations lighting a path in the distance and dies with the knowledge that it is withheld perpetually from him.

Thinking about the different kabbalistic registers outlined above for "the man from the country," readers derive multiple theses about why he never enters the Law. The simplest one argues that since the man doesn't know the Law, doesn't study the Law, then, he is not entitled to enter it at any time, alive or dead.[97] Another possibility hearkens again to the individual's inherent ignorance of the Law, making him akin to Ezra's biblical enemies who attempt to prevent the Jews' building the Temple, fulfilling the Law, or of integrating the commandment into the tradition. He is identified with the Law's enemies.

However, if Kafka writes with an "orthodox kabbalah" in mind, then, the *amhoretz/ am ha'retz* can be read through two different kabbalistic lens, neither of which is particularly optimistic about the individual's future. The PaRDeS approach walks readers through Kafka's short story, discounting each stage of traditional exegesis.[98] The *amhoretz* looks at the gateway to the Law, and it seems simple enough to enter it, to read it. It's literally just a gate; the only obstacle is a gatekeeper and perhaps he can overcome that agent of the Law. After exhausting the literal method, he attempts to "peer into" it, to read it a little more deeply. To accomplish this method, he contorts physically in order to see into the Law, but he sees nothing. Although he ponders that the Law "should" be readable by everyone, his literal and his rational readings fail him.

He sits at the gate "for days and years," attempting to use every "possible" strategy. He continues to reason with the gatekeeper, resigned to its failure. He offers him bribes, all of which the gatekeeper takes, but the gate remains closed to him. Kafka offers then a subtle shift in the narrative, the "man from the country" no longer looks at the gate, but at the gatekeeper—"he fixes his attention almost continuously on the gatekeeper."[99] Reflecting Kafka's earlier diary entries, "the man from the country" only stares at creation and human existence.

His pleas for admission revolve around the knowledge the gatekeeper and he share in common. His attention on how the gatekeeper is just like him and has been able to enter, to cross over into the Law's secret, now preoccupies him. He "grumbles to himself" aware that "where the Kabbalists claimed to be able to penetrate these secrets," the commoner or "secular Jew" is trapped, "impotently paralyzed outside the first gate of the Law."[100] In a final attempt, he begs "the fleas" on the gatekeeper's collar, the lowest denominator of Nature, to make a case to the gatekeeper for letting him enter. He has sat before the gatekeeper, trying to read himself into the Law, for years. In this moment, the *amhoretz/am ha'aretz* has become someone who follows the Law, obeys it, even studies it, but still the secret is withheld from him. Magid identifies this as the unenlightened/enlightened paradox of Hasidism in which the "unenlightened" studies the Law, but cannot read its mysteries.

When "the man from the country" loses his sight—his capacity to read—the last thing he "sees" before succumbing to death is the infinite Light streaming from the gate. With the suppression of his senses in death, he becomes aware of the Torah's emanations, how they fill the entrance to the Law. Moreover, it comes from the same place where he had seen only nothingness while he lived. He has spent his entire life, focused on the entrance to the Law, the gatekeeper preventing his access, and the best outcome of all of his efforts is that at death, he catches a glimpse of the Light of the other side to which he is still denied. If Kafka models the parable on an Hasidic template, then, the "man from the country" encompasses Jews who are both observant and non-observant, indicating that both groups are incapable of reading the "secret." They lack something important that they have jettisoned and it is not obedience to the Law, but something else entirely.

If Kafka's story is read as a Frankist *aggadah*, the broken promises of Frankism/Sabbateanism become legible: the man has made his own redemption and he stands before the Law, determined to cross over its boundary into paradise. He is entitled to it but this entitlement fails him. Its failure enables him to see at death, the emanations of the Law, the streaming "inextinguishable" Light proceeding from the darkness out from the doorway to the Torah. He intuits it only to discover though that while there is "inextinguishable" Light from the Torah, *it is not for him*. With this model, "the man from the country" compels himself to read the darkness through the spaces the gatekeeper fails to obscure, to block. Every day that the man sits before the gateway, he is forced to trace the absence that occupies the space where the Law purportedly remains. He sees only darkness, but the story implies that the Light has been there all along: his senses, his entitlement, his expectations, have prevented him from seeing it.

Here the possibility of *Ezra's* biblical precedent, read through the lens of "the heretical kabbalah," suggests that Kafka's "man from the country" has imagined he has a part in rebuilding the Temple with its ark of the holies of holies, but he has remained ignorant nonetheless of what it means. The Temple remains darkened to him, a signifier of the absence of God rather than His presence.[101] The gatekeeper, like the Temple's high priest, repeats that he cannot enter: he does not merit its redemption even though he has been promised. This version too ends with Kafka's adage ringing in the ears of the reader, "there is infinite hope, but not for us."[102]

What of *gilgul* and the other orthodox kabbalistic reading Grözinger applies to the narrative? In that version, for whatever reason, the man from the country is denied access to the Law and its Light. He stands before the "halls of the Law" as an example of "an unsuccessful life in the Jewish sense." Thus he is compelled in his death to start the process over again. He is on an endless exile, aware of an intuited paradise of Torah, but to which he never actually enters. Like Moses, another biblical precedent, he sits on the other side of the Jordan and peers out to see a promised land that he is unqualified to enter. Scholem underscores that each person's failures trigger the need for more exile.[103] In fact, if "renewed exile" is Kafka's revelation about the modern Jewish subject, then, the subject is compelled to stand before the Law repeatedly, forbidden to enter.

After he listens to the parable, the question becomes for Josef K. in *The Trial*, why does "the man from the country" never merit admission to the Law? The story suggests that the Law as a system only works in its prohibitions.[104] It is a machine that forbids humans from crossing its epistemological boundaries.[105] The kabbalist answers with a resounding voice that since the "man from the country" does not "write" or innovate his own Torah, he can never enter it. Essentially, "the man from the country" remains condemned by the Torah because he has failed to integrate his own innovated text into tradition. The Law remains just out of reach, inflexible in its condemnation. It exists to pass judgment, and there is no new revelation of a supplemental writing that can change its judgment.

In *The Trial*'s extension of the story, flush with the experience of emancipation, the "man of the country," as the priest describes him, "can go where he likes. It is only the Law that is denied to him."[106] To enter history, the modern secular Jew gives up the Law or that which is constitutive of Jewish existence. Here Kafka plays intentionally with the idea of the emancipated Jew, the liberated peasant, any number of new identities that come into being because of political reform. The contrast becomes particularly weighted to emphasize that the "country man" has become liberated while the *halakhic* doorkeeper has remained tethered to his post.

They are interchangeable in this aspect. The priest underscores that the doorkeeper is obsessed with his "duties." These duties prohibit him from seeing both inside the world of the Law, and recognizing the need for the protagonist's entrance. One could assume that Kafka critiques the rabbinic perspective that the Law is under their authority; thus the parable encourages the democratization of the Law, its "accessibility" for everyone. Certainly, the novel's expansion of the parable around the axis of duty suggests this reading. One could also imagine that Kafka undermines the Law's validity: this implication echoes Löwy's account reproduced in Kafka's diary.

However, in all of these examples, the tension between desiring to fulfill the Law, but being incapable of it, desiring Nothingness, but finding instead nothingness, is central to understanding why Kafka thinks about Kabbalah, yet ends up its failed prophet simply because within "infinite" messianism, there remains no messiah. In fact, Kafka skates between these two poles, announcing the revelation, only to fail repeatedly to achieve it. In some ways, he articulates a messianic position that necessarily sees every attempt as a failure; with every step toward the individual's entrance into the Law, he recognizes he will never be redeemed. The individual's liberation is always just out of reach. Moreover, for Kafka, his writing repeats its impossibility: in its repetition, it can only tell the story of his written failure. This is the "secret" of "Before the Law": it repeats the modern Aher's failure.

The Assault of PaRDeS

January 16, 1922, is a fraught day for Kafka because he believes he has suffered a "breakdown." The "breakdown" prompts him to conjecture in his diary that there are "two interpretations" on how to read his distress.

> First: breakdown, impossible to sleep, impossible to stay awake, impossible to endure life, or more exactly, the course of life. The clocks are not in unison; the inner one runs crazily on at a devilish or demoniac or in any case inhuman pace, the outer one limps along at its usual speed …. the two worlds split apart …. Second: This pursuit, originating in the midst of men, carries one in a direction away from them. The solitude that for the most part has been forced on me, in part voluntarily sought by me—but what was this if not compulsion too—is now losing all ambiguity and approaches its denouement …. it may lead to madness … the pursuit goes right through me and rends me asunder. Or I can—can I—…. be carried along in the wild pursuit …. I can also say, "assault on the last earthly frontier," an assault, moreover, launched from below, from mankind, and since this too is a metaphor, I can replace it by the metaphor of an assault from above, aimed at me from above.
>
> All such writing is an assault on the frontiers; if Zionism has not intervened, it might easily have developed into a new secret doctrine, a Kabbalah.[107]

In his first "interpretation," Kafka likens his "breakdown" to the "clocks" of inner and outer life; they are "two worlds split apart." The subjective "clock" runs at a wildly "inhuman pace," so much so that it seems to him to be "demoniac." Meanwhile the objective "clock" that measures the outer world "limps along at its usual speed." Together, their convergence in Kafka forces them to "split apart" repeatedly. Scholem describes them as two kinds of exile, "inner" and "outer," that converge in Kafka. Hence he is the "product" of the "heretical kabbalah."[108]

This rupture prompts Kafka to his second interpretation; he must, is obligated to, embark on a "pursuit" of the inner world that now speeds "at an inhuman pace" away from the "outer" world of human existence. He must reunite these two "clocks" through his writing. The differences in speed suggest that no matter how fast he imagines pursuing his "inner" truth, matter, the outer world, slows him down so that Kafka becomes continuously aware that the answer is always on the horizon and always unrealizable. The substance of human existence is in direct conflict with an "inner world," an "inhuman" drive that moves through him.

Kafka imagines himself at the site of an abyss in which his "pursuit" of the "inner clock" pushes him to abandon the human world; it "carries him away" from human existence. He feels compelled to "pursue" the ideas that spin out of control in his thinking so that he tries to follow them into an unconscious abyss, the inhuman world. He is "compelled" to follow his "inner clock" even if it drives him deeper into the abyss.

The "pursuit" is both "forced" on him and chosen by him. It is a compulsion that leads him, but its aim remains unconscious to him. Since "the pursuit … rends" him in two, Kafka recognizes a cosmic fault line that runs between "inhuman" and human. Picking up "the two worlds split apart" in the first "interpretation," Kafka identifies that while his mind retains the memory of being cut off from the "inhuman," his body prevents him from reuniting his broken pieces. Paradoxically, even though the "pursuit" originates with human existence, to follow it requires its acolyte either to abandon human existence or to surrender to "madness."

Kafka shifts then to declaring his "pursuit" to be an "assault launched from below." The act of pursuing his inner compulsion demands that he scale the heavens, that he mounts an "assault on the last earthly frontier" because in that assault, in a final nihilistic act, he transcends human existence. It suggests that imprinted in the human is a drive to reach the separated world of the inhuman, to regain what has been taken away.

However, in his depiction of the assault, he is forced to use "metaphor" because he cannot resolve the gap between the "infinitude" above and the profane below. He exhibits (*darstellen*) his assault on the "frontiers," but the exhibition (*Darstellung*) only reiterates his failure. His metaphorical "work of art" still expresses its own immanence, taunting him with the trace memory of a world he can never enter. Kafka intuits this aspect of immanence as "aimed at me from above." "From above" gives just enough of a hint of "infinitude," enabling the individual to become aware of its trace, but without the means of grasping it.

In this way, Kafka comes to writing. In writing, Kafka pursues transcendence, only to recognize that the profane text never reveals a "secret." Textuality buries the traces of "infinitude" in words so that even if aware of its existence, he cannot render its message from among its pages. Only able to retrieve discrete fragments, Kafka writes his own *aggadah*, parable, of the unresolvable conflict that offers him three untenable options: he might die, go insane, or abandon his writing, an act of apostasy.

Kafka has found himself within the PaRDeS. With "Before the Law," he recognizes that the heretical kabbalah's promise to redeem all modern Ahers never materializes. Thus he writes an *aggadah* of failure. From within his "breakdown," he wonders if writing's revelation could allow him, like Akiva, to enter and exit the "halls of Torah" at will, to "keep his feet" and "be carried along in the wild pursuit?"[109] In other words, Kafka's 1911 diary entry and his short story, "Before the Law," have led up to this moment when Kafka imagines writing a new *aggadah*, a new kabbalah for himself in which he isn't Aher, but instead Akiva. Moreover, the new story exhibits writing's "assault on all frontiers"; in its materialization of the "unison" of inner and outer "clocks," writing would finally erase the boundary between sacred and profane ontologies. There would be no written, only unending writing.

For Kafka, after Frank, the heretical kabbalah's messianic age could produce only prophets of failure. There would be no more messiahs in modernity, only failed prophets who would bellow the *hineni,* the "Here am I" to infinity, write the Name of God in a profane vernacular, always hoping to hear, read, the sacred again. However, only a distant light could ever be glimpsed. Under the sign of this failure, the prophet realizes that true messianism must forego the written for writing. Only through writing can human existence ever be able to read the revelation again.

5

Being and Nothingness: The Matter of Golems

In Bruno Schulz's short story collection, *Cinnamon Shops,* the narrator's "Father," Jacob, shares an ambiguous textual kinship, with the historical figure of Jacob Frank, and Schulz's own biological father.[1] The stories recount Father's "teachings" on and "experiments" in creation at the family home in Drohobych, Poland. Strikingly, the "teachings'" resonance with Frank's "heretical kabbalah" evolves into aesthetic transgression because Father's heresy begins with works of art. Rather than Judaism and its Torah, Schulz innovates Frankist heresy and aesthetic experience. Thus his "teachings" not only provide alternative blueprints for creation, but also point to alternative revelation, a "Second Book of Genesis," describing another path to redemption.[2]

To that end, the son describes Father's teachings as "regions of great heresy"; his father is "our heresiarch."[3] The teachings not only motivate "all his actions," but also recognize in the patriarch himself a Frankist or at least, a sympathetic gnostic disposition.[4] Although Schulz does not characterize any of the characters in his writings as even ostensibly belonging to any Judaic, Jewish, kabbalistic, or Frankist sects, *Cinnamon Shops* suggests nevertheless that Frankism is a foundational part of Jewish secular life, as well as a metaphysics of heresy that pervades the profane, non-Jewish world too.[5] His stories contain fragments, remnants of occluded kabbalistic narratives. To put it bluntly, with these narratives, Schulz indicates that to be secular and Jewish in Poland in the twentieth century is to be a "product" of the "heretical kabbalah."[6]

However, being a "product of the heretical kabbalah" is not the same as endorsing Jacob Frank's proclamation of apostasy. In fact, in Schulz, heresy and apostasy are not equivalent. With Frank, apostasy is necessary because the world to which humans have been condemned is literally "the other side," or *sitra ara*. Thus humans experience its transgressiveness, accepting that we are not only cut off from a world we can never know, but also that we are encouraged to settle in and become part of this world on "the other side." We are obligated to accept that we travel through illegitimacy to reach paradise's backdoor. The model is gnostic usurpation, blended with Frankist aspirations. The hero or *prostak* of the narrative, the term Frank uses to describe himself, overcomes a Demiurge oppressor, and by his own power, defines the terms for his redemption.

In this way, Frank inverts, "innovates" Luria's doctrine of exile in which exile remains a powerful tool of refining the soul, of remaining attached to the Torah and hence living in alienation from the "other side." Although condemned to live in proximity to evil, we are commanded to walk through transgression without absorbing it. In Luria, the allusion resonates with the Rhineland Hasids several centuries earlier, whose doctrine of "the devout" advocates "entering" the Law without standing "on" it so that the Torah shields the Hasid from evil.[7]

Father's "heresy" is a last redemptive act before his capitulation to the apostasy of the "stupid, witless tribe" of Drohobych.[8] Thus Father's "heresy" contrasts with Frankism's apostasy, the unarticulated foundation both to Drohobych's idolatry, their "golem" state, and to Tokarczuk's last chapter of *The Books of Jacob*, "The Book of Names," in which there are no secret names of God, only inconsequential lists of names, and occupations. The Frankist sect recedes into history. Its hopes and aspirations become synonymous with wealth and "thoughtlessness."[9] In this way, Father represents a heretical project of innovation that searches to restore something missing from Frankism.

Jacob's teachings unfold as a consequence of the family's maid, Adela, arriving "unexpectedly in Father's avian kingdom," a sanctuary of birds Jacob has created among the ceiling rafters and throughout the upper stories of the house.[10] Through "great expenditure and labor," he has imported exotic bird eggs, from around the world, as well as all manner of fowl to incubate his purchases.[11] When the birds hatch, the upper chambers of the house are "filled with the colorful murmuring, the flickering chirping of its new inhabitants."[12] The exotic newcomers intensify Father's desire to bring to light more new beings, a desire nurtured through meditation on "his great ornithological compendia."[13] He studies the book's "colorful plates," until "feathered phantasms .... fly out from them and fill the room with colorful fluttering, with petals of crimson, scraps of sapphire, verdigris, and silver."[14] Father innovates the "compendia," drawing from it these temporal entities, golems of text, that live as long as the duration of his reading.[15]

This idea is not original to Schulz, but is part of the kabbalah. Scholem notes it emerges among the Rhineland Hasids in Eleazar of Worms' work, so that the "concept of the devout" or *Hasiduth*, is juxtaposed to "the development of the legend of the Golem or magical homunculus—this quintessential product of the spirit of German Jewry."[16] For Scholem, the golem and *Hasiduth* are emblematic within German Jewish life; moreover, the golem's appearance testifies to the hasid's devotion.

> Side by side with tracts on magic and the effectiveness of God's secret names ... one finds the oldest extant recipes for creating the Golem—a mixture of letter magic and practices obviously aimed at producing ecstatic states of consciousness .... in the original conception the Golem came to life only while the ecstasy of his creator lasted.[17]

Scholem's reference to *Hasiduth* and the golem is noteworthy because with *Hasiduth*, the Hasids' "original" or "novel conception of the devout" conforms to "a religious ideal which transcends all values derived from the intellectual sphere."[18] *Hasiduth* negates the known and it posits a turn away from Judaism's epistemology—the Law understood as a system—in order to embrace the Law's transcendence of human existence.[19]

Thus the Hasid "transcends" the Law's "intellectual sphere," its outer shell. Trancendence enables the "devout" individual to enter a sphere of the inner Law in order to exceed epistemological obligation. Scholem explains that "the essence of *Hasiduth* is to act in all things not just on but within ... the letter of the Torah; for it is said of God ... The Lord is *hasid* in all his ways."[20] If *Hasiduth* joins the devout to the "letter of the Torah," Torah becomes constitutive for the Hasid in the same way it is constitutive to "the Lord."[21] The premise implies a different relationship to Torah than simple observance of the Law. It indicates the possibility of the Law's external violation while the Hasid remains with the Law, hinting at how a heretical innovative reading—part of the heretical kabbalah—could emerge in Schulz.

Although Scholem emphasizes *Hasiduth* as a mode of sanctifying the self as God is sanctified, it places nonetheless a forfeiture of entitlement next to a sublime experience in which the Hasid must step "into" the Law rather than stand "on" it; by entering the Law in this way, the Hasid engages in a mode of contemplation whose inadvertent effect produces a temporal entity, a golem.[22] The golem is generated by the Hasid's entrance into the Law, a sign confirming the Hasid's entrance into the Law rather than simply conforming to its knowledge.[23] The Hasid experiences what is not reducible to a mimetic performance of *halakhah*.

In this sanctified aesthetic experience, transcendence occurs because the Hasid repeats permutations of God's secret names in the Torah. When released from the Torah, they are free to create. Therefore, the Hasids' "writings" preserve "the oldest extant recipes." The "recipes" produce the "golem" through "a mixture of letter magic and practices" designed to elicit ecstasy. Ecstasy or transcendence is the reward, and the golem is its sign. The golem is the hasid's work of art because he experiences sublimity or enters into the Law. In other words, the Rhineland Hasids' project of permutation offers an aesthetic experience that triggers ecstasy in the Hasid and the work of art or golem is its secondary effect.

The *Zohar* attaches this experience to the innovation of Torah so that the kabbalist liberates the letters from their outer lexical shells in Torah and engages the "secret names of God" through reading, writing, and chanting.[24] In the kabbalist's ecstasy, the letters are free to write creation. In this way, the kabbalist experiences aesthetic affect across multiple registers of sacred text. The practices enable sublimity to cross over to an "other side" of materialization. Scholem underscores that the sign of the golem attests to the kabbalist's move into the Divine flow of being: the kabbalist produces a work of art, creation for the duration of the mystical experience.[25]

The migration of the procedure to a profane text—Father's contemplation of its profane object—implies that the "secret names of God" are available within the "compendia."[26] The "phantasms" released by Jacob testify to his transcendence because of the way he reads the "compendia." Jacob innovates the written, producing creatures that "seduce" him to move beyond "hatching ever new specimens," offering instead the means to create wholly new "structures of beings." In his awakening of these "golems," he does not distinguish between substance and matter, between genus and species. Matter holds within itself infinite possibilities; these potential beings are not constrained by what is already known. Father imagines them outside of any taxonomy, epistemology, system.[27] Hence they are "outside the law."[28]

Father engages, then, in cross-breeding different species in the attic. Some creations don't fly anymore. They have been "lured out of nothingness … blind," misshapen and demanding food so that Father creates "true freaks in shape and coloring …. monsters with enormous, fantastic beaks that ripped themselves wide-open immediately after birth, hissing greedily in the abysses of their throats."[29] These creatures articulate for him, patterns of being, formerly trapped within matter, liberated now by him. Abandoning the compendia, Father innovates natural phenomena and liberated from the compendia, they are no longer golems.

The narrator perceives Father's project of creation as a "deeply sinful and unnatural turn"; it tears through the monotony of everyday life—the illusion—of Drohobych.[30] Jacob turns the "attic's gaps and cavities," the roof itself, into "a Noah's ark to which all sorts of winged creatures flocked from far-off places" so that the whole top of the house, "the enormous gabled and shingled roof" is ceded to the Father's "avian kingdom."[31] His transgression restores color to the house's mundane, profane world. Although the son deems his father's actions both necessary and "sinful," these profane and misshapen creations represent the only way to liberate Drohobych from the emptiness that has become constitutive of the town's existence. The son implies that the town's redemption is contingent on Father's creative power acting on profane phenomena, his messianic materialism.

Due to his "transgressions," Jacob changes physically. Watching him sleep, the son imagines Father shrinks into a "mummified" state.[32] As Father's body declines, the family shunts both creatures and Jacob to "two garret rooms … junk rooms," far removed from the business of the family below.[33] These rooms, now filled with unfamiliar colors, noises, smells, shut Jacob and his kingdom off from the rest of the family, until finally they "lose sight of Father for several weeks."[34] Both worlds live in ignorance of each other. On the rare occasions when Jacob descends the stairs into the world of the household, the family sees the diminished patriarch, mimicking his creations. He speaks their secret unintelligible language. Jacob recedes into an inhuman world where he metamorphoses from one form to another.

Thus, from the illusion of the household below, Adela's ascent to the "avian kingdom" above performs an assault on the cacophony, excrement, detritus of Father's unknown world, his chaos. She attacks him from below. Her venture into the "unnatural" world, with its "stench," compels her to clean the rooms, to restore them to order—to what is known. In the process, she opens a window, forcing any birds who can fly outside the house. She carries out a "dance of destruction" with her broom and annihilates the final remnant of Father's "creations."[35] Standing "alone … on the battlefield," Adela drives Jacob down "the steps from his dominion—a broken man, a banished king," a ruler who has "lost his throne and his kingdom."[36] In this way, Adela mimics a tension between *halakhah* and heretical kabbalah in which she acts, to put it in Scholem's language, as the *halakhic* defender of the "well-ordered house" of Judaism, fighting against Jacob's "anarchic breeze" of heresy.[37]

All of his dreams of a transcendent creation undone, Jacob returns to his family and "the boundless element of boredom stupefying" the town, a "lethargic," and "empty" world.³⁸ The emptiness of the world around him underscores that something fundamental, something constitutive, has been destroyed, and in its place exists an infinite "emptiness."³⁹ The household and the town prefer the emptiness of existence to Jacob's colorful heresies. What has been constitutive for him, the power of creation, has been destroyed by the servants of the household, those in service to monotony, order, and control. Adela, the servant of sanctioned order, bans his heretical kabbalah. "Betrayed by everyone," Father returns from "the locations of his recent glory." Eventually, his family "forgets" him again; he recedes into a liminal space between the "gray twilight" of their consciousnesses and the "colorless" unconscious world motivating his creations.⁴⁰

A kabbalistic pattern emerges. Father performs a vulgar and "tawdry" *tzimtzum* in order to provide a space for his creation. His exile from his hidden "garret rooms" becomes a signifier of the alienation he feels for the world to which he has been condemned. Like his family and town, he is trapped once again in the immanence of matter, incapable of transcendence, and returning to his regions of "glory." Although a memory of the splendor persists, he merges into the "witless tribe" below.⁴¹

In retrospect, his son describes his father's transgressions as a "lonely heroism" in defense of "poetry."⁴² By creating "freaks," breeding across species, Jacob innovates the "colorless" abyss, the immanent darkness, in order to produce singular beings, new entities. Although his creations rarely act according to "classical" forms, for Jacob, the singular principle of their being rips through the mundane world's illusion: it heralds a "poetry" of the abyss, a phenomenal usurpation of "nothingness" and "chaos."⁴³ Moreover, the son associates this "poetry" with the consequences of the "deeply sinful and unnatural turn," Father's inspiration takes. Jacob extracts a singularity from the "truly wretched disintegration and chaos" within him.⁴⁴ Pulled out of this abyss, Father's messy, colorful, vulgar "poetry" redeems existence.⁴⁵ Thus the son associates "poetry" with an animate drive that gives human existence meaning. Humans are predicates for this "poetry," a writing in the universe, unknown to the senses, but persistent, and linked nonetheless to something within Father.⁴⁶

Father's path inverts an older tradition within the kabbalah in which "evil represents an illegitimate road upon the divine realm of light."⁴⁷ Now the illegitimate path of transgression is in the service of "poetry," straining to be liberated and Jacob's art testifies to radical emancipation. By inverting the tradition, Jacob suggests that it has become necessary to take this path if one is to find any redemption at all from the world of "dead matter" surrounding human existence.

As the boundaries between "chaos," abyss, and body collapse, matter is revealed to extend into and from the abyss itself. Essentially, mundane human creation masks the "chaos" within the abyss.⁴⁸ This "void" pervades human existence itself; thus Father's claim that humans exist within a "lower sphere" signals existence shared between the "world of chaos" and the "world of creation."⁴⁹ The implication suggests a sphere in which boundaries between "spirit" and "matter" overlap, where poetry's diverse "spirits" hover over the void. It is a world akin to kabbalah's realm of the *kelipot*.⁵⁰

In kabbalah, the *kelipah*, plural *kelipot*, is subsumed under the theory of "The Breaking of the Vessels." The theory's genealogy extends from the *Zohar* to Isaac Luria, its foremost proponent.[51] In the older projects, the *kelipot* come into being because of the cataclysmic and necessary unfolding "of the Godhead and the *Sefirot*," i.e., in the process of creation.[52] Scholem observes that for Luria's predecessors, "every stage" of that process "is crystalized in a specific world where the creative power of the Creator achieves the perfect expression of one of its many aspects."[53]

Consequently, the *Zohar* introduces a calculus of creation in which four worlds, *atzilut, beri'ah, yezirah, asiyyah*, express the unfolding of Divine Being in creation.[54] These worlds constitute "a series … from above to below," formed around "one basic vector" so that "creation passes from its primeval point to its finalization in the material world."[55] In his outline of the "four basic worlds," Scholem describes the attributes of each one: "the world of emanation—the ten *Sefirot* (*atzilut*) … the world of creation—the Throne and the Chariot (*beri'ah*) … the world of formation (*yezirah*), and … the world of making—which sometimes includes both the whole system of the spheres and the terrestrial world, and sometimes the terrestrial world only" (*asiyyah*).[56] He associates "primeval point" with the world of emanation to demonstrate that the "four worlds" progress toward materialization. Each world appears in early kabbalah as sequential; creation occurs in an order, that is both progressive and regressive, in the sense that each world engages with its counterparts. While the Fall affects all of these worlds, *Asiyah* absorbs the effects particularly. It encompasses both "the domain of the material world and of evil spirits" and "the whole range of creation from the angels … through the ten spheres to the world of matter."[57] Consequently, in at least one interpretation of the doctrine, *Asiyah's* phenomena intersect with *Beri'ah's* created world of objects.[58] Something in phenomena gestures toward "making," discovers itself in materialization.

Even in these pre-Luriannic strains of an "orthodox kabbalah," the boundaries between these worlds are not only shared, but they can be conceivably erased: *Asiyah* occupies the same field, but in different dimensions, or disharmony. Luria draws on these previous projects to advance his own radical innovation of creation.[59]

As Scholem notes, Luria's innovation takes place after the unfolding of Divine Being in the *sferot*, and before the theory of "four worlds," the starting place for creation in older kabbalah. In Luria, the *sferot* are initially "bound together." As Divine Being recedes into itself in order to open up space for creation, the *sferot* unfold, or emanate, proceeding in the linear path or "vector" described above. Their initial unfolding produces primordial *Adam Kadmon*, "the first form that emanation assumes after the *tzimtzum*."[60] In the figure of *Kadmon*, a "realm above the four worlds" not only becomes cognitively imaginable, but also illustrates "how the forces of emanation were organized … in this form" after God's recession into the self or *tzimtzum*.

Kadmon is the site where the ten *sferot* first emerge, appearing as "concentric circles."[61] Upon taking their shape, the *sferot* "rearrange themselves" along the vector familiar to the old kabbalah. Their permutations lead to the emanations writing "the form of a man."[62] Luria's innovation rests on *sferot* performing their own *tzimtzum* to create "the purely spiritual sense of the incorporeal supernal lights."[63] Containing all of the "mysteries beyond human knowledge," within these "incorporeal supernal lights," *Kadmon* "serves as an intermediary link between *Ein-Sof*, the light of whose substance continues to be active in him, and the hierarchy of the worlds still to come," i.e., the four mentioned above.[64] When these "lights" unfold, they concentrate around aspects of *Kadmon's* body until triggered by their own progression and regression, the lights enclose themselves in "vessels."[65]

Luria refers to the lights as a "world of points" or a "world of chaos."[66] The image suggests that the lights themselves reflect the same dynamic of *Adam Kadmon* in relation to the supernal lights: they must be contained individually within form or "vessel." These lights exceed form and produce "the breaking of the vessels."[67] While the "vessels" closest to *Ein-Sof* remain intact, the lower six "break," "shatter and fall" because of the creative power of the light; some of the light is able to "retrace its path back to its source," but "the rest" of the light is "hurled down with the vessels themselves, and from the vessels' shards, the *kelipot*, the dark forces of the *sitra ahra*, take on substance."[68] In this one sentence, Scholem encapsulates not only how the "rest" of the light of *sferot* could become trapped in matter, but also how its liberation from matter could be imagined by Luria as the kabbalist's obligation. The kabbalist must liberate the light from *kelipot*, freeing it from the "other side."

To phrase it in the previous kabbalah's terms, the kabbalist liberates the shards of light from "evil … an illegitimate road upon the divine realm of light … that … becomes evil only because something which is good in its right place tries to usurp a place for which it is not fitted."[69] The "vessels" have become evil because they adhere to light for which they are not "fitted." This "other" path, illuminated by the light of "sin," an "illegitimate road," suggests itself as another entrance to glory, a "backdoor" to paradise, a forgotten and forbidden path.[70] Its route traces an abyss studded with broken shells, the representations of shards of "incorporeal supernal lights."

Luria's innovation of this teaching suggests both God and human engage in mutual *tikkunim* or repairs as a fulfillment of their shared obligation to liberate light from broken vessels, to reveal the original writing of *Kadmon* in the void. In his project, the "shells" or "forces of evil" exist prior to the "breaking of the vessels"; they are "mixed up … with the lights of the *Sefiroth* and the … *Reshimu*, or residue of *Ein-Sof* in the primordial space."[71] Since the shells are embedded in "chaos or anarchy," God expels them from the *sferot*. Divine Being must cleanse "the elements of the *Sefiroth* by eliminating the *kelipot*."[72] Thus God's obligation is fulfilled by "catharsis," and it is the original "cause" for the *kelipot* because it provides "a real existence and separate identity to the power of evil."[73] Catharsis is the discharge of Divine energy, pushing out of matter these shards of vessels that cannot represent the forms of the "incorporeal supernal lights." The remnants create though another testimony to Divine writing. They are the cast-offs, the expunged that form another path. The other's "path" to paradise is "quickened" or illuminated by transgression.

Hence Luria's project of human existence is entangled with the "realm of the *kelipot*." It begins with Eden's Adam, who as a "spiritual being" lives within a "spiritual realm," the world of *Asiyah*, or "making."[74] He is part of the incorporeal, "the purely spiritual sense" of creation. After Adam's fall "into sin," the *Asiyah* world falls as well and becomes "mixed up with the realm of *kelipot* which originally was placed below it."[75] In other words, the abyss and *Asiyah* are entangled so that "the material world in which we live" occupies both the abyss and the "world of making" simultaneously. Humans are "part spiritual" and "part material being," or to put it in Father's terms, "spirit" and "matter."[76] They are always tacking between creator and created.[77]

In this way, Father's "unnatural turn" defends the revelation of another path, a *poetry* of broken vessels, an animation of the mundane. Father reads "against the grain" of creation to evoke divine inscriptions, buried in matter. His "sin" reveals a path, the only path left to Father and perhaps to all of Drohobych.[78] Furthermore, it is a path imbricated in human existence and strewn with "broken shells."

When Father engages in his experiments of creation, he liberates the singular drive of the spirit within, a part of the "multiplicity" from that abyss. He liberates "making" from its entanglements. In fact, Schulz suggests that the "poetry" Father defends is a vestige of a primordial world. It is the *reshimu* or remnant caught in the *tehiru* or void. From a kabbalistic perspective, Father's actions constitute a transgression that illuminates the "other" existence, the "illegitimate path." From a heretical kabbalistic perspective, these same actions reveal a forgotten path to liberation in which humans are compelled to travel to the "other side" as a desperate act.[79] The heretic's journey requires a multitude of narratives in order to get to paradise. However, for both kabbalah and its heretical other, Father engages with mystical phenomena that are trapped in the void. Despite different valences attributed to his actions, the pattern belongs to kabbalah.[80]

Father's creations not only fissure the mundane illusion of Drohobych's existence, but also liberate something within him. He has innovated matter to reveal buried inscriptions, "recipes," that attest to the possibility of creation, even if they are short-lived. Implicitly, these "recipes" have been waiting for Jacob, specifically, to liberate them. In the act of their liberation, they free him. Jacob realizes his own temporality. He can be awakened even as he awakens dormant possibilities in others. He can be transformed into another species altogether, a *metempsychosis* in which Father's spirit migrates between bodies.[81] He bears a poetry within the self, an inscription, struggling to leave matter, whose residue reveals "the world of making."

The son's juxtaposition of "poetry" to "boredom," suggests "poetry" is a representational drive that innovates matter, awakening dormant forms inscribed within it: poetry is *Asiyah's* drive of "making." Since in its "making," it no longer articulates the primordial order from which it comes, it produces beings excluded from Nature's "recipes." To some extent, the son plots how creation can be considered transgression: humans "make" something that exceeds the epistemological structure that governs existence, holds it in place.[82] For epistemology's gatekeepers, excess representation is transgression. Transgression elevates to heresy when in the attempt to harness the power of creation, the human agent mistakes it for a property of the human faculties, an effect of lived experience.[83] Kabbalistically, transgression's heresy derives from a change in status: it no longer signifies hasidic devotion to Torah as a constitutive aspect of the self, but instead reflects a life without that "missing piece" in favor of something of its own "taste" or creation.

In this "world made by the words of … Schulz" "the inanimate" becomes "alive," even "self-aware."[84] Essentially, Schulz exhibits a world of immanent substance that awaits its innovation by poetry in order to embody a flow of animation, trapped in matter, Luria's "lost light" held fast by the *kelipot*. While Schulz echoes Heine's theory of *poesie* as innovation, unlike the prophet/poet, ben Halevi, Father does not limit himself to textual innovation.[85] He innovates phenomena. He is more Faust than poet.[86]

Furthermore, Father innovates the world around him because matter ceases to communicate its singular principle of existence: it lives without "vitality." To restore this principle—the mysterious *principium individuationis*—he must not be distracted by particular "content."[87] Jacob hopes to excavate new "beings" from within matter, "the indistinct smiles," the externalization of "experimental forms," breathing life into a lifeless world.[88]

As a consequence of Adela's housekeeping, Father's experimentation ends. The house reverts back to "gray twilight," overcome by the "mournful grayness of the city." The household is plunged into the town's malaise because Adela has eliminated Jacob's "unnatural" world. No matter what Adela does, she cannot restore "the splendid illuminations" of "winged phantasms" that she has destroyed.[89] Although the narrator believes that "echoes and the possibilities of colorful flashes" are hidden "in the depths of the colorless aura," none of the household are capable of reaching into that abyss, innovating substance, and pulling out from its darkness, Jacob's vibrant and vital missing world.[90] Essentially, only Jacob writes this Torah, only he can integrate it into the heretical kabbalah.

Defeat compels Jacob to take up nightly "wanderings" throughout the house and his tailor shop. On one such walk, he stumbles on the seamstresses, Paulina and Polda, in a backroom, surrounded by "scraps of cloth," "frivolous clippings," and "hundreds of sheared off pieces" so many that "they could shower the entire city like a colorful fantastic snowstorm."[91] On their knees before a mannequin, the women "measure fragments of a dress marked with white basting stitches."[92] They work so intently that the small room becomes "hot": their bodies "burn."[93] Opening a window, they expose themselves to the "dark breeze of night."[94]

The women repeat the ritual every night. Jacob's sudden appearance, on this particular evening, framed "in the dark doorway of the adjacent room with a lamp in his hand," surprises both the women and Jacob.[95] He is "enchanted by the scene full of fever and blushes"; the workshop has become an "idyll … for which the winter night served a background full of meaning, breathing amid the billowing window curtains."[96] The whole scene pulsates with immanence. The wind is caught in the act of "breathing" into the women. At this moment, the Father awakens from his defeat. He puts on his glasses, and draws "closer" to the women kneeling before "Moloch."[97]

The scene revolves around the women kneeling before the lifeless mannequin that is the object of their labors. "Carried in their arms," the mannequin is "a silent, immobile woman," but installed in the corner of the room, "the quiet lady" transforms into their "mistress."[98] As he stares at them, he walks "around the girls, illuminating them with the lamp."[99] In their illumination, the seamstresses transform before his eyes. They are revelations in darkness.

[T]he young women allowed themselves to be examined, twisting at the hips, glistening with the enamel of their eyes, the lacquer of their creaking slippers, the buckles of their garters under their skirts that the wind was billowing out ... while my father gazed attentively at the snorting young ladies ... [he] whispered under his breath, "*Genus avium* ... if I'm not mistaken, *scansores* or *psitacci* ... worthy of attention in the highest degree."[100]

The bearer of light in this darkness, Jacob discovers the two women unselfconsciously "full of fever and blushes" amid colorful "scraps" of fabric. Like Adam, Jacob repeats the scene of creation, observing the wind, the "tellurian spirit" of the world exhaling into creation. The echo is intentional: the women, like his avian creations, nestle among "scraps" of color. With the "winter night full of meaning," a mysterious breeze "has breathed" on Paulina and Polda. Exposed to its life force, they appear to Jacob in their hidden essences. The women share a kinship with his creations, previously unknown to him. They are remnants of his kingdom; he sees through the disguise of their "content" to the "form" of their essences.[101]

The Father desires to touch and examine them. They cavort before him, "twisting at the hips, glistening with the enamel of their eyes." They captivate him with "the lacquer of their creaking slippers, the buckles of their garters under their skirts" that "billow out." The whole scene depicts them coming alive, turning away from their "worship" of "Moloch," in order to exhibit themselves for Father's pleasure. His presence has liberated them from their labors. Jacob imagines them to be evidence of a creative impulse in the depths of the abyss that materializes its "structures of beings" in this world. Hence creation makes visible a boundary between immanent substance and a transcendent drive, enabling the exhibition of hidden beings in time and space, the translation of "indistinct smiles" into "experimental forms."[102]

Moreover, the boundary between these existences of human and inhuman dissolves with Jacob's desire. Desire produces his declaration of the seamstresses' ontological connection to his creations, "*Genus avium* ... if I'm not mistaken, *scansores* or *psitacci* ... worthy of attention in the highest degree." He sees an inner truth because his desire stimulates its visibility, their occluded forms revealed. This discovery encourages him to "start ... an entire series of performances" in which he "enchants" both young women. They even consent to his "fervent ... study" of their "slim, tawdry bodies."[103] He performs his examinations "with dignity and refinement ... such that it removed any suggestive appearance from the most risky points of these investigations."[104]

Carefully removing Paulina's stocking, he exposes her calf, "stripped" of its garter. He "cries out ... the world would be more perfect" if rather than content, "gentlemen demiurges' could gaze on the female form."[105] Here he proposes his own repair of creation because if as a creator, he "could gaze" on the hidden feminine form, its individual principle, obscured by the "tawdry" content displayed before him, the animation trapped within matter, he would add "more perfection."[106]

He stares at Paulina's calf in his hands, and revels "in the form of being" the women have "chosen."[107] The women appear enchanted by him, listening eagerly to his ramblings. When Jacob highlights the female form for "gentlemen demiurges" he implies that the body of the woman can be compelled to capture, express, this mystical, phenomenal drive gushing from the abyss at a precise moment.[108]

As a result of Jacob's charm, the narrator identifies another metamorphosis in which "all things ... retreated to the root of their being," or the *principium individuationis*.[109] The women recede into their essence, exhibited before the Father. They are left in a "golem" state. Walking among these "structures of beings," the "heresiarch" fascinates them. He "infects" and "seduces" them. Father's innovation repeats the creation of "experimental forms," forcing them to reveal immanence.[110] The scene culminates with Paulina's complete surrender to the Father: she becomes his willing "disciple, the model for his experiments."[111] Her capitulation emboldens Jacob to reveal his "Treatise on the Second Book of Genesis."[112]

Like the heretical kabbalah's forebears, the Gnostics, Jacob tells his "disciples" that the world is ruled by a "Demiurge" who has "no monopoly on creation: creation is a privilege of all spirits."[113] There is no Law; there is no soul. There is only "spirit" and "matter" on which "spirit" acts. Anarchy is constitutive of Jacob's world because "making" follows its own singular principle. Juxtaposed to Jacob's anarchic desire, the oppressor "Demiurge" imposes an incomprehensible law on creation and that law demands its violation. Human antinomianism expresses a radical freedom. Jacob Taubes claims it is "the only way that mankind becomes part of history. Nature, and mankind embedded in nature, have no history."[114] In their drive to free themselves from "all laws," they produce existence, history; history is the testimony of their emancipation.

In this way, Schulz posits a world of matter that waits to be enlivened: "spirits" create, and immanent "matter" receives this action because "matter has been granted infinite fecundity, an inexhaustible vital force."[115] If matter embodies the possibility of beings, spirit innovates these possibilities.

Jacob describes the original "Demiurge," as an adversary not only of "all spirits," but also potentially of humans. If humans succumb to the "temptation" to liberate the "inexhaustible vital force"—spirit—they must violate the Demiurge's law since according to this law, humans are not entitled to transcendence. Jacob's Demiurge uses the power of transcendence to enslave immanent matter. Akin to Jacob Frank's description of his own exploits, Father's "heroism" performs a "theft ... of the treasure ... kept away from mankind by a jealous Creator, a cruel or errant demiurge." Consequently, the text erases a boundary between the "Jacobs," highlighting Father's transgressions on behalf of his works of art.[116]

According to Father, matter presents itself as an abyss in whose "depths ... indistinct smiles take shape, tensions are reinforced, experimental shapes solidify," an infinity of beings whose exhale produces "faint shivers" in "matter."[117] Matter extends in all dimensions; it is both abyss and the substance of the human world. While the scene repeats Father's innovation of the compendia, Father has shifted away from the permutation of letters, images, and words to focus instead on the permutation of matter because of these "possibilities" of being. Therefore, matter "waits" for a "life-giving breath" to externalize its being.[118] Father's bold statement is meant to "solidify" the creations, the women before him: they exist as "matter" exposed to "the night wind" and its "life-giving breath of the spirit" coaxes them out of their "seamstress" existence. Jacob believes his illumination manifests the revelation of their "avian" essences. Like a Rhineland Hasid with his golem, the women in their phenomenal essence prove his achievement. Jacob glimpses this phenomenal mystery, but only for the duration of his ecstasy.

Father declares then that matter "[L]acking in initiative, lasciviously submissive, malleable like a woman, compliant in response to every impulse ... becomes a space outside the law, open to every sort of charlatanry and dilettantism, the domain of every abuse and dubious demiurgic manipulation."[119] The force of the simile, "like a woman," reinforces matter in its essence to be lawless and "malleable."[120] Since matter is not bound "by the law," matter can be exploited by the "charlatan," a victim of "demiurgic manipulation." In the likenesses between Demiurge and "charlatan," Schulz implies that the real transgression rests with the "charlatan's" imitation of the "Demiurge."[121] Consequently, Jacob imagines the possibility of "gentlemen demiurges" who resort to neither imitating nor competing with the original creator. His mimesis does not represent the Demiurge's order. It "distills" instead matter's animating principle from the "chaos within."

Although Father's conceptual scaffolding is punctuated by an heretical kabbalah, it shifts self-consciously away from the "charlatan's" aim of controlling phenomena. While the charlatan's illegitimate claim to power reproduces demiurgic oppression, Father's experiments in creation release matter from being trapped by the past.[122] Hence Schulz juxtaposes Father's redemptive transgressions to the charlatan's "ossification" of reality's illusions. The charlatan's desire to control, to make reality permanent, stalls creation, prevents the liberation of being, and inhibits the expression of "new and different forms."

In this way, the charlatan joins those in service to the Demiurge who prefer "ossified forms of being" even though they "are no longer satisfying." "New and different forms" propose a world "outside the law." Together, charlatan and demiurgic servant foreclose the permutation of "life," making human existence reducible not only to death as the end of being, but also to the codification of "legitimate" forms in time and space as the boundaries of that end.

This illusion of reality appears as a mask of "lifelessness ... an external appearance behind which unknown forms of life are hiding."[123]

> The scale of these forms is infinite, their shades and nuances inexhaustible. The Demiurge possessed vital and ... creative recipes .... he created a multitude of species that renew themselves by their own power. Whether these recipes will ever be reconstructed is unknown. But this is not necessary, for even if those classical methods of creation should turn out to be forever inaccessible, there remain certain illegal methods, an infinity of heretical, extreme methods .... Too long have we lived under the terror of the Demiurge's unsurpassable perfection .... Too long has the perfection of his creation paralyzed our own creativity. We do not wish to compete with him. We have no ambition to equal him. We wish to be creators in our own, lower sphere, we desire creative work for ourselves, we desire creative delight, we desire in a word, demiurgy.[124]

"Unknown forms of life" hide behind the mask of "lifelessness"; they are "infinite" and "inexhaustible"; they are "recipes" that "renew themselves." In an eerie echo of those early Rhineland Hasids, Schulz points to "recipes" that tack between orthodox and heretical kabbalahs.

Since matter bears "infinite" forms of being, the world only reflects a portion of these forms; they reflect the narrow vision of the Demiurge, his "classical methods of creation." These "recipes" "terrorize" human existence with "perfection," a "perfection that destroys" human "creativity."[125] In Jacob's teachings, mimesis illustrates the "lower sphere's illusions," condemns humans to copy, to imitate the Demiurge's pleasure, forfeiting any "creative delight" of their own. Father's search for "new beings" implies he "plumbs" for phenomena beyond their mimetic representations. He rejects "lived experience" and searches for the abyss' hidden inscriptions.

Espousing the necessity of the heretical, the antinomian, in order to attain "creative delight," Father advocates the adoption of "illegal methods," heresies humans must use because "those classical methods of creation" remain "inaccessible." The "Demiurge's unsurpassable perfection" destroys humans' "creativity." It fosters fear and "terror." Jacob offers an alternative: abandon the Demiurge's "perfection," his law, in order to become "demiurges" themselves. Father posits an ontological transformation and it takes place "in our own lower sphere." Essentially, he advocates a redemption not only within the realm of the *kelipot*, but also for the "broken shells."

In this way "sphere" intimates the condition that Jacob posits as the locus of human creation.[126] Its "lower" region is filled with possibilities of being so much so that it extends into darkness and "chaos." *Asiyah's* outlines are visible here. It exudes a "colorless" aura that can only be liberated by spirits. Tempted, humans can commandeer the creative process through heresy even if they cannot achieve the "classical" forms. They experience the pleasure of creation, but their creations do not renew themselves. They are finite against the backdrop of the "infinite."[127] Thus Father posits his "Treatise on the Second Book of Genesis" in which human creations, using "an infinity of heretical, extreme methods," rewrite the revelation as "a program ... a second demiurgy, an image of the second generation of creatures that was to stand in open opposition to the present era."[128]

> We do not care about creations with long-lasting breath, about creatures for the long run. Our beings will not be heroes of multivolume romances. Their roles will be short, concise, their characters without plans for the future .... bringing them to life for just one moment.[129]

Intriguingly, Jacob is disinterested in creations that foster identification. They will not be idols. They will not "be heroes of multivolume romances." They will not endure. No one will mistake them for the Demiurge's creation because "if they are to be people, we will give them ... only one side of a face, one arm, one leg—namely the one that will be necessary for their role .... In the back they can be simply stitched up with canvas or whitewashed."[130] Modeling his creations on mannequins, Father continues with the crux of his innovation. "Each individual human being" that he "brings to life" will be in the service of "word" and "deed."[131] No longer measured according to a calculus unavailable to human "taste," new creation finds answers to its unfinished state in the predicates of human existence.[132] Matter will be enlivened, freed from mute passivity to illustrate creative possibilities in a mortal register. Father's fantasy of a meaningful life liberates creation's *poesie*—spirits within matter—to be heard, glimpsed, but only for the brevity of an instant. Humans are entitled to glimpse the phenomenal; however, they are entitled to neither possess nor control it.

His comparison of "first" and "second" creations juxtaposes the Demiurge's transcendental project to human "taste." Consequently, Father "writes" his own heretical Torah in which he replaces the Demiurge's "refined, splendid complex materials" of creation for the "material thrills" of "the tawdry, the cheapness, the shoddiness."[133] The things that excite and stimulate the human senses, "the profound meaning of ... this passion for gaudy tissue paper, for papier-mache, for lacquer paint, for scraggly hair, and sawdust" attest to humans' "love for matter as such, for its puffiness and porosity, for its unique, mystical consistency" in their own works of art.[134] Jacob's creation emerges on a path through the senses and the revelation triggers a human command to violate the Demiurge's law whereby God "makes invisible" this "mystical consistency .... commands it to disappear beneath the game of life."[135] The Demiurge seals off the faculties from the aura of the phenomena underpinning creation, but humans intuit nonetheless their "mystical consistency."

Although "the game of life" continues, its illusions and simulacra occluding the ancient "recipes," the materials' ellipsis elicits humans' "passion" for the "tawdry," leading them toward the extension of matter into the venal, the "shoddiness" of the "carnivalesque." These "material thrills" in their cheap imitations expose the frailty of creation and the deceit of the Demiurge. However, as readers discover, while the illusion of "the game of life" can be undermined by "profound ... passion," it still induces an equally profound forgetfulness.

After Father's discourse, the son reenters the scene, observing that the "girls sat motionless with glassy eyes." The ambiguity of their expressions suggests that they could inhabit either the first or second generation of creation. It creates furthermore the context for Father's conclusion, "we want to create man for the second time, in the image and likeness of a mannequin." A suture term, "mannequin" grounds Father's revision of the biblical, "let us make man in our image," and extends it to the "mystical" essence allegedly dormant or imprisoned within matter.

However, at his pronunciation of "*mannequin,*" Adela intervenes. She interrupts him with her "slowly extended ... foot in its tight-fitting black silk, ... flexed like a serpent's head," the effect of which causes Father to become "silent," to withdraw "in upon himself."[136] He collapses and curls up, appearing "rigid," another entity entirely.[137] Desire erases the boundary within him between spirit and matter, agency and golem, subject and object. Schulz describes him as an "automaton," sinking to his knees before the women, who now occupy the position of "Moloch."[138] They issue commands to him. In that moment, Father is restored to matter. He too is "like a woman."

After Jacob's capitulation to desire, the son hears the lamp's "hissing," and "the whispers of poisonous tongues." He intuits "the meaningful glances" traversing "the thicket of the wallpaper." Boundaries between objects in the room erode to reveal the phenomenality of matter, a second Eden, lurking among them. Finally, he becomes aware of the "zigzag of thoughts," bodiless, but asserting themselves in matter nonetheless. The son shares Jacob's revelatory vision. The lamp "hisses" and the wallpaper "whispers"; unmoored and unembodied "thoughts" pass through matter, the stuff of the workroom, the bodies, "in faint shivers." Kafka calls these God's "nihilistic thoughts"; Schulz refers to them as "unfinished stories."[139]

Witnessing his father's transformation from patriarch to prophet, to one of the "gentlemen demiurges," to an "automaton" under the thrall of Adela, Polda, and Paulina, the son describes Father's discourse as a template of creation in which inert matter—the mannequin state—becomes innovated existence, an enlivened being that lives for only the duration of "the ecstasy of his creator." He espouses a theory of creation that reflects fragments of biblical, kabbalistic, and heretical "recipes."

When Adela takes over the scene, she inverts the order. Father's desire for her causes him to revert to "the root of his being." He becomes "malleable" matter. Previously, his desire to create enables his transcendence, glimpsing its underlying revelation, matter in its "fecundity." However, Adela's intervention tempts him to return to that pliable state in which desire has limitless possibilities of expression.

This "second Genesis" is organized around Adela's agency. She dangles her foot, "like a serpent," and Jacob's metamorphosis occurs. He reverts to a golem state, underscored by Polda's command "Jakob will be reasonable. Jakob will listen, Jakob will not be stubborn."[140] In this way, Schulz's heretical kabbalah links Father's unconscious desire not only to a return to "unformed" existence, but also to be restored to phenomenal matter, awaiting being's stimulation. Jacob recedes into a golem state, listening to the "shivers" of desire.[141]

Every night then Jacob repeats the scene. He appears at the workshop and returns to "his dark and intricate theme" of the "image and likeness of the mannequin." However, his focus is on the world outside of the shop, where the comical wax figures of carnival side shows "are pathetic church-fare parodies of mannequins."[142] These creatures elicit human laughter, but he warns that "matter knows no jokes"; it suffers, "imprisoned," but without knowledge of "who it is and why it exists."[143] Condemned to an existence without meaning, matter lacks as well the knowledge of a destiny.[144]

Incapable of communication, the figure's torment is intensified by the masses' laughter.

> The crowd laughs. Do you understand the terrible sadism, the intoxicating demiurgic cruelty of this laughter? All the same, we should weep, my ladies, over our own fate at the sight of the misery of this matter, violated matter, upon which a terrible injustice has been committed. From this, ladies, there follows the terrible sadness of all those clownish golems, all those hags tragically brooding over their comical grimaces.[145]

These "golems" are aware that they exist in a "clownish" state, are subjected to a "terrible sadism," in which the crowd's "laughter" participates in a "demiurgic cruelty."

The "crowd" though is not the Demiurge: they merely imitate him. They reproduce his laughter at the "misery of ... matter." To put it in Frankist terms, the "crowd" reproduces the Demiurge's laughter at the suffering of these particular "humans."

The golems also evoke Adam unformed and without consciousness. The revelation that onlookers laugh at these beings represents an action in which the Demiurge participates; the crowd is intoxicated by their mimetic reproduction of "his action." Hence Father warns his listeners of "our own fate." Implicitly, Jacob associates "golems" with the "crowd," with the women listening to him, and with himself. In this way, Schulz layers both heretical and orthodox kabbalistic readings of *Genesis* to conflate the boundary between human and golem.[146]

Although this is the first time Schulz mentions "golems," they have been foreshadowed repeatedly in his stories. They are present in the townspeople whose faces wear "golden masks .... of a pagan cult," who move silently through the streets, trapped in the monotony of "business as usual" in Drohobych.[147] They are hinted at in his cousin, Emil, whose "features ... for a moment collapsed back into nothingness ... his face departed into absence, forgot about itself, dissipated" when he stares at "images of naked women and boys" with the "germ of desire."[148]

Golems appear among the townspeople as often as they appear as imprisoned, "violated matter." Houses become animate; their doors are "old and wise," and although they remain "silent witnesses" to their human inhabitants—characters "enter into their life"—the boundary between animate and inanimate disappears because of the narrator's recognition that "we" are "related to them by blood and fate."[149] In other words, Schulz signals that human existence is a golem state; the same desire that calls into being the golem's animation, can also undo it, forcing its return to nothingness. Thus when desire is focused on matter, it either awakens it to life or restores it to "nothingness." It enlivens or it dissipates. Father's heresy recognizes human existence to be a temporary death between metamorphosis and dissolution.[150]

Cinnamon Shops proposes two variants of dynamic innovation, one the short-lived letter phenomenology that Father uses on his "compendia" and one focused on liberating material immanence, no longer the immanence of the text, but rather the innovation of the object world in order to draw out from its phenomenal center, new beings. Father wants to fashion this world according to his own "taste." New beings are intuited from the detritus of human existence, the abandoned, forgotten "scraps" on the workshop floor. *Cinnamon Shops'* entire project affirms Father's "right" to pursue his desire to be a "gentleman demiurge," to create his own world from the residue of the first creation, to construct his own "Torah," from the "trash" of human existence.[151] Jacob's "unnatural turn" or path prompts his experiments: transgression is a necessary mode of his redemption.

In this way, *Cinnamon Shops* repeats creation and destruction. His works of art are repeatedly exhibited and then destroyed by Adela, or some other competing group from below. The repetition forms the heart of Schulz's stories so that the Father's surprise at the "unexpected return" of his bird creations to Drohobych ends with him in a golem state, horrified by their destruction, and aware of his own impotence.

> How moved Father was by this unexpected return, how amazed he was by avian instinct, by this attachment to the Master that the exiled tribe nursed, like a legend, in their soul, so that at long last, after many generations, on the final day before the tribe's extinction, it would be lured back to its primeval fatherland.[152]

Tracing this excerpt alongside its kabbalistic allusions, we have Father, the "demiurge moved" by the return of his creation. He has been hidden from them in that they no longer "recognize him," yet their "return" is inscribed "like a legend, in their soul." After their "many generations" in exile, they have returned to him and the "primeval fatherland" even though it is ominously suggested they come "on the final day before the tribe's extinction."

The revelation of their return prompts Father to "call to them with his former incantation in the forgotten avian language." He has given them this language and while it motivates their return, "those blind paper birds could no longer recognize Father .... they neither heard nor saw" their patriarch.[153] Compelled by an unconscious need to return to the "primeval fatherland," they have no consciousness of who their "creator" is, of the revelation he imparts.

His creation no longer remembers him; he exists as a failed demiurge who must witness their destruction again as "[S]uddenly stones began whistling in the air. It was the jokesters, the stupid witless tribe, aiming missiles at the fantastic avian sky."[154] The attack by "the stupid witless tribe" underlines ironically the posited kinship of the golems below and the golems above. Father's efforts to "warn them ... threaten them with supplicating gestures" are "in vain" because they neither "hear him" nor even "notice him." In their deaths, they revert to formless matter.

> And the birds were falling. Struck by a missile, they drooped heavily and were already wilted in the air. Before they flew down to earth they were already a shapeless pile of feathers.
>
> In the blink of an eye, the uplands were covered with this strange, fantastic carrion. Before Father could run over to the place of slaughter, the whole glorious avian tribe was already lying dead, scattered about on the rocks.
>
> Only now, close up, could Father observe the entire trashiness of that impoverished generation, the total absurdity of that tawdry anatomy.[155]

As the birds fall to their deaths, struck by stones thrown from below, incapable of hearing and understanding "the forgotten avian language," the secret language gifted by creator to the created is no longer intelligible to them. They are not cognizant of its revelation; they cannot remember when the language organized their existence, when it was constitutive of their existence. Like Kafka, Father recognizes that he has "ended up in an abyss of despair," his creations, "failures" easily destroyed. Jacob's heretical kabbalah does not keep its promises to him. Redemption has not been sustained in his works of art. Father might "write his own torah," but he cannot save his creations. His innovation is futile.

In other words, Schulz recognizes with *Cinnamon Shops* the failure of a messianism grounded in a heretical kabbalah. Resonating with Kafka's "man of the country," all of its promises end not only in Father's intuition of a redemption that can never be materialized, but also in the recognition that with his creations, he is condemned matter: the imagination of transcendence, more a burden than emancipated ecstasy.

Part Two

Letter Phenomenologies of Modernist Kabbalahs

God gave us the Torah entire and perfect from the [word] Bereshit *to the [words]* Le-einei kol Israel. *Behold how all the letters of the Torah, in their diverse forms, whether assembled and separated, swaddled, curved or crooked, superfluous or elliptical, narrow or wide, inverted, with their diverse calligraphy, the pericopes open and closed as well as ordered pericopes—all of this constitutes the form of G-d, blessed be He. That resembles* mutatis mutandis, *the act of painting, using [several] colors. In the same way, the Torah is, from the first to the last pericope, the form of God .... And because every man in Israel must consider that the world was created for him, God bound each one to write a Torah Scroll for himself. And the secret, implicit therein, is that each one has made God, blessed be He.*[1]

When the "'world' does not disintegrate ... but the hope of redemption crumbles," the only strategy left to Frankists, Sabbatians, secularists, modern Ahers, "products" of the heretical kabbalah, is either to recede back into old identities, illustrated by Tokarczuk's "Book of Names," or to continue resignedly down the "illegitimate" path, in all of its futility, suggested by Heine's Faust, Kafka's "man of the country," and Schulz's "Father." However, in "Jehudah ben Halevi," Heine hints that *aggadah*'s transformation into *poesie* offers an alternative to these two choices, this fallen dialectic. Heine implies another model for kabbalah's engagement with literature, one in which literary ontology experiences metamorphosis. It is no longer bound to represent mimetically human experience; content is not the source of its revelation.

Thus the individual imagines "redemption is ... an event in the spiritual realm, reflected in the human soul rather than the actual acts of the messianic figure."[2] The messianic idea is preserved through an "interpretative context," a phenomenological experience of the messianic idea derived from another source, a non-phenomenal origin. In this way, literature becomes a messianic site. It motivates both a phenomenological redemption in the subject and a discursive *metempsychosis* in text. As the "messianic idea" abandons expression of the failed messiah's lived experience, its "vitality" emerges through literature's other constituent parts. Literature awakens to its own immanence and it projects a letter phenomenology that elicits more writing, more reading, pushing through the palimpsest of the written, to recover writing's liberation.

In this way, the transformation of literature relies on kabbalah's premiss that Torah "constitutes the form of G-D" because it articulates the Names of God, implying that Torah remains excluded from the Fall. Its letters restore being to "before the Law." Hence we are "commanded .... to write a Torah scroll" for ourselves. The "secret" is in the writing of each one's scroll: humans have "each one ... made G-d." From their multiplicity, they express a singularity "that resembled the *mutatis mutandi*."

This expansion is an implication of Jeffrey Rubenstein's identification of two "interpretive trends" of "the Four who went to Pardes" in which paradise shifts to its suggestive acronym, PaRDeS. The acronym emphasizes intensive study of the Torah through four methods of analysis: *Peshat, Remez, D'rash, Sod*. Beginning with *peshat* and ending with *sod*, the story elevates exegesis to be the revelation itself so that revelation begins with reading; reading "receives" it.[3]

The acronym alludes to the depths of textual engagement available to Talmud's readers. *Peshat* is the literal interpretation of text. The text communicates its lexical meaning unproblematically. *Remez* imposes more work on the reader. The text "hints" at contexts through allusion, allegory, symbolism, and even semiotic connotation. The third term, *D'rash*, is built on the Hebrew root, *d r sh* and its focus is an active study or an exegesis of text. These first three methods encompass the main focus of Judaism as an epistemological project.

However, the last method, *sod*, "secret" or "mystery" anchors the PaRDeS. All exegeses end with "mystery," an aspect of the text unwilling to be disclosed through standard interpretation. It requires an agent to probe the text, to permutate its parts, combining them to form new syntagms. It is the text's transcendent moment when its constituent parts awaken to their immanence. Erich Auerbach represents it foreclosed to human possession, although "glimpsed" in its shadows.[4] Furthermore, its "mystery" is not necessarily found in the first three methods of Judaism's formal study.[5]

Consequently, Akiva chooses companions for the journey to PaRDeS who recognize transcendence not only in the "orchard," with all of its Edenic allusions to place, but also in *aggadah's* textual world of "hidden" spaces, those aspects that are not as they appear. It is a wholly "novel" experience, a world beyond human categories of time and space and therefore beyond the human intellect's efforts to infer, speculate, conjure.

In this way, PaRDeS inflects study of Judaism's epistemology. Akiva warns his companions that trust in the senses, inference, and received knowledge, what is familiar, is prohibited by the "mystery" because it implies the conceptualization of the Divine within Judaism's objects and categories. The *tannaim* must not substitute conceptualization for the *Divine Name*.[6] In the absence of being able to say *The Name*, humans repeat their names for eternity. Tokarczuk's "Book of Names" implies this very gesture: after Frank's failure, his followers abandon reading and writing *The Name* in favor of paradise's materialization, a lived experience of freedom and prosperity.

However, the "secret" of the text does not end in lived experience's materialization. The impact of shifting Pardes to PaRDeS enables the *aggadah* to break apart into discrete patterns in which its constituent pieces deploy independently to suggest new revelation. The letters, themselves, become touchstones for revelation, illuminating the depths of the text, those elements undiscoverable through the normative tradition.

Hence revelation's "secret" is a phenomenological project focused on reading, writing, saying Hebrew letters, in order to remember *The Name*, hidden in the unconscious. The letters not only exhibit a textual path, transcending time and space for the subject, but they also adhere to cognition, restoring themselves to a pre-Fall, primeval writing. In an echo of Joseph Dan, reading "receives" their revelation and the modern Jewish subject begins to write.[7]

6

Golems of Text and Bruno Schulz's "Interminable *Aggadot*"

Although *Cinnamon Shops* preoccupies itself with Father's "regions of heresy," its minor theme, the liberation of letters and words, becomes integral to Josef, narrator of *Sanatorium under the Sign of the Hourglass*, Schulz's second collection of short stories.[1] Unlike Father who releases immanence from matter, the phenomena of lived experience, Josef uses text to transform his cognition. Hence Josef's metamorphosis begins with a missing "Book," and ends with him, an elderly pensioner, enclosed in his childhood room, "like a mouse," alone with *The Book of Creation*.[2] The mysterious "Book" constructs a world of golems within his room; he is "walled in with bricks." Its creations sever the narrator from human connection. Its letters saturate time and space, essentially sealing Josef within its pages so that "The Book" absorbs him. Josef not only permutates its words and letters, but the letters also restructure his subjectivity.[3]

Sanatorium under the Sign of the Hourglass opens with a quizzical first story, "The Book," an anonymous narrator's discussion of a mystical book that his Father possesses. In subsequent stories when the narrator, revealed as Father's son, Josef, discovers pages of "The Book," he experiments with textual innovation. These two themes refine the kabbalistic register identified within *Cinnamon Shops*, refocusing it around Josef's memories of these early textual experiments.

"The Book" exceeds human cognition; it has neither "attributes" nor "epithets."[4] In its lack of identifiable, physical characteristics and without content, "The Book" is not an object of knowledge.

> I am simply calling it The Book without any attributes or epithets, and in this abstinence and limitation there is a helpless sigh, a silent capitulation before the immensity of the transcendent, since no word, no allusion, can manage to shine, smell, flow with that shudder of terror, that premonition of the thing without a name, the first taste of which on the tip of the tongue exceeds the capacity of our rapture.[5]

In the absence of an objective tether, the narrator has only the "premonition" of his own human failure before it. He marks its existence with the knowledge of the imposed boundary of his "finitude," his "limitation," a measurement, against the "formlessness," measureless "Book."

Juxtaposed to his "limitation," "The Book" signifies an entity akin to Abraham Abulafia's "absolute object." In Abulafia's project, Hebrew letters stimulate "the soul's deeper life ... freeing it from ordinary perceptions."[6] Since the letters reflect a dimension outside of time and space, they suppress "ordinary perceptions" of matter and meaning. Hence Schulz's narrator resists anchoring this writing to any content. Its lack of "attributes" compels him to ponder "The Book" as an "absolute object" until it gives up its emanations, its "shine, smell, flow ... that shudder of terror."

In *Cinnamon Shops,* Father's discourse claims that "all matter flows from the infinite possibilities passing through it in faint shivers"; the son's innovation of Father's teaching identifies these "possibilities" to be "The Book's" emanations, its "shudder of terror."[7] Within its pages, emanations of potential being are trapped.

The image resonates with and revises several kabbalistic themes: the *Zohar*'s insistence that Divine Light is hidden within Torah's pages, placed there by God to wait for kabbalists. This hidden revelation becomes with Josef, the story of imprisoned spirits in writing. Their forms, their lights are creation's excess, a "pulsating" residue.[8] It echoes an even older *aggadic* belief that *Sefer Yetsirah* has been hidden, again by God, also within Torah until Abraham, its "author," extracts it.[9] The trope of revelation hidden by God in a text to be discovered later by patriarch, prophet, or poet, for whom it is purposive reiterates that "The Book" is not reducible to a specific object, yet remains the dynamic source of all books.[10] They are copies, reproductions of the "inimitable" writing that creates them.

In this way, the "Book" exhibits a "formlessness" against which the son perceives himself: he is its "limitation": a boundary of finitude, juxtaposed against "the immensity of the transcendent." A gap between humanness, his use of language, "word ... allusion," and the infinite's "immensity" becomes visible. In his recognition of the failure of words to describe transcendent infinitude, he is reduced to "abstinence" and "a silent capitulation."[11] He cannot cross the abyss between himself and the "transcendent." They are two different ontologies. Hence his intuition testifies to "The Book's" Nothingness in relation to his nothingness; his incapacity to communicate acknowledges his senses are sealed against "that shudder of terror." Simultaneously, he apprehends the flow of the "transcendent" at an unconscious level, as it streams into consciousness, exceeding "the capacity of our rapture."

Schulz's text suggests that the interplay between consciousness and unconsciousness around "The Book" repeats *tzimtzum*'s narrative, God's contraction into the self, in order for creation to occur. Associated with Isaac Luria, Scholem observes that *tzimtzum* is unknown to the ancient world, because it negates the possibility of *pleroma*.[12]

> God did not reveal Himself overtly in creation, but confined and concealed Himself, and by so doing enabled the world to be revealed. Then came the second act, the "emanations," the creations of the worlds, the revelation of the divine as mankind's deity, as the Creator, as the God of Israel.[13]

Concealment or *tzimtzum* signifies God's withdrawal into the depths of Divine Being, producing space, and foreclosing *pleroma* within it. An abyss opens up between the surface on which creation takes place and the hidden God. Josef's "limitation" juxtaposed to the "immensity of the transcendent" suggests that humans live, consciously tracing their "limitations" back to their inaccessible, unconscious origins. The tension between unconscious and conscious is the cognitive inscription of *tzimtzum:* the mind remembers what it could not possibly know, what it could not possibly have experienced.

Likewise, in the act of "concentrating" the self, God imposes "limitation" on Divine Being, a receding into a state of "hiddenness," so that the first exile, *galut*, is divine because "He exiled Himself from boundless infinity to a more concentrated infinity. There is a profound inward Galut, not the Galut of one of His creatures, but of God Himself, who limited Himself" in order to permit creation's existence.[14] God recedes and in contraction, he produces a boundary within infinity, a "limitation" that can never be absorbed into boundary-less infinity.

As Josef recognizes himself in "limitation," in negation, against the "immensity of the transcendent," designated as "The Book," he perceives within its pages the exiled hidden concentration of Divine Being. His identification obligates him to liberate it. It is his duty. However, in proximity to the "transcendent," he can neither conceptualize its "immensity," nor communicate the ecstasy it produces in him at its "first taste." He admits to a sensual or corporeal register in which sense impressions bear the trace of the "transcendent," but these impressions cannot be translated into conscious meaning. The "immensity of the transcendent" underscores that the narrator cannot bridge the gap between his existence and "the transcendent." In his "rapture," he is always aware that he cannot extract from within his own "disintegration and chaos" the revelation he seeks.[15] He will never be "transcendent."

In *Cinnamon Shops*, Father's heresy reflects a desire to be a "gentleman demiurge"; in *Sanatorium under the Sign of the Hourglass*, the son recognizes that human substance cannot substitute for "The Book's" transcendence. Like Kafka, like Aher, the narrator stands before the "transcendent" and realizes he will never be "like a divine being."

Josef declares that "the pathos of adjectives and the fluffiness of epithets" cannot assist the communication of its formlessness since it is a "thing without a name," "a thing without measure," an unbounded "magnificence."[16] A being whose "immensity" cannot be named, who cannot be recuperated as part of the phenomenal world, who is notable in its infinity, but never in its "thingness," all of these factors point to the kabbalistic theory of *En Sof* (אן-סוף), or "Nothingness." "The Book" does not reveal its *sod*, but only repeats "Nothingness." Thus it hides Divine Being: it is walled off by lexical meaning. Its ontology conflicts with its representations so that it occludes rather than reveals. In this way, "Nothingness" is constitutive of "The Book."

"No word, no allusion" represents its revelation and the realization triggers the narrator's "helplessness." His apprehension, "premonition," implies that "the thing without a name" is present to an unconscious world, but whose presence extends into the mind of the reader via writing's trace. Hence it cannot be named; it exceeds imagination. Its letters "shine," but they are not knowable as words.

Since this "thing" exists outside any epistemology of knowledge, "The Book" cannot be a "thing." The narrator's persistence in identifying it in negation forces the mind to entertain the possibility of not only being outside time and space, the mode by which humans measure existence, but also being inherent in the text's constituent parts: those elements that are not reducible to meaning. In this way, "The Book" signifies Abulafia's "absolute object." Through its contemplation, the narrator "unseal[s] the soul" and "untie[s] the knots which bind it." In Abulafia's project, Hebrew letters are the only absolute objects. They displace "all kinds of gross natural objects" whose "images" bore into consciousness, with their "stamp of finiteness." In Schulz, vernacular letters also bear infinitude's traces. They affix themselves to the profane, textual excess, their revelations seeping through refuse, discarded, tawdry, meaningless pages.[17]

Severed from its representations, "The Book" creates the narrator's awareness of a chasm between communication's currency—words—and his intuition of the "immensity of the transcendent." Words "name" things, but the book's ontology—its writing—disrupts this process. His faculties can neither harmonize nor disharmonize around this "absolute object." "The Book" both violates aesthetic experience and forecloses the object's relationship to a phenomenon. Schulz broaches the idea of a textual object without a phenomenal tether to time and space.

Since "The Book" is not a phenomenon of this world, it sits outside of any epistemology of knowledge. It does not correspond to any specific text of human transmission.[18] "The Book's" contents are not the revelation: "the immensity of the transcendent" is found in its unarticulated, ontological being, registered as a memory the narrator has never experienced, a writing that persists as a buried inscription. Its trace is hinted at, but remains hidden. Communication's failure produces for the narrator a tension between the words used to express content and the unarticulated plane of memory from which they emanate, as if the words constructed for communication obscure this plane or manifold purposely. His entire quest is the expression of this memory that he feels, but that remains at the edges of his consciousness in shadow.

In the word's failure to represent mimetically "the immensity of the transcendent," "The Book .... exceeds all the capacity for our rapture." The word fails in order for the narrator's "rapture" to occur. However, unlike Abulafia's absolute object, "The Book" does not displace "gross natural objects" with Hebrew letters, rather it exhausts the vernacular. With its profane objects, the vernacular exhausts communication, causing words to fail. The narrator's "rapture" or ecstasy is the sign he has achieved failure.

Even more perplexingly, the failure of all the other books highlights "The Book's" extension into the world, immanent and singular. Therefore, it calls to its own "true reader."[19] By answering that call, the reader joins the narrator, in the recognition of their "shared sense."

> After all, in any event the reader, the true reader on whom this narrative is counting, will understand when I look him deep in the eye and to my very depths begin to shine with that radiance. In that brief and mighty glance, in the transitory squeezing of his hand, he will grasp, accept, recall—and he will close his eyes from rapture at that profound reception. For do we not all hold one another's hands in secret under the table that divides us?[20]

Purposive for the "true reader," the narrator waits. Moreover, when he discovers this "reader," he will "look him deep in the eye." The depth of that glance liberates immanence, within the narrator. Stimulated by being read, writing now innovates the narrator until his "very depths begin to shine with that radiance" of the "transcendent."[21] In proximity to a "true reader," the narrator's "radiance" manifests. Alone, the narrator's proximity to the infinite ends in the narrator's realization of an abyss between the "transcendent" and human existence, but bound to an imagined reader, the liberated narrator emanates "radiance."[22]

The "true reader" innovates the "depths" of both the narrative and the narrator. In that moment, the "true reader" recognizes the narrator as a textual unit, disarticulated from words, pages, text. This "recognition scene" has no precedent in literature because narrative is neither reducible to the text's contents, nor the narrator to "The Book's" characters. The narrator speaks to the reader from a different position altogether. In fact, he implies that between reading and being read, a textual *sensus communis* emerges to link reader and narrator as predicates for "The Book's" untold stories.[23]

His imagined companion's "brief and mighty glance," accompanied by the narrator's "transitory squeezing of his hand," triggers then in "the true reader" the intuition of their connection. The reader "will grasp, accept, recall" the narrator's "radiance" from the depths of "The Book." The narrator points to this "secret" relationship hidden "under the table that divides us." A material boundary that "divides," "table" obscures and protects both reader and narrator so that what is separated on its surface is reunited underneath: they grasp "one another's hands in secret under it." In this moment when reunification occurs, they "recall" a primordial connection, looking past the current world's materiality.

Moreover, primordial connection occurs from within the text where it has been preserved. Reading changes in order for a reader to extract the "Book's" revelation. Its transformation must disrupt communication's narrative. As the reader rearranges "The Book's" words, letters, liberating them from meaning's restraints, both narrator and reader hover over the text; they innovate it.[24] Schulz's model of reading hinges on repeated permutations of a profane "absolute object"; the combining of elements previously separated by meaning forms the "object of contemplation," just like its kabbalistic counterpart. It is paradoxically constitutive to writing but external to the written. It elicits its reader to respond, "here am I," but it does not communicate its meaning.

Implicitly, Schulz's correlation between narrator, and the being associated with "The Book," initially signified by nothingness and Nothingness earlier, is repeated in the action of reading. The narrator cannot be named until he reads "The Book" for himself, discovering among its letters, the narrative he is to inhabit and that act reveals his proper name. Essentially, his name is the product of "writing his own Torah" through the reading of "The Book." His name is contingent on the "innovated text's" existence even though the moment of the name's revelation comes in the second story, "The Age of Genius." This innovated writing issues a commandment to the narrator and reader equally: search for, recover the missing pieces. This is the law. In order to evoke the transcendent, trapped in textual depths, narrator and "Book" discover their names, their connection, through reading's stimulation of immanence.

Once "the Book" is recognized in its immanence, "any *true* reader—and this story is only addressed to him—will understand." In this way, the weight of the sentence shifts to a textual *sensus communis*: the narrator "looks" the reader "in the eye."[25] Thus the nameless narrator declares that both reader and narrator form part of an imagined community, concentrated around their shared experience of "the rapture" of "The Book."

Moving from the shared intuition of "radiance," Schulz's character remembers "The Book's" origin "[s]omewhere in the dawn of childhood, at the first daybreak of life," when "the horizon" grows "bright from its gentle light."[26] The link between "radiance" within the narrator and "The Book's" "gentle light" brightening the horizon suggests that when its emanations extend beyond the text, it transforms the natural world. The narrator remembers it "lay full of glory on Father's desk, and my father, quietly engrossed in it … patiently rubbed … until the blind paper started to blur, to grow opaque, to rave with a blessed premonition."[27] The child witnesses Father's manipulation of the letters. When "patiently rubbed," they lose their forms; and "rave." It indicates an interplay between the "Father" of "Father's desk" and the man who actually handles the book, "rubbing" its "blind" pages: they are not static positions. They change with each innovation. As his "father" handles the text, the pages "blur" until the boy watching him apprehends what is to happen, "a blessed premonition."

He recalls the moments when "alone with The Book, the wind would rustle through its pages and the pictures would rise."[28] As matter changes around him, it loses its permanence. The boundaries between forms collapse and the "wind" stimulates "The Book."

> when the wind quietly paged through those sheets, blowing away colors and shapes, a shudder ran through the columns of its text, releasing among the letters the formations of swallows and skylarks. Thus did page after page fly away, scattering and sinking gently into the landscape, which it saturated with color. Sometimes the Book slept and the wind blew it apart silently like a *centifolia* rose … petal by petal, eyelid by eyelid, all of them blind … dormant, concealing in their core … an azure pupil …[29]

The image of the wind "quietly" leafing through the pages calls to mind the *Zohar's* image of God "reading" His Torah, and writing creation through it.[30] As the "wind" revives the letters, it "unfolds" creation. The "shudder" sutures the "shudder of spirits through matter" in *Cinnamon Shops,* to the son's experience with an innovated text. The wind's animation reverberates through each page's "columns." Although "The Book" signals its kinship to both Talmud with its "columns," and the *Zohar* with its "splendor," these sacred texts are not the site of "The Book's" revelation.[31]

Hence the vehicle for the letters' release is less important than their liberation: for the narrator, redemption of the text—its capacity to create—occurs because of the way the wind hovers unceasingly over its pages, blowing "apart" the pages, "like a *centifolia* rose." As "The Book" falls open, each page flutters into being, "petal by petal." When the "Book sleeps," the wind still continues to stimulate the letters so that the pages "fly away." Their stories sink into "the landscape," bringing color to the world, yet "The Book" still remains "full" of stories.

Depicting the "wind" as the first "*true* reader," the wind stimulates the text, sends a "shiver" through its "columns." As the letters begin to breathe in the wind, with their exhale, flocks of "swallows and skylarks" are created. In their stimulation, their permutation, the letters produce, create a new world. They emanate creation. The material book decomposes or comes apart, and the letters release their phenomena. The new phenomena are the letters' emanations.[32] "Page after page" saturates matter around him and the narrator recalls that he has been a witness at the scene of creation.

The mystical book is forgotten by the narrator as he grows a little older; its memory is displaced by his mother's presence until "I forgot about my Father, my life ran on a new, different track, without holidays and miracles."[33] The memory of "the Book" persists though in his unconscious and one night, it breaks free in a dream in which he is tormented by "the old, forgotten Book."[34] Awakening, he becomes manic, and unintelligible. Incoherent, he "rummages" through his father's library, searching for it.[35] Incapable of communicating "the indescribable thing," to his "stupefied audience," he becomes "disappointed and angry" and finally, he weeps "from impotent despair."[36] His parents hand him book after book, but each one is rejected as a false witness.

His father offers him repeatedly one particular "thick, heavy folio" that should serve as the revelation.[37]

> I opened it. It was the Bible. I beheld on its pages a great migration of animals, floating down the high roads, branching out in processions across a distant land. I saw a sky covered with flocks and fluttering, an enormous, upside-down pyramid whose distant summit was touching the Ark.
> I lifted my eyes, full of reproach, to look at Father.
>
> "You know, Father," I cried, "you very well know; don't hide, don't try to wriggle out of it! This book has betrayed you. Why are you giving me this tainted apocrypha, this thousandth copy, this incompetent forgery? What have you done with the Book?" Father looked away.[38]

Although the son innovates the biblical text, it produces only the expected "great migration of animals." In this way, the Bible constructs, reproduces golems, "familiar" forms, but "the Book" creates new beings. Substituting mimetic representations for "the Book's" living *aggadot*, the Bible signifies a written history. This "tainted apocrypha" reproduces its finished stories—its golems of text—substitutes them for the writing of new beings. In the child's accusation, the Bible is held up as an exemplar of heresy because its stories have already been expressed in time and space; they have already entered history. They are a part of an epistemology that is "incompetent" because it enables the "Father" to "look away." The son lives with the knowledge that "The Book" exists, and that his father hopes to deceive him: its "secret" is withheld from him by his parents.

Thus his father's gift of the Bible reinforces that once "The Book"—its stories—was hidden among that tome's pages. It has been liberated by Father's "rubbing" of the pages, so that "The Book" leaves behind its original repository, an empty husk, proving "The Book's" existence in time and space through its absence, much like a chrysalis bears witness to the existence of a butterfly that is no longer confined within its walls.[39] Its absence testifies to its presence.

When later, his father informs him that "there exist only books. The Book is a myth that we believe in our youth," the narrator has already arrived at his own "conviction": "the image of the Book still burned in my soul with a bright flame, a great, rustling Codex, an agitated Bible through whose pages the wind moved, ransacking it like an immense, crumbling rose."[40] The simile at the line's conclusion picks up on the previous image of "the *centifolia* rose" to suggest the written as an empty crypt. The "wind" destroys the written text in order to liberate its "light."

For the son, heresy imposes time and space on the text, static meaning. The "great, rustling Codex," the "agitated Bible" within him would be imprisoned if its limits were to be rigidly understood as simply history. Thus "The Book" articulates a new obligation for the narrator.

> I knew that the Book is a postulate, that it is a task. I felt on my shoulders the weight of a great mission …. At that time I was already in possession of that scrap of a book, those pitiful remnants that a strange stroke of fate had smuggled into my hands. I carefully concealed my treasure from all eyes, grieving over the profound deterioration of this book about whose crippled remnants I would be incapable of winning anyone's understanding. This is how it happened.
>
> One day that winter, I had caught Adela in the process of cleaning, with a broom in her hand, leaning against a lectern on which a tattered scrap of paper was lying. I bent over her arm …. "Look," she said …. "Is it possible that someone's hair could grow down to the ground? I would like to have hair like that."
>
> I looked at the print. On a large *in folio* sheet was the image of a woman with a rather strong, thickset shape …. From this lady's head flowed an immense pelt of hair, tumbling down heavily from her shoulders, the ends of its thick coils sweeping the ground.[41]

"A postulate …. a task" only he can perform—obey—it is also part of a "great mission." His devotion to it completes a portion of its grander scheme of *tikkun* or repair. The "scrap" he has discovered of the "Book's" revelation, moreover, appears as the "crippled remnants" of a tabloid. It's an abandoned sheet of paper, part of the trash of which the maid Adela intends to rid the house.[42] The tabloid newspaper one might buy for its titillation, emblematically profane, a catalogue of the grotesque, that one disposes of as garbage once desire has been satisfied, emerges as the site of revelation.

The tabloid's image of a woman with hair "tumbling down from her shoulders," so long that it "sweeps" the ground triggers something within the boy so that he knows the "*in folio* sheet" is a page ripped from "The Book."[43] His "treasure" relates a "long story, similar in construction to the story of Job" in which "an act of God" causes the woman to be almost bald. Although she leads "an irreproachable life," she remains cursed with very little hair.[44] Her town and neighbors pray for the curse's removal and finally, she receives the revelation: a "miraculous medicine whose secret she alone knew."[45]

In the tabloids' sensationalism, Josef realizes that he has discovered "the Book," in "its final pages, its unofficial supplement, a rear annex full of waste and rubbish."[46] In fact, the narrator alludes to discarded pages, "unofficial" records full of revelation, but clothed in "waste and rubbish." What has been thrown away, designated as garbage, is in reality, an illegitimate path to redemption.[47] Back in his room, he shakes as he "leafs" through the papers.[48] "Not a single page" is legitimate revelation, yet among the "advertisements and announcements," he sees the liminal outline of other worlds, populated by creatures with "letters" in their mouths, traversing across the folio pages. With the last sheets, he realizes that "The Book" has abandoned "the sphere of everyday affairs" and its writing has moved into "regions of poetry."

Tracing the path of creation through these abandoned pages, he comes to a new realization. The path itself is corrupted because "this wretched document" has fallen "into ever steeper decline" until "disintegrating into scraps," it becomes a "roadless tract of … fraudulent divination."[49] "The Book" is fallen, but its letters still bear their animating force of light. The pages transform before him "into delirious gibberish" and "nonsense."[50] In their heresy, they have become unintelligible, but they are still part of the revelation. He hovers over these pages, still moving from "ecstasy to ecstasy."[51] He is so "engrossed in reading" that he remains in his room, ignoring the world around him.[52] He has finally found "the Authentic, a holy original, even though in such a profound state of humiliation and degradation."[53] However, even in "degradation," "the Authentic" still pulsates with life so that he is "indifferent … to other books!"[54]

The narrator recognizes these mundane "other books" to be limited to a specific space and time.

> For ordinary books are like meteors. Each of them has a single moment, one moment when with a cry it soars like a phoenix, blazing with all its pages. For the sake of that single moment, we love it afterward even though by then it is only ashes. And with bitter resignation, we wander now and again, late at night, through these now-cold pages, shifting with wooden clacking their dead formulas, like rosary beads.[55]

Akin to "meteors," these golem texts articulate only "one moment." Their entire existence moves to speak their singularity. Once it is expressed, it dies and readers are left with "now-cold pages," attempting to animate them with "dead formulas." These "ordinary books" pass into an epistemology of knowledge. They can neither animate nor be innovated. Hence the narrator likens them to "rosary beads," the signifiers of a ritual commemorating death of the sacred.

The analogy prompts Josef to posit a genealogy for these mundane expressions.

> Exegetes of the Book assert that all books aim for the Authentic. They live only a borrowed life that, in the moment of soaring, returns to its ancient source …. books wane but the Authentic grows …. the Authentic lives and grows.[56]

Here too, the son points to a tradition that follows "the Book"; its "exegetes" claim that all books serve "the Authentic" so that they are temporal entities, bound by time and space. When they have expressed themselves, their "borrowed life" recedes back to the hidden "source." In this way, these individual texts die off, while "the Authentic lives and grows." "The Book" is replenished by these discrete texts' "soaring" to the heights of "the Authentic" and falling to "ashes."

"The Book's" animation enables the stories to migrate, to move beyond their initial contexts in order to express new dimensions of the "ancient source." As the narrator marvels at how the creations of "The Book" move between its pages, at times, flying away from it altogether, only to arrive on an unexpected missing page far removed from their original page, and another "unofficial supplement," he encloses himself all the more in these textual worlds where stories transmigrate between page and phenomena. He decrees "The Book's" figures, "Angels of the Countenance" who "forget their mission, and astonished," pretend they have arrived "inside the doors of our kitchens" to ask "for alms."[57]

This casual aside leads Josef then to his most profound description of "The Book." It "unfurls during reading" so that each page's liberation is understood as unfolding, ostensibly by alluding to the "*centifolia* rose" image that crumbles after releasing its ineffable writing.[58] Moreover, each page's porous borders "are open to all fluctuations and flows."[59] These "flows" not only stimulate "the Book" registering creation's pulse, but also enable multiplicity of beings to enter and exit its pages. Through innovation, Josef as a "true reader" performs the profound liberation of textuality so that creation unfolds. Josef recognizes "the transcendent" moving within the text and permutates its words, letters, to release being from its tether. In its liberation, it illuminates a forgotten path, requiring the reader to "journey into the age of genius."[60] The narrator and reader embark on this adventure together "in the name of God."[61]

The "Age of Genius" begins with the explanation that Josef's fear at the end of the "The Book" is due to the transgression of time and space, narrator and reader are about to commit. They unseal their faculties from their lived experiences. Together, they prepare to take an illegitimate path, encompassing events that violate "continuity and succession" because these events "do not have their own place in time"; they have "arrived too late," after "all of time was already distributed, divided, disassembled, and now they've just been left there, unclassified, suspended in the air, homeless and errant."[62] "Unclassifiable," and inimitable, the events are "in the name of God." While reader and narrator travel "down a blind track," the narrator burns the "old folios," "armfuls of old newspapers and diaries," in order to release "the radiance."[63] Josef destroys revelation to force its illumination in the darkness. As he describes in "The Book," these secular pages of print are "like meteors." Their eruptions produce a "flood of dazzling questions with which God is inundating" him.[64] When the pages release their radiance, the son becomes aware of a divine voice, flooding him with questions.

His family watches him in horror, while he feels overwhelmed by "visions" of animals, peoples.[65] They have "crowded in, created roadblocks, until … all the roads and paths were swarming and streaming with parades … the entire country branched out in migrations."[66] The narrator has joined himself to textuality, writing. Previously he witnesses new creation in and out of its pages but now "The Book" encloses him within his room. He is part of its writing. He recognizes himself to be within a pattern, "as in the days of Noah." Akin to the patriarch, the pre-Flood biblical Noah, Josef rearranges the biblical narrative around "these colorful parades."[67] Thus his room "becomes a border and a tollgate. Here they came to a stop, crowded together .... They fidgeted, stamped in place anxiously .... terrified of themselves."[68] His room, filled with new creation, he now wonders what his role in this world is to be? He has presumed that he has been restored as a witness at the scene of creation; however, their terror elicits his sympathy.

> Were they waiting for me to name them, to resolve their enigma that they did not understand? Were they asking me about their name, in order to enter into it and fill it with their essence? Strange monsters arrived—creature questions, creature propositions—and I had to shout and drive them away with my hands. They retreated, lowering their heads and looking from under their brows, and lost themselves in themselves, returned, dissolving into nameless chaos, into a junk room of forms.[69]

As if Eden has become available again, Josef has been restored to an Adamic role. He has come into this world to name these beings that crowd his room. He must "resolve" the enigma of their existence by restoring to them "their name." In that moment, he redeems them because he recognizes their predicates: he assigns them a "name." With this act, they "enter into ... and fill" their names "with their essence."

While he looks at his creation, "strange monsters" attempt to commandeer the name, to come into being. He feels the intensity of their "creature questions, creature propositions." If they can be named, these "strange monsters" can also be redeemed, but the narrator "drives them away" from his creation. They are exiled, condemned, "dissolving into the nameless chaos"; they remain incapable of expressing their forms, a phenomenal excess, glimpsed at and rejected.

The kabbalahs in Schulz's *Sanatorium* are both heretical and orthodox. Josef's desire to be restored to a primordial creation, to inhabit the soul of Adam, is part and parcel of an orthodox kabbalah in which practitioners imagine returning to the scene of creation, to correct past injury there through their innovations. Josef's traverse of the illegitimate path back to paradise resonates too with the heretical kabbalah. In the tension between these two kabbalahs, Schulz, like Heine, advances several "novel" revisions.

They emerge in the chapter, "Spring," when Josef realizes that his path can "lead no further."[70] He sees its terminus as "the end of our words, which are already becoming hallucinatory, delirious, insane."[71] As if he stands at the PaRDeS, with Akiva, with Kafka, "before the Law," Josef observes that his "words" break down, lose purchase on communication, but "beyond their border," traces of "the boundless and ineffable .... begin."[72] Beyond the boundary of words "that dark, boundless element" reverberates.[73] In this other dimension, "the word disintegrates into elements and dissolves, returns to its etymology" and formlessness.[74] Josef witnesses the letters' absorption into "the immensity," their return "into its depths, into its dark root." The pronouns underscore that the letters belong to "boundless" depths. They write from the "depths."

The letters cling to the "root" so that "many tales and ancient stories, pile up under the sod."[75] "Sod" and *sod* intertwine: matter protects its "secret." The letters are filled with "tales ... stories" that threaten to break through the surface, "sod." In the role of a prophet, Josef shifts to command the "true reader."

> Bury one's face .... and in a moment it will be totally dark, soundless .... Then one must press one's eyes like leeches to the blackest darkness, apply light force, squeeze them through what is impenetrable, shove them straight into the dense soil—and suddenly there we are, at the finish line, on the other side of things, we are in the innermost place .... And we see .... the whole interior is pulsing with light .... the darkness is marbled, the wandering, luminous ravings of matter.[76]

The force of the commandment is to immerse the senses in darkness, to "squeeze them through what is impenetrable." Demanding that the reader "shove" the eyes "into the dense soil," the narrator promises the reward will be the reader's arrival "on the other side of things." Essentially, Josef commands the senses to darkness in order to adhere to "the other side," the hidden, "innermost place," where the entire abyss "is pulsing with light." Once the senses are saturated with the abyss' darkness, its "depths," the reader sees a world of supernal lights. Schulz repeats a kabbalistic pattern of creation in which uncontrolled light comingles with the "luminous ravings of matter" within the void. In other words, Schulz's heretical kabbalah builds consciously on an exile in darkness that leads to paradise's entrance, forgotten among the detritus of exile. Moreover, the journey through the abyss is the only way to find the hidden world of "pulsing" light.[77] The foreclosed path reappears because the reader immerses the self in the darkness and filth of rejected revelation. Supernal lights illuminate this illegitimate path; even in the void, their radiance persists.

This heretical kabbalah allows Josef to connect his engagement with "the Authentic," the innovated reading he proposes, to an occluded aim of the unconscious dream world.

> In just the same way .... when we sleep, cut off from the world .... in a reverse pilgrimage back to oneself—we also see .... Thus does regression play out in us .... a retreat into the depths, a reverse journey to the root.[78]

Subtly, the narrator shifts from the discovery of light at the end of the innovated path, to link it to "a reverse pilgrimage back to oneself." He recounts that during sleep, the mind is released from its duties and "we" journey back to "the root" of our origins. In this way, he traces the inscription of creation within the mind calling "us" to "retreat into the depths," to make a "reverse journey" back to a primordial beginning. Hence Josef's declaration that when humans perform "regression" during sleep, they remember "a reverse journey," *tzimtzum*'s unconscious inscription.

Harold Bloom posits that this recollection haunts human existence; it is "the image of a wandering exile .... propelled onward .... along the frontiers between mind and body .... illuminated only .... by the strong light of the canonical .... the light of the perfection that destroys."[79] The "pulsing light" inscribed within human existence draws us further and further away from creation, the origin, until we return to it through an alternative route on which we ignorantly travel, unaware of the consequences. Our inability to recognize a path inscribed within our unconscious proposes that this "illegitimate" path is still "evil"—we traverse evil to find ourselves redeemed.

"Interminable Stories"

The narrator follows the path to a "roadless tract" and discovers he must abandon his world, "bury" his face in the "dark, soundless .... innermost place." In order to discover that which drives him unconsciously, bringing him ever closer to that "journey to the root," he must recede into matter.[80] While its pattern invokes "A Treatise on Mannequins or the Second Book of Genesis," in *Cinnamon Shops,* the son repositions the pattern to evoke a recollection of the original genesis at which he could not have been present, yet appears to him in dream.

> Thus do we branch out into the depths of anamnesis, shuddering from the subterranean shivers that run across us, and dreaming subcutaneously beneath the entire phantasmal surface. Because only above in the light .... we are a trembling, articulate cluster of melodies .... in the depths we disintegrate once again into .... babble, into a host of interminable stories.[81]

Mapping a new path in the dream world and one that is intermingled with the abyss' roots, narrator and reader "branch out into the depths of anamnesis." Following these roots, he feels "the subterranean shivers that run through us" as if Being "hovers" over him and all matter. In an echo of the biblical Genesis, the boundary between "true reader" and Being conflates so that the narrator understands that he too is being read by an other. The "true reader" accompanies him into these "subterranean shivers" permeating matter—and creation continues to "branch out."

It leads Josef to bracket existence between two stages, "in the light .... we are a trembling cluster of melodies," but within "the depths we disintegrate once again into .... babble, into a host of interminable stories."[82] Being extracts "forms" from matter and brings them into light. In their creation, a "cluster of melodies" is expressed: a music beyond the human senses that reverberates. When these songs cease, we recede into "a host of interminable stories."

Translators have struggled with this particular line. In the older Wienewska English translation of *Sanatorium,* Wienewska defines *nieskończonych* as "unfinished."[83] Her translation implies that in the darkness of "the depths," the stories remain incomplete. Readers might think the stories become complete when they emerge in the light, when they gain their human predicates above. Schulz's belief that human interiority consists of disintegration and chaos undermines the idea of completion and Wienewska recognizes this by noting that humans remain a "jumble of tunes." In a sense, Wienewska thinks the translation through Kafka, where condemned to know there is music in the universe, humans never hear it. Eventually we recede into disintegration, "black murmurs, confused purring, a multitude of unfinished stories."[84]

With Wienewska's translation, the effect of the line reinforces life as a property of the light because in disintegration, we return to incompletion. We become golems again.[85] Completion of the story only occurs in living. Thus receding into the depth or abyss is a return to being "unfinished," waiting for another story to which the self can affix. All the weight of the passage suggests that human existence, consciousness itself perhaps, is the necessary predicate to being. We exist as "unfinished stories" before and after consciousness; each individual's responsibility is to finish a story. In the recession into incompleteness, Schulz posits a model of human existence as the attempt to finish one story since each individual's existence is tethered to a narrative in need of a particular human ending. "Unfinished stories" struggle repeatedly to come to light and thereby complete themselves. This produces an echo with *Cinnamon Shops* where the Father extols, as I note earlier, the affinity between golem and human.

Levine treats the same passage somewhat differently: "we are a trembling, articulate cluster of melodies .... in the depths we disintegrate once again into black muttering, into babble, into a host of *interminable* stories" (my emphasis). Levine removes "jumble" and freights "cluster of melodies" as an articulation of a music, tenuous true, but nevertheless, voiced. Taking *nieskończonych* to mean "interminable," Levine shifts the line subtly to reflect that the stories within human substance are "endless" or "infinite": they are "interminable" in the sense that they continue to produce their narratives and they can never be completed. They continue to write themselves into existence. They do not end. We are the products of this endless writing; we exist only for the length of time that our bodies last, but the writing that produces us continues into eternity. We are writing although we often aim to be written.

Ironically, both translations reflect an association that Schulz makes about human existence and the transmigration of the writing that produces us. The drama of this moment enables Schulz to advance a theory of the transmigration of the soul, its *metempsychosis*, but instead of identifying it as the soul, he identifies it as writing, "an *aggadah* drive" that motivates, underpins human existence. Borrowing from Bloom, Norman Finkelstein identifies it to be a part of the "ritual of new creation" in Jewish tradition. It is writing's "repetition." Attempting to finish the story, writing pulls Josef into unconscious "depths," the abyss of beings.

Thus the collection, *Sanatorium under the Sign of the Hourglass*, describes Josef's "interminable" stories writing themselves as a "cluster of melodies" until arriving at "Loneliness," the collection's penultimate narrative. Josef, now a pensioner, returns to his childhood room where he once innovated the secret "Book," and liberated creation from its pages.[86] On his return to the room, he alludes to it haunting his childhood. He names it the *Book of Creation*, or *Sefer Yetsirah*, the Jewish mystical text that now has "bricked" him into his room again.[87] It has closed off all other forms of life and sustenance. In his "dead room," he metamorphoses into a "careless field mouse, living from day to day .... confident in my talent as a starveling."[88] He presses the metaphor to declare that even if he starves to death, hunger cannot destroy him. "The Book's" writing sustains him.

> at the tail end of the Book of Creation—I will manage to live on nothing." And so I do live on nothing in this dead room .... only I, an immortal mouse, a lonely posthumous child, am rustling about in this dead room, endlessly running ....[89]

Even in his diminished state, he relies on the promise of the *Book of Creation*. He has crossed over to "the other side"; thus he can "live on nothing." Nothingness conflates with "The Book's" "Authentic Nothingness" so that Josef, aware that he has been "walled" into the "Book," recognizes he is severed from the world outside. He realizes that by forfeiting history, Josef consents to being sealed into *Yetsirah's* writing. He stands at a crossroads: he can remain in history, be written, or he can be writing, enclosed within "The Book's" pages. A profound loneliness forces him to "imagine doors, good, old doors," to reopen his story. Writing takes place in desire's fulfillment. Instead of sinking into matter, the matter of his room, instead of receding into the "unfinished stories" of the abyss, Josef liberates his "cluster of melodies" and returns to the light.

In *Cinnamon Shops*, the compendia's liberated entities remain golems of text; they last only as long as the Father reads. In *Sanatorium*, they infuse matter with new creation when they are freed from their existence in "the Book." In this respect, they articulate a kinship between writing and reading. Limited to a textual existence on the page, they remain "unfinished" narratives, but freed and released into the elements, they are endless, "interminable stories."[90] In this way, stories continue to write the universe.

7

The "Absolute Object" in Argentino's Basement

Like Bruno Schulz, Borges' fictive use of the kabbalah engages a range of kabbalahs.[1] Borges too takes up the golem and the creative power of the Hebrew letters; he too recognizes the power as well as the inevitable limitations of the *Sefer Yetsirah*, the *Book of Creation*. Akin to Schulz, he embeds the formal triggers of these kabbalistic projects in his narratives, and in their repetition, he inscribes a liminal crack in his writing, a small rupture, the tiniest disclosure of transcendence.

In this way, as Jaime Alazraki observes, "Borges has turned us all into inquisitive Kabbalists" because these disclosures focus our attention repeatedly on the "secret" writing we hope to discover, the mystical meaning "subtly intimated between the lines."[2] While scholars, like Edna Aizenberg, Saul Sosnowski, Jaime Alazraki, often recognize the disparate kabbalistic traditions that Borges innovates, two thirteenth-century sources in particular, Abraham Abulafia's *Hokhmath ha-Tseruf* or "combination of the letters" and *The Zohar*, appear to dominate Borges' use of the kabbalah in "El Aleph," his iconic short story.[3] By repeating kabbalistic patterns in that narrative, Borges reopens an older archive of stories in order to reveal the suggestion of another writing.[4]

Edna Aizenberg recognizes that in his "repetition of certain timeless fables and metaphors," the texts transform into an "original" writing.[5] In this respect, the "repetition" of stories from older traditions could suggest a strategy employed by many writers; in that register, the modifier "original" denotes simply a representation of an object, a story, already known, already intelligible to readers, but repositioned by the writer to produce something new. She adds that in Borges' critical methodologies—the structure of his "literary universe"—the pattern, the "repetition," and innovation of stories derive from "the Bible."[6] With this statement, though, the valence of "original" shifts to suggest Borges transmits "original" writing. If the Bible is the archive of the stories from which the writer draws, then, Aizenberg has placed him in the role of a prophet. His writing is not a retelling of the tradition, but rather its innovation. As such, it excavates new ground; it pulls outs "original" writing, previously unimaginable. Intriguingly, she alludes to his project as an innovation of *aggadot*.

In this way, she suggests Borges adopts aspects of the kabbalah. The innovation of *aggadot* is the foundation of *The Zohar* in which the kabbalist innovates biblical narrative, extracting from it previously unknown aspects of the revelation. In Abulafia, when he develops his "prophetic kabbalah," he is commanded to "write something new."[7] Since Borges reads the biblical stories purposively, he gleans patterns that have awaited him specifically, just as they awaited Abulafia and the Zoharist, so many centuries earlier in Spain.[8] The patterns have been hidden within Torah itself and Borges extracts them from the stories or shells of text. Borges looks to parse an unarticulated aspect of something deeper, and constitutive of the writing itself, to make legible something previously unwritten in time and space, yet immanent in the innovated text.

Thus the stakes of Borges' deployment of aspects of kabbalah resonate with these two projects in which the Hebrew letters, liberated from human attempts to stabilize their meanings, form patterns of the Name. In that moment, these patterns illuminate writing within the Divine flow of Being. The kabbalist reads or receives the patterns, liberating them. In their liberation, they inscribe a path in Being that Abulafia believes can be followed by "skipping and jumping" from "sphere to sphere," traveling the trail of the letters, their light, into the Transcendental Flow or *shefa*.[9] For him, the first step is a "prophetic ecstasy" that enables the kabbalist to become an active agent for the duration of the experience.

As a consequence of it, a mystical disassociation occurs in which the acolyte "encounters his own self confronting and addressing him."[10] Suddenly liberated, the self "remembers" or becomes aware that the path to the *shefa* is imprinted on the soul, an inscription in the soul previously "forgotten" or displaced by the faculties.[11] The soul also becomes an interlocutor of the human agent. When the kabbalist "encounters" the self, he actually meets his soul "restored" to him.[12] However, in order for that "encounter" to take place, the soul must be "unsealed" from the faculties.

According to Abulafia, the soul has been cut off from the mind because God has sealed the faculties purposely from it. As a result, the mind preoccupies itself with the phenomena of existence.[13] In its focus on phenomena, the mind organizes itself around time and space. The categories of time and space inhibit the soul through their distraction of the mind. This distraction prevents cognition from slipping into the depths of Divine timelessness—the flow—and the subsequent judgment that redemption has been lost since the moment of creation.

Abulafia's program intervenes at this moment to declare that the kabbalist "having climbed the … last step of the mystical ladder … consciously perceives and becomes part of the world of divine light, whose radiance illuminates his thoughts and heals his heart."[14] In that moment, he gains "the stage of prophetic vision in which the ineffable mysteries of the divine Name and the whole glory of its realm reveal themselves to the illuminate."[15]

Abulafia's "prophetic kabbalah" implies a change in human ontology for that moment.[16] To that end, Abulafia frames his project as an innovation of the biblical "call" to the prophet Isaiah.[17] He dreams that God calls him twice and he responds with the biblical *hi-ne-ni* or "Here I am."[18] In his dream, his adoption of "the call narrative" introduces a wholly new aim or mission. Instead of the original *aggadah*'s ending with God's promise to Abraham about his descendants, Abulafia is instructed "to write something new."[19] The unique command not only reveals a new dimension of sacred writing, an aspect of the immanent text that has not been known before, but also indicates the re-authorization of the role of prophecy in Abulafia.[20]

"Prophetic kabbalah" proposes to unseal the mind by focusing it on an "absolute object, one capable of stimulating the soul's deeper life and freeing it from ordinary perceptions."[21] By unsealing the faculties, the human mind stops holding mental space together. It ends effectively the segmenting of Being, imposed by the mind's cognitive limits.[22] Since the faculties no longer constrain the world within to conform to the world without, the "absolute object" liberates the soul because the absolute object "stimulates" the soul's response to *it*.[23] In the absence of the faculties, mimesis forfeits its phenomenal register, engaging instead with the world of "absolute objects."

In the suppression of time and space, Abulafia's "absolute object" directs the mind to another dimension, one emptied of human existence. Scholem describes it as the moment when the boundary between human existence and the dimension of the Divine is erased.

> All that which occupies the natural self of man must either be made to disappear or must be transformed in a such a way as to render it transparent for the inner spiritual reality, whose contours will become perceptible through the customary shell of natural things.[24]

With the boundary between the dimensions made "transparent," the "contours" of this "inner spiritual reality" are revealed. Their edges exceed human cognition of time and space. Positing this "reality" as the horizon to which the kabbalist must journey, Scholem explains how Abulafia ascertains the Hebrew letters to be "absolute objects."

> Basing himself upon the abstract and non-corporeal nature of script, he develops a theory of mystical contemplation of letters and their configurations, as the constituents of God's name. For this is the real .... and the peculiarly Jewish object of mystical contemplation: the Name of God, which is something absolute, because it reflects the hidden meaning and totality of existence; the Name through which everything else acquires its meaning and which to the human mind has no concrete, particular meaning of its own .... Abulafia expounds a peculiar discipline .... *Hokhmath ha-Tseruf*, ie "science of the combination of the letters."[25]

The Hebrew letters are "abstract," "non-corporeal," and most significantly, "the constituents of God's name." Scholem identifies them to be the linchpin to Abulafia's *Hokhmath ha-Tseruf*: the "configurations" of the kabbalist's "contemplation." The kabbalist permutates the letters and in their permutations, they write "the Name of God," even though the adherent does not know that Name, only that the letters are constitutive of it. Moreover, "the Name of God .... reflects the hidden meaning and totality of existence." The letters embody it so that theoretically every time the letters are repeated, they voice the "Name of God."[26] Every time they are written, they express the Name of God. Whenever they appear, they imprint the Name of God on matter.[27] Scholem declares the Name to be a "peculiarly Jewish object of contemplation"; by this designation, he hints at an historical preoccupation of the kabbalah: it is a letter phenomenology.

Joseph Dan explains this property of the Hebrew letters as their "creative—rather than communicative" essence.[28] They "preexisted in God before creation"; they are the sounds of Divine Speech, "the actual word of God in its original language."[29] Thus they are the "word of God as actually uttered by him even before humanity was created."[30] The realization produces the Jewish belief that "God's utterance was not a semantic one: there were no people, nobody could be listening."[31] Dan concludes with the profound, "the very utterance was the deed," and he declares that "[O]nce language is recognized as an aspect of infinite divine wisdom, it cannot have finite meanings .... so one cannot glean the real, finite semantic message of any word of God."[32] The letters are active in creation: they are constitutive of it because they bear within themselves something more than their lexical, or orthographical status that we have accorded them.

The critical point of this discursus from Borges to Abulafia underscores not only how Abulafia's "letter phenomenology" becomes an integral part of Borges' kabbalistic "literary universe" exemplified by the short story, "El Aleph," but also how an "absolute object" induces in the narrative's fictive Borges character the realization that the written cannot substitute for "En Soph."[33] Borges merges the Zoharist's understanding of "I" (*Ani*) and "En Soph" (*Ain*) in the Abulafian experience of "prophetic ecstasy" in order to ground why he denies the experience at the end of the story.

From the start of "El Aleph," the reader encounters a fictional Borges who relates how the *aleph* comes to dominate his faculties.[34] It suggests the character's account to be both a "received" and "transmitted" revelation; it mimics the reception and transmission of kabbalah itself. In this way, the fictional Borges "encounters his own self .... addressing him," an encounter that we witness as readers.[35]

The story is ostensibly about the fictional Borges' unrequited love for Beatriz Viterbo who has recently died and his willingness to tolerate her insufferable cousin, Carlos Argentino Daneri, in order to be close to the place where she lived. Every year after her death on her birthday, Borges returns to her family home where he dines and drinks Armagnac to her memory with her cousin. He describes his annual performance as "an irreproachable and perhaps unavoidable act of politeness" that he fulfills because "now that she was dead, I could devote myself to her memory."[36]

To "justify" his regular visits to Daneri's home, Borges brings "modest offerings of books."[37] However, he discovers "months later" that his gifts "lay around unopened." There they sit ignored in Daneri's house. This anecdote sets the tone then of the narrative: Argentino is neither a man of books nor does he recognize their significance. He does not valorize texts although he holds "a minor position in an unreadable library out on the edge of the Southside of Buenos Aires."[38]

Over the course of these annual dinners, Borges characterizes Argentino to be "authoritative, but unimpressive." Although his Italian forebears are at "a remove of two generations," Daneri still affects "the Italian 'S'" in his speech and uses "demonstrative Italian gestures."[39] He is particularly self-absorbed and coupled to the earlier awareness that Daneri possesses but has never read any of Borges' gifts, Borges sketches a dilettante; Argentino pontificates "fatuously" on "meaningless" topics, and "pointless analogies."[40] In his obsessions with current fads, he smugly assumes the profundity of his own conclusions.

Surprised by Argentino's "foolish .... ideas," Borges recommends humorously that he "write them down."[41] The recommendation elicits Daneri's declaration that he has already "opened the floodgates of his fancy" to produce "the Proem, or Augural Canto, or, more simply the Prologue Canto of the poem on which he had been working for many years now."[42] Daneri imagines himself to be a great writer.

The fictional Borges' recollection establishes that Argentino has no real commitment to art; he attributes a depth to himself although he has no justification to do so. Furthermore, Borges' suggestion to "write" his fantasies down strikes Daneri as confirmation that Borges recognizes his literary "better" before him. While he reads his poem to Borges, he punctuates each stanza with "his own approval and .... lengthy explications."[43] Borges concludes, "there was nothing remarkable" about the work.[44] After hours of Argentino's endless reading and explication, Borges finally escapes "at midnight."[45]

Consequently, he stops coming to the house; he eventually forgets even his concern that Beatriz's cousin might demand his help in promoting the poem. After a lengthy period of time, Argentino's call to solicit his help in another matter surprises him. The bar next door plans to demolish the Daneri/Vitterbo house. Borges is struck by the intensity of Daneri's anger; he threatens that if the owners "persist" in this "outrage," he will sue them for damages.[46] Suddenly, his voice becomes "impersonal," and he confesses to Borges that he cannot finish the Canto without the house because the house possesses a secret related to the poem. Beneath it, "in the cellar, there was an aleph .... one of the points in space that contains all other points."[47] This treasure will not only be destroyed by the bar's expansion, but his poem will also remain incomplete. The fame he imagines will never occur.

Puzzled by Daneri's declaration of what an "aleph in the cellar" signifies, Borges listens to the rest of the man's account of its discovery.

> "It's in the cellar under the dining room," he went on, so overcome by his worries that he forgot to be pompous. "It's mine—mine. I discovered it when I was a child, all by myself. The cellar stairway is so steep that my aunt and uncle forbade my using it, but I'd heard someone say there was a world down there. I found out later they meant an old-fashioned globe of the world, but at the same time I thought they were referring to the world itself. One day when no one was home I started down in secret, but I stumbled and fell. When I opened my eyes, I saw the Aleph."[48]

What strikes Borges first is the loss of "pompous" affect when Daneri relates his "worries." The memory of his childhood discovery of the mysterious "world" in the cellar is joined to his aunt and uncle's prohibition against entering it. Its staircase is too "steep" for the boy to climb in the dark, but after he hears a rumor of a "world down there," their rule for his safety transforms into a law that demands its violation. In this way, the depths of the house signify both a place forbidden to him and the mystery of another "world." The child's imagined transgression leads him "in secret" to climb down the stairs in darkness, but inevitably, Carlos Argentino "stumbled and fell."

Evoking the pattern of the biblical *Genesis*, Argentino presents his discovery as something to which he is entitled—"it is mine"—and he possesses it "all by myself." He imagines it to be something the adults keep for themselves.[49] His desire to know their secret causes his fall. However, his transgression is also the instance of his revelation: after he falls, he sees "the Aleph." He *knows* the secret hidden in the cellar. It is his prize after "falling."

Borges' ignorance elicits from the man more information. He explains that it is "the only place on earth where all places are—seen from every angle, each standing clear, without any confusion or blending."[50] The *aleph* allows the individual to experience omniscience, to see "from every angle." The letter emanates this vision so that the individual, in proximity to it, draws from the emanation, a transcendence, the clarity of which confirms the special nature of the individual. Daneri admits he keeps his secret revelation to himself, returning regularly, to the cellar to gaze at his prized *aleph*.[51] His possession relies on his aunt and uncle being unaware of his actions. Their lack of knowledge preserves his possession.

Although Borges suggests that Argentino's childhood recollection could be flawed, Daneri accuses him of a "closed mind" that can never know the "truth."[52] Borges' disbelief compels him nevertheless to insist on going to the cellar and seeing Daneri's mysterious treasure for himself. He intends to prove him wrong.

As he races to the house, he concludes that "Carlos Argentino was a madman as were all the Viterbos." In the knowledge of their weakness, he is "filled …. with spiteful elation": he recognizes the insanity in Argentino.[53] Up to this point, neither the fictive Borges nor Daneri elicits any kind of identification with the reader; the story is humorous, but not exceptionally provocative. Borges' interest in humiliating Daneri reciprocates Daneri's own condescension toward Borges. In fact, the possibility of exposing Daneri's delusions compels Borges to rush to the house, if only to reenact his host's "fall." There is no revelation in the cellar.

After his arrival, Borges receives precise instructions from Daneri on the requirements for seeing the *aleph*. The pattern for seeing the *aleph* resonates with the Abulafian method. Borges must enter the darkness of the cellar, lie on his back, and focus his vision on the "nineteenth step."[54] He also must be "alone," and although Daneri will lead him into the space, he will have to seal him, alone, into the darkness by closing the cellar's trapdoor.

As a last caveat, his host underscores that if Borges does not see the *aleph*, his "incapacity will not invalidate what [Daneri] has experienced": it will only certify Borges' ignorance in relation to Daneri's superior sensitivity.[55] As he leaves Borges, sealed in the cellar, he adds that soon enough Borges will "babble with *all* of Beatriz's images."[56] The sentence intimates something unexpected, and potentially a threat.

As Borges hurriedly descends into the cellar, accompanied by his host, he registers that the cellar is "barely wider than the stairway"; in fact, it is more like a "pit" or an abyss.[57] Instead of looking for the *aleph*, he tries unsuccessfully to find the globe that prompts Argentino the child to descend initially into the cellar's darkness. Daneri breaks the silence and hands him a canvas sack, "folded …. in two," telling him to lay down on the sack, at a specific place, and "there you'll lie, feeling ashamed and ridiculous."[58] For Borges to see the abyss' treasure, he must enter its darkness, feel "ashamed," isolated, and "ridiculous." He must feel some aspect of unknown threat that promises *pleroma*, and he must be cognizant that he transgresses a law he does not know.

The whole story hinges on this encounter between the fictive Borges and the mysterious Hebrew letter, the *aleph*, how it transforms him for the duration of his experience with it.

> I arrive now at the ineffable core of my story. And here begins my despair as a writer. All language is a set of symbols whose use among its speakers assumes a shared past. How, then, can I translate into words the limitless Aleph, which my floundering mind can scarcely encompass?[59]

Sequestered alone in the cellar, he recalls "the ineffable core of his story," implying that something immanent within the story motivates events outside of it.[60] Humans want to reduce the *aleph* to a lexical object. In this way, Borges reframes the text's construction around "the ineffable," an agency he does not control. It is an inexpressible "core" that is distinct from the events his character has related up to this point. From an intuition of something that exceeds the actual narrative, the fictive Borges ponders his awareness of a "world" within the story, constitutive of it, but external to language's "shared past." If the short story is a palimpsest of another writing, then, the fictive Borges might also be the palimpsest of another writer. Implicitly, Borges' character recognizes that language as the medium of the text's communication has become invalidated because of what he sees. The inexpressible has displaced the story of his relationship with Daneri, his affair with Beatriz. By evoking a "creative—rather than communicative" essence, the "ineffable" writes another story from within "the petty rivalry" of Borges and Daneri.[61]

In "despair," he wonders how to "translate into words the limitless Aleph," that his "floundering mind can scarcely encompass?" His admission implies that his faculties have ceased to legislate his cognitive experience. In Spanish, the line moves decisively into a kabbalistic register: *¿como transmitir a los otros el infinito Aleph, que mi temerosa memoria apenas abarca?*"[62] By using the infinitive *transmitir*, Borges suggests that in his reception of the "infinite aleph," he adopts the obligation to "transmit to others." Moreover, his "fearful memory" can scarcely "encompass" the received revelation. With "the infinite" saturating his human memory, in that moment, Borges becomes more than a writer. He loses control of the narrative and transforms into its instrument; that is, it writes through him and he inhabits the role of its prophet. Borges recognizes that he is obligated to "write" and that likewise, he is obligated to fail at writing it. Juxtaposed to Daneri, who hides his treasure, hoarding it for himself, and reproducing its secret for his own gain, Borges emerges as a redeemed failure who intuits the presence of the "other writing," but who fails to reproduce it.

As he contemplates his failure before the *aleph*, he realizes his dilemma has only ever been experienced by those individuals who have been deemed "mystics."[63] They alone have experienced something "analogous," a "trance," and their recourse to that problem of incommunicability has been "to fall back on symbols," layering the experience with signifiers of a code that barely "encompasses" the revelation.[64] These analogous experiences prompt his rejection because if "the gods might grant me a similar metaphor," "the ineffable" would be "contaminated by literature, by fiction."

Literature absorbs representation, through mimesis, reducing it to the known. A simulacrum, an idol, would substitute for Divine Being or Divine writing.[65] It would propose an image, captured in text, frozen in time and space, a false god of the literary, its symbols signifying its permanence.

Simultaneously, Borges experiences an ontological metamorphosis in which Divine writing rewrites him for the brief duration of his proximity to the *aleph*. When he attempts to write the "impossible," its representation falters in its stability because "any listing of an endless series is doomed to be infinitesimal."[66] He might "lavish" signifiers on human experience, yet language always fails. The writer always testifies to failure. The contrast between Daneri's "Canto" and Borges' failure is erased in the knowledge that human understanding cannot recuperate "one single instant" of the "millions of acts both delightful and awful" he sees in the *aleph*.[67] Although he sees everything "simultaneously," his attempt to "transcribe" the experience is condemned to time and space; it becomes "successive, because language is successive."[68] Borges uses *transcribiré* to suggest that in his transmission of the encounter, an attempt to just record what he receives, Borges is still condemned to language and language follows a sequence. It reflects cognition's organization around its two defining categories, time and space.

It prompts the fictional Borges to finally "recollect" the experience for the readers now bound to the story.[69]

> On the back part of the step, toward the right, I saw a small iridescent sphere of almost unbearable brilliance. At first I thought it was revolving; then I realised that this movement was an illusion created by the dizzying world it bounded. The Aleph's diameter was probably little more than an inch, but all space was there, actual and undiminished. Each thing (a mirror's face, let us say) was infinite things, since I distinctly saw it from every angle of the universe.[70]

The *aleph*, "a small iridescent sphere of almost unbearable brilliance," appears to "revolve." Borges realizes his perception is "an illusion." In his attempt to define the "object" exhibited before him, through his categories of time and space, he experiences the *aleph* as chaos, a "dizzying world."[71] Its inexpressible "vertiginous spectacles" trigger physiological and cognitive reactions within him.[72]

Although the *aleph* or "sphere" is "probably little more than an inch," he experiences "all space" there, "without diminishing its size."[73] As the events of human history multiply within the *aleph* and are reflected back to him, he "lists" each one until he arrives at images from the archive of his own experiences, "a summer house in Adrogué .... a copy of the first English translation of Pliny .... and all at the same time .... each letter on each page (as a boy, I used to marvel that the letters in a closed book did not get scrambled and lost overnight)."[74] He recognizes the child who sees "each letter" alive in the *aleph* as cotemporaneous to the Borges whose love affair ends with "the rotted dust and bones that had once deliciously been Beatriz Viterbo."[75] Concentrating itself on the fictive Borges, the *aleph* exhibits to him "the circulation of my own dark blood."[76] The entire description alternates between "I saw" and discrete images, the predicates of human existence, reflected back to him by the *aleph*. The piling up of these strings of images, interrupted only by Borges' "I," produces a sense of vertiginous speed, increasing with each event's intuited proximity to Borges. As Borges attempts to follow the *aleph* and "each thing" it exhibits before him, he realizes the *aleph* inscribes matter with its "name."

The fictional Borges depicts the experience as one familiar to kabbalists: he witnesses all of creation, all of time and space, within the letter itself. Moreover, being is exhibited before him unsegmented, with "each thing" expressing its place in the infinite; it is akin to "a mirror's face" except reflected back to Borges is the inscription of "infinite things" within the thing itself. He sees time and space "from every angle of the universe." The "illusion" of a multiplicity—the chaos within him—is rewritten before him as the expression of a singularity.[77]

> I saw the Aleph from every point and angle, and in the Aleph I saw the earth and in the earth the Aleph and in the Aleph the earth …. I felt dizzy and wept, for my eyes had seen that secret and conjectured object whose name is common to all men but which no man has looked upon—the unimaginable universe.[78]

In its reflection of the *aleph*'s ontology, Borges witnesses "the Aleph from every point and angle, and in the Aleph I saw the earth and in the earth the Aleph and in the Aleph the earth." Instead of refracting light, mediated by the external lens of time and space, the *aleph* discloses its infinitude. From its boundaries, the *aleph*'s emanations make perceptible the intuition of the transcendent for the Borges character. Hinting that the fictive Borges has been transformed from the petty writer who hopes to humiliate Argentino into a witness at the moment of creation, he speaks now to himself and to us from the state of his metamorphosis. In Abulafian terms, the fictive Borges confronts Borges the writer as he struggles to "write something new." It is the mystical moment of disassociation that attests to the soul's liberation and the incapacity of the faculties to transmit that liberation. In fact, the transformation changes the whole purpose of Borges' life as a writer: he becomes a prophet obligated to testify to another writing in the text, in him, in the universe.

In a *Zoharist* register, Borges' repeated "I saw the Aleph and in the Aleph the earth" has followed the "passage from ain to ani …. the transformation by which the Nothing passes through the progressive manifestation of its essence in the sefiroth, into the I—a dialectical process whose thesis and antithesis begin and end in God."[79] Each time Borges begins from the position of "I saw," he moves between "ani" and "ain"; through these positions, he gazes at the *aleph* in order to produce "I saw." Since *Ain* or "En Sof" refers to the Hidden God or "Nothingness," and *ani* refers to the Divine "I" within the sephirotic tree, Borges reproduces the pattern of climbing the tree or "jumping from sphere to sphere." For the Zoharist, the ascent and descent of the tree is done to stimulate Divine Being: it triggers creation. For the Abulafian, moving between spheres reflects the kabbalist's entrance into *shefa*. For Borges, the pattern attests to his illegitimacy. Humans, no matter how gifted, are not permitted to articulate *ain-ani* in time and space.

The *aleph*'s magnitude overcomes Borges; he feels "dizzy." He weeps because of "that secret and conjectured object whose name is common to all men but which no man has looked upon—the unimaginable universe." The English phrasing suggests a *sensus communis*, shared between humankind, and emanating from the *aleph* in that "all men" bear a common sense of something indeterminate and outside themselves.[80] The translation freights Borges' awareness that although the "secret" is common to all, the world continues without knowledge of it, and this enables a reader to assume that at the end of the story when Borges denies seeing the *aleph* to Argentino, he expresses its loss somewhat ambivalently. No one is entitled to the *aleph*.[81]

The phrasing in Spanish accents though a contrapuntal relationship between the *aleph* and matter in that the "eyes" see both entities "in various combinations."[82] While the English translation shares the intensification conveyed in Spanish, "in the Aleph I saw the earth and in the earth the Aleph and in the Aleph the earth," the Spanish implies almost a dialectical relationship, in which the Aleph and the earth switch places continuously with each other in his vision.[83] The speed of their alternation not only exhibits them becoming synonymous with each other, but also reflects their many combinations, the permutations of multiplicity in the *aleph*'s singularity.[84] To return this to a kabbalistic register, the revelation indicates that the illusion of matter's multiple forms is an emanation from the *aleph*. The faculties produce the illusion of time and space and that illusion insinuates itself in the mind as the diachronic, synchronic segments of reality.

The English translation emphasizes *aleph*'s repetition to imitate the intensity and speed of the character's experience, the rapidity of the *aleph*'s permutations of matter in creation. However, in freighting a sense of the world around Borges spinning out of control, plunging him into vertigo, the translation leads the reader to interpret that Borges weeps because of the intensity of the experience. The Spanish produces though another possibility: Borges' realization that the boundary between the *aleph* and the phenomenal has been erased; he has experienced that which should have been foreclosed to him. The *aleph* overwhelms, invades, occupies his senses and like Akiva's companion, ben Zoma, before the PaRDeS, they threaten to drive him insane unless he answers the call to transmit the revelation.[85]

Thus Borges intuits his physiological reaction in relation to the revelation of the *aleph*'s illegitimate possession, in which the "name" is used by "men" who "appropriate" it, "even though no one has looked on it."[86] Moreover, the series, "*aleph*," "secret object," "name," introduces a sequence of mediations, which culminate with the "name." The "*aleph*" becomes the "secret object," and the "secret object" becomes the "name." They are permutations, rapidly occurring, suture points where Borges posits *aleph* as an "absolute object" that articulates the Name of God. In this way, Borges collapses any difference between these entities while simultaneously the "name" endures as the sign of the secret that humans "appropriate." Humans focus on the "name" as the sign of their usurpation.

Borges links a human usurpation—the force of the verb, *usurpar*—to "the unimaginable universe." The English translation of *inconcibible* introduces the existence of a universe outside of what the imagination can represent. Hence it freights the inadequacy of the human imagination. The Spanish term, *inconcibible*, shifts the valence to a structural register, centered on human understanding. The understanding cannot conceive of this "universe"; it cannot reduce its experience to a concept. In fact, it suggests that the imagination bears the trace of the *aleph* within it. However, in that trace is the resignation of failure. The imagination cannot represent the "universe" of the *aleph*. In English, the difference appears to be a philosophical one of little consequence—imagining versus conceiving—but the Spanish *inconcibible* hews more closely to a traditional kabbalah because "conceivable" denotes an epistemological characteristic: all objects are knowable through their concepts and can be subsumed into categories of knowledge. This Kantian adage underpins as well what Scholem describes as the condition triggering the kabbalah, "the dogmatic object of knowledge." When burdened by the "dogmatic object of knowledge," humans seek the "novel intuition" of the tradition's "living experience."[87]

Thus Borges' earlier conclusion that human attempts to possess the *aleph* fail because these attempts are "successive" rather than "simultaneous" is grounded in the concepts of temporality and spatiality, legislated by the understanding. In this way, the *aleph* elicits a "shared sense" that is never known. Humankind shares in its failure to perceive the *aleph*. Nevertheless, he attempts to write its revelation. He feels obligated to write although his representation is a failure necessarily.

This obligation is the foundation of why Borges denies seeing the *aleph* to Daneri. He refuses to assist in any attempt to possess the letter for gain. When Carlos Argentino returns to the cellar, he accuses Borges of "spying into places where you have no business."[88] He still though wants to force Borges into admitting "this revelation."[89] Regaining his feet, Borges listens to Daneri's "hated but jovial voice" taunting him with it. In that moment, Borges returns to himself and "found …. revenge" by refusing "to discuss the Aleph."[90] Borges plays with Daneri while simultaneously insisting that he should "get away from the pernicious metropolis, which spares no one—believe me, … no one!"[91] The story ends with Borges, happily being able to slip into "oblivion."

In his midrash to the story, a "postscript," Borges returns the *aleph* to its kabbalistic register, only to distinguish it from his own experience.

> For the kabbala, that letter stands for the En Soph, the pure and boundless godhead; it is also said that it takes the shape of a man pointing to both heaven and earth, in order to show that the lower world is the map and mirror of the higher; for Cantor's *Mengenlehre,* it is the symbol of transfinite numbers, of which any part is as great as the whole. I would like to know whether Carlos Argentino chose that name or whether he read it—applied to another point where all points converge—in one of the numberless texts that the Aleph in his cellar revealed to him. Incredible as it may seem, I believe the Aleph of Garay Street was a false Aleph.[92]

Borges acknowledges first that the Aleph "stands for the En Soph"; the admission is important specifically in relation to how "En Soph" is understood by kabbalists. As Scholem explains, it is an epithet for God that means "Nothingness" and at times, even "No One."[93] It refers both to the "God who is hidden in Himself" and to "that which is infinite."[94] Borges accents for the reader that the epithet acknowledges a God who cannot be read or derived from human cognition. Taken with Scholem's observation on Abulafia earlier, that the Name of God "has no concrete, particular meaning of its own" relevant "to the human mind," Borges signals that "En-Soph," or "No One" must not be the property of any one person, telling Daneri to "get away from the pernicious metropolis, which spares no one—believe me, …. no one!" While the fictive Borges announces his denial is for "revenge," in his transformation during "the ineffable" experience, he realizes that humans are not to possess this knowledge.

The tension between these two positions is resolved then in Borges' declaration that "the Aleph on Garay Street … is a false aleph." Daneri has followed an "illegitimate path" that results in his poem's publication. The subsequent accolades he garners for it are another "triumph" for "dullness and envy."[95] Borges declares Daneri's act is akin to a false witness; its success relies on deception and a forbidden entitlement. The real *aleph* cannot be written.

In his failure, Borges bears witness to *aleph's* "infinite wonder and infinite pity." His redemption occurs through his denial of Daneri's possession of the letter. While he slips back into "oblivion," he does so with the knowledge that he has preserved the *aleph* from its unlawful possession. In "El Aleph," letter phenomenology only redeems the writer who fails to transmit its revelation, a failed prophet. The one who, like Daneri, reveals the *pleroma* of the scar, is condemned.

8

Lost Letters

Romy Achituv's "lost communities," an installation at Israel's Ghetto Fighters House Museum, represents the losses of Jewish lives during the Holocaust in the spatial metaphor of Hebrew letters fading into the cosmos.¹ Shrouded in darkness, "on the eastern wall, a ten and a half meter" display cycles through forty-five hundred placenames, the "indigenous names" of Jewish towns, villages, ghettos, farms.² At first, these detached names appear as isolated letters that "rise from a rubble-like base, comprised of a random mass of letters."³ They ascend the wall, toward the ceiling. As the letters continue upward—"in their ascent—they come together to form a name, only to thereafter break apart."⁴ These temporal formations, briefly signified by their names, in Polish, Ukrainian, and other European languages, begin to transform into Yiddish. Some are partial translations; they exist incompletely in both vernacular and Hebrew orthographies. Some of the Yiddish names flow in parallel with their indigenous counterparts, translations of each other. However, the formations collapse immediately as if the burden of existence from within this chaos is too much to bear. These lexical vessels are shattering repeatedly. The names dissolve into their constituent

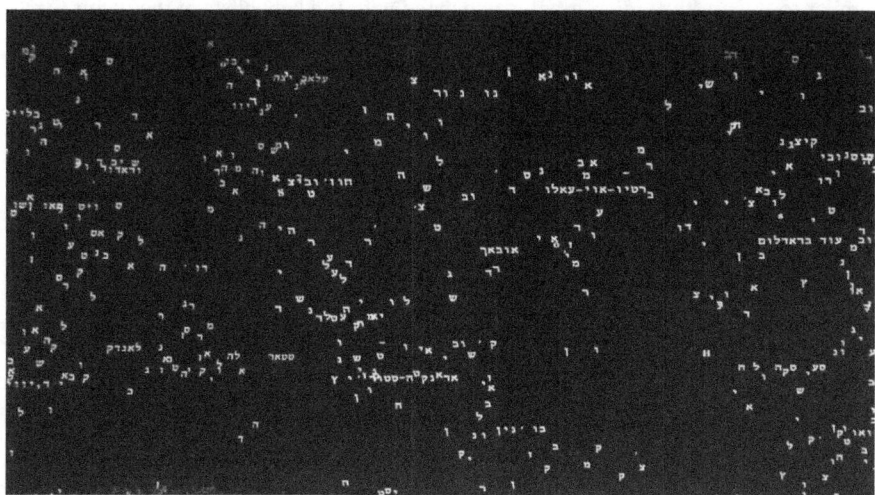

Figure 8.1 Achituv, Romy. Still, "Lost Communities." Ghetto Fighters House Museum, Western Gallilee, Israel (used by permission of the artist).

parts, revealing discrete isolated Hebrew and vernacular letters.[5] They are condemned to this isolation: they are condemned to recede into the darkness, bearing the burden of their loss in silence. They are the lost letters of Jewish existence.

Although the letters attempt metonymically to identify their "lost communities," they no longer form proper names.[6] The people for which these names stand no longer exist. As the letters get further and further away, they become blurry, unrecognizable to the people standing in the darkness of the Museum. In their dim outlines, they look like stars as they continue to recede into the darkness until they extinguish. Onlookers are left to wonder about their absence. Finally, the lights come up, signaling the installation has ended. People slowly move to the exits. Conversations resume as the crowd leaves the Museum.[7]

Achituv's more well-known, "Text Rain," an interactive installation, and collaboration with Camille Utterback, is also preoccupied with letters. In that work, visitors stand against white projection screens in which letters cling to their every move.[8] The body becomes a physical metaphor for writing so that it expresses an objective relationship to the letters as phenomena. Each movement reflects a phenomenal writing in the universe; each body is its expression. With the letters clinging to each individual body part, Achituv and Utterback suggest that humanness is animated by an indiscriminate textuality, a chaotic writing that finds its specificity uniquely on, through, and by each individual's cluster of letters.[9] The letters' embodiment enables each individual to write one's own story. By the introduction of an unseen writing that adheres necessarily to bodies in the universe, the artists suggest that humans represent particular permutations of letters. These permutations not only combine to form individuals, peoples, worlds, but also suggest the letters are active in their own permutations. In this way, "Text Rain," resonates with kabbalistic principles.

The computers' generated letters, randomly adhering to bodies, impose a pattern similar to the mystical micrography associated with the kabbalists of the Iyyun Circle in Spain.[10] They posit the Torah as an aggregate of Hebrew letters unconcerned with the finite meanings humans attribute to them so that as an aggregate of Divine Being, the letters articulate the secret and unknown Names of God. They form a writing unreadable as finite meaning.[11] Since the letters exceed the roles humans give to them, the historical practice of micrography as "ornamentation" of the Hebrew Bible is more than "an artistic convention"; it reflects "invisible .... hidden exegetical .... mystical meaning."[12] Thus the "translation" of the letters into aesthetic images illustrates permutations for which we have no corollaries.

Likewise, in his focus on the Hebrew letters as "absolute objects," Abulafia reminds his followers that according to the *Sefer Yetsirah*, the letters themselves are each "coordinated to a special member of the body."[13] He teaches there is an intimate relationship between the letters and substance. Achituv and Utterback's project echoes this sentiment: they intimate that each individual comprises a unique combination of letters adhering to the body. Each personality, each individual, composes a unique text, expressed as a singular aggregate of letters. Furthermore, the letters are dynamic and they can shift to articulate new singularities. The artists' work suggests kabbalistic patterns produce individual existence; their work resonates as well with the anonymous thirteenth-century kabbalist's declaration that each individual is commanded to "write one's own Torah."¹⁴ In other words, the letter phenomenology of these early kabbalistic projects relies on an unarticulated belief that humans are commanded to be writing, even though they exist in the condemned state of the written.

By the sixteenth century, Isaac Luria, the Safed kabbalist, innovates Abulafia's principles of "sealing" and "unsealing," linking a condemned or "sealed" creation in the process of unsealing through exile, to his teaching of *tzimtzum* in which creation takes place through a radical act of Divine self-negation. God recedes into the Divine Self and empties a space within the Self in order to create the cosmos, the universe. Within His hiddenness, He pushes the chaos of letters within the Divine Self out. The letters stream, then, from within the Hidden God, the new epithet that Divine Being must be in order to inaugurate creation. The legacy of *tzimtzum* demands the letters' emanations.[15] Hence the letters are traces of Divine Being in the world, traces that have been sent into exile with us in order to redeem our human existence, to save us from reverting to our golem and silent selves. To redeem a fallen world, and in their immanence, they have waited for "prophets" to receive and to transmit their revelations. However, in the absence of "prophets," in the absence of Jews, the letters themselves bear the weight of a Divine writing, exhibited before us.

Thus Achituv's aesthetic statement in "Lost Communities" is stark and from a kabbalistic perspective, damning since the letters are forced to abandon the world in the absence of the bodies to which they have adhered.[16] This destruction is more than even they can bear, even they can represent. As a result, they move away from humankind. In their singularity, each one recedes into the darkness, severed from the other. They no longer present the "music of the universe," a belief recorded in Judaic liturgy.[17] Thus their flight portends a grave moment in human history: the letters have been prevented from performing creation and redemption by a human act of extermination. Redemption no longer exists because the constituent parts of revelation have been compelled by the act of extermination to abandon or disengage from human existence. They flee its "rubble."

They now must forget this world, and in exile, untethered from their purpose, they recede into the hidden God. As the prophet of this vision, Achituv has recognized the one outcome every kabbalist, even Shabbatai Zvi, fights against: the abandonment of the Divine trace and with it the foreclosure of revelation. The world has been left with only "objective statement .... and the kapo barks 'left!' and the soup was watery."[18] As the letters recede into "nothingness," the installation ends. Visitors are invited to leave the exhibit.

A handful of Jewish writers and artists have experimented with kabbalistic patterns to describe the damage of the Shoah and these resonate with Achituv's installation. Elie Wiesel calls it "night."[19] In the context of his memoir of the same name, Elie the boy has just arrived at Auschwitz. For the young Elie Wiesel, staring at the crematoria on that first night, he realizes there is no promised *shefa* or Divine cosmic stream of transcendence. Auschwitz has exterminated that possibility for ever.

> Never shall I forget that night, the first night in camp, that
> turned my life into one long night seven times sealed.
> Never shall I forget that smoke.

> Never shall I forget the small faces of the children whose
> bodies I saw transformed into smoke under a silent sky.
> Never shall I forget those flames that consumed my faith
> forever ….
> Never shall I forget those moments that murdered my God and
> my soul and turned my dreams to ashes.[20]

The repetition of "Never shall I forget" anchors a series of images to produce a chant that can only articulate the destruction of the children's "small faces," the "smoke" of their bodies burning "under a silent sky." This produces the "murder" of God and the transformation of Elie's "dreams to ashes." Linked to the first night as "one long night seven times sealed," Wiesel inverts a kabbalistic register to suggest that in the camp, the boy, Elie, realizes that he is not only cut off from Divine Being, but also that Divine Being has been severed from him. God no longer reaches into human existence through Hebrew letters; God no longer rescues anyone. Thus there is only "nothingness." In Wiesel, Elie's "nothingness" testifies only to death, the absence of being, of En Sof: the camp has erased a barrier between Divine and human, but instead of the revelation of God, the restoration of creation, the recovery of paradise, there is only the condemnation of nothingness.

From a hasidic family, Wiesel has grown up with the belief that Nothingness, or *En Sof*, both surrounds and is hidden from human existence. The epithet for this aspect of God, Scholem tells us, freights God's infinite Being: God must not be conceived as an object. God is not a thing, but rather infinite No-Thingness. It is a dimension that humans cannot enter in their condemned state.

In the Abulafian kabbalah, the soul is sealed by God as an act of mercy so that in our conscious states, we cannot see the extent of the violation through time and space, categories that come into being because of the Fall. As the kabbalist endeavors to draw closer to God, he attempts to "untie the knots which bind it" by concentrating on—also an act of "innovating"—the Divine Names as the Hebrew letters present themselves to him.[21] This "unsealing" releases the mystic into a realm of liberation and transcendence, "the cosmic stream."[22] As Scholem describes it, "[T]he seals, which keep it locked up in its normal state and shut off the divine light, are relaxed, and the mystic finally dispenses with them altogether."[23]

For kabbalists, while the letters proceed from and remain tethered to *En Sof*, "Nothingness," or "the Hidden God," the attempt to draw near to *En Sof* through the letters is supposed to elicit "sublimity" in the kabbalist. For Wiesel, that possibility has been exterminated with his people so that the letters, reduced to lifeless units, inanimate instruments, reproduce the conditions of an existence without being, without "structures of beings."[24] They are representations of objects, statements of fact, but there is no path for or possibility to constitute missing subjects among them. Like Achituv's "ruins," they represent "nothingness" in and of themselves.

Bruno Schulz recognizes the letters' original mandate to be the transformation of their "unfinished stories" into unique "clusters of melodies," but this is a "luxury" denied now apodeictically. Human existence supplies these predicates; we read and attach ourselves to finish these stories, bringing our songs bodily into being. Due to the cataclysmic moment when there are no more predicates in proximity to them, the letters are lost within "nothingness." The letters' inability to fulfill their "obligation" in Hebrew, and all of the vernaculars of Achituv's installation, implies that these "interminable stories" remain "unfinished" for eternity.

On a work detail at Auschwitz, Jean Améry "recalls that particular lines from Hölderlin's poem had previously elicited in him a subjective liberation, 'an emotional and mental response,'" but after his experience at Auschwitz, Hölderlin's poem, "Half-Life," "no longer transcended reality."[25] It voices "half-death" instead.

> I recall a winter evening when after work we were dragging ourselves, out of step, from the IG-Farben site back into the camp to the accompaniment of the Kapo's unnerving "left, two, three, four," when .... a flag waving in front of a half-finished building caught my eye. "The walls stand speechless and cold, the flags clank in the wind," I muttered to myself in mechanical association. Then I repeated the stanza somewhat louder, listened to the words sound, tried to track the rhythm, and expected that the emotional and mental response that for years this Holderlin poem had awakened in me would emerge. But nothing happened. The poem no longer transcended reality. There it was and all that remained was objective statement: such and such, and the Kapo roars "left," and the soup was watery, and the flags are clanking in the wind.[26]

As Améry repeats the words, the "expected .... emotional and mental response" no longer occurs. The writing within the poem "no longer transcends," and he realizes the absence of the aesthetic in him is now expressed as a phenomenology reduced to "objective statement."

Likewise, the French dramatist, Liliane Atlan, presents Shoah's Jewish victims, condemned to hover almost within reach of the *sferot* or spheres' "messiahs," only to continue "floating," blind, unmoored, abandoned in the cosmos of their incomplete lives.[27] For that writer, herself a "hidden child," kabbalah's redemption is lost. Its victims and its "messiahs" wander lost in the cosmos, incapable of ever facing each other. There is no illuminated path to redemption.

Her "messiahs" are tethered to their planet, a decaying "wooden spiral, staircase."[28] Their names make no sense and reflect their impotency: these entities never voice the "Great Name of God." They are "moored" and appear "tied up."[29] They speak "an imaginary language," partially encased in "huge plaster casts"; they are archaic, obsolete, and powerless. Strung up and down their "ladder," they evoke the *sferot*, and simultaneously their inconsequential status. They are perched on the "tree of life," reimagined now as a ladder of missing rungs, suspended between Nothingness and nothingness. Like the *sferot*, they wear rags and mumble. These messiahs are incapable of saving anyone. Displayed in their pettiness, preoccupied with how they once were worshipped, readers are struck by their disconnection from the world below. It is dissolving into ashes, and the Jews who once followed them no longer exist.

Juxtaposed to these divine failures, the Nazis' victims below meet for Rosh ha-Shanah dinner on Krystalnacht. They are rounded up and deported; Atlan relates fragments of their experiences. By the story's end, their shadows traverse the universe on a raft, much like the one, on which they try to escape, but this "celestial chariot" never stops at the *Pardes* and their cries, the sounds of Krystalnacht's pogrom, mingle "with the sound of the spheres."[30] The spheres' emanations repeat their screams, but the messiahs do not listen. Instead "they write in their *Pell Mell* Book about their own losses." Only the "GALAXIES" bear witness to these Jews on a raft. They carry them, "dispersed, wrinkled .... their litanies are feeble."[31] Eventually, the "cries of the galaxies" and the screams of the Nazis' victims transform into "the chirping of the spheres." Nature and the universe cannot bear to hear these victims.

If as the *Zohar* puts it, God reads the letters in order to create, then, God has stopped reading His Torah. He has become incapable of reading it. Although Isaac Luria believed humans would repair God, perform the *tikkun*, by reading, they have instead preferred the void of their own dissolution amid the destruction of the Jews so that God's *tikkun* never occurs. All of these projects state fundamentally that the kabbalah has ended with the Shoah.

Harry Mulisch's *Discovery of Heaven* explores a similar theme in which the Hebrew letters of the Mosaic tablets, abandoned and forgotten, buried under a staircase, covered with centuries of dust in the Cathedral of the Popes in Rome, elicit something uncanny in Quinten, the prodigy child of the novel.[32] The letters wait for him; they call to him from the unconscious. He intuits their occluded presence on the tablets. He recognizes the tablets must be restored to their origin. With his father's help, he steals the forgotten treasure, imprisoned in the Vatican, and returns these "tablets of testimony" to Jerusalem, depositing them in his room's safe.[33]

The tablets draw him to the safe; its combination commandeers his hands. "He doesn't have to think" about the letters because they present themselves to him.[34] "Without knowing what else has to happen, he takes the two heavy stones in his hands" and mysteriously he is transported to the "golden cupola of the Dome of the Rock" and the Temple Mount.[35] He "crosses the threshold" to stand before its "Golden Gate." He recognizes around him that he has entered "the small sanctum": he can stare into "the dark interior of The Dome of the Rock."[36] At this point, Muslisch has Quinten achieve what "the man from the country" could not and it underscores Mulisch's use of an heretical kabbalah to address the loss of Jewish lives during the Holocaust.

Quinten "begins walking toward that black hole" and hears sounds that appear to be "coming from the stone tablets" he carries.[37] As he looks on "in astonishment at what is happening," he becomes aware that something on the tablets "is trying to fight its way out from underneath, to free itself."[38] In looking at the Mosaic Tablets, Quinten witnesses the letters' liberating themselves; "their tiny, glassy, translucent creatures appearing all over the surface, freeing themselves from the crusts of thousands of years, leaping and swarming around him." Moreover, he "sees" it happening; his sensual perception of revelation's embodiment is the sign of the heretical kabbalah because Quinten materializes divine writing.

> Letters! They are letters! Letters of light! At the same moment the sapphire plates have become so heavy that he can no longer hold them .... They slip from his grasp and smash to smithereens .... but he does not care—he must have the letters; they must not escape! The ten words! Thou shalt not steal! Thou shalt not kill! He grabs at them with both hands, but the swarm rises .... and disappears.[39]

In their liberation, "the letters of light" break the vessels holding them. The substance of the "plates .... become so heavy," that Quinten cannot bear them. They drop from his grasp and shatter. They "smash to smithereens." The tablets don't break because of Moses' anger at the Jews "golden calf"; they slip because the human body cannot support them. In Mulisch, humans enact a physical manifestation of "the Breaking of the Vessels"; they are condemned to repeat the narrative.

Quinten's reaction to the "perfection that destroys" is to attempt to "grab" at its letters. The intensity of Mulisch's lines conveys that the letters' glory compels Quinten to try desperately to hold them together. His desire to possess is thwarted though because the "swarm rises and disappears." In the text, there's even a slight indication that the letters in their liberation are ecstatic to leave behind Quinten's world, to be free of human meaning. Trapped in the forgotten tablets, imprisoned on earth, the letters almost seem to mock human existence in their ecstasy to be free.

In proximity to the letters, Quinten becomes obsessed with their experience. He must possess them and in his failure, like ben Zoma and ben Azzai before him, he experiences madness, and death, yet his pursuit doesn't end.

> He chases after them in despair .... the letters dance and gleam up and down above the holy rock .... he is standing on the rock .... sees the arabesques .... and at that moment Moses' swarm of letters envelops his naked body with such an endless, dazzling Light that his body disappears in it.[40]

"Despair" motivates his pursuit and he "leaps" onto "the rock." From this vantage point, he "sees the arabesques," the patterns of divine writing in matter. In one last gesture, he gives up, "spreads his arms" and "Moses' swarm of letters" reappear. Quinten does not imitate Aher and abandon the revelation, but instead he "gives up" and continues to stand before the letters. The "swarm" overwhelms him, "envelopes his naked body with endless, dazzling light." Reminiscent of Enoch's transformation, Quinten has transcended. He disappears into the letters writing their liberation. His human substance has been erased for that writing to take place. In this repetition of the PaRDeS, Quinten's transcendence occurs in spite of his attempts to materialize redemption and hold on to the letters. He experiences the letters' "secret" because he desires to know it and they awaken the "testimony" inside him.[41] His ontology is transformed into "a divine being" in the sense that Quinten no longer exists. He has been taken by the letters. Quinten's performed *tikkun* requires his life and his repair is not directed to God, but to the letters as distinct entities.

The novel has two endings, one with Quinten's aging father "standing in the hallway," and knocking on Quinten's room door. He only opens it "an inch or so" peering through the slit of the chained door. His fear that "something impossible has happened" overtakes him and he breaks down the door, to search for Quinten, but absence and silence testify to his "impossible" conclusion. Quinten has left this world and his father behind.

The other, the novel's "Epilogue," takes place among divine beings. They have amused themselves by controlling human fate throughout the novel. Their only goal is to keep the "testimony" for themselves and so they engender events the outcome of which ends with Quinten's death and his liberation of the Hebrew letters. They mock human existence although they also envy human writers who in their writing experience infinity, and the "stamp of finitude": the writers are "always having the best of both worlds."[42]

Thus readers discover that the divine beings discussing human events which they control are not angels, but the *sferot* themselves.

> *The main thing is that we've got the testimony back just in time. Where's our man now?*
>   –Returned to the Light.
> *By now you might just as well say: to the Twilight. And what happened to the fragments of the two tablets?*
>   –Collected by the Jerusalem Sanitation Department. Taken to a rubbish dump with all the other rubble in the Dome of the Chain ....
>   –*Well for that matter the testimony itself is a mess too .... the language of a world that we've no use for anymore .... My strength is exhausted. We're done for. The world is done for. Humankind is done for. Everything is done for—except Lucifer .... The only thing left after 3000 years is to take back those ten words .... the Chief's contract with humankind, concluded with its deputy, the Jewish people, represented by its leader, Moses in the role of the notary.*[43]

The *sferot* unfold creation; they send forward the "testimony," but now the Tablets' contract between divine beings and humans has been voided. At the beginning of the novel, these beings discuss that in the Jews' extermination, Lucifer has revealed another path to paradise, but not for the Holocaust's victims. Extermination of the Jews has foreclosed access to paradise; hence the letters must abandon the earth. Thus the *sferot* have manipulated human events in order to place the tablets in Quinten's hands. His act allows them to save the letters "just in time." The letters will not be repurposed; will not pave the way to heaven's discovery. In their discussion, the "spheres" recognize this truth too. The world is in its "twilight."

The "fragments" that bore the letters are taken as "rubbish." Mulisch's prose traces another heretical kabbalistic pattern that Scholem also fears.[44] By taking the "fragments" to the city dump, the "Jerusalem Sanitation Department" performs a violation that Jews for centuries refused to commit: they have not only thrown away the vehicle used to carry the revelation, but they have also discarded the animate letters steaming from within Divine Being. For centuries, Jews have deposited in genizas all texts bearing Hebrew when such documents are no longer in use, but now these shards of revelation have become reducible to trash.

As the conversation between these divine entities ends, they admit "they have no use" for humans, "the world," everything. Mulisch applies a gnostic register here and in their resignation, these divine beings outline the end of their roles in creation. Even though one voice among them refuses to leave human existence, for Mulisch, these divine beings are resolved to abandon humans.

Mulisch's resonance with the preceding projects is clear in the sense that the letters leave earth: they are forced or they choose to abandon the world. The principles are dissimilar though around why the letters leave human existence. With Achituv, Atlan, Wiesel, Améry, the Shoah destroys something fundamental that cannot be repaired. God is incapable of rescue. In Mulisch, this is also true, but the divine entities entrusted with the world are unmoved by human suffering. This is the gnostic, heretical element. Mulisch posits entities—like a demiurge—who intend to keep the "testimony" for themselves. Thus human existence becomes an adversary of these guardians. They ignore the suffering of the Nazis' victims on earth. They appear like Atlan's "messiahs" to be more inclined to squabble among themselves than to rescue Jews. In Mulisch's characterization, these divine beings are mimetically aligned with humans. There is no gap between divine and human ontologies. In Mulisch's reckoning, redemption has never existed, and will never exist. There are only discrete moments of human connection, but the world exists in a gnostic dream world, a fantasy of powers that exceeds time and space. The most that humans can hope for is to be taken in with the letters, becoming part of a divine narrative that no longer "has any use for" human existence.

9

"There Must Be Other Songs beyond Mankind"

Written in 1965, Paul Celan's "NO MORE SAND ART" exhibits words and letters unmoored from meaning. The poem's trajectory begins with cryptic declarations and ends with meaningless sounds in which the letters appear to have become "sensible" non-sensible units, or phenomena of nothingness.

> NO MORE SAND ART, no sand book, no masters.
> Nothing won by dicing. How many
> dumb ones?
> Seventeen.
> Your question—your answer.
> Your song, what does it know?
> *Deepinsnow,*
> Eeepinnow,
> Ee-i-o.[1]

As the words stop communicating, the letters become exposed to new combinations—"Deepinsnow, Eeepinow"—but even these rearranged constructions strike readers as meaningless. Without the capacity to communicate sense, the new words exist without reference, without phenomenal likenesses. They reduce to their constituent sounds, expressed in the poem's last line, "Ee-i-o." Language appears to have lost its revelatory "place" among humankind.

The poem has motivated writers and critics to attempt to parse Celan's meaning only to stop short of its last lines, the letters that seem to say nothing, repeating the intonation of a children's rhyme: "deepinsnow, eepinnow, ee-i-o." Anne Carson notes that Celan writes the poem at a time when he is "disheartened by the resurgence of anti-Semitism in Europe and also by the deaf ears with which .... the European literary community listened to his verse."[2] Her observation hinges on Celan's aesthetic project initially being a mimetic one, reflective of his lived experiences, that he eventually rejects: the poet represents his experiences during the Holocaust in his earlier work, but his audience has proven incapable of recognizing, of "hearing" him and "seeing" them, so he "turns away" from that project.[3]

She ties the poem explicitly to Celan's first book, *The Sand from the Urns* and an earlier version of the poem, "Death Fugue" (*Todesfuge*), written in 1947.[4]

"Death-fugue" .... concerns the concentrationary universe and contains the refrain "Death is a master from Germany." Both the book *Sand from the Urns* and the poem "Deathfugue" were repudiated by Celan himself, the former because of the many misprints that appeared in the text when it was published, the latter because he came to think it spoke too directly or explicitly about things that could not be said.[5]

Since he has spoken too "directly.... explicitly" about his experiences, Celan determines that these "are things that could not be said." In other words, Carson recognizes in Celan a condemnation of mimesis inherent in his rejection of lyric poetry. In this way, she echoes several scholars who see "NO MORE SAND ART" as a direct movement away from Celan's earlier aesthetic projects since it repudiates "a kind of art and a stage of himself that no longer suffice; a stage in which he had sought to 'poeticize' reality (as he says) rather than simply to 'name' it."[6] Implicitly, Carson points to Celan's rejection of "aestheticism" or more appropriately aesthetic experience and aesthetic judgment as the purposive principles underpinning his poetry, the principles that give shape to his poetry's "structures of being."[7]

However, in Celan's rejection of his former "aestheticism," Carson attributes still a relationship to mimesis inherent within "NO MORE SAND ART." He cannot liberate himself from the burden of bearing witness. Thus Celan represents a structural disfigurement in poetry because of the Jews' extermination during the Holocaust. The poem's lack of explicit meaning testifies mimetically to this damage so that the poem expresses their injury and absence, sutured through the signifier of "naming." He remains focused on the representation of his experiences although his initial poetic register fails him.

Shoshana Felman identifies the poem too to be part of an aesthetic strategy; however, she describes it as "less explicit, less melodious, more disrupted, and disruptively elliptical verse."[8] Like Carson, she locates the strategy in relation to Celan's disappointment over the reception of "Todesfuge" or "Deathfugue." She links his rejection to his sudden prominence within the German-speaking world due to its "success."[9] Felman suggests "NO MORE SAND ART" is intentionally "elliptical" to prevent its appropriation by generations of Germans belatedly. Enthusiastically, identifying with the previous lyricism of "Death Fugue," they have subsumed Celan's work into the canon of the Beautiful, precisely within the register of lyric and all that such a move implies.[10]

Consequently, she explains that Celan alters "his writing style," foreshadowing Adorno's critique of lyric poetry.[11]

> The whole endeavor of Celan's poetic work can be defined .... in Adorno's terms, as poetry's creative and self-critical *resistance to the verdict* that it is barbaric, henceforth, to write lyrically, poetically; a verdict which the poetry receives, however, not from the outside, but from inside itself; a verdict which "Death Fugue" encompasses already and in fact .... sets in motion the master's usurpation of the singing of the inmates. Something of that usurpation has, however, inadvertently reproduced itself even in the very destiny of "Todesfuge," whose immense success

and frequent anthologization in the German-speaking world had soon turned Celan into something like another celebrated "master." Celan .... in later years, turned against his early poem .... and changed his writing style.[12]

Felman observes that Celan makes lyric self-conscious of its own barbarism; it receives the "verdict .... from inside itself." In the juxtaposition of "the master's usurpation" to "the singing of the inmates," Felman highlights an aspect of Celan's poetics that seems to get lost in scholars' attempts to historicize Celan's "turn away" from the "lyricism" of "Death Fugue." In "Death Fugue," Celan forces lyric to reveal how the master "usurps" the Jewish inmates "singing," implying that the master commandeers the "songs of humankind" while murdering his victims. He arrogates to himself *poesie* as he slaughters the Jews.

Felman reminds readers that "something of that usurpation" persists "in the very destiny of 'Todesfuge'" so that the success of the poem continues "that usurpation" through the processes of aesthetic experience. In that moment, Celan recognizes that he has become "something like another celebrated 'master.'"[13] At the heart of this reckoning is his realization that the Nazis' absorption of lyric has so overwhelmed the tradition that, even when used by Celan, a survivor himself, it is incapable of restoring Jewish voices.

As I demonstrate in these two examples, most Celan scholarship cites some form of biographical link between Celan's "writing style," and his aesthetic choices.[14] While the poet's biography is imbricated in his poetic project, it is not exclusively about the attempt to represent the damage done to Jews because of the Holocaust in the sense that it evolves. It is also about the need for *poesie* to regain its redemptive power through the restoration of Jewish voices, Jewish being, to be able to renew human existence through the diversity of its representations. When Celan realizes that *poesie's* redemption cannot come through any traditional means of aesthetic experience, he moves into the very Jewish register of kabbalah to try to liberate the letters themselves. They must be awakened to their immanence and not remain the dead property, inanimate signifiers of an aesthetic tradition that extinguished Jewish presence in the pursuit of transcendence.

Hence I want to press on the nuances of Celan's refusal to see himself as a transcendent "master" of poetry because in that refusal, the context for "NO MORE SAND ART" becomes critical to understanding what exactly Celan has tried to do with this poem, his poetry, and *poesie*. I believe it exceeds both Carson's thesis of "naming" and Felman's claim that it is made solely to forfeit "sense," or to exist as language no longer capable of meaning, even though these two perspectives in particular point indirectly at an aspect of Celan's overall strategy.[15]

In other words, Celan's aesthetic project in "NO MORE SAND ART" does not just mimetically bear witness to *poesie's* damage and injury, although modern readers find this thesis more than compelling, if not comforting. Rather he attempts a new aesthetic, "a song beyond humankind," perhaps a lyric "beyond humankind," because for Celan, the stakes of his "turn away" from "poeticization" are grounded in a kabbalistic register in which the letters themselves must be liberated to address new "structures of being."[16]

To imagine Celan's later project, the earlier "Todesfuge" has to be placed in relief to it. "Todesfuge" relies on a lyricism, "a song .... of humankind."[17] It juxtaposes how a subject can "write and write" while simultaneously sending "his Jews" to gas chambers. In that poem, Celan's outrage and horror are palpable and intuitable.

> Black milk of dawn we drink you at night
> We drink you mornings and noontime we drink you evenings
> We drink and we drink
> A man lives in the house he plays with the snakes he writes
> He writes when it turns dark to Deutschland your golden hair Margarete
> Your ashen hair Shulamit we dig a grave in the air there one lies at ease[18]

The lyricism of each line builds two parallel destinies, the Nazis, articulated in the figures of the "master" and "Margarete," are juxtaposed to the Jews in "ashes" and "Shulamit." The poem's engagement with aesthetic experience requires Celan to use its principles: *mimesis,* a mode of representing the "unity, integrity or continuity of conscious meaning," in relation to *Sinnlichkeit*, understood as "the sensual world," or the world of the senses. He juxtaposes carefully the phenomena of extermination to the master's work of art, expressed as "he writes and writes." "Death Fugue" intervenes in an aesthetic experience determined to ignore or overlook the Nazis' actions. It "resists" from within its own interiority by requiring readers to map the phenomenologies of both Nazis and their victims simultaneously.

Thus these two organizing principles of aesthetic experience, mimesis and *Sinnlichkeit*, present readers with an imagined subject position of "a master from Germany" who "writes" and the lack of a subject position, the lived experience of Jews who "dig a grave in the air." In this way, Celan sutures the master's revelation to "Shulamit's" destruction, evoked by the signifier of "ashen hair." The two trajectories are intimately linked for Celan through the possessive adjective, "your" so that "your golden hair, Margarete …. your ashen hair Shulamit," establish both an intimacy with and a distance from Celan the poet.

Together, they produce a tension that Celan attempts to solidify through the repetition of the poem's last lines in which "death is a master from Deutschland" emerges as the real predicate of "Black milk of dawn we drink …. and drink."[19]

> Black milk of dawn we drink you at night
> We drink you at noon death is a master from Deutschland
> We drink you evenings and mornings we drink and drink
> Death is a master from Deutschland his eye is blue[20]

Interrupting the previous stanza's "a man lives in a house," the real predicate "death is a master from Germany" links consciously the destruction of Jews to the transcendence of "he writes and writes." The mimesis of the death camps becomes inscribed then within Celan's concluding refrain, "Your golden hair Margarete …. Your ashen hair Shulamit."[21] The refrain traps the reader between the two phrases.

Beauty belongs to the Germans; absence and ash belong to the Jews. "Todesfuge's" stark conclusion is that the tradition of the aesthetic, of transcendence, is permanently bound to Jewish extermination. Again for Celan, there is no synthesis, no resolution in the poem: both poem and poet are forced to bear witness to this binding together of transcendence and extermination so that "Death Fugue" states effectively, the master has commandeered the music, "lyric," and there are no "songs beyond humankind."[22]

In this way, Celan stages a testimony of silence, framed as the *Sinnlichkeit* world of ashes and its mimetic representation through the continuous murder of the Jews, hour by hour—"we drink and drink." Bracketed by these images, "a master from Deutschland .... writes and writes." With the interplay between mimesis, and *Sinnlichkeit*, Celan represents the relationship as the horror of a Faustian bargain in which German culture colludes—"he writes he writes"—with the action of extermination and the stark revelation of "we drink and drink." The text hardens around the recognition that the master's time and space remain unaffected by his actions; within the exterminator's world, transcendence continues to be available in a way that no longer exists for Jews.[23]

Continuing to write his lyrical verse, both during and after his destruction of anonymous Jews, the transcendent subject, the "master," transforms even Jewish proper names to ashes. Consequently, the master usurps "the singing of the inmates" because he purges the faculties of their dissonance.[24] Their songs belong no longer to the "songs" of humankind.[25] To some extent the whole tradition of transcendence allows for this "master" to emerge unscathed from the crimes of the Holocaust.[26] Catharsis has guaranteed it.[27]

This "consciousness" sutures an uncomfortable dissonance between the "master's" articulation, and its foreclosure for Celan. Felman reminds readers that the poem "Todesfuge" forces recognition of the aestheticization of "violence ... its own dehumanization," its transformation of "its own murderous perversity into the cultural sophistication and the cultivated spaces of a hedonistic art performance" so that the poem "works to dislocate this masquerade of cruelty as art."[28] The critical moment in the poem is precisely when Celan's opposition of "the melodious ecstasy of .... aesthetic pleasure" intersects with "the dissonance of the commandant's speech acts."[29]

It is continuously repeated by "your golden hair Margarete" and "your ashen hair Shulamit"; the refrain forces the faculties to position themselves around the *"unforgettable return of what the aesthetic pleasure has forgotten."*[30] With "Todesfuge," Celan reminds Germans and the world then that there can be no forgetting: victims never have the luxury of forgetting. There is no Beauty in the displacement of the Nazis' victims through the transcendence of *poesie*. In fact, with "Todesfuge," Celan stages the production of "transcendence" to be contingent on the reproduction of Jewish extermination.

The possibility that his readers might find the Beautiful in the depiction of a "master from Germany" exterminating Jews forces Celan to construct thereafter his poetry in a different key or at least to search for another combination of the words themselves in order to construct "another universe."[31] Both Felman and Carson are correct that

Celan, in becoming aware of how "Todesfugue" has been received and transmitted, shifts to another aesthetic project altogether, represented by "NO MORE SAND ART."[32]

Felman hints though at the striking "innovation" of Celan's later poetic project in which he begins to break apart words in subsequent poems in order to inflect their lexical meanings.[33] These inflections occur between the possibility of the aesthetic in "Death Fugue" and the testimony of its complete collapse in his later poems, exemplified by "NO MORE SAND ART." On the one hand, with "Death Fugue" the tradition of *Wissenschaft*, of aesthetics in a secular register, is used by Celan to accent the dissonance between the master's capacity to continue to write and his extermination of the Jews. On the other hand, Celan moves in "NO MORE SAND ART" to "dislocate his own aesthetic mastery by breaking down any self-possessed control of sense .... by disrupting any unity, integrity, or continuity of conscious meaning."[34] In her reading of the later poem as a "disruption .... of conscious meaning," Felman stops with that disruption and so does Carson, as if the "disruption of conscious meaning," its inflection, is Celan's sole aim. In this way, both scholars' perspectives anchor "Todesfuge," to the problem of an aesthetic experience that could elicit transcendence while simultaneously discharging Jews to the ash pits of Belzec, Sobibor, Treblinka, Chelmno, and Auschwitz.[35]

As Felman reiterates, Celan, the survivor, knows this, even though with "Todesfuge," he still aims to use lyric to preserve traces of Jewish existence. Written just after his own liberation, amid the ruins of his life, he wants his readers to hear the "singing of the Jewish inmates," to imagine "your ashen hair Shulamit" in time and space. When their songs cannot be heard, Celan determines to pursue that "there must be songs beyond humankind."

Thus Celan severs his poetic project from "any self-possessed control of sense" because he realizes the allure of transcendence has been too great for his readers. Time and space have not been altered for them; they read "Death Fugue's" lyricism and they fall into the illusion of Goethe's Faust.[36] The importance of Celan's rejection of *Sinnlichkeit,* the foundational mode of human experience, demands that Celan reject the path to becoming both "a master from Deutschland" and becoming a subject, since both positions seek transcendence from the world depicted in "Todesfuge."[37]

In his mimetic representation of the process whereby "a man in the house" forgets, Celan realizes the larger problem remains how poetry or *poesie* must change ontologically.[38] As both Felman and Carson illustrate, mimesis rather than staging a conscious rejection of the transcendent "master" has instead enabled it. Although the enabling of the subject is not his goal, Celan lives with the horror. Not only have lyric, *mimesis, Sinnlichkeit* failed to transform his readers into witnesses, but they have also communicated it within the subject's privilege. Thus Celan begins writing a refusal of communicability.

Celan's realization that his readers remain subjects in spite of these acts haunts Celan's *poesie*—to the extent that he turns quite literally to its constituent parts, the words and letters themselves in search of another kind of redemption, a mysterious redemption beyond communicability. He begins to permutate these elements in order to extend his word creations beyond "conscious meaning," to restore to these abandoned morphemes their music, the "other songs beyond humankind."[39] Like Celan's anagrammatic transformation of his given name, Antschel, to "its Romanian spelling, Ançel, into Celan," the poet begins to imagine the permutation of letters in order to restructure poetic ontology.[40]

By 1963, Celan's *NoOnesRose* has integrated Jewish and kabbalistic principles in its trajectory, and these poems point to the creative power of Hebrew letters, "the letters' mortal-immortal soul."[41] His translator Pierre Joris, notes that this text is "where for the first and last time" Celan makes visible his relationship to a diverse array of Jewish sources, ranging from "Osip Mandelbaum, to Gershom Scholem, from Nelly Sachs to Margarete Susman."[42] As Joris suggests, *NoOnesRose* is Celan's "revelation," in which he juxtaposes the possibility of an "innovated" text, producing and restoring creation, returning to him a multiplicity of presences, voices and beings lost irrevocably to the world of lyric and mimesis.

Esther Cameron remarks that the revelation "seems addressed to the assembly of poets .... from all time."[43] However, her first example isn't known as a poet at all.

> Indeed, [the book] sometimes seems addressed to the assembly of poets ("all poets are Jews") from all time, with one rabbi—Rabbi Loew, the Maharal of Prague—included in the company, and the masters of the Kabbalah, through the influence of Gershom Scholem, also present.[44]

Identifying two audiences, poets and kabbalists to whom Celan directs *NoOnesRose*, Cameron's insertion of Rabbi Loew's presence on the side of the poets responds to an undercurrent running through Celan's poetic project. Loew or the Maharal is well known because of the "legend of the golem of Prague." If only known through the golem legend, though, the Maharal's presence as a poet signifies an error. He should be counted as a kabbalist and not a poet.

However, as John Felstiner observes, Celan's family has Hasidic roots.[45] He would recognize the Maharal as a kabbalist and with that recognition is the knowledge that the Maharal's sources for kabbalah are tied to the Rhineland Hasids of the eleventh century, the *Sefer Yetsirah*, and the *Zohar*, all three of which understand texts of revelation to be "innovated" through their constituent parts, the Hebrew letters themselves, for the sole purpose of renewing Jewish life. By placing the Maharal within the "poets" rather than "masters of the Kabbalah," Cameron signals that the poet's relationship to *poesie* has changed. With this text, Celan has "turned away" from the poetic pursuit of transcendence to the poet's obligation to liberate writing's immanence in order to restore some form of redemption for the Nazis' victims.[46] The poet bears a responsibility to the letters' liberation from their *logocentric* stasis because the poet occupies subject positions of both creation and redemption. In this way, Celan creates a bridge between the poem and the poet; like the Maharal, Celan hopes to awaken the letters from their golem state.[47] He will write himself into another existence, to "speak in an other's matter."[48]

Implicitly Celan's early texts, those written before *NoOnesRose*, reflect Celan's growing disappointment in *poesie*'s ability to force readers to confront the implications of the Holocaust and Jewish loss. In their incapacity, "they, who sowed it, they wrote it away with mimetic bazooka fist."⁴⁹ The freighting of mimesis here intentionally points back to "Death Fugue". His earlier text is akin to a golem for his readers, but it is still a testimony to the dead for Celan, even though the master "wrote it away with mimetic bazooka fist." Thus Celan posits *NoOnesRose* as the site for his *poesie's* "innovation."

Even the book's title, *NoOnesRose* or *Niemandsrose* alludes to the fragile relationship between the poet, Jewish existence, and *Eyn Sof* (אין-סוף), the Hidden God, or "Nothingness." Celan freights *Niemand*, to underscore how Jews have been abandoned by "mankind"; Pierre Joris' translation repeats the gesture with *NoOnesRose*.⁵⁰ The "Rose" belongs to "No One." Implicitly, though, the translation also hints at the Name of God in kabbalah, "Nothingness," or *Eyn Sof*. In this work, Celan' engages explicitly with the kabbalistic signifier of the "rose" from *Zohar*.

"Nothingness" (אין-סוף) underscores for kabbalists that God is reducible neither to "thingness," nor to the senses. In German, it is translated as *Nichts*.⁵¹ Since God is infinite and cannot be conceptualized within human terms, there are no temporal or spatial limitations to the Hidden God. The Jews as the "rose" of "No One" propose allusively the possibility that even though Jewish existence has been destroyed, it might be preserved on another textual plane, one "beyond mankind," and by "NoOne."⁵²

The first poem in *NoOnesRose* merges then the abandonment of the Jews by this world with the presence of a "strange" phenomenon, signified specifically by the final stanza's last line.⁵³

> THERE WAS EARTH INSIDE THEM, and
> they dug ....
>
> O one, o no one, o noone, o you:
> Where did it lead, as it led nowhere?
> O you dig and I dig, and I dig myself toward you,
> and on our finger the ring awakens.⁵⁴

Like "Death Fugue" this poem is almost iconically recognized as one of the most important of Celan's poems because of its image in the first line, "there was earth inside them." However, the first line begins to contrast, implicitly, the revelation later expressed in the poem's last stanza, between the ones with "earth inside them" and "no one." To get to that contrast, Celan introduces a progression of terms, "O one, o no one, o noone," *einer, keiner, niemand* in the last stanza above that he will use to intensify the sense of abandonment. Essentially, he constructs a *Sinnlichkeit* of abandonment. The translator's choice of translating *niemand* as "noone," the progression of *einer*, "one" to *keiner*, "no one," and finally to the fused "noone" conflates to produce this overwhelming sense of abandonment. The world is not only implicated in a complete abandonment of the Jews, but this abandonment has also usurped the phenomenal world so that the subject becomes a subject by pushing through the *Sinnlichkeit* boundary of Jewish absence. The line finishes with the ambiguous "you," who is both one who "digs" and to whom the "I" narrator "digs .... toward." Both "dig," but their digging leads to "nowhere" even though "I dig myself toward you." The futility expressed by "nowhere" inclines readers to overlook then the end of the poem itself.

The last line ends with a symbol, "the ring" that "awakens." The importance here isn't in the "ring" in and of itself, but rather in its ontology's lack of animation. It is inanimate matter, but it "awakens." Thus Celan indicates a new form of existence within the inanimate "ring" as those "with earth inside them" lose the boundaries of their individual bodies, contrasted by "our."

Celan returns to "No One" more forcefully in "Psalm" to suggest a different "song" or prayer in which *Niemand*, translated by Joris as "NoOne," is transformed.

> NoOne kneads us again of earth and clay,
> no one conjures our dust,
> Noone.[55]

Previously, *Niemand* is associated with humans. No one has come to save the Jews. Here though "NoOne kneads us .... conjures our dust." Of the many ways to read these lines, readers might suppose the one word, "NoOne," includes the Hidden God, reminding Divine Being, in the tradition of the Psalms, that the Hidden God has remained absent while the Jews are murdered.[56] In that absence, creation stops; that is, "no one conjures our dust." In this respect, as the agent of creation, *Niemand* is left isolated and incomplete, signified by "no one." Moreover, Joris' translation of the repeated *Niemand*, fused as one word, "Noone," reiterates that *Niemand* now includes or at least is beginning to signal a specific transformation in the word itself, diverting away from human existence and toward Divine Being.

In the poem's second and third stanzas, Celan introduces the possibility of "we" also being transformed into another kind of existence that addresses the isolated "NoOne."

> Praised be thou, NoOne.
> For your sake we
> want to flower.
> Toward
> you.
>
> A Nothing
> we were, we are, we will
> remain, flowering:
> the Nothing—, the
> NoOnesRose[57]

Like a hymn, and included in the "we," the poet begs "to flower"; the line reiterates again that "we" act "for your sake" so that in the third stanza, "we" becomes renamed as "we were, we are, we will remain ... Nothing." In that moment, "we" has a share in "Nothingness." Celan uses the term *Ein Nichts,* "A Nothing" that he revises in the penultimate line as "The Nothing." In this way, he signifies that they will be a remnant in "the Nothing." He is pressing on the name of God, as *Eyn Sof*, to suggest an ontological transformation of the Nazis' victims whereby they "remain .... the Nothing—,the NoOnesRose." Celan reveals the new name for "we" to be "NoOnesRose." Celan writes a new psalm to perform an ontological transformation: as a "Rose," the Jews might continue in "Nothingness." They are hidden away, preserved in a Hidden God.[58]

With Book II, in "Radix, Matrix," Celan begins to trace the rose as "Abraham's root, Jesse's root, NoOnes root."[59] The patriarchs, "NoOne," and the poet share a root that expresses itself in "o ours." Now he foregrounds the possibility that "as one speaks to stone .... you, with my hands grab .... onto nothingness." In the poet's "hands," "you .... grab onto nothingness" becoming part of "nothingness." Here Celan uses *Nichts* consciously, to suggest that the "you" absorbed in *Nichts* attempts to reach out and touch "stone." The "you" retains a form of connection to the poet even though the poet recognizes that "you" has become part of "Nothingness" (*Nichts*).[60] Between these two forms of nothingness, the "NoOne" of the world (*Niemand*) and nothingness, or the absence of human beings (*Nichts*), Celan "writes" a bridge in order to restore Jewish voices "beyond humankind."[61] Rather than a master whose "writing" is contingent on Jewish dissolution, Celan the poet attempts a writing that would enable them to touch "with my hands" from within their "nothingness." He suggests that they still have voices—they sing—and it is his obligation to provide the textual path whereby they can be heard. Still they speak "as one speaks to stone." The poet and the reader appear as the inanimate partners toward whom "Nothing" reaches.

From the vantage point of addressing "Nothing" as a potential space for redemption, Celan pronounces "I opened my word."[62] Breaking apart the words to form new pathways for beings, he performs an act of creation, "the chirping manikin" comes alive and in this context, he calls to Rabbi Löw. Löw becomes a poet because he is needed to "circumcise" the "word." In an act of innovation, Celan has attempted to recreate Jewish being in the form of a new "word." "This one's word" is the space of redemption; for this word, "write the living Nothing on his spirit."[63]

In the very next poem, "Mandorla," Celan continues the innovation of "Nothing" in order to reveal, "the King .... in Nothingness (*Nichts*)—what stands there? The King .... There he stands and stands. Jew's curl, you'll not turn gray."[64] In placing "the King" within "Nothingness," he joins apodeictically *Nichts* to אֵין־סוֹף.[65]

Dramatically, Celan performs a poetic *tikkun*, in the tradition of Luria. He stages the repair, repeats its pattern to "write the living Nothing on his soul." By going beyond the injury done to both the Hidden God and the Jews—"(all poets are Jews)"—he offers writing as the mode of their redemption. In writing, he liberates the poem's consciousness of "itself as an act of freedom."[66] This "extreme formulation" of the poem "in its self-sublation," becomes linked in Celan's mind to the liberation of *Nichts* from the inanimate "nothingness" embodied in *Niemand* and "no one" from the first book of *Niemandsrose*.

By substituting a new form of nothingness for God, Celan imagines a world where Jews remain "structural beings." This foray moves Celan to "open" more words in order to perform new Jewish "blessings." In "Benedicta," the first two stanzas purposely break the first word, forcing the reader to see the words "open." In their brokenness, they form new words that lead in the last stanza to the Yiddish word for blessing, "*Gebentsht.*"

Dr—
unk.
Bl—
essed.
Ge—
bentsht.⁶⁷

Each preceding word is broken open and from within their fissures, Celan declares "*Ge—bentsht.*" From the ruins of language, these broken words, in several different tongues, end with a Yiddish blessing that also must be broken open. Transliterated into a Roman orthography from the Hebrew letters, Celan makes clear that even Yiddish must transform if Jews are to be heard again.

Celan continues this thread with the next poem, the last one of Book 2, "A la Point Acérée." Yiddish breaks open and reveals "the ores are exposed, the crystals … Some unwritten, solidified into language, lays open a sky."⁶⁸ Implicitly, Celan traces a revelation that exists at an "unwritten" level, but when animated by writing, "the exposed ores …. open a sky." Likening their exposure to precious gems that have been entombed in or "solidified into language," the stanza ends with the "ores'" effect on the natural world. It opens up the phenomenal as well as the phenomenological—the "word-matter" of existence.⁶⁹

The operation shifts then to "we too lie" and fragments of intermingled memories emerge. Their proximity to the "exposed ores'" opening "a sky" suggests a correlation between the "crystals" …. unwritten, solidified into language" and these untethered bits of memories.⁷⁰ Buried in the solidity of language, memories and "ores" conflate, but they now can "belong to a—reading?—eye." Enigmatically, Celan suggests that he and the lost, with their shared memories, are preserved in the exposed "crystals."⁷¹ They can be excavated by a "reading …. eye." However, to perform that excavation, the words still must be broken, "opened up." He has obligated "reading" to break up the text with him in order to say their names.

Book III opens then with "THE BRIGHT STONES pass through the air."⁷² The awareness of their presence forces Celan to return to his point of view as the poet in the last stanza.

I see you, you gather them with my
new, my
everyman's hands, you put them
into the Bright—Again no one
has to weep for or name.⁷³

At this moment, Celan reenters the poem as the vehicle for the "you." His "everyman's hands" are used to "gather" these ethereal gems. As "you" animates his "new …. hands," the poet watches them being collected and restored to the "Bright—Again." To some extent, Celan has become golem-like, and animated by an innovated writing: he works to collect their missing sparks. In this way, he demonstrates the full significance of the poetic *tikkun* he has proposed: he remains on the side of the mute, the "singing" usurped by the "master," but writing has been able to animate him again.

In this capacity, he has attempted to search for a writing that must still be available to them as well. In other words, Celan proposes that an "other" being uses his "hands" to speak an "actualized language, set free in the sign of a radical individuation .... It is the poem that does not forget that he speaks under the angle of inclination of his being .... of his mortality."[74] The poem alive to itself collects the sparks of disconnected memories, lost to language, and innovates them. They liberate the poet so that "in the angle of inclination of his being," he writes and "no one has to weep for or name." Celan insists on a poetic intervention that in its liberation from the deafness of aesthetic experience, repairs the abandonment of "no one."

Emblematically, another poem within the section, "Les Globes," proposes the process in which the "reading eye's" repetition of the unintelligible, the incommunicative, liberates writing, and repairs the "living Nothing."[75] The poem opens with the command, "read there:" because as the next stanza presents "the deaths and everything" are "buried," and "still hangs here, in the ether, edging the abysses."[76] These unarticulated beings need writing to expose their "crystals." Celan's levied commandment implicates then readers and the poet in a shared textual project.

> All
> the faces' writing, into which
> whirring wordsand drilled—Mini-eternal,
> syllables.
>
> Everything,
> even the heaviest, was
> fledged, nothing
> held back.[77]

"All the faces writing"—*Aller Gesichte Schrift*—alludes to the פרצופים or the "faces" and aspects of the *sferot*, the "globes" that emanate the image of the Tree of Life in the kabbalah. The "Mini-eternal, syllables" are produced because of "all the faces' writing." All the *sferot* are now engaged in creation and that process, "the whirring wordsand drilled," produces an infinity of syllables. "Everything .... was fledged, nothing held back" implies that the entire array of the spheres' emanations produce these "syllables"; thus we are commanded to break the idols of our language to reveal their voices.[78]

Book IV takes up the process of speaking "the faces' writing," by reducing words to their newly animated letters. Emblematically, "Hutwindow," with its condemnation of a writing that kills with its "mimetic bazooka fist," repeats the isolated chanting of the Hebrew letters, "the letters' mortal-immortal soul."[79]

> With alpha and aleph, with yod,
> With the others, with
> Them all: in
> You,
>
> Beth,—which is
> The house, where the table stands with
>
> The light and the light[80]

As Celan introduces the Hebrew letters, he does not give them a context beyond their enclosure within "Beth." In fact, he alludes to the "Haqdamat" of the *Zohar* in which creation is tied to the letter Bet.[81] He's simply repeating the letters and in their cadence, they are being reawakened. Throughout the rest of Book IV, Celan adds to the Hebrew letters, Cyrillic, among other alphabets, in order to continue the new poetic project he envisions and until he reaches the volume's conclusion where he "burns the meaning into a language they waken to, they—:."

What Celan attempts in *NiemandsRose* is the permutation of the letters, a reimagining of the poet in the subject position of *baal ha-kabbalah*.[82] In this position, Celan engraves, combines, rearranges, and permutates the letters, breaking open words into syllables that don't exist.[83] Like Abraham and God in *Sefer Yetsirah*, he rejects "conscious meaning" to restructure "new beings," to liberate the "Mini-eternal syllables" a path of letters to which the lost can adhere.

For most Celan scholars, Celan's rejection of "conscious meaning" in "NO MORE SAND ART" represents what has happened to existence, the cosmos, and redemption, because of the Holocaust. It is both a testimony to an injury and the inauguration of a new aesthetic project testifying to Jewish victimization. If "conscious meaning," that which the faculties can articulate, can understand, around which the faculties harmonize, becomes for Celan the evidence of a profound crime and its injury to the Jews, it also suggests that poetry bears that burden perpetually. In other words, the new aesthetic project that scholars routinely identify in Celan's later work still only "names," points to the burden literature must bear after the Holocaust. It assigns the victims to a permanent place of disfigurement and damage, anchored through the valence of mimesis.

Pierre Joris identifies though the stakes of Celan's revelation to be the articulation of another aesthetic project—"there must be other songs beyond humankind"—to perform the restoration or redemption for which Celan has hoped.[84]

> [E]arly Celan uses metaphors or metaphorical images in a more classically trained poetic sense, whereas in later Celan the author's intent is to fuse, coagulate, join, transmute—however you want to speak of it, and you can speak of it from several different areas or fields of endeavor—those juxtaposed images into a concrete whole, or, as I put it elsewhere, 'into the actual cornerstones of a new universe Celan was proposing, for him a necessary new universe after the Holocaust.'[85]

Joris' terms describing Celan's "intent" are particularly important for understanding how Celan presses *poesie* into another aesthetic and kabbalistic register. The poet is "intent to fuse, coagulate, join, transmute" the letters themselves, in order to create, as he created a new identity for himself. These permutations perform a creation, a wholly and "necessary new universe after the Holocaust." Joris sees the project in the "juxtaposed images" that produce "a concrete whole" so that Celan reveals "the actual cornerstones of a new universe."

While in passing, Joris, like Felstiner, mentions that "both his parents came from orthodox and, on one side, Hasidic family backgrounds," with *NoOnesRose*, Celan makes visible the kabbalistic patterns, foundational to his new aesthetic project, gleaned from his background.[86] What Joris' translation has highlighted is Celan's abandonment of aesthetic experience in favor of a letter phenomenology associated with kabbalist theories of creation and redemption. By focusing his intention (*kavvanah*), Celan attempts to permutate *poesie*'s constituent parts, in the hopes of projecting "another song" of redemption beyond the failure of this world, where the letters repeat the names of his family, people, to "NoOne."

His project rests then on the very enigmatic lines of "NO MORE SAND ART." In their brevity, Celan's cryptic "no more sand art. No sand book. No masters" suggests a fundamental break within the universe. Readers might associate the signifier of "sand" with Jewish culture, so that Celan points effectively to the trace of an older tradition becoming impossible, their interpretation purely semiotic. In fact, John Felstiner argues that "[T]hrough this experiment," of "NO MORE SAND ART," Celan illustrates that "two paths coincide: poetic language and Jewish existence."[87] Thus it signifies the termination of an aesthetic project founded in the desert. "No sand book" forecloses that revelation given in the "desert," until finally, the last statement of the line, "no masters" appears. Celan's language appears to endorse a one-to-one correspondence between "sand" and Jews until the line stops at "masters."[88] Using Felstiner's calculus, "master" of the book evokes a permanently lost Jewish world. In this reading, the loss or damage produces a mimetic effect in its absence. The representation is non-sensical. Scholars have been looking at that non-sensible element as the entire aim of the poem: since language has been damaged indelibly because of what has happened to the Jews, language can only repeat their absence, and its "nothingness."

Therefore, when "master" ends the line in "NO MORE SAND ART," Celan produces an apodeictic break between an aesthetic project that died in the camps, even for those outside of it, but especially for those trapped within it. It rewrites "Death Fugue" through the *nothingness* that adheres to language now. Celan writes literally the void of language that has opened up through the word "master." This void, the place of untethered "half-death," where nothingness resides, where life cannot be, exists as the cipher that these three short declarative statements form. That Celan would choose to write them brings Felman to her stunning conclusion, the poet engages in "breaking down any self-possessed control of sense" because the sensual world is exactly the illusion "the master" deploys in order to ignore the nothingness unleashed at the core of language itself.

At this moment, Celan's poetic arc moves from the poet's control over "sense," the natural order, or the realm of *Sinnlichkeit*, to indict transcendence: the poet must not be a "master" in Germany, condemning him within a Faustian register. He offers instead with "NO MORE SAND ART," the obligation to bear witness to inescapable and interminable damage, written as meaninglessness. Thus the poet and the reader stand at the precipice between wielding the Beautiful and the gaping void, the intersection of an illusion and the revelation of its nothingness.[89] He can map the *pleroma*, represent the full revelation of the Beautiful in transcendence for his readers, creating a simulacrum of life, or he can write the void, and in this final representation he and his readers search for the "songs beyond humankind," only to confess we cannot hear the silenced "singing" of the Jewish inmates, but our inability to hear does not invalidate their voices.[90]

As Celan moves deeper into the void, he breaks the syntax of the next lines so that readers bear witness to sentences disconnected from any context, "Nothing won by dicing. How many dumb ones?" Fragments of missing conversations, they are objects detached from phenomena. Whole dialogues seem to have transpired and disappeared in the space between "dicing" and "how many," until finally, there is only one word, "seventeen."[91] Reduced to discrete words, readers trace poetry's lost immanence. The word cannot bear this burden: it shatters and readers are left with "*Deepinsnow*, Eeepinnow, Ee-i-o." Tracking this development, syntax loses the sense of the poetic line; finally, the letters themselves are reduced to isolated sounds. They howl in the universe.

In other words, with "Todesfuge," Celan points to the loss of transcendence for Shulamith and the anonymous Jews who "drink black milk" until they choke to death while the "master" of Germany "writes and he writes." The "master" transcends through the transformation of Jews to ashes. With *Niemandsrose*, Celan "burns the meaning into a language they waken to."

However, while it is compelling to read "NO MORE SAND ART" as indictment, Celan teeters at the edge of the abyss with other questions: has writing lost its immanence? If the letters cannot be permutated, if they cannot combine and be combined, then, is the world condemned to "objective statement."[92] This is the reality and the revelation of the death camp.

In this trajectory, reading no longer permits the subject to permutate the letters and the letters are incapable of bearing permutation themselves. The "master" signifier gains a Jewish dimension at this point in the poem because it signals that there are no more subjects who could permutate, innovate, the letters to bring revelation to life; "(all poets are Jews)" either utters a condemnation or inaugurates a mysterious permutation that Celan finishes in "NO MORE SAND ART." For Celan, the possibility of producing a "song beyond mankind" not only motivates his "changed writing style," but also challenges the inhuman world of the Shoah. Thus he lingers, hovers over the void, contemplating, fighting against, resisting the erasure of those letters, the sparks of memories, of beings, their "unfinished stories." The letters must not be lost for eternity. They encapsulate the names and memories of Jews and it is his hope in permutation that drives Celan into attempting a "necessary and new" aesthetic universe by permutating the letters of *poesie*, "Ee-i-o."

Celan, the survivor, has been trapped within the ruins of language, aware that God has stopped reading His Torah and this Celan, the poet remains impotent to repair, to perform the *tikkun* that would restore both God's and their memories, their stories, the "wonder of their voices."[93] In this reading, the sounds of the letters are howls in the abyss. Humans and Divine Being remain forever estranged from each other. However, Celan the poet/kabbalist/prophet posits still "there must be other songs beyond mankind," songs that the poet is obligated to hear, to receive, to transmit: "Ee-i-o." With "Rabbi Löw I rasped, circumcise the word," innovate it to bring the "Living Nothing" forward, and expose "the ores." In permutating the letters of "NO MORE SAND ART," Celan releases the "songs beyond humankind" even if he and his readers cannot hear them and we collect the sparks of their memories.

Conclusion: Literature's Messianic Moments

Literary Messiahs

Olga Tokarczuk ends *The Books of Jacob* with Yente, whose body, since swallowing an amulet's Hebrew letters at the beginning of the novel, has been moored to earth, "waiting." Suspended in matter since 1752, she has witnessed the births and deaths of the world around her; she has also watched Hebrew letters inscribing and circumscribing the universe. Finally, her "waiting" ends with her evolution into a crystal that saves her descendants during the Holocaust. With their survival, she has finished the work that she starts so long ago. Her *metempsychosis* is complete and she begins to ascend into the light.

She looks at Poland below her, the "flash of the Dniester .... the lighthouses communicating by means of little scraps of light," and she hears the sound of her name, but she cannot be sure.[1] She sees a woman, sitting at a computer screen far below her. Yente is not omniscient so she doesn't recognize the screen; she "just watches letters appear out of nowhere from under this figure's fingers."[2] The letters are unrecognizable to her; she thinks they are unintelligible, like "tracks in the snow." Unlike the Hebrew letters, these letters do not hold her to earth. She ascends until she "vanishes" in the light. Yente disappears, but the figure below, a fictional Tokarczuk, continues to write "YENTE YENTE YENTE" on her computer.[3] The narrator confesses that "wherever we are .... the grim sound of matter" persists, testifying that "the world is made of darkness" and "we find ourselves on the side of darkness."[4]

Tokarczuk places the novel's curious ending as the last scene of its last chapter, "The Book of Names." The entire chapter comprises short summaries about Frankism's surviving members. They recede into history, while the fictional Tokarczuk ponders Yente's name, written in "darkness." The contrast between Tokarczuk's writing and the written form on her screen traces a gap in which those who continue on earth, preoccupied with matter, never see Yente whose final metamorphosis is immaterial.

Thus Frank's followers recede into history, as lists of names: Jews who lived as Jews, Jews who lived as Christians, Christians who lived as Jews, Christians who lived as Christians and who wanted Jews to be Christians, Christians who wanted to identify the Jews among them, Jews who died as revolutionaries, charlatans, messiahs, has-been prophets, crowds who lived nameless, anonymous in history. The heretic messiah and his followers become interchangeable with millions of names. They disappear in the crowd; they exist as historical fiction, a mimetic representation of a group whose desire for more requires them to abandon Judaism's obligation for less. Moreover, they merge with the modern aspirations of peoples far beyond Poland and intellectually distant from the figure of Jacob Frank.

However, as I state in Chapter 1, Tokarczuk brackets her stories of Frank, with Yente, his relative, whose illegitimate use of Hebrew letters transforms her into a being who does not die, instead she lingers at the margins of human existence, on the edges of consciousness, "waiting" to save her family once more and after that rescue, she disappears. She is not Enoch, content to leave her people and transform into Metatron.[5] She waits or more appropriately, her story waits.

In the process of writing Yente's narrative, Tokarczuk arrives at the literary messiah: Yente represents a "novel" intuition, an inadvertent "messiah" who surrenders herself to Hebrew letters because her lived experience has become a burden to her family. She seems "golem-like," living and conscious of creation, but incapable of agency. In this state, she eventually loses the capacity to read her own name. In other words, even a messianic Yente must be construed as a failure.

The people she "rescues" negotiate her as a "spirit" trapped in matter who waits for release, akin to the fantasies of Schulz's Father in *Cinnamon Shops*. Although the story of Yente horrifies and fascinates them, they do not recognize her as messianic, but rather the last form she has on earth, the crystal becomes their redemptive sign. The rumor of its existence draws her great grandchildren to flee the Nazis, hiding in the cave where it is entombed. Their escape occurs because of the repetition of Yente's story; her crystalline form left in a cave has been retold for generations.[6] She persists in their memories as both matter and narrative.

While Yente ascends, the fictional Tokarczuk still sits at her computer, aware that "wherever we are," we remain on the other side of "darkness." This consciousness of being on the other side of Yente's ascension prompts Tokarczuk's final articulation of hope.

> Nonetheless it is written that any person who toils over matters of Messiahs even failed ones, even just to tell their stories, will be treated just the same as he who studies the eternal mysteries of light.[7]

Essentially, Tokarczuk recognizes the human capacity to tell stories is vested with the messianic because stories of "Messiahs even failed ones" still elicit innovation. She can innovate a failed messiah's lived experiences in order to study "eternal mysteries of light" because even these *aggadot* of failure, heresy, and lived experience, are necessary to literature's *tikkun*. Even if not Torah, and even if in darkness, literature compels Tokarczuk to write "words" that bear "half the world inside themselves." Literature has absorbed the human need for messiahs and it produces writing that even if it always ends in being written, it still retains the trace of another. Consequently, if messiahs must fail, literature's messianism persists, "waiting." To that end, literature suggests prophets who not only bear witness to new stories, but who also innovate them.

Literary Prophets

In 1911, when Kafka writes in his diary about "The Four who went to Pardes," he glimpses through the figure of Elisha ben Abuya, the possibility of mental liberation.[8] However, Abuya or Aher "the free-thinker" never achieves transcendence. Kafka traces this failure, realizing with his protagonist in "Before the Law," that although the Law's transcendence should be for everyone, it excludes him. Kafka writes this exclusion repeatedly until in 1922, he fears he has had a "breakdown."[9] He writes, but he never reaches that glimmering "horizon of infinitude": the written never encompasses writing's transcendence.

In fact, he experiences with those *tannaim* in "The Four who went to PaRDeS" that writing might drive him insane, kill him, or compel him to reject it altogether. Harold Bloom remarks that Kafka experiences "the vessels .... breaking for him as his demoniac, writerly inner world and outer life 'split apart'": Kafka is condemned to rewrite "the breaking of the vessels" in every iteration of his work.[10] In this way, his writing has become both an "assault from below" and an "assault from above."[11] He inhabits this tension as he writes, but his *aggadot*—those popular "parables"— remain written objects. His writing is a "perfection that destroys." Although Kafka is not a messiah, his *aggadot* retain messianic aspirations. He imagines he could "write a kabbalah."[12]

When Scholem reads Kafka, he recognizes in him an "inimitability" that derives from a "strangeness" inherent in his fiction.[13] Although it inspires imitation, its uniqueness resists categorization.[14] "Inimitability" leads Scholem to include Kafka with "[T]he Hebrew Bible," and "the Zohar," as one of "three sets of canonical texts."[15] Readers examine and re-examine them because they express the "light of the canonical, a quality inhering in certain privileged texts that compels the reader to endless exegesis."[16] In this way, "strangeness" becomes synonymous with the "light of the canonical," compelling "endless exegesis," and infinite innovation.

Scholem's "light of the canonical" proposes that literature bears within its mimetic representations, another phenomenal writing, "a living intuition" that is never reproduced as an "object of knowledge." Thus "canonical" indicates a quality beyond a canon, a writing that rejects its static placement in any genre.[17] In its unboundedness, writing exceeds the written, and readers are not only compelled to ponder the text, but they are also liberated from its meaning because juxtaposed to the written, this writing denies a "stereotypical obedience" to one meaning.[18]

To put it another way, Scholem's "canonical" texts elicit in their readers an "endless" process of "innovation" in which each source-text becomes an archive of perpetually new meanings, waiting for the next prophet to retrieve. In these "three sets," Scholem posits, therefore, a connective thread of revelation and innovation. Furthermore, their revelations are not precepts, but stories. They suggest independent "sets" of *aggadot*, narratives, so that Kafka is in the same stream of inspiration as *Hebrew Bible* and *Zohar*. By placing these "sets" together, Scholem outlines a pattern of innovation that in its repetition produces "Kafka." It begins with *Hebrew Bible*'s received revelation, the innovation of which transmits *Zohar*, and ends with heretical innovations of *Zohar*, producing "Kafka" and "secular kabbalah."

As Robert Alter notes, Scholem's "fascination" with Kafka occurs because Kafka's work is "a secular representation (*Darstellung*) of a mystical and sacred sense of the world."[19] Alter's insight hints at the stakes of Scholem's "metaphysics" of the kabbalah. For Scholem, the implication of *Darstellung* forces Kafka to exhibit "sacred" phenomena in profane registers, and these cannot be constituted as objects.[20] Hence his stories are "inimitable." If kabbalah's introduction into the aesthetic is via *Darstellung*, then, literature transmits a multiplicity, but emanates an unknowable singularity. Writing's singularity becomes multiplicity when written: it breaks apart, rearranges itself, transmitting new revelations, all of which push at profane vessels' attempts to contain it. Scholem believes Kafka's writing is emblematically Jewish; it articulates the condition of the modern Jewish subject entering history. These vessels carry Hebrew into the world.

When Benjamin reads Kafka, as he remarks in a letter to Scholem, he sees in Kafka's profane outline, failed redemption too. Ostensibly, his letter criticizes Max Brod's biography of Kafka as "unsuitable" for his "own image of Kafka."[21] The freighted signifier "image" points to an ineffable "aspect" of Benjamin's "Kafka" that must be apprehended in writing his "image of the past."[22] Therefore, when Benjamin writes "Kafka," he isn't looking for the historical Kafka, but rather a phenomenal figure at the edges of representation. He has already begun to think "Kafka" as part of an "inimitable" writing.

Consequently, "Kafka's work is an ellipse with foci that lie far apart and are determined on the one hand by mystical experience (which is above all the experience of tradition) and on the other by the experience of the city dweller."[23] Renaming "experience of tradition" as "mystical experience," Benjamin not only points to kabbalah implicitly—kabbalah means "tradition"—but he also makes its "living intuition" synonymous with Kafka's writing. He posits a dialectic, akin to Scholem's. Kafka writes as "living intuition"—the "experience of tradition"—juxtaposed to the lived experience of the modern Jewish subject or "city dweller," who surrounded by a "vast bureaucratic machine" of "dogmatic objects," is controlled by "authorities" he never encounters.[24] In this way, Benjamin innovates "Kafka": writing and written become, for example, the "image of the past" and "historical materialism" or the work of art's "aura" and "mechanical reproduction."[25]

Like Scholem, Benjamin believes Kafka's *aggadot* form a "secular kabbalah," but unlike Scholem, Benjamin expands these stories to be emblematic of modernity's crisis because Kafka's stories testify that kabbalah "is falling ill" and it affects all humans.[26] A heretical movement substitutes its messianic materialism for an ailing mystical "tradition." In this moment, Benjamin expands the mystical synthesis to warn that the foundation of modern human existence is at risk.

There is an "aura" to the human, "truth in its [h]aggadic consistency" and "this consistency of truth .... has been lost," yet the vessel of its transmission, its residue, remains.[27]

> Kafka's real genius was that he tried something entirely new: he sacrificed truth for the sake of clinging to transmissibility, to its [h]aggadic element. Kafka's writings are by their nature parables .... that is their misery and their beauty, that they had to become *more* than parables. They do not lie at the feet of doctrine, as [H]aggadah lies at the feet of Halakhah. When they have crouched down, they unexpectedly raise a mighty paw against it.[28]

In Kafka's attempt to write something "new," Benjamin recalls for Scholem, his interlocutor, that Kafka, like Abulafia, hears a mystical command. Benjamin adds that in his "sacrifice" of truth, Kafka discovers *aggadah's* revelation: truth has an *aggadic* "shell," its "transmissibility," and it is not mimesis." Benjamin speaks to Scholem as a Jew, who recognizes "tradition" in its kabbalistic dimensions. Hence Kafka's stories are "*more* than parables" because they perform a *tikkun* both for God and for humans. They are not the same as Christian parables. These textual *kelipot*, "the products of decay," cause Benjamin to rethink Kafka's writing as *aggadah's* resistance to being *halakhah's* instrument—it "raises a mighty paw against it." In *aggadah's* revolt, this "storyteller" acts to repair something broken even though he fails.

Kafka's failure does not prohibit his stories from trying to finish their work. Liberated from *halakhah*, from "dogmatic objects of knowledge," these textual shells migrate, telling stories in every vernacular, scribbling in all spaces. Thus Benjamin proposes a writing whose persistent "mystical experience" is heard from the shadows, even though outlined against the "miseries" of humans' lived experiences.

In this way, Benjamin believes Kafka "surrendered" to tradition, a "mystical experience" he never has, but on which he could "eavesdrop." He "listens hard," but "does not see."[29] As a result, "Kafka" does not prophesy about the future because there is no future.[30] These are snippet views of "tradition" foreclosed.

However, with *aggadah's* repetition, the messianic is still available even if a messiah is not. The *aggadah's* "aura," even if it lacks the "consistency of truth" still underpins a secular kabbalah's new stories. This phenomenal excess constitutes both *kelipot's* revelation and failure's redemption.

> To do justice to the figure of Kafka in its purity and its peculiar beauty one must never lose sight of one thing: it is the purity and beauty of failure. The circumstances of this failure are manifold. One is tempted to say: once he was certain of eventual failure, everything worked out for him en route as in a dream. There is nothing more memorable than the fervor with which Kafka emphasized his failure.[31]

By removing "Kafka" from history, "the figure of Kafka in its purity and its peculiar beauty" emerges, signifying for Benjamin a "failure" that redeems because it becomes visible from within the profane: shards briefly flash, clinging to their profane prophets. Although the "figure of Kafka" recognizes the certainty of "eventual failure," that certainty does not negate the "figure's" attempts to reveal writing's "infinitude," even if obscured by written objects.

Benjamin declares it "memorable" that Kafka writes "his failure" with "fervor." In this one sentence, he links Kafka to key themes throughout his own work: Kafka's "failure" to experience the materialization of redemption in *aggadah* forces the shells in their exile to absorb the light in darkness until they shatter. Simultaneously, the vessels' fragments remain discarded in time and space, a "memory," or residue that must be apprehended before it is lost.

Although the optimistic messianism of the eighteenth and nineteenth centuries never illuminates the "other's path" to paradise, glimpsing its possibility in "Kafka" suggests to Benjamin that redemption can be materialized, even if not "for us."[32] To put it another way, in spite of modernity's textual crypts, its "shells," revealed to be nothingness, Tokarczuk's "darkness" of human existence perhaps, Benjamin imagines he sees a "residue" of creation's original paradise, a "shard" that remains here. Kafka *must* write it, repeating it in every parable, *aggadah*, novel and diary entry because this repetition is *aggadah's mitzvah* for these ruined and abandoned vessels. Thus Benjamin innovates Kafka's literary "consistency of truth" to evoke the "aura" of the work of art in the "memory" of its absence, the fleeting "memory" or "image of the past."[33]

He innovates history too, insisting that "every image of the past that is not recognized in the present as one of its own concerns threatens to disappear irretrievably." It will be "lost in a void." Like the "aura," lost in the work of art's reproduction, "every image of the past" unrecognized in the present will be forgotten, erased because it falls outside of one's "own concerns," or lived experience.[34] Benjamin associates this erasure with "conformity," against which he juxtaposes memory's inimitability. "Memory's" obligation demands "conformity's" violation.

When he writes his innovation of history, he turns to his "angel" who "would like to stay, awaken the dead, and join together what has been smashed to pieces."[35] He writes in response to Scholem's poem, "Greetings from Angelus." However, Benjamin only quotes one stanza in which the angel ponders human existence.[36] In Scholem's poem, the angel is condemned to live among humans, incapable of communicating to them the one "announcement" he is commanded to give. Therefore, the angel declares "there is no sense in me."[37] It laments that even "if I were to stay to the end of days, I would still be this forlorn."[38] Scholem's angel wants to leave, has no connection to human history, and remains an unwilling witness to human destruction.

Benjamin's response revises and innovates Scholem's poem by attaching a predicate to what the angel sees and transforming the angel's desire to flee into a desire to fix what has been "smashed to pieces." The angel "stares" at "wreckage after wreckage" of human history, wanting to reunite what has been destroyed, to collect destruction's remnants and perform history's repair. However, it is prevented from this act, acknowledging that history's "catastrophe" is one continuous "storm" that begins in "paradise," progressing to the present, and for which it has no remedy. Simultaneously, the "future" pulls the angel away from what has been broken. A spiritual being, the angel only watches helplessly history's endless "catastrophe." Neither angel nor writer can perform a *tikkun* to repair history because this "storm" has never ended. Human history appears to be the continuous experience of the "breaking of the vessels," inscribed within the unconscious, and expressed in the pile up of "wreckages."

In her English edition of Walter Benjamin's *Illuminations,* Hannah Arendt notes that Benjamin's work resonates with kabbalah. When she reads Benjamin, she characterizes him as living in the "present tense" and this aspect of his life makes him "unclassifiable."[39] She uses the dialectic that grounds Scholem's "metaphysics" of the kabbalah to describe Benjamin in the stream of inspiration as well.

Benjamin is "unclassifiable" because his essays are "inimitable." They have a "strange quality" that causes them to be "'*schlechthin unvergleichlich*' ('absolutely incomparable')."[40] Arendt notes there is nothing like them "in existing literature" because "everything Benjamin ever wrote" has "always turned out to be *sui generis.*"[41] "*Sui generis*" implies a phenomenon without an object of knowledge. Nothing in "existing literature" bears its pattern. As a result, his essays are "unclassifiable ones"; they can neither be subsumed under "the existing order" nor can they constitute "a new genre that lends itself to future classification."[42] Benjamin's writing evades "classification."

Furthermore, Arendt's "Benjamin" is an archive of "novel intuitions," continuously creating representations of elusive phenomena, peering out from behind "objects of dogmatic knowledge."[43] He lives among these "novel intuitions," their prophet rather than their master. His essays reflect "the theological type of interpretation for which the text itself is sacred."[44] Their foundation rests on a "sacred" ontology of writing, an immanence that when stimulated emanates the "inimitability" of "Benjamin." Hence Benjamin focuses on writing's immanence and not a Messiah's transcendence.

For Arendt, Benjamin's writing rests on the "sacred" attempting to break through "the order of the profane."[45] The gap between them expresses a lingering hope. If the sacred constantly tries to materialize in the profane, but the profane cannot contain this materialization and shatters, then, even though the "profane runs counter to the Messianic direction," it still "assists," still intimates that there is hope among the condemned for a "messianic kingdom," just "not for us."[46] In this way, Arendt sees in his work, sacred shards adhering to the written profane. Benjamin's innovations transform him into a prophet of the "secular kabbalah."[47]

When Harold Bloom reads Scholem, he characterizes him as "inimitable" too; his "peculiar and complex originality" identifies a "continuity in Jewish esotericism, so as to establish a counter-tradition to the normative."[48] In constructing the field of kabbalah, Scholem recovers a sanctioned aesthetic experience that enables Jews to challenge "the normative," the "dogmatic object of knowledge" of Judaism, with their own "living intuition." Since the "ritual of Rabbinical Judaism makes nothing happen and *transforms* nothing," the "normative" functions epistemologically.[49] Scholem presents his "counter-tradition," or "metaphysics" as a way of thinking about how humans liberate themselves from epistemology, the "conformity" of the object.[50]

> Creation out of nothing, from the void, could be nothing other than creation of the void, that is, of the possibility of thinking of anything that was not God. Without such an act of self-limitation, after all, there would be only God—and obviously nothing else. A being that is not God could only become possible and originate by

virtue of such a contraction, such a paradoxical retreat of God into Himself. By positing a negative factor in Himself, God liberates creation.[51]

For Scholem, "creation," "nothing," "void," and "the possibility of thinking about anything that was not God" are synonyms, opposed to an infinity, "God." They are ontologically different from Divine Being. In a gesture to Luria, Scholem posits that God's contraction imposes a boundary on Being in order to bring "we who are not God" into existence. Implicitly, we express the negation of Divine ontology in our creation. Our boundary severs God from us. Its difference imposes itself as a Law, but paradoxically, "God liberates creation" through it. By underscoring the human, as a necessary boundary, imposed by an ontological difference, Scholem intimates the necessity of the profane and secular kabbalah. In this way, Scholem becomes its prophet too.

All of these "prophets" read, write, and rewrite secular kabbalahs. Hence the memory of what is on the other side of the Law still reverberates. In this way, Scholem, Benjamin, Arendt, Bloom, Kafka, and Tokarczuk testify to its memory even if we cannot recover it ourselves. The trace of an infernal and inspiring memory, literature's messianic moment, repeats its ontological difference in every iteration. In other words, writing's "inimitability" stimulates the expression of prophets' written innovations, just as received revelation stimulates its transmission. In the fragility of these written vessels, fragments of redemption and condemnation proclaim the "perfection that destroys."

Consequently, we chase Heine's *poesie*, and we live with Halevi's martyrdom. We search for a "missing book" and recognize in the chaos of Schulz's "interminable stories," these "unfinished narratives," a "catastrophe" of "endless aggadot." We fail with Borges in writing "Aleph," and we retain a memory of the letters' impossible obligation. When heresy, tradition, kabbalah, and literature collide with the Shoah, as Atlan, Achituv, and Mulisch remind readers, messiahs no longer redeem history's victims and God no longer reads his Torah. Although humans have lost the ability to hear the letters' music in the universe because of the Shoah, we join Celan in the letters' permutation, hoping that a secular, profane kabbalah can still fill the cosmos with "songs beyond humankind" even if we never hear them. A writing still reverberates in literature, discovered among the fragments of the "void," those "shattered vessels of creation" in which God "dispersed himself" in order for our liberation to take place.[52]

In the introduction, I argue literature's ontology transforms because of its absorption of the kabbalah. Literature awakens to self-consciousness and realizes that beneath palimpsests of texts, there is more writing. Writing is God's infinite attempt to stream into the profane, concentrated in discrete letters. Hence literature absorbs the obligation of the kabbalist and strives to perform writing's *tikkun*, to reunite what has been broken. Literature's messianic moments are these brief disclosures of transcendence, the ecstasy of the PaRDeS, when readers and writers fulfill the command, "to write something new, "to write their own Torahs,"" even if their attempts fail.[53] They are also those moments when letters exhibit themselves, reveling in their immanence, revealing a sacredness in the profane awaiting us. Thus literature transforms because of the kabbalah and we are transformed by it.

Kabbalah and Literature represents the first movement of kabbalah's migration into literature. Using its innovated principles to stimulate an immanent, silent, secular text, its prophets and messiahs explore the "razor's edge" between the aesthetic "and nihilism"[54] In an echo of Bruno Schulz, kabbalah emerges from rubble, a revelation hiding amid forgotten, discarded trash. As literary prophets collect the sparks of sacred writing in darkness—the depths of shadows—the boundaries between reader, writer, character, dissolve because these entities remain connected in spite of their differences.

Erich Auerbach's scar and shadow reemerge, reminding us that literature encompasses *pleroma* and *kenoma*. We desire the full revelation, but are forbidden to enter that hiddenness, yet the light continues to stream into our world through letters and stories. We glimpse it, we chase it. We command its materialization, like Frank, Faust, don Isaac, only to realize we cannot quite catch up to this mystical writing. Although our creations are doomed to finitude, we, modern Ahers strive to fail repeatedly, but with each failure, we recognize that redemption is intuitable, even if beyond our grasp. Under the sign of the messiah, redemption fails in this human world.

However, under the sign of the prophet, the text remains redemptive, but not in its content. It is messianic, but it is not a messiah. Its constitutive pieces, letters, carry redemption's burden; they transmit a phenomenological liberation from lived experience, sequestered away within writing itself, even if its exhibition testifies to our failure and condemnation. In other words, literature's prophets not only bear witness to the vessels' fragility, but also still stimulate us to imagine the possibility of our future redemption.

The nexus between kabbalah's messiah and literature's prophet rests on a thesis about human ontology's transformation and is related to Aher. On the one hand, the messiah posits that human ontology has been permanently transformed in the world. The gap between human and divine ontology is remedied by the messiah's materialization. Furthermore, in this posited transformation, revelation is the messiah's to control. On the other hand, the prophet makes no such claim to a transformed and static ontology. The prophet retains a fallen human existence, a fallen human ontology. In this state, the prophet experiences "prophetic ecstasy," expressed as discontinuous moments of transcendence that last only for the duration of the experience. He, she, they collect writing's sparks. Literature's prophets extract the "memory" of the past even though its revelation occurs too late to redeem. Literature's messianic moments repeat redemption's hope, even if they do not rescue. *Kabbalah and Literature* freights this gesture through its insistence that kabbalah is in literature: from the moment *aggadah* becomes *poesie* and leaves the ghetto, its shards buried, but waiting. It offers both scar and shadow.

Notes

Introduction

1. David Biale (2010), *Not in the Heavens*; Elliot Wolfson (2014), *Through a Speculum That Shines*.
2. The reference comes from Walter Benjamin's enigmatic comment in "Theses on Philosophy of History" in which the historian's articulation "of the past …. may be lost in a void the very moment" the historian presents it. See Walter Benjamin (1968), *Illuminations*, 257.
3. In a conversation with the French dramatist, Liliane Atlan, her translator, Marguerite Feitlowitz, notes Atlan's "alienation" to French, that Atlan's syntax follows a "music" familiar to the translator, but alien to French. Atlan responds that her work "cannot go simply from French to English, because it not written simply in French. It is a mixture of my everyday language, Hebrew, Ladino, Yiddish—in short, it is written in a language of the Jewish subconscious" (qtd. in Liliane Atlan [1985], "The Messiahs," 18). In her declaration that her work derives from languages of the "Jewish subconscious," Atlan implies that "the Jewish subconscious" is filled with diverse orthographies, exceeding what she consciously knows. See Marguerite Feitlowitz (1985), "Translator's Note."
4. Joseph Dan (2002), *The Heart and the Fountain*, 1. See also Robert Alter (1987), "Scholem and Sabbatianism," 86.
5. Olga Tokarczuk (2022), *The Books of Jacob*, 677.
6. See Kitty Millet (2018a), "Introduction," 1–29. In the *Faultlines* "Introduction," I discuss this reflex extensively.
7. Agata Bielik-Robson (2014), *Jewish Cryptotheologies of Late Modernity*, 30.
8. Harold Bloom (1987), "Scholem. Unhistorical or Jewish Gnosticism." *The Strong Light of the Canonical. Kafka, Freud and Scholem as Revisionists of Jewish Culture and Thought*/The City College Papers, No. 20. (New York: CCNY), 57.
9. Abraham Abulafia (n.d.), *Iggeret wezod lihudah*, 15. Qtd. in Sandra Valabregue (2016), "Philosophy, Heresy, and Kabbalah's Counter-Theology," 253. Valabreque identifies in Abulafia letter phenomenology as a formal method.
10. I refer to *Darstellung/darstellen* in aesthetic experience in which *darstellen* exhibits the work of art to the individual.
11. Harold Bloom (1987), "Scholem. Unhistorical or Jewish Gnosticism." *The Strong Light of the Canonical. Kafka, Freud and Scholem as Revisionists of Jewish Culture and Thought*/The City College Papers, No. 20. (New York: CCNY), 76–7.
12. S. Ansky (1926), *The Dybbuk. A Play in Four Acts*, 46.
13. Gershom Scholem (1995), *Major Trends in Jewish Mysticism*, 132.
14. Kabbalah refers to an aggregate of Jewish mystical projects beginning in the Middle Ages; it is also used as shorthand for all Jewish mystical traditions even though that application is historically inaccurate.
15. "Dogma," "Hex," "Supernatural," and the reboot of "Charmed" are exemplary of the trend. The latter produces a golem through a magical spell, without reference

to Jews or Hebrew, implying the golem is a creature that any spell in any language can summon, even though the show's characters use the Maharal's methods. The popularity of these isolated figures has even shown up on YouTube where NBA player, Amar'e Stoudemire, uses Hebrew letters as powerful weapons in Nissim Black's "Win" (https://www.youtube.com/watch?v=jsX5LzGmRBw).

16 While there are exceptions, their perspectives reflect often the religious studies scholar identifying a writer or an isolated work as having kabbalistic content and then relating that content to a larger psychoanalytical or historical perspective. My book presumes the kabbalah in specific writers in order to examine how its integration into a literary tradition transforms literature. Since Scholem's essays on literature have recently appeared in German, more scholarship will appear on this aspect of Scholem's oeuvre. See Gershom Scholem (2019), *Poetica*. See Eliot R. Wolfson (2005), *Language, Eros, and Being: Kabbalistic Hermeneutics and Poetic Imagination* (2014), "In the Mirror of the Dream: Borges and the Poetics of the Kabbalah," 362–79, Moshe Idel (2002), *Absorbing Perfections: Kabbalah and Interpretation*; Klaus Grözinger (1994), *Kafka and Kabbalah*. See Scholem (1995), 25.

17 See Nicklaus Largier (2009), "Mysticism, Modernity, and the Invention of Aesthetic Experience," 37–60.

18 See Dan (2002), 7.

19 This structure should also be familiar to scholars of Judaism since kabbalah introduces new narratives, but always with a view to showing how mystical *aggadot* illustrate *halakhah*. My depiction of religious studies reflects how Scholem's conceptualization of kabbalah mediates the field for literature professors.

20 See Northrup Frye (2002), *The Great Code. The Bible and Literature*, xi–xiii.

21 Robert Alter (1991), *Necessary Angels. Tradition and Modernity in Kafka, Benjamin, and Scholem*.

22 See Harold Bloom (1987b), *The Strong Light of the Canonical* (1981), *Kabbalah and Criticism* (2002), *Genius: A Mosaic of One Hundred Exemplary Creative Minds*, xi. The latter text proposes the *sferot* stimulate "genius" in the arts.

23 Eliot R. Wolfson (2002), "Assaulting the Border: Kabbalistic Traces in the Margins of Derrida," 475.

24 Many thanks to Anne Tomiche for reminding me that Derrida taught Scholem seminars at both Irvine and Paris.

25 Cixous signals her interest in designating Derrida *un Saint Juif* because he lives between "two deaths," "Literature" and "Amnesia." However, she continues this "thread" through Marranism. That link reintegrates him into kabbalah through its heretical afterlife. See Helene Cixous (2005), *Portrait of Jacques Derrida as a Young Jewish Saint*, viii; 87.

26 Agata Bielik-Robson (2022), *Derrida's Marrano Passover*, 25.

27 Qtd in Bloom (1987b), 70.

28 Bloom (1987b), ibid.

29 See G. Gebauer and C. Wulf (1995), *Mimesis: Culture, Art, Society*, 1.

30 Stephanie Dalley, trans. (1989), *Myths of Mesoptamia. Creation, the Flood, Gilgamesh and Others*, 109.

31 This approach is not Judaism's *halakhic* tradition; it is however representative of the Bible as literature.

32 Paul Guyer traces how ancient aesthetic tradition is recuperated by German philosophers in the eighteenth and nineteenth centuries. For a discussion of Plato and

Aristotle in relation to *Wissensschaft*, see Paul Guyer (Fall 2020 edition), "Eighteenth-Century German Aesthetics," 1. https://plato.stanford.edu/archives/fall2020/entries/aesthetics-18th-german/, 1–84.
33 See Guyer (2020), 5.
34 Guyer (2020), ibid.
35 Benedict Anderson (1983), *Imagined Communities*. Of course, the exclusion of others presents for Anderson evidence of how "imagined communities" are built on exclusion historically, 47.
36 Robert Alter (1996), *The Pleasures of Reading in an Ideological Age*, 49. I make use of Alter's description in Chapter 5 because of its resonance with the Rhineland Hasids' "recipes" for golems.
37 As I have noted elsewhere, the formulas of persecution remain embedded in the histories of slavery, colonization, and the Holocaust in spite of emancipation, withdrawal, and liberation. See Kitty Millet (2017), *Victims of Slavery, Colonization, and the Holocaust*, 157–166.
38 Ariel Dorfman (1998), *Heading South, Looking North. A Bilingual Journey*, 248
39 See Kitty Millet (2007), "An Old Family Narrative: Gender and *Testimonio*", 63–81.
40 Benjamin Moser (2009), *Why This World? A Biography of Clarice Lispector*, xx.
41 Veza Canetti (2006), *Viennese Short Stories*, 71–76.
42 Erich Auerbach (1953), "Odysseus' Scar," 3–23.
43 Auerbach (1953), 9–10.
44 Auerbach (1953), ibid.
45 See Benjamin (1968), "Theses on the Philosophy of History," 253–264.
46 David Ratmoko notes that Auerbach's thesis about the *figura* resonates with Taubes' thesis of "inwardness" and "outwardness" in which he links individual repentance and revolution to the collective expression of antinomianism. To get to Auerbach's figura though Taubes has to think through the implications of these two scenes. His connection implies that a necessary antinomianism, latent in literature, finds its full expression in modernity. Like Jonas Wehle, Taubes links his thesis through Hegel and Kant, making these writers suture points between Jewish messianism, kabbalah, and German philosophy. For a brief discussion of Taubes' "inwardness/outwardness" thesis and a synopsis of his thought in relation to Auerbach, see David Ratmoko's "Preface" to Jacob Taubes (2009), *Occidental Eschatology*, xiv–xvi.
47 *Genesis*, 2.
48 Auerbach (1953), 7.
49 MacDonald claims the Homeric scene underpins the depiction of Christ's reappearance to the apostles after the resurrection. He hints that Christianity inherits a pagan Greek expectation of immediate transcendence. See Dennis Ronald MacDonald (2000), *The Homeric Epics and the Gospel of Mark*, 6.
50 *Genesis*, ibid.
51 Erich Auerbach, *Mimesis*. German edition, p. 17. *Das Gott ein vorborgener Gott ist.*
52 Robert Alter, trans. and ed. (1997), *Genesis: Translation and Commentary*, 105. Alter's translation of "The Akedah" or the "Sacrifice of Isaac" story freights another aspect altogether. He offers "see to" rather than Auerbach's "will provide"—the "idiomatic force" of the line—because his alternative reinforces the line's poetic resonance with Abraham's previous actions of "seeing." The biblical verse implies, furthermore, that God places himself in the same subject position as Abraham in order to feel the burden of his command from the perspective of his human servant. By "seeing" the

world through Abraham's eyes, God is compelled to compassion. Alter's translation, unlike Auerbach's, emphasizes God's identification with Abraham. It flows from God to Abraham and not from the reader to Abraham. God's compassion is elicited by His identification with the patriarch, but the biblical context implies that it is not about human to human identification. In other words, the story is a representation of the relationship between God and patriarch. However, both perspectives on the scene end with mimesis allowing God to see humans where they stand; that is, God intuits humans by reading them.

53 Auerbach's critics often ignore how Judaism reads "lacunae" and the gap between human and Divine. Most recognize Auerbach's attribution of an absence of lacunae to Homer in order to overlook Auerbach's Jewish experience in his discussion of "the common man." See G. Gebauer, C. Wulf (1995), 13.

54 *Genesis*, ibid.

55 This realization is also constitutive of Talmud's Elisha ben Abuya in "The Four who went to Pardes." See Part 1, "The Other's Path."

56 See Idel (2002), 32. Auerbach's choice of the "Akedah" freights so much more than a mimetic representation of Abraham's sensual perception of the commandment's fulfillment. In fact, the play of the German, *Schatten,* in its dual meaning of "shade" and "shadow," resonates with Bezalel of biblical narrative, whose name in Hebrew suggests, as Idel notes, being both "in the shade of" and "in the shadow of God" (צל). Here, biblical narrative hints at a creative drive in Bezalel that shelters him when he imitates the Divine act of creation in his "creation of the tabernacle." Since the tabernacle is fashioned according to God's instructions, Bezalel's aesthetic creation performs a mystical mimesis.

57 See Part 1, "The Other's Path." The "Four who went to Pardes" suggests that if humans attempt to experience the *pleroma*, they die, go insane, or become apostate.

58 Used by kabbalists and Jewish mystics in antiquity, this epithet signals for Auerbach an incredibly important moment in Hebrew literature: the "Hidden God" speaks to Abraham through representation's shadows. It also indicates the pervasiveness of kabbalist epithets at the very least circulating among some German Jewish scholars, unassociated with formal Judaism.

59 Robert Alter (1996), *The Pleasures of Reading in an Ideological Age*, 49.

60 Introductory texts for the study of literature often build on literature's capacity to represent reality in a palpable form through insignificant details. See James Woods (2008), *How Fiction Works*, 87.

61 Dan (2002), 16.

62 See Scholem (1995), *Major Trends*, 132.

63 See Norman Finkelstein (1992), *The Ritual of New Creation. Jewish Tradition and Contemporary Literature*, 76. Although Finkelstein discusses Bruno Schulz's theory of "heretical" creation in which "fiction, that profane secondary means of creation" competes with tradition, I contend that Schulz's "method" extends it necessarily.

64 Robert Alter (1993), "Kafka as Kabbalist," 87. Scholem stresses that from early on, he knew his project to be a "metaphysics" rather than a history. The claim establishes that Scholem examines kabbalah from the perspective of its concepts and principles rather than its events and historical footprints. Although many now challenge Scholem's historical accuracy, his contrast hinges on the metaphysical implications of "living" and "lived."

65 Scholem (1995), ibid.
66 The *Wissenschaft des Judentums* is both an intellectual and academic project, founded by Leopold Zunz, and organized around the idea of Jewish Studies as a formal discipline in German universities during the nineteenth century. Scholars affiliated with it model the project after the idea of *Wissenschaft* in the German university, signifying that Jewish Studies is part of the organization of knowledge in its entirety. For another perspective on *Wissenschaft des Judentums,* see George Kohler (2019), *Kabbalah Research in the Wissenschaft des Judentums (1820–1880); The Foundation of an Academic Discipline.*
67 Scholem (1980), 3. *Die Judische Mystik.* Moshe Idel concludes similarly in his analysis of "classifiable" and "unclassifiable" in relation to Scholem. See Moshe Idel (2007), "Arnaldo Momigliano and Gershom Scholem on Jewish History and Tradition". *Momigliano and Antiquarianism: Foundations of the Modern Cultural Sciences,"* 318.
68 In his discussion of *Zohar,* Scholem locates the tension to be at the heart of kabbalah: the movement's "vitality" is juxtaposed to the reification or "book learning." It punctuates Scholem's entire theoretical project so that "unclassifiable" juxtaposed to "classifiable" signifies a specific kabbalistic dimension. See Scholem (1995), 205.
69 The idea of the kabbalah as aesthetic experience almost never emerges in scholarship about Scholem's kabbalah. Of those texts that discuss Scholem in relation to aesthetics, see Bloom, Harold (1987a), *Gershom Scholem.* David Biale (1982), *Gershom Scholem. Kabbalah and Counter-History*; Robert Alter (1993), "Kafka as Kabbalist," 86–99.
70 Scholem (1995), 1. Echoing Scholem, David Biale observes that these historians were "convinced that Judaism was primarily a religion of reason"; thus Jewish mysticism had to be either "ignored or despised." Echoing Scholem, Biale concludes that "Judaism has no dogmatic 'essence' but rather is made up of whatever Jews have done or thought no matter how outlandish or even dogmatic." See David Biale (2018), *Gershom Scholem, Master of Kabbalah*, ix. For most scholars familiar with Jewish history, Scholem's meaning points to a popular belief that he did not share, in which Jews' eagerness to jettison the ghetto causes them to abandon the particularity of Judaism in favor of an unparticular minority identity acceptable to their non-Jewish neighbors.
71 See also Gershom Scholem (1957), *Die jüdische Mystik in ihren Hauptströmungen*, 11 (10, English; 11, German). Scholem freights the indefinite article to characterize both the original state and its transformation: an object of knowledge to the novel intuition. It refers to the necessity of inversion in Scholem's thought: Judaism needs to be reimagined regularly in order to preserve Jewish participation. Essentially, he uses philosophical and religious registers to posit that Jews renew their Judaic world historically through kabbalah. In this statement, Scholem makes explicit why kabbalah is more than an object of knowledge. The English version opts for "object of dogmatic knowledge." I've changed the order somewhat even though the English reflects Scholem's original choices simply because of the tension Scholem's use of the German philosophical tradition imposes on the statement. In seeing a dialectic at the heart of Judaism and Jewish lived experience, Scholem posits the object behaves "dogmatically," so that in its epistemology—Judaism—it deems its concepts to legislate in all fields, a gesture designated as ideology since Kant.
72 Bloom (1987b), 55–77.
73 Scholem indicates that under the lens of reform, Jews still need a process by which they can constitute themselves as subjects outside of its epistemology. Although

Judaism does not require individuals to be subjects, only to fulfill *mitzvot*, to follow the Law, to learn its precepts through *aggadot*, when Moses Mendelssohn argues for the rationality of the religion, he includes the experience of the subject, constituted in sublimity. Mendelssohn's radical suggestion implies we are most in God's image, when we are subjects. See *Philosophical Essays*, 192 "on sublime."

74 Elisheva Carlebach (2001), "The Sabbatian Posture of German Jewry." *Jerusalem Studies in Jewish Thought* 16–17: 1–29.
75 We need only recall Scholem's correspondence with Benjamin in which the two men ponder the sublime failure of Kant to understand how closely attuned Scholem is to his historical moment.
76 As I demonstrate in Chapter 2, "Heretics of Innovation," and following Scholem, Haskalah-era Sabbatians in Prague believe the political reforms of modernity resonate with their Sabbatian-Frankist heresies in that these reforms share with these heretical kabbalists, the desire for a full and total liberation from the bondage of an antiquated law. Scholem adds the striking influence political revolution would have mentally on the Sabbatians. Scholem (1971), *The Messianic Idea in Judaism and Other Essays on Jewish Spirituality*, 137.
77 This meaning is always reinforced for Scholem because of the emergence of Kafka. Scholem draws a line between what is done in the eighteenth century, the nineteenth century, to the twentieth century, in to demonstrate that Jews need a way to constitute themselves as subjects and that path relies on kabbalah's aesthetic interventions.
78 Here Scholem swerves away from the "heretical kabbalah" introduced by Sabbateans and Frankists into the discourses of reform because their revision of the kabbalah erases Jewish specificity in order to gain social, cultural, and political mobility. This point is underscored by the mass conversions that Frank orchestrates.
79 David Biale argues that Jews "converted or not" see in *Bildung* "a kind of German Jewish subculture"; it is "a secular belief system founded on German culture, but with a peculiarly Jewish twist" (36). *Wissensschaft* and *Wissensschaft des Judentums* enjoy a similar relationship.
80 See Kitty Millet (2018), "Our Sabbatian Future," 134–52.
81 Scholem (1995), 39.
82 Scholem lays the groundwork for understanding kabbalah's migration into culture, politics, philosophy; thus Jews' entrance into history encompasses metaphysics too.
83 See Scholem (1995), 60. Later, he also demonstrates what happens to Judaic observance when Jews abandon kabbalah. In subsequent publications, Scholem comes back repeatedly to a crossroads of the modern Jewish subject in modernity. See my discussion of this in the Part 1, "The Other's Path." Harold Bloom extends Scholem's argument to include non-Jewish writers as well.
84 Scholem works in three different languages as he writes: German, his native tongue; Hebrew, his new national language; and English, the language of his audience for the *Major Trends* lectures. Hebrew's mediation of German compels him to "irresistibly experience Hebrew even in the German language" and Hebrew's inflection adds new valences to German philosophical principles. See Gershom Scholem (2007), *The Diaries of Gershom Scholem, 1913–1919*, 200. In Judaism's written and oral Torahs, the relationship of *halakhah* to *aggadah* remains unchanged: *aggadot* illustrate the law's application. While the implication of Judaism as an "object of knowledge" entails the Dual Torah system, the German phrase, "the object of knowledge" (*Objekt des Wissens und der Dogmatik*) alludes via its translation into Hebrew (מושא הידע) not

only to the oldest Jewish mystical genre, the *Hekhalot/Merkavah* traditions, but also to the idea of "*ma'aseh bereshit*" or the "work of creation." "Knowledge" and "Creation" act as synonyms for profane and sacred. The pairing implies that the "work of creation" is infinite although the creation is finite. For orthodox kabbalists, it signifies that the work of creation continues in their study of the Torah. For heretical kabbalists, "reading" creation requires abandonment of the earthly Torah.

85 *Zohar* (2003), 29. The text hints that the work of reading and writing is the work of creation and that when God reads, God stimulates the letters in order to create.
86 Moshe Idel (2007), "Jacques Derrida and Kabbalistic Sources," 113. See also Moshe Idel (1990), *Golem. Jewish Magical and Mystical Traditions on the Artificial Anthropoid*, 9–27.
87 The basis for this claim derives from Luria's two Torahs, the higher Torah that God reads—the *Torah of the Atzilut*—and the earthly Torah, the *Torah of the Beriah*. If taken with Idel's reference to the thirteenth-century kabbalistic text, commanding each Jew to "write his own Torah," then the command is to write a Torah on earth in order to bear witness to the higher Torah, inscribed within them.
88 *Zohar* (2003), ibid.
89 Scholem (1995), 129.
90 Millet (2018), 134–52, ibid.
91 See Scholem (1995), 299. Since kabbalah renewed Judaic subjects so that they would continue to be Jews, with its migration into secular literature, Jews realize an existence without Judaism. It becomes an anachronism.
92 By recognizing Zvi's inflection of the "given," Scholem conflates Jews' lived experience of oppression with the "givenness" of *Sinnlichkeit*. At this moment, he implies that Zvi offers an alternative to Jewish suffering by pointing to another world accessible through the path of the false messiah. In this way, Zvi's intervention becomes somewhat inevitable: he offers an alternative to Jews living historically with oppression.
93 Scholem believes that when Frankism inherits this tension, its members pursue revolution and politics. See Gershom Scholem (1981), *Du Frankisme au Jacobinisme. La vie de Moses Dobrushka, alias Franz Thomas von Schonfeld alias Junius Frey*.
94 Scholem (1995), ibid.
95 Yosef Hayim Yerushalmi (1982), *Zakhor: Jewish History and Jewish Memory*, 86.
96 See Herbert Levy (2001), "A Note for the General Reader," in Alexandr Kraushar (2001), *Jacob Frank. The End of the Sabbatian Heresy*, 4.
97 I discuss this further in Chapter 4, "Kafka, Prophet of Failure."
98 See Idel (2007), ibid.
99 As Alexandr Kraushar, Frank's nineteenth-century biographer identifies, these narratives circulate under the title of the *Deceptive Bible*, incorrectly translated by Skimborowicz in his account of Jacob Frank's life and his influence on Polish history. See Krauschar (2007), 36–37.
100 Technically, everything outside of the purview of halakhah constitutes transgression (299). Scholem identifies one such example, the anonymous, eighteenth-century Sabbatian treatise, "The Adornment of Days" that circulates within Jewish communities, sometimes marked as an heretical treatise and sometimes as kabbalistic tract. Its heresy is its status as a beautiful "poetic" work. Thus the modern Canadian writer, Aryeh Lev Stollman, innovates it in his short story of the same name to reimagine its ritual as a transgressive obligation the story's protagonist must fulfill.

See Amir Engel (2017), *Gershom Scholem: An Intellectual Biography*, 125. Engel contextualizes this reflex or "behavior" as a social phenomenon in Scholem, a paradox that allows for "belief" to adhere to "the improbable, the strange…the paradoxical" and even "the impossible."

101 With this claim, Scholem demonstrates that the constellation of Jewish Studies scholarship opposed to kabbalah includes within its ranks already numerous figures, tropes, and narratives derived from the very experience they hope to displace.

102 Gershom Scholem (1973), *Shabbatai Zvi, the Mystical Messiah. 1626–1676*, 130. In Scholem's analysis of Nathan of Gaza's *Treatise on the Dragons,* he cites Nathan's "inversion" of Luria's thesis on *tehiru* and *reshimu*. Nathan and Zvi justify adhering to transgression because when God contracts into the self through *tzimtzum*, he leaves a space behind the withdrawal. It is *tehiru*, the substance of the void or abyss. However, something of the Divine remains stuck in the substance: Luria calls them sparks. This is *reshimu*, the residue of Divine Being. Nathan picks up on Luria's thesis to suggest that in the act of catharsis, Divine Being expels "thoughtless" sparks, abandoned to the void where they are discovered by *kelipot*—the shattered containers of Divine Being. These *kelipot* adhere to the mysterious shards of Divine Being, trapping them in the abyss and preventing them from finding their predicates in creation. The Messiah must recover and restore them from their imprisonment in *tehiru*.

103 Scholem (1971), 126. Also see chapter 1.

104 See Joy Williams (2023), "All art is about nothingness: our apprehension of it, our fear of it, its approach." (https://web.archive.org/web/20150908051728/http://www.reaaward.org/Williams/Williams.html); quoted in *Porter House Review*. https://porterhousereview.org/articles/directly-to-the-heart-an-interview-with-joy-williams/.

105 Scholem, ibid in English. In German, see Gershom Scholem, *Die Judische Mystik in ihren Hauptströmmen*, 324. Scholem applies this description in his characterization of Sabbateanism; however, it foreshadows how he understands Kafka's emergence in the twentieth-century. remarks that Nathan had begun his "interpretation" of antinomianism in response to Zvi's "personal peculiarities and the strange and paradoxical traits" of his character.

106 Scholem, *Judische,* ibid. (*etwas Gewaltiges*).

107 See Pawel Maciejko (2011), *The Mixed Multitude. Jacob Frank and the Frankist Movement*.

108 Moshe Idel (1988), *The Mystical Experience in Abraham Abulafia*, 17. Idel implies a similar relationship between thirteenth-century Abraham Abulafia and eleventh-century Rhineland Hasids.

109 I refer to any text outside the canon of the Torahs.

110 See Paul Sherwin, "Introduction," in Harold Bloom (1987b), *The Strong Light of the Canonical*, xii.

111 Scholem (1995).

112 Gordin (1906).

113 As I discuss in Part 1's introductory comments, Elisha ben Abuya is held up by the Yiddish dramatist, Jacob Gordin as a messianic figure for modern Jews.

114 Olga Tokarczuk (2021), *The Books of Jacob*, 10.

115 See Scholem (1995), 304.

116 See Scholem (1995), ibid.

117 Heinrich Heine (1851) *Der Doktor Faust*.

118 Kafka sees the play in 1911 and records its plot in his diary. See Klaus Grözinger (1994), *Kafka and Kabbalah*, 46–51.
119 See Bruno Schulz (2018), *Collected Stories*, 25.
120 See Benjamin Balint (2023), *Bruno Schulz, an Artist, a Murder, and the Hijacking of History*, 164; 267–8. Balint follows Wladyslaw Panas' thesis—as do I—that Schulz refers to *prawdiziwa ksiega blasku* or *The Book of Radiance* as *The Zohar* is known in Polish. However, *The Zohar* is not Schulz's "missing book." As Panas notes, Schulz "treats his own narrative art as a work of restitution" where his stories recover aspects of missing writing. Panas calls it a *tikkun* in which Schulz believes writing repairs the chaos of his lived experience. As I note in the chapter, Schulz understands writing to be a distillation of the chaos within the self, a creation writing over his lived experience. The true *Book of Radiance* is the one *Sanatorium's* narrator writes for himself, i.e., all other identified books, whether *halakhah* or *kabbalah*, would be copies, simulacra because "he writes his own torah." See Wladyslaw Panas (1997), *Księga blasku. Traktat o kabale w prozie Brunona Schulza*, 221. I quote Underhill's English translation, reproduced in Balint's text.
121 Borges (1978), *The Aleph and Other Stories*, 30.
122 See Max Brod (1937), *Franz Kafka*, 74.

Part 1

1 Jeffrey Rubenstein (1999), *Talmudic Stories. Narrative Art, Composition, and Culture*, 65. See also Gershom Scholem (1965), *Jewish Gnosticism, Merkabah Mysticism, and Talmudic Tradition*, 14–19; Alon Goshen Gottstein (1995), "Four Entered Paradise Revisited," 69–133.
2 Rubenstein (1999), 65.
3 Rubenstein (1999), ibid.
4 Rubenstein (1999), ibid. Rubenstein offers a compelling revision and reordering of this part of the story.
5 Sandra Valabregue (2016), "Philosophy, Heresy, and Kabbalah's Counter-Theology," 254. Valabregue traces the phrase's genealogy through several centuries. In Talmud, it is synonymous with a heresy that "isolates and separates one dimension from another." It signifies any "rupture to the sferotic realm." Its dualism is recuperated now as a "heresy that fractures Divine Unity." By the Medieval era, it transforms into kabbalistic "innovation."
6 Rubenstein (1999), 65.
7 By the Medieval era, the celestial Pardes will be replaced by the acronym, PaRDeS. As I explain in Part 2, "Letter Phenomenologies of Modernist Kabbalahs," the acronym refers to the four sanctioned ways of reading the revelation in Judaism: *pshat, remez, d'rash, sod*. These four methods enable the believer to move between the literal or *pshat* understanding of Torah in time and space eventually arriving at the Torah's secret or *sod* outside of time and space. This secret modality in text comprises the second half of this volume.
8 Scholem (1965), 39; Dan (2003), 18.
9 Scholem locates this nihilism occasionally within Judaism itself; however, he develops the theory in relation to a dialectic, as Alter notes in his introduction to *Major Trends*. Scholem (1995), xviii.

Chapter 1

1. See Olga Tokarczuk (2022), *The Books of Jacob*, 963.
2. Tokarczuk (2022), ibid.
3. Tokarczuk (2022), ibid.
4. Tokarczuk (2022), ibid. Tokarczuk leaves open the idea of the letters in matter, but forecloses their presence in ensouled creatures.
5. Tokarczuk (2022), ibid.
6. Torkarczuk (2022), 909–10. Elisha suggests that by writing "המתנה" on the amulet, the letters command the displacement of Yente's imminent death until after the wedding.
7. Tokarczuk (2022), ibid.
8. Tokarczuk (2022), ibid.
9. Tokarczuk (2022), 907. However, Yente still appears to witness the letters in creation, akin to an Adamic state in which Adam exists as "golem" before being ensouled.
10. See Gershom Scholem (1969), "The Idea of the Golem," 161-2. Scholem's extended analysis of Talmudic, *midrashic*, and *aggadic* sources adds considerable depth to Tokarczuk's depiction of Yente. "At a certain stage in his creation Adam is designated as 'golem'"; although the Hebrew word appears only in Psalm 139:19, "Jewish tradition" attributes it to "Adam himself." It means "unformed, amorphous" and philosophically, "it is used as a Hebrew term for matter, formless *hylé*." Thus Adam is "'golem' before the breath of God had touched him." In another tractate, in which Adam's golem state lasts twelve hours, Scholem observes that Adam is described "as a golem of cosmic size and strength"; additionally, "while he was still in this speechless and inanimate state," God shows the creature "all future generations to the end of time." Thus Scholem concludes, "[E]ven before Adam has speech and reason, he beholds a vision of the history of Creation, which passes before him in images."
11. The key element for Yente's transformation is the character's realization that she is dying, that she will soon return to "dead matter" and her soul will leave her body. Her desperate act of swallowing the letters, to invoke "waiting," essentially suspends her body, soulless, within matter. As Scholem notes in relation to so many *midrashic*, and kabbalistic sources discussing Adam as a golem, Yente gains "a hidden power to grasp or see bound" up within her. See Gershom Scholem (1974), *Kabbalah*, 351. Chapter 5 in this volume explores the golem further in relation to Bruno Schulz, Tokarczuk's compatriot, whose *Cinnamon Shops* resonates with much of *The Books of Jacob*.
12. See Ron Charles (2022), "Olga Tokarczuk's 'The Books of Jacob' is finally here. Now we know why the Nobel judges were so awestruck."
13. While Pawel Maciejko argues for "charlatan" instead, Frank was and is primarily known as a false messiah in Jewish tradition. See Pawel Maciejko (2010), "Sabbatian Charlatans: The First Jewish Cosmopolitans," 361–78. DOI: 10.1080/13507486.2010.481930.
14. Scholem (1995), 315. I use "fabulist" in the sense elaborated by Saadiya Hartman to suggest a history in fiction when a traditional history doesn't exist.
15. Charles (2022), ibid.
16. Tokarczuk (2022), 686.
17. Although Tokarczuk contrasts Yente's actions to "save her family" with Frank's desire for power and freedom, both actions are technically transgressions.
18. Tokarczuk (2022), 652.

19 Tokarczuk (2022), 698. These villages, both Polish and Ukrainian, noteworthy for their pogroms. Yente sees geography as the letters' emanations: they write the universe.
20 Tokarczuk (2022), 696.
21 Tokarczuk follows very closely here the historical accounts given by Pawel Maciejko, some of which I will examine later in this chapter.
22 Tokarczuk (2022), 695.
23 Tokarczuk (2022), 50. The novel suggests the other's path is the only road to redemption, an illegitimate, but actual entrance.
24 Tokarczuk (2022), 691. Frank believes that he is in fact the "real Jacob," and not the Jacob who has a vision of angels and a ladder, but rather the one who wears an animal skin to deceive Isaac into giving him Esau's blessing. Hence his followers understand his narrated autobiography to correct errors in Jewish history, "repairing" the injuries inflicted because of their adherence to the Torah of *Beriah*, and not the Torah of *Atzilut*.
25 Tokarczuk (2022), 691.
26 At one point in the historical accounts of Frank's last moments, he is identified as the reincarnation of Jacob, whose return to Edom and Esau becomes the necessary condition for all Jews to experience redemption. In fact, the novel's title, *The Books of Jacob*, alludes to a little known detail from the ancient pseudopigraphical text, *Jubilees*, in which Jacob gives to Levi the purported "books of Jacob .... books of his forefathers .... to preserve and renew his children" (433). They are considered "books of wisdom" that are ignored at the Jews' peril (ibid). See Lawrence Schiffman (2004), "Pseudepigrapha in the Pseudepigrapha: Mythical Books in Second Temple Literature," 429–38.
27 Scholem (1995), 272.
28 Tokarczuk (2022), 470. Tokarczuk posits then the suggestion of an ethnic Jewish identity that forfeits Judaism in order to belong to the nations.
29 Tokarczuk (2022), 685.
30 We might also consider Yiddish here because that language is written with Hebrew script. To some degree, Frank advocates the loss of ghetto, shtetl, and *halakhic* markers.
31 One cannot help but think of Frank's admonition in relation to Freud's later discussion in *Moses and Monotheism* in which he describes the "disingenuousness" of the Jews over millennia as a historical phenomenon. See Sigmund Freud (1939), *Moses and Monotheism*.
32 Zohar, 29. When God reads his Torah, he shifts from being the repository of the letters in chaos to becoming letters of Divine writing. He streams out of darkness, the undifferentiated lights of the letters pushing out from His Hiddenness.
33 Idel quotes "the Book of Unity," an anonymous kabbalist tract from the thirteenth century. See Idel (1981), "The Concept of the Torah in Hekhalot Literature and Kabbalah," 62–4.
34 Idel, ibid. One has to wonder if when Yente swallows the amulet, and the letters become formless in her, if she has in reality performed a violation of the heavenly Torah since in their unnatural adherence to her, she loses the capacity to die and gains knowledge as well as a perspective to which she is not entitled. Moreover, the letters have lost the form of God too. At the same time, though, her metamorphosis by the end of the novel into "crystal" suggests that the letters still refine matter

so that a future redemption awaits her. The sheer optimism of Tocarczuk's novel hinges on Yente—not Jacob Frank—because Yente continues on her "other's path" to redemption.

35 Moshe Idel, "Jacques Derrida and Kabbalistic Sources," 113. The implications of this kabbalist tract are disturbing because in this formulation; human existence's significance is only to furnish God with predicates to His story.
36 See Scholem (1995), 138. Abraham Abulafia uses *Sefer Yetsirah* to posit that each Hebrew letter corresponds to a "special member of the body." If an unprepared mind engages in prophetic ecstasy, and inadvertently rearranges the letters associated with that individual specifically, that person not only could emerge from the experience missing a limb, dying, or going insane, but also would damage the "name of God" in its singular iteration within that individual.
37 Maciejko (2010), "Frankism," ibid.
38 Tokarczuk (2022), 480.
39 Tokarczuk (2022), ibid.
40 See Joseph Dan, (2002), *The Heart and the Fountain*, 4.
41 Tokarczuk (2022), 480.
42 Tokarczuk (2022), ibid.
43 Tokarczuk (2022), ibid.
44 In the next century, Jacob Gordin will make "the incomprehensible Law" the basis for Aher's apostasy so that Aher, a "free-thinker," tries to save the Jews from their Judaic overlords. Gordin's play introduces the Talmudic figure to Kafka. See Chapter 4, "Kafka, Prophet of Failure."
45 Tokarczuk (2022), ibid. This particular teaching was meant to undermine the "old kabbalah" specifically by demonstrating that their exegetical aim of innovating the Torah of *Beriah* both with Talmud and with the written Torah was in actuality affirming Samael's treachery. It also revises Luria's theory of "collecting the sparks" to be the Frankist's collection of the fragments of *Atzilut*, the "new Law."
46 Tokarczuk (2022), 685.
47 Tokarczuk (2022), 689.
48 Tokarczuk (2022), ibid.
49 This innocuous phrase is used whenever Talmud's *tannaim* or *amoraim* find themselves forced "to fulfill a command through the violation of another command" (*mitzvah ha-ba'ah ba-averah*). David Biale underscores that it not only motivates Scholem's kabbalah scholarship, but also resonates with his view of Zionism.

> Zionism had made it possible for Jews to explore the most heretical moments in Jewish history since it freed them from the need to justify themselves in the eyes of the non-Jewish world …. in later years, Scholem would emphasize repeatedly that Zionism should not dictate a particular view of Jewish history but rather make possible the fullest exploration of all facets of the Jewish experience.

In this brief comment, Biale recognizes within Scholem's metaphysics of the kabbalah, the profound desire to reintegrate heresy as a part of "Jewish experience." See David Biale (2018), *Gershom Scholem, Master of the Kabbalah*, 125.
50 Pawel Maciejko (2011), *The Mixed Multitude. Jacob Frank and the Frankist Movement*, 21.
51 Tokarczuk (2022), 684.
52 Tokarczuk (2022), 683.

53 Tokarczuk (2022), ibid.
54 Tokarczuk (2022), ibid. Maciejko indicates that there is proof that Frank may have purposely left the windows only partially covered in order to enable the scene to be viewed surreptitiously: he essentially wants to provoke the rabbinate by the display. See Maciejko (2011), 32.
55 Tokarczuk (2022), ibid.
56 Tokarczuk (2022), ibid.
57 Tokarczuk (2022), 682.
58 Whether or not Tokarczuk intended to suggest a cognitive link in readers' minds between Frank and Faust, it is certainly an implication of the narrative. The link encompasses also the earlier figure of Joseph della Reina. For an introduction to Joseph della Reina, see Jean Baumgarten (2018), *La légende de Yosef della Reina, activiste messianique: Trois versions traduites de l'hébreu et du Yiddish*. Scholem underscores the connection too. See Scholem (1995), 145.
59 It is a troubling account. The example resonates with Jacob Taubes in the twentieth century and suggests that the erotic *tikkun* was foundational to his project of liberation even though Muller rejects Taubes as a Frankist. See Jerry Z. Muller (2022), *Professor of Apocalyse. The Many Lives of Jacob Taubes*, 253.
60 Maciejko (2011), *Mixed Multitude*, 26.
61 Maciejko (2011), ibid.
62 Maciejko (2011), 27; 273. He cites *The Zohar*, 3:256b.
63 Maciejko (2011), 27.
64 The novelist, Anna Leznai, inverts the pattern to suggest another variant in which the male body is the readable Torah and the woman is the subject who reads that body, stimulating it as an articulation of the *sferot*. Many thanks to Maria Remelyi for this insight.
65 Maciejko (2011), 27.
66 See Eliot R. Wolfson (2005), "The Body in the Text: A Kabbalistic Theory of Embodiment." 481.
67 See Harris Lenowitz (1998), *The Jewish Messiahs from the Galilee to Crown Heights*, 192. Lenowitz argues persuasively that "Rabbi Nahman of Bratslav .... learned from Frank's dicta or his followers." Although Lenowitz does not endorse or even come close to a revisionist understanding of Frank and his possible relationship to Hasidism, in subsequent writers, Hasidism's "borrowing" of Frankist motifs, and the interaction between Hasidim and Frankists is presented as a given. See Klaus Samuel Davidowicz (1998), *Jakob Frank, der Messias aus dem Ghetto*. The weakness of this text is the writer's lack of nuance with kabbalist writers who influenced Frank. See Elisheva Carlebach (2000),"Review of *Jakob Frank, der Messias aus dem Ghetto* by Klaus Samuel Davidowicz," 163–6. See also Isaac Singer (November and December 1970), *"Der man fun haloymes." Forverts*. The translation can be found in Pawel Maciejko (2017), "The Man of Dreams," 183–92.
68 Lenowitz (1998), 181.
69 Lenowitz (1998), ibid. Lenowitz's discussion of the many implications of the Yiddish *amhoretz* and the Polish *prostak* illustrates furthermore that early Hasidism proposed a transformed valence for "simpleton" because of its resonance with Hasidim. In Tokarczuk, it is suggested by the reference to "masa duma."
70 Maciejko (2010), "Frankism," ibid.

71 Reuven Hammer (2015), *Akiva Life, Legend, Legacy*, 3. Hammer observes that Akiva uses *am ha'aretz* to describe himself as previously a peasant who would not know how to treat one who studies Torah.
72 See Eli Schonfeld (2016), "Am Ha'aretz: The Law of the Singular. Kafka's Hidden Knowledge," 107–29.
73 See Lenowitz (1998), 181.
74 The Polish demiurge will resurface again with Bruno Schulz. Schulz makes it clear that the new Jewish messiah commandeers creation through this figure.
75 Lenowitz (1998), ibid.
76 Lenowitz (1998), ibid.
77 Lenowitz (1998), ibid.
78 Lenowitz (1998), ibid.
79 In an eerie foreshadowing of *sensus communis,* Frank advocates a shared human sense that is the foundation for an imagined liberation from suffering and persecution.
80 Lenowitz (1998), "dicta 130," 186. Frank instructs his followers to embed themselves with the Austrian emperor in order to eventually to establish his own country. For an overview of the strategy, see Scholem (1981), *Du Frankisme au Jacobinisme. La vie de Moses Dobrushka, alias Franz Thomas von Schonfeld alias Junius Frey*.
81 Carlebach also makes this claim in relation to Frank. See Carlebach (2000), Review of Jakob Frank, der Messias aus dem Ghetto by Klaus Samuel Davidowicz, 163–6. ibid.
82 Lenowitz (1998), 189.
83 In other words, there are many heretical kabbalahs.
84 The audience for the narratives were the Frankists themselves since they practiced secretly due to existing rabbinical bans and potential papal excommunication should their actions be discovered.
85 In fact, most scholars accept that Frank crossed many boundaries that would be unacceptable to even the most zealous of Sabbatians. Carlebach notes that when Frank and his followers "later took part in public disputations against rabbinic representatives, they breached an invisible line that no Sabbateans before them, even those who had converted, had dared to cross. After they affirmed the ancient canard that Jews used Christian blood for Jewish religious ritual, most Jews turned away from them in disgust, and the last vestiges of respectability of Sabbateanism in the Jewish world received their death blow." See Carlebach (2000), 163. In the later Sabbatianism that emerges after Zvi's death, the "believers" still adhere to his teachings, but they don't necessarily follow his actions. Consequently, many continue to live among orthodox communities without their actual religious practices being known.
86 Lenowitz (1998), 190.
87 This represents a radical rethinking of *nefilim* since it suggests that the coupling between the angelic and human ontologies might have been a step to the eventual restoration of Eden and the Tree of Life or Torah of *Atzilut*. Popular culture has been somewhat faster to imagine these possible scenarios.
88 Strikingly, Frank implies that human existence bears within itself a testimony that the restoration of *Atzilut* can only come through *Beriah's* destruction.
89 One can see Frank's conflation here: after the patriarchs, human mortality is shorter, akin to our own lifespans and tied to the articulation of formal Judaism and law. In his thinking, Judaism suppresses human potential.

90 Harold Bloom (1987b), *The Strong Light of the Canonical*, 70.
91 Lenowitz (1998), 193. As I note in the "Introduction," Tokarczuk makes a similar claim at the end of the *Books of Jacob*.
92 Lenowitz (1998), ibid.

Chapter 2

1. See Vaclav Žáček (1938). "Zwei Beiträge zur Geschichte des Frankismus in den böhemischen Ländern," 343. While today, it might be considered obscure, Wehle and the Prague Circle are well known in Bohemia in the eighteenth and nineteenth centuries. The group inherits and integrates previous generations of Sabbatians whose backgrounds remain "secret" for fear of their excommunication or ban by the rabbinate. Jonathan Eibeschütz is but one example of someone who lives as an orthodox Jew, but who practices Sabbatianism. This preceding generation will have significant contact with Swedenborg, the Moravian Protestant Church, and other Christian groups who believe that "the Sabbateans' version of Kabbalah are close to Christian beliefs and that it could end the ancient divisions between Judaism and Christianity." See Marsha Keith Schuchard (2011), "From Poland to London Sabbatean Influences on the Mystical Underworld of Zinzendorf, Swedenborg, and Blake," 252.
2. See Pawel Maciejko (2011), *The Mixed Multitude: Jacob Frank and the Frankist Movement, 1755–1816*, 248; and Pawel Maciejko (2010),"Frankism." https://yivoencyclopedia.org/article.aspx/frankism. Maciejko identifies the three centers of Frankism to be "Offenbach, where Frank lived the last four years of his life and where he established the court that served as a pilgrimage center for followers from different countries; Warsaw, where the majority of the converted Frankists lived; and Prague, whose importance grew in an inverse ratio to Offenbach." Wehle's financial support of the court implies Prague as the de facto power behind the court.
3. Maciejko (2011), 249.
4. Vaclav Žáček (1938), "Zwei Beiträge zur Geschichte des Frankismus in den böhemischen Ländern." *Jahrbuch der Gesellschaft für Geschichte der Juden in der Cechoslovakischen Republik*. Ed. Samuel Steinherz, trans. Anton Blaschka, 343.
5. Gershom Scholem (1974), "A Frankist Document from Prague," 787–814. Scholem argues that Wehle's son-in-law may have been the author of tracts previously attributed to Wehle; however, for our intents and purposes the critical element is the target of Wehle/Hönig's efforts. Scholem also identifies that Hönig comes from a Frankist family and is related to Frank as well. See also Žáček (1938), 398. Zacek implies that their Frankist orientation reflects a modern Bohemian cosmopolitanism, an eclectic attitude toward "the novel," cultural trends of a new Europe.
6. Harris Lenowitz (1998), *The Jewish Messiahs from the Galilee to Crown Heights*, 196. Lenowitz suggests that while Offenbach is the main center of the sect, Prague's adherents remain its main benefactors.
7. Maciejko (2011), 248.
8. Maciejko (2010), "Frankism," "ibid." Maciejko describes it as an "open secret" among Prague's Jewish communities. See also Maciejko (2011), 248. Maciejko also notes that the Prague Circle leans more toward Sabbateanism than Frankism in their daily lives.
9. Žáček's perspective characterizes the persecution as ongoing although Maciejko sees the conflict occurring after Frank's death.

10 See Vaclav Žáček (1938), 343.
11 Žáček (1938), ibid.
12 Žáček (1938), ibid.
13 Stuart Taberner (2021), "Redemption through Sin: Benjamin Stein's *Das Alphabet des Rabbi Löw* and the Heretical Dynamism of Contemporary German Jewish Literature and Identity." 482.
14 Žáček (1938), ibid.
15 Žáček posits the popularity or at least the notoriety, of Sabbatian and Frankist movements among Jews and non-Jews. Ironically, Hönig invites Zunz to speak at Prague's first Reform Synagogue of which he is the founder and benefactor. Whether or not Zunz actually gave a sermon there, he most certainly would have recognized the possibility that his hosts were known Frankists and Sabbatians.
16 Žáček (1938), 344.
17 See Pawel Maciejko (2010), "Sabbatian Charlatans: The First Jewish Cosmopolitans," 34–5. Maciejko comments on Elisheva Carlebach's work on secrecy among Sabbatian Jews in Prussia.
18 Maciejko (2010), ibid. With so many Frankists converted to Catholicism and embedding themselves in Prussian, Central European, and French social and political milieux, it is not surprising that kabbalah, the underwriting tradition which Frank innovates to propel himself as messiah, would be extremely popular suddenly among Christians, that its signifiers, principles, themes would circulate in cultural and social movements.
19 See Maciejko (2010), ibid.
20 Although kabbalah is a "fad," Jews remain excluded from certain professions. As both Maciejko's scholarship demonstrates and Tokarczuk's novel illustrates, Frank not only manipulates this popularity to his own advantage, but he also deploys his revision of the kabbalah through several generations of followers across Europe, ie he exploits antisemitism to further his social and political project.
21 This is in and of itself quite unique: that non-Jews might recognize kabbalist innovations suggests the prevalence of kabbalist practices at a greater scale than imagined previously. It implies that Sabbatianism and Frankism were popular trends and not the minor affairs that their critics had made them out to be. Also intriguingly, Žáček doesn't identify whether his sources are exclusively Jewish or if they include non-Jews too.
22 This is the sense of *prostak*, the Polish word for "commoner." See Lenowitz (1998), 186. As I've noted earlier, "the common man" is used an epithet to describe Akiva, and at other times, to suggest in Yiddish, a "simpleton."
23 Scholem's discussion of prayer as an "intensification," lends itself to my mind as a necessary step to innovation as a theory. Scholem (1995), 101–2. In the German version of *Major Trends*, the role of innovation becomes a bit clearer. See Gershom Scholem (1957), *Die Jüdissche Mystik in ihren Hauptströmungen*, 112. For a brief history of the Kalonymides or Kalonymous family, see Joseph Dan (2002), *The Heart and the Fountain*, 82.
24 Dan (2002), 117–20. Although Joseph Dan discusses an anonymous early attempt to "bridge the chasm between traditional prayer and a mystical one," he implies nonetheless that the intensification of prayer is a new practice associated with early kabbalah. This intensification gains momentum so that in the *Zohar*, it is linked to prayer and text. To the innovate suggests to the Zoharist, the stimulation of the Hebrew letters.

25 I believe this theory is compelling to Kafka who surely would have been exposed to theories of kabbalistic innovation in Prague, especially since as Grözinger notes, kabbalah is discussed openly at the dinner table as Kafka grows up. See Klaus Grözinger (1994), *Kafka and Kabbalah*, 4.
26 By "Zohar generations," I mean those groups who both introduce and study the *Zohar* as the defining text of kabbalah.
27 Scholem (1995), 203.
28 Scholem (1995), ibid.
29 Daniel Matt (2003). Matt, *Zohar*. 25; 1:4b.
30 Qtd. in Harold Bloom (1987b), 70.
31 Matt (2003), ibid. A striking recuperation of kabbalist innovation occurs with post-Holocaust writers, especially the French dramatist, Liliane Atlan. She uses the Luriannic tradition of the *sferot* and the Tree of Life to demonstrate how innovation fails because of the Holocaust. Atlan explores the theme of the *sferot* in "The Messiahs." See Liliane Atlan (1985), "Les Messiahs," 89–165. Likewise, Paul Celan and Romy Achituv illustrate the letters' abandonment of the world because of the event and its significance to them. See Chapters 8 and 9 on their letter phenomenologies and the Holocaust. Atlan explores the theme of the *sferot* in "The Messiahs." See Liliane Atlan (1985), "The Messiahs," 89–165.
32 Matt (2003), ibid.
33 Scholem expresses his fear to Rosenzweig in 1923 that modern Hebrew is used as if the letters themselves are simple instruments of human communication. See Jacques Derrida (2002), "The Eyes of Language: The Abyss and the Volcano," 195.
34 Joseph Dan (2002), *The Heart and the Fountain*, 10–11. See Derrida (2002), ibid.
35 Joseph Dan (2007), *A Very Short Introduction to Kabbalah*, 2–3.
36 Žáček (1938), 343. A similar thesis is advanced by Agata Bielik-Robson in relation to Derrida's *Marrano* declaration in "the Toledo statement." She suggests that not only does Marranism offer the ground of Derrida's Jewish identity, but it proposes itself also as "absolute secret" of Judaism. See Agata Bielik-Robson (2022), *Derrida's Marrano Passover*, 1–5. A heretic might even take it as an implication of the "other side" of *tzimtzum*.
37 Scholem has pointed out that Žáček's acceptance of the veracity of his "sources" is a little skewed since Hönig's family has several connections to Frankism, thus suggesting that the marriage between Hönig and the Wehle family is part of Frank's dynasty-building stratagem. See Scholem (1981), *Du Frankisme au Jacobinisme. La vie de Moses Dobrushka, alias Franz Thomas von Schonfeld alias Junius Frey*, 8.
38 Žáček (1938), 343. See Gershom Scholem (1981), *Du Frankisme au Jacobinisme. La vie de Moses Dobrushka, alias Franz Thomas von Schonfeld alias Junius Frey*, 14. Whether Žáček's portrayal of the two men's repeated discussions of philosophy and kabbalah can be verified isn't the point: what their discussions cause Žáček to infer though remains relevant to the heretical kabbalah becoming a redemptive apostasy of ideas.
39 Scholem believes that Hönig's Frankism is pronounced, but is expressed in a vernacular mixture of Hebrew and German in a "barbarian" form the son-in-law's attribution of the higher teachings of Frankism in relation to German idealism to Wehle makes some sense in that Wehle would possess a more nuanced vocabulary than Hönig. Hönig's "testimony" is given to force Czech authorities into acting on Wehle's behalf against the rabbinate who are coming closer to a possible "ban" on the

group according to the son-in-law. Thus he doesn't explicitly tell the authorities what Wehle's kabbalah portends, only that his father-in-law teaches "love." Gershom Scholem (1974), "A Frankist Document from Prague," 789.
40 Žáček (1938), ibid.
41 Žáček (1938), ibid. Hönig's use of a recognizable Christian narrative suggests an atteempt to sway sympathies for the sect with Christian authorities.
42 Zacek (1938), 363.
43 See Maciejko (2011), 252. He cites the *The Prophecies of Isaiah*, a text written by the Prague Frankists and in tenor, completely unlike Jacob Frank's *Sayings of the Lord*. The difference in tone and content suggests to scholars that there has been a cognitive shift in Frankism with its leader's death. I believe this to be true overall, but an aspect of Kant's theory of the aesthetic remains pertinent to the Frankist movement. For Frankism and Sabbatianism to migrate into literature in modernity, they need to establish cultural markers or affinities with modern philosophical themes; that is, the markers would need to demonstrate a cognitive relevance to literature in order to influence how subjects constitute themselves. These affinities would have to suggest at the very least the possibility of identification. In other words, the identification that Frank elicits from Polish hasids, disenfranchised Jews, "the revelation of the prostak," does not elicit the same response in Prague's Jewish society. For this world of Sabbatian and Frankist adherents, identification must be underwritten by the rational nature of the intellectual and political project they advocate. Thus the Kantian aesthetic experience becomes available as an archive for the Prague Circle.
44 Scholem gives further description of how far Frankism would go to realize its political aims of messianism by sending Junius Frei to fight alongside Robespierre and the Jacobins during the French Revolution. Junius Frei, the alias of Moses Dubrushka, and a relative of Jacob Frank, was sentenced to death by guillotine in 1794 because of these actions. Scholem (1981), 8–9.
45 Hannah Arendt identifies this new perspective in imagining Jewish collectivity as a theme emerging in Sabbatianism. See Hannah Arendt (2008), "Jewish History Revised," 303–311. For an interesting overview of how Arendt contributes to modern Jewish thought, see David Biale (2015), *Not in the Heavens. The Tradition of Jewish Secular Thought*, 127. Intriguingly, Frank wanted a kingdom of his own. Wehle appears to be more inclined to be part of an assimilated tradition where the heresy would be constitutive of the subject.
46 Žáček, 343.
47 As I note in the previous chapter, Frank's hagiographies advocate this principle.
48 In this respect, Žáček repeats the long-standing German belief that in order for Jews to be "elevated," to German status, they would have to "shed" the Judaism of the past in all of its markers.
49 For an extended analysis of Frank as a "charlatan," see Pawel Maciejko (2010), "Sabbatian Charlatans: the First Jewish Cosmopolitans," 361–378.
50 Žáček (1938), 343.
51 Žáček (1938), 344–5.
52 As I note in the previous chapter, Frankists call themselves the "believers" to distinguish their beliefs from Judaism.
53 Scholem (1995), 304.
54 Adam Mickiewicz, the Polish poet, for example, declares himself a Sabbatian, comes from a Sabbatian family, but sees himself as a "liberated" Pole. He advances a radical

sense of Polish nationalism as a consequence of this intuited liberation. See Gershom Scholem (1974), *Kabbalah, a Definitive History of the Evolution, Ideas, Leading Figures and Extraordinary Influence of Jewish Mysticism*, 308
55 I use this term specifically to point to how kabbalah's theories of "essences" could be transmuted by the heretical kabbalah to suggest an aesthetic project of essences, or potential suture points between Wehle's project and its extension beyond him.
56 In fact, as Scholem notes, at least one of the founders of the *Wissenschaft des Judentums* comes from a Sabbatian family. See Scholem (1971), *The Messianic Idea in Judaism*, 167; n. 11, 358.
57 Žáček (1938), 343–4.
58 This is Hönig's phrase in his complaint registered with the authorities. The whole text has been translated by Gershom Scholem. See Gershom Scholem (1974), "A Frankist Document from Prague," 787–814.
59 See Maciejko (2011), 252.
60 See Maciejko (2011), ibid. See Scholem (1975), ibid.
61 See Scholem (1971), "A Sabbatian Will from New York," 172.
62 Scholem (1971), 169.
63 See Scholem (1971), ibid.
64 See Scholem (1995), 320; also Gershom Scholem (1981), *Du Frankisme au Jacobinisme. La vie de Moses Dobrushka, alias Franz Thomas von Schonfeld alias Junius Frey*, 11. Thomas von Schoenfeld is one of the several pseudonyms Moses Dubroshka uses for his many "metamorphoses" from Jewish rabbinic student to French revolutionary who dies by guillotine.
65 See Maciejko (2011), 239. His historical account is helpful in understanding the timeline and its relevance to Edom's emergence in literature after Frankism no longer has any public figures associated with it.

> At the very end of the century, the Frankist leadership in Offenbach dispatched circular epistles to Eastern and Central European Jewish communities. Some were written in red ink; on this basis, Peter Beer, the first scholar to analyze the dispatches, coined their name, under which they became known also in later scholarship. The first copies reportedly started to circulate around 1798, but most of the letters can be dated to January 1800. The epistles included a full text of two letters written by Frank during his imprisonment in Częstochowa in 1767-8 …. and another lengthy message signed by three "elders" of the Offenbach court: Franciszek Wołowski (Solomon ben Elisha Shorr), Michał Wołowski (Nathan ben Elisha Shorr), and Jędrzej Dębowski (Yeruham ben Hananiah Lippman of Czarnokozienice). The message was addressed to "the entire House of Israel" and purported to be a "final warning."

66 Elaine M. Kauvar (1986), "An Interview with Chaim Potok," 291–317.
67 Heinrich Heine (1910), *Heinrich Heine's Memoirs from His Works, Letters and Conversations*, 148. Included in a letter to Moses Moser, Heine's poem "To Edom" reflects elliptically on conversion.
68 See Kitty Millet (2018), "Our Sabbatean Future," 141. See Yerushalmi (2011), *Zakhor, Jewish History and Jewish Memory. Zakhor*, 86.
69 While Scholem describes the scholars of *Wissenschafts des Judentums* as inimical to the kabbalistic projects of the preceding centuries, he recognizes they still embrace aspects of the kabbalah detached from its religious roots. To some degree, the hidden

sabbatianism of this generation's scholars, even when rejected, clings to them so that they deploy, unconsciously perhaps, kabbalistic elements within the very structure of the *Wissenschafts* project.

70   *Genesis* 3:5. Jacob Frank's nihilist, materialist antinomianism is transformed by Wehle into a necessary cultural intervention to the extent that the biblical sin of Genesis 3:5 becomes aspirational for modern Ahers rather than a signifier of their condemnation.
71   Jacob Taubes (2009), *Occidental Eschatology*, 90. Taubes' discussion of Hegel implies Wehle's cultural intervention.
72   Taubes (2009), ibid.
73   Although the *Haskalah* movement is not the result of Frankism, or any Jewish messianic movement, these sects see in it a kinship with their own beliefs and goals. They share an imagined *sensus communis* in which liberation from perceived and real injustices can be overturned by a messiah, one whose grasp of the future enables them to finally sever themselves from the past. Indeed Frank believes he can manipulate *Haskalah* for his own desires. However, as has been pointed out, *Haskalah* absorbs these sects, stripping them of their particular messiahs, and transforming the conceptual scaffolding of the messianic into an imagined political possibility.
74   The *Wissenschaft des Judentums* scholars' objection to the public display of Hasidism has its roots in the memory of German Hasidism whose settlements in the Rhineland dominate German Jewry's historical past. While the two movements are not the same, the memory of an earlier orthodoxy that dominated Jewish life becomes associated with the image of a dark, pre-enlightened, ghetto past.
75   See Lenowitz (1998), 193; see my discussion in chapter 1.
76   This is the textual echo of *1 Samuel* 8:5 in the *Bible* in which Jews demand a king so that they can be like everyone else in the land.
77   Walter Benjamin constructs a similar thesis in his discussion of Goethe for his dissertation. See Howard Eiland and Michael W. Jennings, eds. (1991), *Selected Writings*, 177. See also Peter Osborne and Matthew Charles, "Walter Benjamin," https://plato.stanford.edu/archives/fall2021/entries/benjamin/

Chapter 3

1   Max Brod notes that Heine's uncle impresses Heine because of the uncle's travels and his commitment to the kabbalah. The uncle not only makes several trips to Safed to study kabbalah, but he also shows up regularly at kabbalist centers, associated with Frankist and Sabbatian sects. See Max Brod (1957), *Heine. The Artist in Revolt*, 5ff.
2   Most recently, Chaim Potok echoed Heine's sentiment in his claim that literature enables writers to "handle good and evil in a way the *halakhah* never can." Elaine M. Kauvar (1986), "An Interview with Chaim Potok," 291–317.
3   Jeffrey L. Sammons (1979), *Heinrich Heine, a Modern Biography*, 108.
4   Jeffrey L. Sammons (1969), *Heinrich Heine, the Elusive Poet*, 351. Presumably, Sammons thinks of Max Brod's quotation of Heine's comment to Sethe in which he states "[O]nly in the infinite depths of mysticism can I cast off my infinite pain." See Mark H. Gelber and Hans Otto Horch, eds. *The Jewish Reception of Heinrich Heine*, 176.
5   In fact, the majority of scholarship has historically followed Sammons' perspective.
6   Sammons (1969), ibid.

7   Sammons (1969), 353. While Heine apparently learns about Swedenborg's "visions of the world" from Fichte's son, it does not necessarily lead to Heine's claim that *poesie* transforms the poet's ontology. In his disavowal of any "mystical Enlightenment" for Heine, Sammons stumbles over the *Romanzero* title itself and its resonance with Zvi and Frank. He ignores as well Swedenborg's place in the "erotically-charged mystical underground in mid-eighteenth-century Europe" in which he was in contact regularly with "Sabbateans, Frankists, and prominent Christian mystics" who all relied on a lingua franca of kabbalist symbols. See Glenn Dynner's "Introduction," in Glenn Dynner, ed. (2011), *Holy Dissent. Jewish and Christian Mystics in Eastern Europe*, 7. In the same volume, Marsha Keith Schuchard has made perhaps the most significant intervention in demonstrating the path that Swedenborg and others take in order to come into contact with kabbalist, Frankist, and Sabbatian figures. See Marsha Keith Schuchard (2011), "From Poland to London Sabbatean Influences on the Mystical Underworld of Zinzendorf, Swedenborg, and Blake," 252. David Biale, Scholem's definitive biographer, argues that Heine's "spiritualism" reflects a pantheism and derives from his admiration of Spinoza's writings. See also David Biale (2011), *Not in the Heavens: The Tradition of Jewish Secular Thought*, 36–7.

8   Gershom Scholem (2006), *Alchemy and Kabbalah*, 94–5. Scholem notes that Goethe not only has von Welling's text on kabbalah on his desk, but he also writes about it in *Poetry and Truth*. Scholem recognizes though that Goethe's resonance with Jewish kabbalah is "in name only." However, there is an argument to be made that Heine draws on Welling too. Schuchard's work on Blake's recuperation of Frankism in *the Marriage of Heaven and Hell* reiterates the pervasiveness of kabbalah for Christian writers throughout Europe. See Schuchard (2011), 250.

9   Heinrich Heine (1987), "Jehudah ben Halevi," 102–3.

10 Heine (1987), ibid. Heine employs a "wondrous child" signifier to set up Halevi's work as akin to revelation. Under these terms, he produces an "innovated text" from which readers, "initiated readers," extract pieces of the revelation.

11 With Chaldean identifying not only the language Abram speaks, but also the region from which Abram comes before his transformation into Abraham, the patriarch, Heine associates Hebrew with a revelation belonging to a primordial Jewish existence.

12 He posits Hebrew to be a part of the unconscious primordial world.

13 Harold Bloom (1975), *Kabbalah and Criticism*, 86. In his discussion of poetry and kabbalah, Harold Bloom explains that "poetry works to *remind* us of what we may have never known, yet need to believe we have known. Such reminding may be only a lesser restitution, but it does strengthen the mind, almost literally it *re-minds*." Heine suggests that *poesie* reminds Halevi of that unconscious world which he could not know, but he could recognize.

14 This trope has also been used by Harold Bloom to stake reading as constitutive for the modern subject. Harold Bloom (1997) *Anatomy of Influence. A Theory of Poetry*, 30ff. With Heine, Hebrew becomes not only the center of primordial creation, but it is also a continuing dynamic force that moves away from the original site of the Fall as it continues to emanate creation.

15 That the project of Eden must be "finished" by humans reiterates allusively Luriannic kabbalah's thesis of a human *tikkun* for the Divine. The repair attaches a human predicate to Divine alienation so that human exile eventually leads to the other side of Divine. Luria's thesis borders on violation of *halakhah* because Eden and the Fall have not been taken away due to sin for infinity, only that the project of time and

space, the refinement of substance, starts at that moment and on the condition of God's alienation from the self. It is an obstacle that humans must overcome in order to restore something to God.

Additionally, the poet is called to finish Eden's story since the Fall cuts off the narrative God hopes to tell, leaving the universe imbalanced because this one story cannot be completed until all the stories of the multiplicity are completed in human predicates. Thus the poet or poets are called to *poesie*. Celan recognizes this implication when he states "(all poets are Jews)." See Chapter 9, "There Must Be Other Songs beyond Mankind."

16 Eli Schoenfeld describes this process as well although he comes to a different conclusion than I do. See Schoenfeld (2016), "Am Ha'aretz: The Law of the Singular. Kafka's Hidden Knowledge," 107–29.
17 The process is different from the scene in the first chapter of Tokarczuk's *Books of Jacob*, and which I analyze in Chapter 1. It differs precisely in the mode of reception. The letters are presented as narrative and they constitute the tradition of transmission. When Yente swallows the letters, she consumes them as things in themselves.
18 See Willi Goetschel (2003), *Spinoza's Modernity: Mendelssohn, Lessing, and Heine*, 272.
19 Goetschel (2003), ibid. Although Goestchel aims to prove Heine's relationship to critical theory, a modern field of intellectual inquiry and a phenomenon of the twentieth-century, his identification of "innovation" in Heine indicates that scholars have recognized something uncanny about the term for almost two centuries. The nature of this uncanniness I believe stems from its origin in kabbalah.
20 Heine's phrase in German is particularly apt here: *Zwei verschiedne Sorten Lichtes*. The revelation of Torah comprises "two different kinds of light."
21 Technically, the period of the ghetto never occurred in Spain, but for Heine, the term signifies a perspective in which the world is divided between the ghetto where Jews are forced to live, and everything outside of it is tainted by a non-Jewish orientation. This goes to the heart of Heine's new investment in the ghetto as the condemned site forced on Jews after the Fall. In this logic, Jews belong there, and nowhere else. Biale has suggested that Heine embraces an Hegelian dialectic of sorts; I believe that this dialectic is transformed with Scholem.
22 Heine's phrasing hints at a latent messianism. This could be thought exactly in the terms of sacred and profane, in the sense, that sacred embodies the received tradition that cannot be communicated, and profane signifies that absence.
23 Scholem (1995), 239.
24 Scholem (1995), ibid.
25 Heine (1987), "Jehudah ben Halevi," 105. While in German, *Garten* is a cognate of English "garden," it could also be a synonym for "orchard." This submerged resonance with *pardes* I believe underpins Heine's thinking.
26 One could be tempted here to think of a historical parallel to which Heine alludes: Talmud begins in Babylon at the Pumbeditha and Bagdad academies; that is, he's merely rehearsing the historical origins of Talmud among diasporic Jews. However, the conflation of *aggadah* with a rival garden, Queen Semiramis' "wonder of the world," suggests that the revealed stories of *aggadah* might not only exceed their Judaic use, but also might purposely extend into the abyss of Babylon.
27 Heine (1987), 107.
28 Heine (1987), ibid.

29 Sammons argues that the poem actually reveals Heine's ignorance of the Jewish tradition because he mistakes ha-levi as Jehudah's patronym, when in fact it is ben Samuel. See Sammons (1969), 390. To some extent, Sammons accuses Heine of being *am ha'aretz/amhoretz*.
30 Many identify sexual desire and passion as both trope and shortcoming in Heine's work. As trope, seeing their importance only in relation to events in his life; however, Heine's "fascination" with Babylon as a necessary step to revelation might also reflect the poet's sympathies with Sabbatian and/or Frankist principles.
31 While the poem ends with Halevi's martyrdom, in his recognition of the elusive possibility of *poesie*, Heine accents the poet's capacity to make legible a forgotten revelation of the text.
32 The question is: does Heine follow Jacob Frank or Isaac Luria?
33 I'm freighting "Jewish" in contrast to "Judaic." Within Judaism, the revelation is exclusive to Jews; outside of Judaism, Jewish suggests a mode of being a Jew, a revelation without Judaism.
34 Halevi the poet becomes a prophet because he resolves the tension between a Jewish mystical nihilism and nihilism and a secular Jewish aesthetic experience.
35 Although Benjamin applies "unfolding" to Kafka and it connotes impossibility, if applied to Heine, it signifies an incredible possibility. See Walter Benjamin (1968), *Illuminations*, 122.
36 This underscores Sammons' gloss that Heine's "spiritualism" is "undogmatic" and "non-institutional" since it does not reduce to just one object of knowledge, or one revelation.
37 Irene Zwiep, "To Remember and to Forget—Jerusalem in Jewish Poetical Memory," 54–66. *JSTOR*, www.jstor.org/stable/43740607 (accessed November 26, 2020). This also resonates with Idel's citation earlier of an obligation levied on each Jew to write his own Torah. See Moshe Idel (2007), "Jacques Derrida and Kabbalistic Sources," 115.
38 His term is a synonym for the splendor of the *Zohar* in German-(*Glanz*). Later Heine uses the term to describe Faust's engagement with Mephistophela in dance. See Heine (1952), 27.
39 Scholem (1995), 10.
40 Heine (1987), 106.
41 Heine (1987), ibid.
42 If as the *Zohar* states "each innovated word" produces a world, then, Heine's role as poet obligates him to innovate the form of literature, by liberating *poesie* from the exile of a strict mimesis. *Poesie* must produce worlds. See Daniel Matt (2003), *Zohar*, 25; 1:4b.
43 Sammons (1969), 390.
44 Derrida comes to mind here because it underpins his project of a writing that remains unwritten.
45 Heine (1987), ibid.
46 Scholem (1995), 10; Robert Alter (1996), *The Pleasures of Reading in an Ideological Age*, 49.
47 Hence Heine innovates a heretical kabbalah even if he is not a Frankist.
48 The collision proposes itself as a crossroads: the reader either moves to possess, to own transcendence, thereby condemning the soul for eternity, or abandons the soul to writing emanating from the text.
49 Heine (1987), 107.

50 Heine (1987), ibid.
51 See *Exodus* 13:21 for the account of God sending Moses a "pillar of fire" to lead the Hebrews out of their desert exile at night so that their journey is illuminated both "day and night."
52 Heine's imagined biography for Halevi even transforms exile into a necessary subjective condition. It's not surprising that Freud would see in Heine a kindred spirit because "Heinrich Heine was the exemplary cultural Jew for late nineteenth century Austria." See Sander Gilman (1992), "Freud Reads Heine Reads Freud," 78.
53 The poet is a secondary emanation of God and this too is a Jewish mystical thesis, reminiscent of Rhineland Hasidism during the eleventh-century and within the historical or temporal locus of Halevi's purview.
54 Joseph Dan (2002), *The Heart and the Fountain*, 72–3.
55 Related to the Rhineland Hasids' ecstasy and Alter's "pleasure of the text," *poesie* inscribes cognition with a memory from before the human is subject to condemnation.
56 Heine (1987), ibid.
57 Heine (1987), ibid.
58 The relationship to psalm, and *poesie* is overt here.
59 In this respect, this inner phenomenon is none other than the Hebrew letters.
60 Heine (1987), ibid.
61 Heine (1987), ibid.
62 Heine (1987), ibid.
63 Heine (1987), 108.
64 Heine (1987), ibid.
65 By innovated, I mean that Heine does not reproduce the Frankist/Sabbatian model of the messiah, but rather "refines" it. He draws from it a "kernel" of revelation. Although Biale understands these aspects of Heine's work to indicate "pantheism," underscored by Spinoza's metaphor of Nature that Heine adopts, he still notes Heine's attempt to restore the legacy of the Hebrew prophets in writing. See Biale (2011), 17.
66 Heine (1987), ibid. Heine creates a link between Spinoza and Halevi in his role as poet.
67 Heine (1987), ibid.
68 Scholem notes that Zvi and Frank both sing *romanceros* as part of their rituals. See Scholem (1973), Shabbatai Sevi, 838.
69 Heine (1987), ibid.
70 I am aware that Heine still appears to follow aspects of the heretical kabbalah, but he does not end with the project.
71 Heinrich Heine (1952), *Doktor Faust.*; Heinrich Heine (1851), *Der Doktor Faust. Ein Tanzpoem nebst kuriosen Berichten über Teufel, Hexen und Dichtkunst*. Although written in French first, Heine's German translation anchors the play to philosophical, kabbalist, principles. For a fuller literary history of Heine's text, see Beate I. Allert (2014), "Heine's Doctor Faust, a Dance Poem," 66–77; Gerhard Weiss (1966), "Die Entstellung von Heines 'Doktor Faust': ein Beispiel deustch-english-franzözicher Freundschaft," 41–57. For the original French text, see Heinrich Heine (1847), *La Legende du Docteur Jean Faust*.
72 Qtd in Allert (2014), 69. She cites Heine's letter to Julian Campe, his publisher. Interestingly, scholars designate Heine's "innovation" to refer to new technologies or theatrical practices, but fail to see its relevance as a Jewish term.

73 For example, Emma Lazarus' identification of *The Rabbi of Bacharach* as a mimetic representation of Jewish persecution presents an obstacle to Heine: he simply can't find a way to resolve the dialectic in which Don Isaac and Rabbi Abraham are caught. See Emma Lazarus (2008) "A Biographical Sketch of Heinrich Heine," in Heinrich Heine (2008) *The Rabbi of Bacharach*, I–XVI.
74 Heine (1847), *La Clef des Enfers*, 6. Heine (1952), *Doktor Faust, a Dance-Poem*, 41. In all three versions, the text refers to a manual for controlling Hell's powers.
75 Heine (1851), 17.
76 The *Power of Hell or Der Höllenzwang* was a book purportedly authored by the legendary figure of Faust. Such books were alleged to enable the possessor power to compel demons to act. Heine (1851), 18; Heine (1847), *La Clef des Enfers*, 6. All three versions refer to a manual for controlling Hell's powers.
77 It cannot be Latin since Latin, a scholastic language, is contemporaneous with Faust, the lingua franca of the period and the text declares it an "ancient language."
78 Heine (1952), 42.
79 Unlike Goethe's *Faust*, Heine changes Mephistopheles' gender.
80 Heine, ibid. The English translation takes some license here. Thus I'm reproducing the original French text to explain and correct some of the choices of the translator. See Heine (1847), *Le Legende du Jean Faust*.

> *mais, cette fois, les ténèbres ont disparu, l'espace s'éclaire d'innombrables lumières; ce n'est plus le tonnerre qui éclate, C'est une musique de contredanse delicieux qui se fait entendre, danseuse en costume de ballet, en gaze et tricot, voltigeant ça et là en pirouettes vulgaires.* (7)

Heine's English translator, Basil Ashmore, translates the country dance (*contredanse*) of "vulgar pirouettes" as a *pas de seul*. However, his translation elevates the performance before Faust to classical ballet and Ashmore's translation points to Faust's desires for classical beauty in Act 4. Essentially, it misrepresents the first encounter with Mephistophela. It is not a seduction scene grounded in the Beautiful, but rather a crude and vulgar encounter. Mary Chan suggests that the dances are sexually explicit and condemned as inappropriate for English masses. Thus Mephistophela seduces Faust with the English Country Dance although its tradition didn't actually exist in France at this time. The genre is subsumed in England under the ban of theatre and "related arts." These "arts" are "prohibited," between 1642–60 because they are associated with "the Vices of the Age, …. too lively and smartly represented"; English commoners are not to "divert ourselves with these humours and pieces of Plays." See Mary Chan (1979), "Drolls, Drolleries and Mid-Seventeenth Century Music in England," 117. What is more striking though is the imagery of "innumerable lights" that fill the empty space.
81 Scholem (1995), 265.
82 Scholem (1995), ibid.
83 Heine (1952), ibid.
84 Heine (1952), ibid.
85 Heine (1952), 43. Ashforth translates *Kunstwerk* as "a hundred *objets d'art*," but I think "works of art" is truer to Heine's meaning.
86 Heine (1952), 42–3.
87 Concha Zardaya (1973), "El Espejo de Federico Garcia Lorca," 237. While Zardaya's essay concerns Lorca, her discussion of "the mirror" as aesthetic symbol relates to

Heine's distinction between *poesie* and the poet in relation to magic and Faust. The mirror allows Heine to juxtapose the materialization of Faust's desire to Halevi's liberation of *poesie*.

88 Heine (1952), 17.
89 Heine (1952), ibid.
90 Heine (1952), ibid.
91 Heine (1952), 16.
92 Heine (1952), ibid.
93 Sammons (1979), *A Modern Biography*, 287.
94 Heine (1952), 16.
95 Again, the ambiguity of Heine's language drives another secondary, kabbalistic narrative. Faust uses Hebrew to manipulate the elements, essentially directing the power of the letters to serve his own desires. Hence he is an apostate. The letters don't animate him because he attempts to control them.
96 Heine (1952), ibid.
97 Heine (1952), 16–17.
98 Heine (1952), 17.

Chapter 4

1 Klaus Grözinger (1994), *Kafka and Kabbalah*, 30. Jacob Gordin (1906; 1910), "Elishe ben Avuya." Kafka uses Eliezer for Gordin's "Elishe." When referring to the play, I use "Elishe," when referring to the Talmudic narrative, and secondary sources, I use the standard "Elisha," and for Kafka, I retain his Eliezer when necessary. Grözinger believes Kafka's error is due to Löwy.
2 Franz Kafka (1948), *Diaries of Franz Kafka, 1910–1913*, 122. See also Franz Kafka (1948, 1949), *Tagebücher 1910–1923*, 128. In the Brod edition of the Diaries, Joseph Kresh translates the names idiosyncratically and creates some confusion about whom Kafka discusses in the excerpt. In German, the identities are clear: Elieser, Akiba, Meir.
3 Scholem (1995), *Major Trends of Jewish Mysticism*, 239. In his description of the *kelipah*, "or the 'bark' of the cosmic tree or 'the shell' of the nut," Scholem reveals that Elisha's sin is actually his adherence to the "shells" of Tree of Life.
4 Obscured by the play Avuya's actions is in the Talmudic narrative and their implications are still pertinent to Kafka's thinking about the play.
5 See Jacob Gordin (1907), *Elisha ben Abuyah: drama in fir akten*, 10.
6 Grözinger (1994), 30. Beth Kaplan sees the play depicting Elishe as "his most autobiographical character." Beth Kaplan (2007), *Finding the Jewish Shakespeare: the Life and Legacy of Jacob Gordin*, 152.
7 For Yiddish audiences familiar with Shabbtai's story, Gordin's narrative produces a loud echo. Although Beth Kaplan argues that Gordin follows a Christian pattern, Gordin reproduces Shabbatai's life story, subtracting its kabbalistic claims, and retelling the entire narrative as Elishe's fictionalized "biography." See Beth Kaplan (2007), 152–3. Shabbatai Zvi's story is so well known at this time that Austrian writer, Leopold von Sacher-Masoch, someone outside of the Jewish community, makes it an organizing trope of his novel, *Sabbathai Zewy: Die Judith von Bialopol* in 1886. See Leopold von Sacher-Masoch, (1886). Sabbathai Zewy: Die Judith von Bialopol. In 1908, Sholem

Asch writes his Yiddish play, "Sabbatai Zevi," in which "redemption through sin" underpins both Sabbatai's marriage and his messianism. See Sholem Asch (1930), Sabbatai Zevi, *a Tragedy in Three Acts*.

8   See Chapter 1. As Biale notes, Scholem sees the connection too.
9   *Volke* in German and the term is pertinent because it's a synonym for people in Hebrew, i.e., עם a term that will be important to analyses of Kafka's "Before the Law."
10 See Biale (1985), "Gershom Scholem's Ten Unhistorical Aphorisms on Kabbalah: Text and Commentary," 88.
11 As I note in Chapter 2, the persecution of the Wehle family prompts its last heirs to immigrate to America where they read the narrative of emancipation as part of their own revelation. Maciejko gives extensive details about how the Wehle family ends its sojourn in Prague, the very public riots in the city's streets around Wehle's funeral and the profaning of the corpse that ensues. See Pawel Maciejko (2017), *Sabbatian Heresy*, 252.
12 In the move to prove the demise of Frankism with its founder, Scholem displaces slightly the general pervasiveness of the heretical kabbalah in German-speaking countries. He has suggested, Wehle's "inverted" method of reading secular texts actually inspires an entire generation of writers, Jews and non-Jews, so that Kafka's emergence is inevitable because of heresy. In *Major Trends*, he inserts Kafka into a genealogy that runs from to Sabbatianism. In fact, as I note in the Introduction, Scholem understands Kafka to be tied to a whole range of "orthodox" and "heretical" kabbalistic projects.
13 The English translation in Brod's edition uses "Meyer" for "Meir," but Meir is the recognizable figure in Talmud and the *aggadah* of Avuya riding on Shabbat is so well known that for the sake of familiarity, I use Meir.
14 Indirectly, we can glean an aspect of Kafka's understanding of the apostate in relation to the Jewish community since Avuya never stops being Jewish. He remains a Jew even though he is outside the Judaic community of *tannaim*.
15 Evelyn Torton Beck (1971), *Kafka and the Yiddish Theatre. Its Impact on His Work*, 153. As a result, Evelyn Torton Beck argues that Gordin "chastises the Orthodox for the futility of their efforts in keeping a Law which is neither reasonable nor comprehensible, and which does not even result in the justice promised to those who uphold it." Her characterization of the rabbinate's promise of redemption and justice, and its repeated failure to liberate Jews either from a world of physical persecution or even from the spiritual effects of the Fall, alludes to how Elisha ben Avuya becomes the sign of the modern Jewish secular subject.
16 Beck (1971), 152. She translates and quotes Gordin's play in Yiddish.
17 Löwy's "pun" also recalls another aspect of the heretical kabbalah in that the nut's shell is *kelipah* but the nut itself remains valuable. See Cengiz Sisman (2015), *The Burden of Silence: Shabbatai Zvi and the Evolution of the Ottoman-Turkish Dönmes*, 172.
18 Beck (1971), 152. To some degree, Gordin's Elishe resonates with Heine's don Isaac; both are thoroughly Jewish, and both wear the distinction of being apostates. Like don Isaac, he is a Jew without Judaism and he remains living among Jews.
19 Grözinger (1994), 30.
20 Like all the other kabbalist content Grözinger identifies within Kafka's many works, he treats the diary's version of "the Four who Went to Pardes" as evidence and then moves on to identify more potential kabbalistic precedents without interpretation of the identified source-text. Indeed, Grözinger actually excludes interpretation from the purview of his study, *Kafka and Kabbalah*. He prefers instead to "give context" which translates to identifying possible sources from which Kafka may or may not have

drawn. The upshot of his strategy is that his analysis concentrates on parsing Hasidic tales and placing them in "historical proximity" to Kafka. See Grözinger (1994), 6.
21 Grözinger (1994), 31.
22 David Suchoff (2011), *Kafka's Jewish Languages: The Hidden Openness of Tradition*, 156.
23 Harold Bloom (1987b), *The Strong Light of the Canonical. Kafka, Freud, and Scholem as Revisionists of Jewish Culture and Thought*, 2.
24 This problem concerns Heine too. His Faust wants "to think, love, live," but he lacks the abilities and the rights to achieve these aims. When his Faust picks up the *Book of Hell*, and recites a Hebrew incantation, he essentially engages in a theurgic kabbalah that will enable him to manipulate physical appearance, the phenomena of the *Sinnlichkeit*. Gershom Scholem (2006) *Alchemy and Kabbalah*, 94–95. Gershom Scholem (1981) *Du Frankisme au Jacobinisme. La vie de Moses Dubruska alias Franz Thomas von Schönfeld alias Junius Frey*, 130–131.
25 Grözinger (1994), 30.
26 Grözinger (1994), 4.
27 While *The Trial* is published in 1924, "Before the Law" is published in 1915, just four years after Kafka summarizes "Elishe ben Avuya" in his diary. Thus the story has both a relationship to the novel and a significance to another context beyond that later novel. Consequently, I will cite the short story independently from *The Trial*. See Franz Kafka (1961), *In the Penal Colony and Short Pieces*, 148-9.
28 See Eli Schoenfeld (2016), "Am Ha'aretz: The Law of the Singular. Kafka's Hidden Knowledge," 107–29; and George Steiner (1996), "A Note on Kafka's Trial," 250.
29 Walter Benjamin (1968), *Illuminations*, 122.
30 Theodor W. Adorno, "Notes on Kafka" ("Aufzeichnungen zu Kafka"), 243–71, 246.
31 Grözinger (1994), 1–14.
32 Freud and Lacan refer to it as the "death drive." See Jacques Lacan (1977), *Ecrits: A Selection*, 301; Sigmund Freud (1961), *Beyond the Pleasure Principle*, 59. Likewise, Deleuze and Guattari's "rhizome" thesis removes Kafka's particularity per se, although the rhizome does operate as a singular principle. See Gilles Deleuze; Feliz Guattari (1986), *Kafka. Toward a Minor Literature*.
33 Grözinger (1994), 1–14.
34 Grözinger (1994), 84.
35 See Iris Bruce (2007), *Kafka and Cultural Zionism*, 99.
36 Suchoff (2011), 160. Suchoff's perspective suggests a parallel as well with Gordin's "parable."
37 See Suchoff, ibid. See Scholem (1995), 10.
38 Scholem (1995), from cut section.
39 Alter, "Kafka as Kabbalist," 87. See Biale, (1985), "Gershom Scholem's Ten Unhistorical Aphorisms on Kabbalah: Text and Commentary," 88.
40 Biale (1985), ibid.
41 Sandra Valabregue (2016), "Philosophy, Heresy, and Kabbalah's Counter-Theology," 233–56.
42 Bloom (1987b), 63.
43 Modernity brings diverse populations closer to each other than ever before. Furthermore, they come in their difference and theoretically in equality. Although oppression persists, Kafka remains rich in these registers of diversity.
44 For the most part, I'll follow Grözinger's translation and keep the character a gatekeeper. However, there is a case to be made for "doorman."

45 Grözinger asserts that the gatekeeper is supposed to resonate with the hasids' gatekeeper tales which he claims Kafka learns by visiting different Hasidic communities, "wonder rebbes," as well as hearing them at synagogues, and Yiddish theaters. See Grözinger (1994), 51–52.
46 Schonfeld (2016), 110. He draws on Heinz Politzer (1966), *Franz Kafka: Parable and Paradox*, 165–217.
47 Schonfeld (2016), 109.
48 Schonfeld does not tell his readers how *am ha-aretz* transforms from "people of the country" to "man of the country."
49 Implicitly, the distinction is between the exiled Jews, coming back into the Land, and a population that sees the Jews rebuilding the temple, and insists that they participate in its construction in order to undermine the project. It is unclear as to whether the group should be understood as non-Jewish or a related group, i.e., a group with some kind of "kinship" to the returning exiles. When their offer is rejected, they reveal themselves to be the Jews' enemies. Here the word, עם, is meant to imply a "mob" or at least a group all related to each other who oppose the returning exiles. See Ernest Klein (1987), *A Comprehensive Etymological Dictionary of the Hebrew Language for Readers of English*, 474; 490.
50 Schonfeld (2016), 111.
51 Schonfeld (2016), ibid.
52 See Schonfeld (2016), 109.
53 Magid describes how late Hasidism inherits this idea so that one who lives in the sacred can "sin" without "sinning." See Shaul Magid (2003), *Hasidism on the Margin. Reconciliation, Antinomianism, and Messianism in Izbica/Radzin Hasidism*, 216.
54 Schonfeld (2016), ibid.
55 See Hannah Nesher-Wirth (2009), *Call It English. The Languages of Jewish American Literature*, 117; Hans Peter Althaus (2010), *Kleines Lexikon deutscher Wörter jiddischer Herkunft*, 41; Heinz Politzer (1966), *Franz Kafka. Parable and Paradox*, 173–4.
56 Dan Miron (2010), *From Continuity to Contiguity: Toward a New Jewish Literary Thinking*, 354.
57 Grözinger (1994), 50.
58 Grözinger (1994), ibid. In fact, in this application, Kafka's metamorphosis becomes the ultimate sign of failure.
59 Scholem (1995), 281.
60 Scholem (1995), ibid.
61 Lawrence Fine (2003), *Physician of the Soul, Healer of the Cosmos: Isaac Luria and His Kabbalistic Fellowship*, 306.
62 Fine (2003), 306–7. The hierarchical division to which Fine refers are Luria's five categories. While for Kabbalah, these categories are important, for literature, only the fifth category warrants our concern.
63 Fine (2003), ibid.
64 Scholem (1995), 281–2.
65 Scholem (1995), 282.
66 Kafka (2010), 150.
67 Kafka (2010), 148.
68 Grözinger (1994), 49–50. He quotes Luria, *Schaär ha Gilgulim* (*Gates of Reincarnation*), c.17, 50b. Although Hayim Vital is technically the alleged writer of the text, Lawrence

Fine notes that Vital reproduces Luria's teachings. See Fine (2003), 391–2, fn 3. Fine works from a copy that Luria's son revises and that is published in Palestine/Israel in the nineteenth century.

69 Grözinger alludes to the final metamorphosis when kabbalah reveals itself to be Divine writing.
70 Grözinger admits the influence of Hasidic and Luriannic kabbalah on Kafka's work. Grözinger and Scholem both recognize and identify Kafka as "the product" of heretical kabbalah, but neither scholar cedes to Kafka the explicit use of Frankist and Sabbatian materials.
71 See Maciejko (2017); Lenowitz (1998), *The Jewish Messiahs from the Galilee to Crown Heights*, 181.
72 I include the Czech here not only to show how the words are related in the mind of the Yiddish speaker, but how the term signifies something particularly critical to Jacob Frank's heretical kabbalah.
73 Lenowitz (1998), ibid.
74 Kafka (2010), 148.
75 Martin Buber (1991), *Tales of the Hasidim*, IX.
76 Buber (1991), ibid. Here the echo with Heine's *Glanz* and *Glühende* in the previous chapter is dramatic.
77 Shaul Magid (2003), *Hasidism on the Margin. Reconciliation, Antinomianism, and Messianism in Izbica/Radzin Hasidism*, 203.
78 Magid (2003), ibid.
79 Magid (2003), ibid.
80 Suchoff (2011), 160.
81 See Daivd Biale (1985), "Gershom Scholem's Ten Unhistorical Aphorisms on Kabbalah: Text and Commentary," 88. I'm reading "the perfection that destroys" ("etwas von dem strengen des Kanonischen-des Volkommenen, das zerbricht.") in the last line of Scholem's Satz 10 as a "breaking apart."
82 The Gatekeeper's phrase "Jetzt aber nicht" focuses the mind around a possible redemption that will come. The commoner only has to wait for it to be revealed.
83 Grözinger (1994), 46. The quote is from Gershom Scholem (1970), *Über einige Grundbegriffe des Judentums*, 112.
84 Scholem (1995), 129.
85 This is the pattern of the Pardes narrative that Kafka reproduces in his 1922 diary entry discussed at the end of the chapter.
86 See Franz Kafka (1935), *Der Prozess Roman*, 256. The German suggests that he's contorting himself to see redemption beyond the gatekeeper.
87 Kafka (1961), 148.
88 In Biale's description of this scene, he freights the frustration of the *amhoretz* who recognizes that the gatekeeper can access the law at any time, live in its halls, while the man from the country cannot.
89 Grözinger (1994), 46–51.
90 Grözinger (1994), ibid.
91 While Schonfeld is right to be critical of Agamben's and Derrida's respective readings regarding messianism, he overlooks how much Kafka leans into on its possibility.
92 Kafka (1961), 148; See also Franz Kafka (1935), 256.
93 Kafka (1961), 149.
94 Kafka (1961), ibid.

95 Kafka (1961), 149.
96 Kafka (1961), ibid.
97 These questions are related to the chapter's three introductory questions about how much Jewish content one needs to read Kafka earlier in the chapter.
98 In "Letter Phenomenologies" Section 2, Pardes becomes an exegetical site instead of an actual place. Hence "The Four who Went to PaRDeS" reflects four different modes of reading revelation. When "the man of the country" ponders his choices for entering the Law, he traces "blindly" the four methods. These are the stages of "*Nigleh* revealed."
99 Kafka (1961), 149. This is the place in the narrative that Biale highlights in his analysis of Before the Law: when the man from the country looks at the "doorman" before him and sees that he has entered the PaRDeS, but the common man can read and read, yet never access this mystical, mysterious experience.
100 Biale (1985), 88.
101 Scholem tells a story about Baal Shem who when faced with a difficult task would go to the woods, light a fire, ponder what to do, and say a prayer. The next generation, the Maggid of Meseritz must perform the same task, but when he arrives in the wood, he doesn't remember all of the ritual, but only the prayer. This motif is repeated every generation until Rabbi Israel of Rishin sits on "his golden chair" among his followers and states that we do not know the place, we cannot light the fire, we cannot speak the prayers, but "we can tell the story of how it was done." As he retells the story, it has the same effect as the previous prayer and ritual. In other words, we have the outline or shadow of its absence: we are licensed to imagine a new version of the ritual and that imagined version is as good as the older one. Rachel Gross explores this thesis as nostalgia in *Beyond the Synagogue*. In a very Kafkaesque mode, the reader accepts the loss of whatever Judaism was supposed to be in order to embrace what it is now, imagined memories of customs, rituals, and allegiances. See Scholem (1995), 350.
102 Max Brod (1937), *Franz Kafka*, 74.
103 Scholem (1995), 281–2.
104 See Franz Kafka (1956), *The Trial*.
105 See Kafka (1961), *In the Penal Colony Stories and Short Pieces*, 179.
106 Kafka (1956), 179.
107 Franz Kafka (1949), *Diaries of Franz Kafka, 1914–1923*. Vol. 2, 202–3.
108 Biale (1985), 88.
109 Grözinger (1994), 50.

Chapter 5

1 See Bruno Schulz (2018), *Cinnamon Shops*. This ambiguity leads scholars often to assume that Schulz's work mimetically represents his "lived experience." See Jerzy Ficowski (2003), *Regions of the Great Heresy. Bruno Schulz, a Biographical Portrait*, 92.
2 See Bruno Schulz (2018), "Treatise on the Second Genesis," 22–3. The Wienewska translation uses "Second Book of Genesis." See Schulz (1977), 59.
3 Schulz (2018), 22.
4 See Bruno Schulz (2018), "Mannequins." *Collected Stories*, 24. I will tack between the older and more familiar translation by Celina Wieniewska for material and

implications omitted from the Levine text. See Bruno Schulz (1977), *The Street of Crocodiles*, 58.
5   Schulz does occasionally mention Jews and he uses several signifiers to suggest kabbalah outright. See Schulz (2018), 77.
6   See David Biale (1985), *Gershom Scholem's Ten Unhistorical Aphorisms on Kabbalah: Text and Commentary*, 88. Although Scholem refers to Kafka, his declaration implies the dissemination of kabbalistic content and principles across Europe; that is, Jews and non-Jews are familiar with the agents of heretical kabbalah and their heresies. This orientation circulates, as I show in Chapter 2, through an array of aesthetic, philosophical, political, and religious sources. If such content is linked to the use of vernaculars among disparate Jewish groups, Schulz's implication is hardly surprising, especially in light of Frankism's origin in Poland. In *Księga blasku. Traktat o kabale w prozie Brunona Schulza,* Wladyslaw Panas argues that Schulz is not only familiar with kabbalist content, but also innovates it and Agate Bielik-Robson advances Panas' claim, innovating it further by linking it to psychoanalysis. While English-speaking scholarship concedes aspects of Schulz's work to kabbalistic influences, few remark on Schulz's Frankist signifiers, preferring instead to subsume them under gnosticism. Wladyslaw Panas (1997), *Księga blasku. Traktat o kabale w prozie Brunona Schulza*, 7–171; Agate Bielik-Robson (2014), "From Therapy to Redemption: Notes toward a Messianic Psychoanalysis," 86–99.
7   Scholem (1995), 93.
8   Schulz (2018), 79.
9   Tokarczuk makes it clear that by the end of her novel, the Frankists are interchangeable with their non-Jewish neighbors through assimilation, they return to the Jewish community of post-*Haskalah* Europe, and they immigrate to the Americas as reformers building a modern secular world. In these cases, they have managed to obscure their families' Frankist roots.
10 Schulz (2018), "Birds," 19.
11 Schulz (2018), ibid.
12 Schulz (2018), 18. Even here Schulz plays with kabbalistic signifiers, suggesting that the house shares space with the "upper chambers" where the Father's glory is exhibited, i.e., perhaps unselfconsciously, but nonetheless significant, Schulz introduces *Hekhalot/Merkavah* imagery into the domestic scenery of Drohobych. While not a part of kabbalah proper, it represents the earliest strata of formal Jewish mysticism. For kabbalists, it is the archive from which they draw in order to posit their new narrative visions.
13 Schulz (2018), ibid. Several Schulz scholars identify the compendia with the *Zohar*; however, that conflation ignores how Schulz shifts the site from text to image and why his innovation matters. See also Benjamin Balint (2023), *Bruno Schulz. An Artist, a Murder, and the Hijacking of History*, 164.
14 Schulz (2018), ibid.
15 As I remark earlier, Alter uses the phrase to describe the "pleasures of the text," suggesting that innovation is an effect of reading. In *Sanatorium under the Sign of the Hourglass,* Schulz repeats the scene substituting the son's innovation of text for Father's actions in *Cinnamon Shops*. The son's innovation is the theme of Chapter 6.
16 See Scholem (1995), 92–99; Gershom Scholem (1974), *Kabbalah*, 37ff. The Rhineland Hasids are organized around three main figures of the Kalonymus family, Samuel, Judah, and Eleazar, spanning the eleventh to early thirteenth centuries. Known as *Hasidei*

Ashkenaz, the group introduces an early theosophical kabbalistic project in relation to an ethical program, called *Hasiduth*. Hasiduth is a system of devotion in which the Hasid practices "ascetic renunciation … serenity of mind, and an altruism." While the Rhineland Hasids are arguably a transitional movement prior to kabbalah, they articulate foundational concepts pertinent to the movement's evolution in the next century.

17 Scholem (1995), ibid. As I discuss later in this chapter, and following Scholem's logic, Schulz inverts the principle. When Father witnesses the seamstresses exposing themselves to the wind, he is plunged into ecstasy, and when that ecstasy dissipates, he returns to a golem state.
18 Scholem (1995), ibid.
19 Shaul Magid (2003), *Hasidism on the Margin. Reconciliation, Antinomianism, and Messianism in Izbica/Radzin Hasidism*, 203.
20 Scholem (1995), 93.
21 *Hasiduth* obligates the hasid to a forfeiture of privilege, even though the Law permits or entitles the believer to claim privilege. Thus the hasid is bound to act "within" the Law, to inhabit an aspect of the Torah unrepresented by its literal meaning.
22 Scholem associates it with prayer, but after the *Zohar*, it signifies an ecstasy bound to the reading, writing, and saying of the Hebrew letters as they articulate unknown names of God.
23 When Kafka's "man from the country" encounters the Hasid-gatekeeper, the presumption is that the Hasid even while speaking to this character remains within the "inner essence" of the Law. However, one could argue that the gatekeeper stands "on" the law while simultaneously he prevents the "man from the country" entering it. If the gatekeeper is to be read as Hasid, then, the one who stands before *him*, the "man from the country," the *amhoretz* discussed in the previous chapter, signifies a person who is ignorant of the Law can be prohibited from entering it because this individual is akin a golem in that the Law is not constitutive in him.
24 In fact, Scholem suggests that they are liberated from human meaning, free then to express a Divine message that the Hasid does not know.
25 In the thirteenth-century, the *Zohar* introduces a sacred writing that produces sublimity and Abulafia posits a sacred form of reading that accomplishes the same thing.
26 I explore the theme again in Chapter 6, "Golems of Text and 'Interminable *Aggadot*.'"
27 If in its immanence, matter has multiple beings, then, implicitly there are multiple identities, multiple genders.
28 Schulz (2018), 25–6.
29 Schulz (2018), 17.
30 Schulz (2018), ibid.
31 Schulz (2018), 18.
32 Schulz (2018), ibid.
33 Schulz (2018), 19. Even with this depiction of the household's desire to shunt aside the heretical, Frankist gnosticism underpinning secular Jewish life in order to construct a semblance of the status quo, Schulz implies that the forces motivating Frankism still pulsate. They still look for a way of escaping the mundane world of Drohobych.
34 Schulz (2018), ibid.
35 Schulz (2018), ibid. To some degree Tokarczuk echoes this defeat in the last chapter, "The Book of Names" from *The Books of Jacob*. In that chapter, the Frankists have

receded into both Jewish and non-Jewish communities, no longer aware of the significance of their sect. They remain just names, inconsequential lists attesting to the dissolution or disinvestment of the movement.
36 Schulz (2018), ibid.
37 See Scholem (1971), 21. Scholem describes Judaism as a "well-ordered house" that is in "danger" of a messianic apocalypticism threatening to overrun its order and it is against this messianism that *halakhah* is used for defense. In Scholem's analogy, Judaism is a structure buffeted by the desire for a messiah in this world that would liberate Jews from oppression. From the perspective of the heresy, struggling to take root in this "house," Judaism is a "hard shell" adhering to the world. Its tenets obscure rather than relieve human suffering. David Biale also notes the analogy in relation to the "Ten Unhistorical Aphorisms on Kabbalah." See David Biale (1985), "Gershom Scholem's Ten Unhistorical Aphorisms on Kabbalah: Text and Commentary," 82–3.
38 Schulz (2018), 20.
39 The intersection of the heretical kabbalah is implicit here; Jews forfeited Torah in order to enter history: they give up essentially "entering the Law," in order to enter the emptiness of human existence without it. For Schulz, who never identifies as an observant Jew, the profound emptiness of missing what has been constitutive for Jews continues for infinity under a variety of signs: nostalgia, transgression, business, really every social institution reaffirms its absence. One can also follow Harold Bloom here and think of Freud who points to the compulsion for the uncanny as testimony of the modern subject's dilemma.
40 Schulz (2018), ibid.
41 Schulz (2018), 79.
42 Schulz (2018), ibid.
43 Michal Pawel Markowski depicts Panas' analysis as a brilliant "overreading," built on the postulate "that matter is evil and everything should be done to redeem it." However, Schulz's "fecundity of chaos" suggests that Panas' argument follows Schulz's textual path through Drohobych; that is, he follows writing through time and space. Bozena Shallcross depicts it as a "retextualization" in which writing emerges out of the chaos to create new being. Markowski and Shallcross are quoted in Balint (2023), n. 48, 268.
44 Jerzy Ficowski (2003), "Letters." *Regions of the Great Heresy. Bruno Schulz, a Biographical Portrait*, 188. It's a pattern that Schulz deploys purposely to reshape his interiority. He writes with a view to rewriting his own ontology.
45 Inverting Heine's *poesie*, in which *poesie* lights up Jehudah's path, Jacob's "poetry" journeys through darkness.
46 Schulz picks up this theme again in *Sanatorium*, when he declares the cosmos is filled with "unfinished stories" as translated by Celia Wienewska. See Schulz (1977), *Sanatorium under the Sign of the Hourglass*, 47. In this example, Wienewska captures a theme in Schulz that is not implied in Levine's "interminable stories."
47 Scholem (1995), 239. For Schulz, all human existence is chaos. He writes to be free of this fallen state.
48 Scholem (1995), 131. This too inverts an orthodox kabbalah. Since human faculties have been "sealed" by God to prevent the memory of the primordial world before the Fall, the kabbalist aims to "unseal the soul, to untie the knots that bind it'" in order to fulfill his call to be a prophet. However, Scholem's description alludes to a tension

between multiplicity and singularity as a consequence of unsealing. Citing Abulafia, Scholem notes that humans live in multiplicity, but "'when their knots are untied they return to their origin, which is one without any duality and which comprises the multiplicity.' The 'untying' is ... the return from multiplicity and separation towards the original unity." Since all souls are inherent in Adam, they are "separated" and "distributed" across time and space in "bodies" because of the Fall. The range of "multiplicity" extends through time and space so that all individuals are "sealed" in differences. Abulafia implies, as Scholem notes, that by "untying" the soul, it is free—liberated—to return to "the original unity," an unbound singularity. Abulafia grounds his optimism in his own existence as a prophet; God has given him the knowledge because presumably individuals are now ready for redemption. Multiplicity signifies incomplete existence, and the only way to survive in this world. Thus Father's creations signify more "multiplicity" and more "perfection." By innovating the void's "dead matter," Jacob liberates "multiplicity" itself from condemnation and judgment: he binds it to "the oldest extant recipes."

49 Schulz implicates the *sferot* themselves in the fall and its consequences.
50 It is the *tohu va bohu* of *Genesis*, where the *kelipot* reside, adhering to the shards of Divine Light after the breaking of the vessels. Implicitly, Schulz rewrites *Genesis* through the Father. He posits an addenda to Torah.
51 Scholem identifies *Tikkunei Ha-Zohar*, a commentary on *Zohar*, written as its continuation, as the primary impetus for later innovations of the doctrine. Scholem (1995), 170.
52 Scholem (1971), 118.
53 Scholem (1971), ibid.
54 Scholem (1971), 119. As discussed in Chapter 1, Jacob Frank focuses on *Atzilut* and *Beriah*.
55 Scholem (1971), ibid.
56 Scholem (1971), ibid.
57 Scholem (1971), ibid.
58 Frankism reverses the doctrine so that *Beriah* is no longer relevant to *Asiyah*. The messianic age unmoors phenomena from *Beriah*, revealing a path for *Atzilut* to express itself in *Asiyah's* world. In his essay "On the Mimetic Faculty," Benjamin alludes to this possibility. Walter Benjamin (1978), "On the Mimetic Faculty," 333–336.
59 Gershom Scholem (1978), *Kabbalah*, 119, 138.
60 Scholem (1978), 137. *Adam Kadmon* has nothing to do with the biblical Adam.
61 Scholem (1978), ibid.
62 Scholem (1978), ibid.
63 Scholem (1978), 138.
64 Scholem (1978), 137.
65 The body referenced here is not in any human dimension, but spans the cosmos. It is the first form and within it are the "incorporeal supernal lights." Scholem also notes that the vessels consist of a thicker light that is distinguishable from the supernal.
66 Scholem (1978), 138.
67 Scholem (1978), ibid.
68 Scholem (1978), ibid.
69 Scholem (1995), 239. Scholem's phrasing alludes to Kant's description of the understanding overreaching its boundaries to substitute its knowledge for reason's

thought. By depicting the breaking of the vessels as akin to the conflict of the faculties in Kant, even if unintentional, Scholem intimates that a trace of "the Breaking of the Vessels" remains cognitively imprinted in the mind. Although Kant describes the understanding's gesture as ideological, Scholem observes that the Zohar and "old" kabbalistic projects deem the strategy as "something good" becomes "evil" through occupying a place for which it is not suited.

70 Scholem (1995), ibid.
71 Scholem (1995), 267.
72 Scholem (1995), ibid.
73 Scholem (1995), ibid.
74 This is the realm of *Asiyah* or "making" and one of four realms that Luria identifies as mediations between the Hidden God and human existence.
75 Scholem (1995), 280.
76 Scholem (1995), ibid.
77 Scholem (1995), ibid. "Creator and created" mirrors the severing of subject and object because of the cosmic catastrophe of the breaking of the vessels. Schulz depicts how the disjunction between creator and created/subject and object, forces Father to recoil into himself, reliving this split repeatedly. The two pieces neither can be reunited nor can their differences be erased; thus they cohabit for the duration of human existence. The idea leads Luria to posit *metempsychosis* as a remedy for separation. The human soul is reborn continuously in exile until it has achieved perfection or refinement. It pushes Kafka to declare "there is endless hope, but not for us." It drives Schulz in *Sanatorium* to abandon remedy altogether, choosing human connection over "loneliness."
78 Agata Bielik-Robson adopts this approach in her analysis of center to periphery, the valorized versus the trashy, in Schulz. See Agata Bielik-Robson (2022), "At the Edges of the World. Diasporic Metaphysics of Bruno Schulz." Bielik-Robson's thesis develops the antipathy in Schulz between the town's center, with its shops and commerce, and the margins of the social, the human, where discrete figures have been sequestered. Thus Father's being shut away in junk rooms underscores the marginalization of creative power, suborned to business, the systematic, the status quo. If the tension is between *halakhic* and an unfettered kabbalah, then, the Father's marginalization occurs because of an overweaning *halakhic* authority attempting to control the Father's creations within the *kelipot*. In this heretical reimagining, *halakhah* is part of the *kelipot* universe, the world of the damned in which the *kelipot* adhere to their structures, organizing them around the trapped shards of light embedded in the void. The Law or *halakhah* in this model is the "hard structure" the *kelipot* impose in order to imprison these lights.
79 It is the heretical kabbalah's innovation of Luria's theory of exile and *metempsychosis*. Scholem (1995), 280–4.
80 While readers might still question how Schulz knows kabbalah if he never identifies as a kabbalist, never studies the tradition, as I note earlier, Frankism and Hasidism saturate aspects of Polish culture.
81 In this way, Kafka's Gregor Samsa, and his animal stories genre attest to *metempsychosis*. Iris Bruce's thesis of *gilgul* in Kafka, points to his innovation of the terms in Luria. Schulz's use indicates the pervasiveness of Luriannic principles in several secular registers. See Iris Bruce (2007), *Kafka and Cultural Zionism*.
82 Humans create beings "outside the law" or excluded from *halakhah*, i.e., idolatry.

83 Ironically, the Father recognizes this aspect of heresy in his discussion of golems which I analyze later in this chapter.
84 Rivka Galchen (2018), "Foreword." *The Collected Stories of Bruno Schulz*, vii.
85 Schulz innovates Faust to reveal Father the failed prophet.
86 Hence Schulz posits a crossroads at the heart of the heretical kabbalah: follow Frank's example and abandon Torah completely, materializing a wholly "other" world, substituting stories of lived experience for *aggadot* or recognize in *poesie*, the necessity of an unbound *aggadah*, a representation drive writing throughout the universe.
87 Schulz (2018), 23; for the *principium*, see p. 265. The term is used by the narrator in "The Comet," originally bound in the older *Street of Crocodiles* as part of the novella. In the Levine translation, *Collected Stories*, it appears as a short story outside of the initial *Cinnamon Shops* collection. For an overview of *principium individuationis*, see Arda Denda (1991), "*Principia Individuationis*" *The Philosophical Quarterly*, 212–28.
88 Schulz (2018), 25.
89 Schulz (2018), 21.
90 Schulz (2018), ibid. The implication of "aura" intrigues: does Schulz think "aura" as a field or dimension of the phenomenon on which the object is mapped? Or is it part of the "manifold" underpinning creation and from which the subject expels the self (*darstellen*) in order to be? Within that process of extracting the self from an unconscious archive, each individual would be a conglomeration of letters within, an existential micrography whose temporal expression lasts only for the duration of the subject's representation.
91 Schulz (2018), 23.
92 Schulz (2018), 22–3.
93 Schulz (2018), ibid.
94 Schulz (2018), ibid. The gesture is reminiscent of an analogy in Scholem regarding "the messianic idea in Judaism." In that analogy, Judaism is a "well-ordered house," defended by the *halakhah*. The representatives of the *halakhah* fight against the nihilistic and heretical aspects of messianism: when messianism shifts from an abstract idea to its material possibility. Thus Scholem refers to it as "the anarchic breeze of messianic apocalypticism."

> From the point of view of the *Halakhah* .... Judaism appears as a well-ordered house .... Something of Messianic apocalypticism penetrates into this house .... a kind of anarchic breeze. A window is open through which the winds blow in, and it is not quite certain what they bring in with them. As vital as this anarchic airing may have been for the house of the law, it is certainly easy to understand the .... misgivings with which other significant representatives of *Halakhah* regarded everything that makes up Messianic utopianism .... As long as Messianism appeared only as an abstract hope .... deferred to the future which had no living significance for the life of the Jew in the present, the opposition between .... conservative rabbinic and .... Messianic authority .... could remain without tension .... But whenever .... the Messianic idea entered the mind as a power with direct influence the tension .... became noticeable .... They could be preserved next to each other, but they could not be united in their execution. (22)

In Scholem, the "anarchic breeze" signifies a "Messianic apocalypticism" that innovates the kabbalah. In Schulz's scene, the women expose themselves to the wind and are permutated by it. See Scholem, (1978), 22.

95 Schulz (2018), 22.
96 Schulz (2018), 23.
97 Schulz (2018), 22.
98 Schulz (2018), ibid.
99 Schulz (2018), 23. This iconic scene might also underpin Tokarczuk's version of Lankoronie.
100 Schulz (2018), ibid. *Genus avium* is the category of birds in general. *Scansores* refers to a classification of birds within that larger category of the *genus*; *psitacci* refers to bacteria that infect bird hosts, specifically parrots. As the father contemplates the seamstresses, he imagines them to part of the bird *genus*. Their human existence manifests the bacteria's infection. He imagines their human appearance is at the expense of their avian essences.

   Additionally, the scene bears some relationship to Tokarczuk's description of Hayah before the Frankist elders in Lanckoronie, in that Tokarczuk innovates Schulz to tell her story of Frank. Like Frank, the Father mumbles almost incomprehensibly as he circles the women. Like Frank, his desire stimulates his liberation.
101 Instead of the "supernal lights" within Adam Kadmon, the women, like all humans, have a chaos inside them that must be liberated through its expression in material creation. The predicate of human existence is the sign of liberation.
102 Schulz (2018), 25. The implications of Schulz's remarks are dramatic: if there are "experimental forms," then, *Adam Kadmon* as the first form and the "Breaking of 'his' Vessels" suggest that perhaps God the creator intends these two original events as part of "the experimental" or rather as an aesthetic experience like "the Beautiful and the Sublime" in which creation is intrinsically unmoored from order, the epistemological, in its expression. Perhaps creation has never been constrained by order or permanence. Perhaps God the creator intended to shower the world with lights, all illuminating potential disclosures of paradise, demarcating unauthorized entry points to a Divine Being hidden away and damaged by its own alienation/separation from creation. Isn't this the force of something being "inimitable?"
103 Schulz (2018), 23.
104 Schulz (2018), 24. While Schulz engages in humor here, the reader is also aware of Father's inability to see desire as *his* motivating principle so that when Adela uses it to reduce him to his "root," he forgets its significance.
105 Schulz (2018), ibid.
106 The scene's similarity to Tokarczuk's depiction of Jacob Frank and the Lanckoronie Affair is striking. Like Jacob Frank, the Father imagines that he engages with something other than just the female body in his performance of possessing the essence. See Chapter 1, "The Heretic of Kabbalah."
107 Schulz (2018), ibid.
108 While Schulz demonstrates that the women control Jacob even when he pontificates about their implied "golemness," the narrative Jacob tells himself and his listeners espouses a teaching reminiscent of the heretical kabbalah where women incarnate "the higher *Torah Atzilut*," the Torah through which God pours the power of creation. Anna Lesznai innovates the theme in her novels so that women not only embody the higher Torah explicitly, but also articulate the "Divine I" position in the *sferot*. Many thanks to Mari Rethelyi for this insight.
109 Schulz (2018), 24. The term is the structuring principle for the story of Uncle Edward's transformation by the Father in "The Comet." See Arda Denda (1991), ibid.

110 In fact, in "the Comet," Edward is stripped down to his bare inscription, embedded in the wall of the house. Schulz (2018), 251–264.
111 Schulz (2018), ibid.
112 Schulz (2018), 25.
113 Schulz (2018), ibid.
114 Taubes (2009), 5.
115 Schulz (2018), 20. Although this construction appears to suggest that women are immanent nature waiting to be determined or "created" by transcendent men, Schulz demonstrates that neither gender controls or possesses "spirit" exclusively: spirit always recedes into matter.
116 See Lenowitz (1998), 181; Schulz (2018), ibid. For a fuller picture of how closely Schulz follows Frankist teachings in the construction of his character, see Pawel Maciejko (2010, August 6), "Frankism." *YIVO Encyclopedia of Jews in Eastern Europe*. Galchen's remarks imply that as the stories interact with each other, they seem "self-conscious."
117 Schulz (2018), 25.
118 Resonating with the heretical kabbalah, Father's "messianic" liberation of matter demands "materialization."
119 Frank enters history as the charlatan. See Pawel Maciejko 2010 "Sabbatian Charlatans: The First Jewish Cosmopolitans," 361–378.
120 Schulz (2018), ibid. I am tempted to read Schulz according to gender critique, but in that reading, I would reproduce what I feel is not actually the implication of Schulz's heretical project. Its heresy lies in matter's "fecundity." The possibility of multiple existences, spirits, within matter, links woman to the original state of all creation. In this revision, Father only testifies to the manifold possibility of matter whereas the simile suggests a secret depth, he glimpses. The diverse spirits within matter materialize "structures of beings" that are reducible to neither the Demiurge's nor the charlatan's commands and intentions.
121 If the Demiurge is behind creation, then, when the text says, "let us make man in our image," the template to which the Demiurge refers encourages humans to imitate jealousy, power, greed.
122 Schulz shifts away from Jacob Frank's doctrine of the Demiurge as adversary toward a theory of kabbalistic creation more attuned to Heine's *poesie*. Transgression's valence is poetic resistance to demiurgic epistemology.
123 Schulz (2018), 25.
124 Schulz (2018), 25–6.
125 The kabbalistic phrase is revised by Jacob to signify that it is an aspiration that condemns rather than liberates human existence. As I demonstrate in the previous chapter, Kafka intuits this when he imagines the infinite on the horizon and he cannot reach it no matter how fast he runs.
126 Schulz uses the Hebrew *sfera* in Polish to designate a zone or "sphere" surrounding human existence.
127 Readers might recall this image in the previous chapter on Kafka.
128 Schulz (2018), 26.
129 Schulz (2018), ibid.
130 Schulz (2018), 27.
131 Schulz (2018), ibid.
132 Schulz (2018), ibid.

133 Schulz (2018), ibid.
134 Schulz (2018), ibid. Taubes comes closest to this idea in his description of apostasy as the ultimate expression of freedom. See Taubes (2009), ibid.
135 Schulz (2018), ibid. The command revises a kabbalistic belief in the sealing of the senses. See Scholem (1995), 132.
136 Schulz (2018), 27.
137 Schulz (2018), ibid.
138 Schulz (2018), 28.
139 Schulz (2018), ibid.
140 Schulz (2018), ibid.
141 Schulz suggests desire's fulfillment is not in the object, but in its demand to abandon the subject position so that in Jacob's surrender, he is restored to immanent matter, awaiting stimulation. Through its stimulation, the golem state reunites with unconscious desire. Father craves feeling spirit's "shivers" through matter; he equates that experience with an obligation to create and be created. Thus he returns to an unformed state, waiting. In the absence of form, the implication is that Father experiences radical liberation from the Fall because in the restoration to matter, he is no longer bound by the law of human condemnation. To put it another way, the unconscious appears to harbor the memory of being unformed, matter before its condemnation to consciousness. Desire moves to write this memory outside the law of time and space, to materialize it.
142 Schulz (2018), 29.
143 Schulz (2018), ibid.
144 Imre Kertesz makes this severance of destiny from the Nazis' Jewish victims a constitutive experience of the camps. While Schulz has no knowledge of this future, this Jewish future, it is quite striking that his "Frankist" character espouses the horror of a creation condemned both to a "slavery" and to a "future-less" existence. Since Schulz's "golems" only exist as long as their maker's ecstasy, the intersection between Frankist redemption from a lifetime spent outside of history and a Demiurge who has abandoned his creation to history because they no longer please him suggests the crisis of a Jewish modernity. Like Kafka's "hunger artist," and like the Father himself, when such ecstasy ends, when the creation ceases to please, these "golems" are left to decay, unwanted, and ignored.
145 Schulz (2018), ibid.
146 Of the many theories of creation in kabbalah, one implies that the first creation exhibits a dialectic between humans and Divine Being in which Adam, a golem of matter, witnesses the first creation before being ensouled. With his ensoulment, God resolves the dialectic of creation. Scholem notes that "the golem is a creature, particularly a human being, made in an artificial way by virtue of a magic act through the use of holy names." Gershom Scholem (1974). *Kabbalah*, 351. Since the Father's innovation of the compendia implies that the "holy names" can be innovated in the profane world, there is some precedent for Schulz's conflation of human and golem.
147 Schulz (2018), 4.
148 Schulz (2018), 9.
149 Schulz (2018), 7.
150 In this respect, desire emanates from writing.
151 *Cinnamon Shops*' resonance with Heine's "innovation" of the Faust legend has never been explored, but notably, both writers see their projects in relation to desire's repression.

152 Schulz (2018), 79.
153 Schulz (2018), ibid.
154 Schulz (2018), ibid.
155 Schulz (2018), ibid.

Part 2

1. Moshe Idel (2007), "Jacques Derrida and Kabbalistic Sources," 113. He cites "the Book of Unity," an anonymous kabbalist tract from the thirteenth century which he identifies as *Sefer ha-Yihud*, MS. Milano-Ambrosiana 62, 113b ff., and discusses further in Idel "Concept of the Torah," 62–4.
2. Jacob Taubes (1982), "The Price of Messianism." *Journal of Jewish Studies* 33 (1–2): 596.
3. Dan (2006), *Kabbalah, A Very Short Introduction*, 4.
4. Erich Auerbach (1953), "Odysseus' Scar," 9–10.
5. The acronym alludes to *Nigleh / Nistar* whereby Judaism's formal study of Talmud and Torah—*Nigleh*, the revealed revelation known to all Jews—is contrasted to Nistar, the hidden revelation. *Nistar* implies that there is something more, mystery hidden in the text. Moreover, one does not necessarily gain *Nistar* through the *Nigleh*.
6. Scholem's metaphysics of "living intuition" and "dogmatic object," as I note in the introduction, rests on this tension. Likewise, it resurfaces in Chapter 2, with Wehle's claim that the rabbinate instrumentalizes the revelation, transforming *halakhah* into punitive system. Conjecturally, I have been tempted to see repetition in much of Kafka's work.
7. Dan (2006), ibid.

Chapter 6

1. Bruno Schulz (2018), "The Book," *Sanatorium under the Sign of the Hourglass*, 83.
2. Schulz (2018), "Loneliness," 231. Scholars' belief that "The Book" refers to *the Zohar* ignores that Schulz identifies it as "the Book of Creation" at the story's end. Their desire for an object underpinning the book misses consequently the implications of *Sefer Yetsirah* in relation to Schulz's overall project. Moreover, the Polish text's translation into Hebrew refers explicitly to that text. *Yetsirah* functions as a set of mystical triggers; thus it is not a book in the conventional sense of the term.
3. When reduced to letters, his stories or *aggadot* permutate cognition, chaos within Josef, until he recognizes his own transformation into writing. See Jerzy Ficowski (2003), *Regions of the Great Heresy. Bruno Schulz*, 188.
4. Bruno Schulz (2018), "The Book," 83.
5. Schulz (2018), ibid. For the more familiar older edition, see also Bruno Schulz (1977), *Sanatorium under the Sign of the Hourglass*, 1. I refer to the Levine translation of the *Sanatorium* within *Collected Stories* primarily. On occasions when I revert to the older translation by Celina Wienewska, I note it as Schulz (1977).
6. See Scholem (1995), 132. Associated with Abraham Abulafia, the "absolute object" focuses the faculties on nothingness until they collapse and the soul is unsealed. With that unsealing, the "absolute object" reveals Nothingness, or *Eyn Sof*.

7 See Schulz (2018), 25. As I demonstrate in Chapter 5, Father experiences emanations while he studies his "ornithological compendia" during which he liberates beings from its pages and they "seduce" him to go beyond innovating text to innovate nature.
8 Schulz (1977), "Spring," 47. See Matt (2003), *Zohar*, 255.
9 Scholem, *On the Kabbalah*, 177–8.
10 The trope derives from *nigleh-nistar* introduced at Qumran, and absorbed into Talmudic tradition. See Lawrence Schiffman (1975), *Halakhah at Qumran*, 22ff.
11 If the boundary between the narrator and infinite "immensity" connotes "otherness," the narrator's occupation of that boundary suggests otherness is an aspect within infinite being. Aher's discovery that he will never achieve Divine ontology drives him to apostasy, abandoning pardes. Schulz inverts Aher's "other path" to suggest that apostasy transforms to ecstasy because humans occupy an otherness in text. In *Cinnamon Shops*, he rewrites kabbalah's dialectic—either apostasy or ecstasy—to be the heretical kabbalah's apostasy, therefore ecstasy. Father abandons the infinite but with "The Book," Josef reads the self into ecstasy. Human "limitation" makes Father and son Aher, other to God by necessity, or perhaps, their human boundary constitutes "otherness" in God.
12 Scholem (1995), 44.
13 Scholem (1995), ibid.
14 Scholem (1995), ibid.
15 See Jerzy Ficowski (2003), *Regions of the Great Heresy. Bruno Schulz*, 188. Ficowski cites a letter to Romana Halpern, dated August 1, 1936, in which Ficowski identifies with Rilke because they both share an interior "disintegration and chaos." Chaos requires them to "lie, to convincingly present as existing and real what inside" them reflects an abyss of despair, an abyss closing in on them.
16 Schulz (2018), ibid. Levine translates the phrase "*przeczuciem tej rzeczy bez nazwy*" as "premonition of the thing without a name." However, if Schulz implies a kabbalistic connection, then, the indefinite article inferred in the phrase produces a correspondence between "a thing without a name" and אֵין סוֹף in Hebrew so that the "immensity of the transcendent" and the namelessness of being signify "Nothingness," one of the ways Scholem translates the Hebrew term for the Hidden God, the Divine Being who cannot be accessed through the faculties, who cannot be depicted in language, but out of whom the Hebrew letters proceed, and in whom the letters are moored. The image is so freighted: the formless being, Nothingness, who is one unity, distributes the self across the cosmos in the multiplicity of the letters, their "limitations." These letters—propelled outward in exile—seek to return to the oneness of Divine Being. Their liberation is the *tikkun* hinted at by Luria, in the sense that Luria posits the need for a human agent to enact the necessary repair. The human agent's innovation of letters, following them into exile, and releasing them from their diaspora, signals for kabbalists, the messianic moment when the liberation of the letters repairs Divine Being and in the process redeems the soul of the agent. That Schulz traces this relationship even faintly suggests the importance of the indefinite article to "a thing without a name" because it accents the incapacity to even conceptualize "transcendent." Bruno Schulz (2014), *Sklepy cynamonowe; Sanatorium pod Klepsydrą*, 100.
17 Scholem (1995), 131. While Scholem quotes Abulafia's unpublished manuscripts, the applicability of Abulafia to Schulz is evident. Schulz's narrator attempts not only to "unseal" the immanent text, but also to unseal the human faculties through its reading.

18 Such attempts have been made, all with a view to bringing kabbalah within an epistemology of knowledge. For example, Rolando Pérez declares that "the book to which both Borges and Schulz are referring is the book of the Zohar, one of the many texts that make up what is called the Kabbalah in Judaic mysticism." In Pérez's analysis, he conflates "The Book" with the *Zohar*, and in that move, he stabilizes it, tethers it to an existing object of knowledge. Panas makes the claim too, inferring that Schulz's use of "splendor" identifies "The Book" as *The Zohar*. However, the designation suppresses Schulz's theory of the text's immanence by attempting its capture, locating it within a register of knowledge. *The Zohar*, like the *Bible*, or any other "revelation," is excluded by Schulz as a "copy." In fact, when Josef identifies the text in "Loneliness" as the *Book of Creation*, the supposition that he has been "studying" it all these years underscores that Josef meditates on strings of letters since *Sefer Yetsirah* has no plot. Hence Josef realizes the impossibility of human connection: the letters are either unbound, liberated from this world or they are bound to creation, in exile from the world of supernal lights. See Rolando Pérez (2016), "Borges and Bruno Schulz on the Infinite Book of the Kabbalah," 41–56; Wladyslaw Panas (1997), *Księga blasku. Traktat o kabale w prozie Brunona Schulza*, 203.
19 Schulz (2018), 83.
20 Schulz (2018), ibid.
21 Schulz uses *blaskiem*, translated by Levine as "radiance." Intriguingly, it resonates with the German Glühende, familiar from Heine, and in reference to the revelation of *aggadah* as it transforms into *poesie*.
22 For the narrator, "being read" by the "true reader" allows the chaos within to be distilled into "radiance." Schulz describes the process when he fantasizes that he can write a new existence that will transform his lived experience. See Ficowski, Jerzy (2003), 188.
23 While there is a resonance with Kantian "subjective universalism," Kant's principle doesn't activate the kind of transformation Schulz suggests because "subjective universalism" changes neither the phenomenal, lived experience of a reader nor the exhibited aesthetic object. Subjective universalism only promotes a fleeting imagination of connection.
24 One might even argue that every time the reader engages in innovation, he, she, they, inhabit the subject position of God and that capacity is the meaning behind "let us make man in our own image."
25 Schulz (2018), ibid.
26 Schulz (2018), ibid.
27 Schulz (2018), ibid.
28 Schulz (2018), ibid.
29 Schulz (2018), 83–4. The simile of the "*centifolia* rose" is an important one to Schulz. Centifolias are also known as old garden roses, *Rose de Mai*, and the cabbage rose; they are a hybrid, but what is most compelling here is that the "wind" sweeps through them, unfolding their petals.
30 See the *Zohar*, 1:1a.
31 See fns. 121, and 699.
32 The image is akin to Tokarczuk's Yente seeing the Hebrew letters in the landscape of Poland. As I show in the next chapter, it is also a premise of Borges' "The Aleph."
33 Schulz (2018), 84. The son evokes consciously *Cinnamon Shops* when the family repeatedly "forget" Father, leaving him to his experiments and avian kingdom.

34 Schulz (2018), ibid. Dutch novelist, Harry Mulisch, repeats this gesture in *Discovery of Heaven*. See Chapter 8, "Lost Letters."
35 Schulz (2018), ibid.
36 Schulz (2018), ibid. Like ben Zoma in the *Pardes*, the son craves the "Book" and he goes insane.
37 Schulz (2018), 85. The image of the biblical scroll grants an implied authority to the proffered text.
38 Schulz (2018), ibid.
39 Intriguingly, Schulz seems to allude to a kabbalistic theory of the *Sefer Yetsirah*, the text identified in the collection's penultimate chapter, and that is believed to have been bound within, hidden away in, the Torah. At times it is represented as a "special book" in Adam's possession, that remains in Adam's possession even after the Fall. "The Book" is concealed within the Torah in order presumably to keep the power of creation out of the hands of the fallen, while simultaneously its dynamism punctuates a *pshat* revelation. The epistemology of Judaism and kabbalah recognizes that the Bible's literal meaning is secondary to this "secret" revelation within the Torah.
40 Schulz (2018), ibid.
41 Schulz (2018), 85–6.
42 Schulz repeats the scene familiar from *Cinnamon Shops* in which Adela, the housekeeper, regularly deems the revelation trash and destroys it. The repetition though of the pattern here demonstrates the son's ability to divert her attention and save the revelation.
43 Schulz (2018), ibid.
44 Schulz (2018), ibid.
45 Schulz (2018), ibid.
46 Schulz (2018), ibid. The narrator's discovery alludes to another story of a secret revelation abandoned in the "rubbish," the anecdotal story of the *Zohar's* discovery by Moses de Leon. Scholem reprises the story in Scholem (1995), 190–1.
47 Reminiscent of the requirement to never throw away anything with Hebrew on it, the abandoned folio page carries with it metonymically an entire archive of Judaic and kabbalistic significations.
48 Schulz (2018), 87.
49 Schulz (2018), 89.
50 Schulz (2018), ibid.
51 Schulz (2018), ibid.
52 Schulz (2018), ibid.
53 Schulz (2018), 90.
54 Schulz (2018), ibid.
55 Schulz (2018), ibid.
56 Schulz (2018), 90–1.
57 Schulz (2018), 91. The term is not inconsequential since it too refers often to the Jewish mystical figure of Metatron, the four *ḥayyot* or angels who carry the chariot of the Countenance in which Metatron is depicted to travel.
58 Schulz (2018), ibid.
59 Schulz (2018), ibid.
60 Schulz (2018), 93.
61 Schulz (2018), ibid.
62 Schulz (2018), 94.

63 Schulz (2018), 95.
64 Schulz (2018), 96.
65 Schulz (2018), 97.
66 Schulz (2018), ibid.
67 Schulz (2018), ibid.
68 Schulz (2018), ibid.
69 Schulz (2018), 97–8.
70 Schulz (2018), 119.
71 Schulz (2018), ibid.
72 Schulz (2018), ibid.
73 Schulz (2018), ibid.
74 Schulz (2018), ibid.
75 Schulz (2018), ibid.
76 Schulz (2018), ibid.
77 Frankist illegitimacy has become legitimately redemptive.
78 Schulz (2018), ibid.
79 Harold Bloom (1987b), "Freud," 53. He quotes Scholem on Kafka.
80 One might see Freud's "death drive" in this passage, to apply it and Schulz. The narrator's "journey" to the "depths" suggests human existence is condemned to destroy itself. Like ben Azzai, the "depths" are too much for cognition. However, Bloom questions a literal reading of Freud that ignores the unarticulated, or as Agata Bielik-Robson calls it, the "precursorial lineage" behind Bloom's reformulation of the death drive: "[t]he aim of life, Freud says, is death, is the return of the organic to the inorganic, supposedly our earlier state of being." If taken without Bloom's revised genealogy, the quote encourages nihilism. However, as Bielik-Robson demonstrates, a failure to see in Bloom's revision the introduction of Jewish and kabbalistic material tethers Bloom's argument to a static reading.

   > It starts with Jacob's struggle with the Angel of Death, which ends with the latter bestowing on the Hebrew hero the blessing of *more life,* and continues with further troping of death as the dark mythic land of *mizraim-*Egypt, symbolizing the bondage to nature and its repetitive cycle of becoming and perishing. Bloom thereby redefines Freud's Eros as the force of Exodus, the power of getting out: "the defense of life as a drive towards agonistic achievement, an agon directed not only against death but against achievements of anteriority, of others, and even of one's earlier self" (*A*, 97). Thus, in yet another imaginative twist, Bloom tropes death into everything that bears a trace of mere citation, literal repetition and "deadening reduction" which drowns a new subject in an endless sea of influence, thus annihilating his "newness." "*Literal meaning equals anteriority equals an earlier state of things equals death equals literal meaning.* Only one escape is possible from such a formula, and it is a simpler formula: *Eros equals figurative meaning*" (A, 107; Bielik-Robson's emphasis).

   Defenses of life are thus essentially the same as defenses of a poem: they both use the same power of figuration that defends against the return of deadening literality. Taking up the narrative of Jacob wrestling with Angel of Death and the patriarch's subsequent gift of "*more life,*" Bielik-Robson traces a dialectic between the death drive and the blessing of "*more life.*" Juxtaposed to "Egypt," the signifier of a "dark, mythic land" where matter is condemned to a "becoming and perishing," a temporal life and eventual death, one might suppose that Bloom recognizes all earth to be caught in this cycle: "the organic" strives to return to its origin as "inorganic." However, as Bielik-Robson points out, Bloom's dialectic hinges on *more life*; thus he reveals "the defense of life as a drive towards agonistic achievement, an agon directed not only against death but against achievements of anteriority, of others, and even of one's earlier self" (*A*, 97). Bielik-Robson underscores that in Bloom, Freud's concept of Eros is "the force of Exodus, the power of getting out" so that Jacob articulates Scholem's "novel intuition." Thus *more life* signals a defense not only against the cycle to which human existence is condemned, but it also imbues *poesie*, to go beyond "deadening literality."

81 Schulz (2018), 119–20.
82 The term means "endless" or "infinite" and Levine's translation obscures it a little. Josef's revelation is that prior to our transformation into a "cluster of melodies," human substance appears to be "infinite" writing or "endless stories."
83 See Bruno Schulz (2014), *Sklepy cynamonowe; Sanatorium pod Klepsydrą*, 145. Also see Bruno Schulz (1989), *Opowiadania Wybór Esejów I Listów*, 158.
84 Schulz (1977), 47. As I show Chapter 9, "There must be other songs beyond mankind." Wienewska's translation resonates with Celan's innovation too.
85 Wienewska's translation creates a conscious echo between Father's discourse on golems in *Cinnamon Shops* and the son's realization that in matter, humans are "unfinished stories."
86 Schulz (2018), 231.
87 In the Polish the text says "in the Book of Creation" (*w ksiedze stworzenia*). Its Hebrew equivalent is ספר יצירה—the title of the Jewish mystical text, *Sefer Yezirah*. Levine's English translation capitalizes the title to point explicitly to it. Bruno Schulz (2017), *Sanatorium pod Klepsydra*, 192.
88 Schulz (2018), ibid.
89 Schulz (2018), ibid.
90 Schulz (2018), "The Spring," 120.

Chapter 7

1 Rolando Pérez (2016), "Borges and Bruno Schulz on the Infinite Book of the Kabbalah," 41–56.
2 Jaime Alazraki (1988), *Borges and the Kabbalah and Other Essays on His Fiction and Poetry*, ix. Alazraki not only articulates a premise of the kabbalah, but also ignores its aim: when kabbalah inflects literature, it intensifies the reader's belief that the discovered "secret" has been waiting for that individual. It may have been "recorded" by another, but that does not invalidate its importance. In fact, it integrates it into the tradition. In "Una Vindicacion de la Cábala," Borges describes it as the "cryptography" of the text in which kabbalists' "hermeneutic procedures" examine words and the "cryptography" that underpins them. See Jorge Luis Borges (1984), *Obras Completas 1923–1972*, 200.

Jose Isaacson links that essay as well to the theme of a Divine Writing hidden in the text. While Borges and Isaacson attribute it to Francis Bacon and John Donne both of whom identify the writer as the Holy Spirit, its principle appears earlier in the *Zohar* in the images of God as writing and God burying or hiding Himself and/or His Light in the Torah. See Jóse Isaacson (1987), *Borges entre los nombres y el nombre*, 29–30.

3   Scholars identify "The Aleph" as proving various points about Borges' diverse uses of the kabbalah. While I lean heavily on Abulafian principles, cases can be made for several kabbalahs in this one story. The four main texts on the topic remain Edna Aizenberg (1997), *Borges, el Tejedor del Aleph y otros ensayos: del Hebraismo al Poscolonialismo*; Saul Sosnowski (1976), *Borges y la Cábala; la búsqueda del verbo*; Jaime Alazraki (1988), *Borges and the Kabbalah and Other Essays on His Fiction and Poetry*; and Jóse Isaacson (1987), *Borges entre los nombres y el nombre*. Several scholarly articles and chapters explore the topic too. See Virginia Gutierrez Berner (2009), "Mystical Laws: Borges and Kabbalah," 137–64; Ilan Stavans (2016), *Borges the Jew*, 50; Eliot R. Wolfson (2014), "In the Mirror of the Dream: Borges and the Poetics of the Kabbalah," 362–79. Remarkably very few scholars analyze kabbalah in Borges through his fiction. Scholars prefer to point to the claim that he uses kabbalah rather than demonstrate where, how, why he uses it. For a discussion of Abulafia's "combination of the letters" doctrine, see Scholem (1995), 133.
4   Jorge Luis Borges (1984), 775.
5   Aizenberg (1997), 65. "La reelaboración de ciertas fábulas y metáforas intemporales en una escritura 'original.'" Although I have taken a slight license in translating "repetition" for reelaboración or "retelling," the sense of the quote underscores how "repetition" becomes "original."
6   Aizenberg (1997), ibid. She notes that not only is Borges' project grounded in the practice of Judaic interpretation or *midrash*, but it is also specifically kabbalistic.

> Borges' introduction to sacred texts, the first source of religious ideas that he could handle aesthetically and on which he could base his aesthetics, was the Bible, which he considered entirely the product of the Judaic spirit. From the Scriptures, or the Judaic intrepretations of the Scriptures .... Borges' basic ideas about literature are derived: .... From the Jewish commentaries on Scripture .... especially Kabbalah .... other cardinal points of Borges' vision about his literary work are born, its importance, his themes, and his methodology (my translation).

Like Aizenberg, Elliot Wolfson concludes that Borges' project resonates with the "kabbalistic dialectic of tradition and innovation." In this way, he implies "tradition" to include the Torahs and subsequent midrash in relation to kabbalistic innovation of that tradition. See Eliot Wolfson (2014), "In the Mirror of the Dream: Borges and the Poetics of Kabbalah," 365.
7   Scholem (1995, 129).
8   Unlike the *Zohar*, Abulafia is not associated with the innovation of Torah. He practices an innovation of the letters. In the way, the letters await both Abulafia and the *Zoharist*.
9   Scholem (1995), 135. For Abulafia, the letters' liberation articulates the Name of God; prophetic ecstasy is the reward for this achievement, or rather, the restoration of the soul to the *sferot*. Scholem points out that "Abulafia calls his method 'The Path of the Names,' in contrast to the Kabbalists of his time, whose doctrine .... of the divine attributes" is identified as "The Path of the *Sefiroth*." Abulafia posits both paths "form the whole of the Kabbalah." The difference between the two programs rests in the nature of Abulafia's contemplated object. The *sferot* "are to become objects of quickened imagination," elsewhere understood as absolute objects, "rather than objects of an external knowledge acquired by merely learning their names as attributes or even symbols of God." Abulafia excludes them necessarily as objects

of knowledge because such objects are subsumed under human categories of time and space. These objects become transitional points for the soul's redemption. The soul repeats the names and stimulates the *sferot*. The "path of names" glimmers for a moment and the soul is restored for that moment. By comparison, when human faculties convert phenomena to objects of knowledge, they are categorized and bound to an epistemology. See Scholem (1995), 143.
10 Scholem (1995), 141.
11 Scholem (1995), 129–34. The הנה אני remains the most important textual response to God's call in the Bible. It reinforces the individual's particularity to God. When the individual responds, "Here am I," it is implied that 1) God always answers; 2) that a specific obligation is imposed; and 3) that the imposed obligation is part of a redemptive plan to bring human existence back to "walking with God," i.e., the primordial state lost because of the Fall.
12 By "restored" I mean it engages with consciousness. Thus the soul counsels and leads the individual through the flow.
13 Scholem (1995), 137. Not just phenomena, but the process of converting phenomena to objects of knowledge becomes the preoccupation of the faculties.
14 Scholem (1995), ibid.
15 Scholem (1995), ibid.
16 See Scholem (1995), 143. Although Scholem references "prophetic kabbalism" for the majority of the chapter, "prophetic kabbalah" is used by Scholem to depict when Abulafia actually enjoins "the path of the sefirot" to "the path of the Names" in order to form the "whole of kabbalah."
17 Scholem (1995), 129.
18 Although Abulafia "compares his mission and his place among his contemporaries with that of the prophet Isaiah," Abulafia "dreams" the *Genesis* pattern of Abraham's call. Scholem (1995), ibid.
19 Scholem (1995), ibid.
20 The reauthorization of prophecy suggests multiple meanings recognizable to Jewish readers. With its restoration, God fulfills the promise of a physical presence among his people, and the Shekinah returns from exile. Additionally, the role of the prophet has become necessary again because of idolatrous and magical practices that distort the powers of the letters for personal gain. Its restoration can even signify that the new prophet transmits another layer of the revelation. Scholem notes that Abulafia commits himself "to reach beyond my grasp" even though the Judaic and kabbalistic hierarchies of the era designate him a "heretic and unbeliever." Moreover, Abulafia claims the restoration of prophecy through him is directed at "those who walk in darkness. Sunken in the abyss, they and their kind would have delighted to engulf me in their vanities and their dark deeds. But God forbid that I should forsake .... truth for .... falsehood." See Scholem (1995), 130. As I note in the previous chapter, Abulafia's project comes close to the heretical kabbalah, but it does not cross over to that path. Thus Borges intimates a kinship with Abulafia.
21 Scholem (1995), ibid.
22 A particular problem of epistemology, from its perspective, all existence can be categorized: every phenomenon can be made into an object, defined by a concept, and subsumed under a category. The mind's categories of time and space divvy up existence under their rule. To segment Divine Being suggests that the entire project of epistemological knowledge hinges on bracketing existence between time and space.

The premiss is simply that there is no world beyond this one, no object that cannot be contained within knowledge's categories.

23 Scholem (1995), ibid. For Scholem, Kafka's revelation, as I present in Chapter 4, is the horizon of infinity and the knowledge of the impossibility of ever closing that gap. Even as Kafka fantasizes that he might hold his ground in the whirling flow within him, he has already conceded defeat before the infinite. He stands, with the country man, "before the Law," incapable of entering it. It signifies furthermore revelation's "fall" within the "heretical kabbalah" and its presumption of another path to redemption.

24 Scholem (1995), 132. Scholem identifies phenomena as the "shells of natural things." He is too much of a philologist to use "shells" without knowing the connotations of a term he has elsewhere developed in relation to the *kelipot*.

25 Scholem (1995), 133. *Hokhmath ha-Tseruf* means "the wisdom of the combination." The designation is critical to the project because it locates permutation in the higher levels of the *sferot* and as a practice in the mind of God.

26 Initially, the Rhineland Hasids use this idea to underpin the intensification of prayer which I believe is a precursor to innovation. See Scholem (1995), 80–118. In a related text, Scholem worries that the Jewish people have made Hebrew a bridge over the abyss and when it collapses, they will be plunged into that abyss. Printed and discussed in Jacques Derrida (2002), "Eyes of Language: The Abyss and the Volcano," 189–200.

27 Scholem explains that Abulafia posits a "peculiarly Jewish object of contemplation" in which the letters are tasked with creation, but in their fulfillment of that task, they also purify or refine it. Scholem recognizes it as a tension within Judaism, its nihilism since the letters' repetition of the Name performs ideally the purification of substance. Implicitly, embedded in fallen creation, a path to the "perfection that destroys" becomes visible. Abulafia's *hokhmah* or "wisdom" is the eventual redemption. With this implication, we "encounter" Schulz and the command for new creation. In Borges, though, fulfillment of this command is prohibited.

28 Joseph Dan (2002), *The Heart and the Fountain*, 11.
29 Dan (2002), 10.
30 Dan (2002), ibid.
31 Dan (2002), ibid.
32 Dan (2002), 11.
33 Borges (1978), 29. The term *En Soph* refers to God as Nothingness or literally Nothing-ness. See Scholem (1995), 25 ff.
34 In fact, three "Borges" figures interact with the text: the writer, the reader, and the fictional character.
35 One could see the narrator in Schulz's stories as a textual representation of Schulz's soul as well in that the narrator not only chronicles but also interprets for the reader the true meaning of the characters' actions of reading, writing, and permutating.
36 Borges (1978), 15.
37 Borges (1978), 16.
38 Borges (1978), ibid.
39 Borges (1978), ibid.
40 Borges (1978), 17.
41 Borges (1978), ibid.
42 Borges (1978), ibid.
43 Borges (1978), ibid.

44 Borges (1978), 19.
45 Borges (1978), 20.
46 Borges (1978), 23.
47 Borges (1978), ibid.
48 Borges (1978), ibid.
49 The echo between Schulz's Josef and Borges' Daneri underscores a fundamental concept of the heretical kabbalah, the transformation of an illegitimate claim of a mystical "thing" or power into a human right or entitlement.
50 Borges (1978), ibid.
51 The English translation doesn't place the emphasis in quite as dramatic a way as the Spanish: "*A nadie revelé mi descrubimiento, pero volví.*" The line starts with "*to no one did I reveal my discovery*" (my italics) and underlines Daneri's greedy possession of his secret. The verb *revelar* creates though multiple significations. The child doesn't "disclose" his discovery as if his transgression, his disobedience, might be revealed. His aunt and uncle are not omniscient so he can walk among them, and return to the cellar without their condemnation. This element of *revelar* builds on his ability to hide what he has done—he is not exposed. In another aspect, the child has experienced a revelation that he chooses to not externalize, to bring into the light of the house above. His "secret" fall rehearses Eden with a new materialist ending. As I show later, Daneri's choices are contrasted by Borges with the human inability to communicate Aleph's creative power. For the Spanish, see Borges (1974), 623.
52 Borges (1978), 24.
53 Borges (1978), ibid.
54 Borges (1978), 25.
55 Borges (1978), ibid. In fact, the line is actually, "*Claro está que si no lo ves, tu incapacidad no invalida mi testimonio.*" With this phrase, Daneri signals his use of the revelation: "Certainly, if you don't see it, your incapacity does not invalidate my testimony." "Testimony" goes forward and backward in time here; the child's experience is neither invalidated nor is Daneri's representation of it later. Borges' host declares essentially that he can represent, communicate, this revelation because of his lived experience; he possesses it. For the Spanish, see Borges (1974), 624.
56 Borges (1978), ibid. Implicitly, Daneri alludes to the possibility that in Borges' experience with the Aleph, he might die, go insane, or become a skeptic.
57 Borges (1978), 25.
58 Borges (1978), ibid.
59 Borges (1978), ibid. Although I cite the English translation above, the Spanish is much more illuminating of the path Borges takes to transmit this experience. Borges calls the "shared past" an alphabet of symbols (*un alfabeto de símbolos*), leaving open the possibility that the letters, constitutive of the alphabet, are also constitutive of the "Infinite."
60 A theme he explores in other texts, scholars often recognize it as something "Jewish," but even that assessment is a misunderstanding. In effect, Borges is saying that he is being written through the story—the story writes through him as matter. To recall Bruno Schulz here, it is a writing that "shudders" through him. See Evelyn Fishburn (2013), 59–60.
61 Fishburn (2013), 59. The real problem with Fishburn's analysis is its lack of knowledge about the multiple kabbalahs from which Borges draws. As a result, Fishburn's claim that "the majesty of the vision is disturbed" by "grotesque surroundings,"

"sordid details of lust and betrayal," that it lacks a "spiritually uplifting effect" because of Borges' "pettily vindictive reaction in denying the experience" ignores the implications of the writer's use of *aleph* for literature's transformation.

62 The critical element is tied to Borges use of *memoria* because it not only points to his recent past, but it also echoes an inscription of memory that exceeds Borges' experience.
63 Borges (1978), 26. This subtle shift has been misread by scholars to indicate that Borges' lived experience is the lens through which the story should be interpreted. See Fishburn (2013), 56, 59.
64 Borges (1978), 26. The Spanish verb, *prodigan*, actually means to "lavish" something on someone. Borges suggests that in a "trance," the mystic realizes the failure of language and ultimately produces multiple symbols or signifiers to carry the weight of the experience, with a view to increasing the experience's excess in order to catch the flow of infinity. No one signifier bears the meaning in its entirety, but instead the mystic "floods" the description with an excess of signifiers so that in their excess, a trace of the experience persists. In his critique of "mystics" who "fall back on symbols," Borges also alludes to a problem of symbol: in the realization that language cannot communicate the *aleph*, the mystic imagines coded signifiers that stand for it, but that have no real relationship to it. They are derived and constructed by the transmitter, and not part of the original received revelation.
65 Borges (1978), ibid. I read "Divine Being" for *la divinidad*.
66 Borges (1978), ibid.
67 Borges (1978), ibid.
68 Borges (1974), 625. While Daneri describes it similarly to Borges before the encounter, what Borges presents is the transformation of his mental experience. In this respect, the two figures are quite different since Daneri wants to possess the *aleph* power, retaining it for his benefit, and Borges, in the role of the prophet, experiences ecstasy, awakens to its obligation, and recognizes his inability to fulfill it. Hence he becomes a prophet, but a failed prophet.
69 Borges (1978), 26.
70 Borges (1978), 26–7.
71 As a result, the *aleph* is akin to a globe, spinning on its axis, the rumored "world" that inspires young Carlos Argentino to break the rules and "fall."
72 Borges (1974), 625. My translation.
73 Borges (1974), ibid. *Sin disminución de tamaño*. Additionally, Borges uses *esfera* an intriguing word to suggest not only the "globe" or "world," but also the kabbalistic *sfera*, the aspects of Divine Being, or "spheres" more familiar in other forms of kabbalah, but still part of Abulafia as well.
74 Borges (1978), 27.
75 Borges (1978), 28.
76 Borges (1978), ibid.
77 Scholem calls it the kabbalistic theory of unity. If readers link it to Borges' previous comments, Borges experiences his "self" being exposed initially in its chaos and multiplicity with the hope of being rewritten into *aleph*'s singularity.
78 Borges (1978), 28.
79 Scholem (1995), 218. What I'm suggesting is not that "Ain" is "Aleph", but rather that Borges has extracted a pattern from the kabbalah—Ain/Ani—and shifted its

coordinates so that *aleph* takes the place of *ayin*. Thus the text imitates Ani/Aleph with Borges tacking between them.

80 In fact, the translation leads readers to suppose the *sensus communis* is the presence of something all humans share but no one individual knows.

81 Fishburn overlooks this passage to argue that Borges' denial of seeing the Aleph illustrates that the experience does not change him. One can look at Borges' postscript to the story, his "midrash" to support Fishburn's literal reading. However, if Borges employs a kabbalistic register, then, there are two writings, and Borges' fictive transformation doesn't need to continue past the character's experience. See Fishburn (2013), ibid.

82 In this respect, Scholem in his discussion of Abulafia's *Tseruf*, likens the combination of the letters to music in which "the ear hears sounds from various combinations" so that the secrets of the letters are made legible through their combinations and the soul "delights" because it "acknowledges its God." See Scholem (1995), 134.

83 As noted earlier, Elliot Wolfson describes it as Borges' "affinity with the kabbalistic dialectic of tradition and innovation." Although his thesis freights dream rather than writing as the motivation underpinning this dialectic, it is notable that "aleph" and "earth" resonate indirectly with tradition and its innovation. See Wolfson (2014), 365.

84 See Borges (1974), 626. The rhythm of the Spanish, Borges' conscious repetitions, produce the effect of a mystery, glimpsed but incapable being captured.

> *vi el Aleph, desde todos los puntos, vi en el Aleph la tierra, y en la tierra otra vez el Aleph, y en el Aleph la tierra, vi mi cara y mis vísceras, vi tu cara, y sentí vertigo y lloré, porque mis ojos habían visto ese objeto secreto y conjectural, cuyo nombre usurpan los hombres, pero que ningún hombre ha mirado: el inconcibible universo.*

85 Borges is too much of a reader to not know the PaRDeS narrative, especially since he reads scholarship that all mention it.

86 Borges (1974), ibid. Borges' curious phrasing, "*cuyo nombre usurpan los hombres*," suggests the *aleph* is a sacred name of God that humans have appropriated or usurped.

87 Scholem (1995), 10. As I demonstrate in Chapter 1, Jacob Frank shifts this formula to be Jewish "lived experience," rather than "living intuition" in order to emphasize his teaching of the *prostak* and to freight a messianic materialism.

88 Borges (1978), 28.

89 Borges (1978), ibid.

90 Borges (1978), ibid.

91 Borges (1978), ibid.

92 Borges (1978), 29–30. For a brief introduction to Mengenlehre and set theory, see Joan Bagaria (2019), "Set Theory," https://plato.stanford.edu/archives/win2021/entries/set-theory/. Cantor's *Mengenlehre* (1895) refers to Georg Cantor's nineteenth-century text on mathematical set theory. Borges' reference makes a subtle distinction between "the mathematical theory of the actual—as opposed to potential—infinite." As Bagaria explains, Cantor works with "the linear continuum, that is, the real line," which he understands "is not countable, meaning that its points cannot be counted using the natural numbers." It is "boundless infinity." Borges refers though to *aleph* and in this subtlety, he substitutes writing for counting so that the writing of the universe cannot be read in human terms. It is infinity in contraction. His thesis of a

"false Aleph" presumes that infinity concentrated in a singular point or the letter is part of the hidden God: humans have no access to it.
93 Scholem (1995), 1–27.
94 Scholem (1995), 12. Scholem derives it from Isaac the Blind, the Spanish kabbalist of the late twelfth and early thirteenth centuries. This period is understood as the "early kabbalah." See Joseph Dan (1986), "Rabbi Isaac the Blind of Provence," 71–87.
95 Borges (1978), ibid.

Chapter 8

1 See Figure 8.1. Romy Achituv (2007), "Lost Communities" *Ghetto Fighters House Museum*, Galilee, Israel. http://m-a-p.net/yizkor/Yizkor_Hall.html (used by permission of the artist and the Museum). The exhibit ran as the last installation at the *Ghetto Fighters House Museum* in Israel.
2 See Romy Achituv (2007), 3:39–5:37.
3 Achituv (2007), 5:01.
4 Achituv (2007), 5:07–5:18.
5 See Figure 8.1.
6 Achituv's installation suggests that literature, language, words, have all been held together by the letters. To put it another way, the letters inhabit the bodies of words; words tether the letters to the universe and when language's destruction conflates with human extermination, the letters choose to abandon all fallen existence. They cannot redeem or repair the world after such crimes. They flee.
7 Celan produces an even more damning conclusion: in their fallenness, they are forced to exist untethered from human existence—no longer capable of creation and left to extinguish in the cosmos. There Divine Being would have to suffer with them, the emanations of unending grief, perpetual sorrow, replacing the *shefa* with the tears of the Divine.
8 Romy Achituv and Camille Utterback (2000), "Text Rain." Permanently available at 21c Museum Hotel, Louisville, KY, and online, http://camilleutterback.com/projects/text-rain/.
9 My analysis displaces Utterback's intention that the artwork enables participants to "lift and play with letters that do not really exist." For the full description of this installation, see Achituv, Utterback (2000), ibid.
10 Suzy Sitbon (2005), "Intersections between Artistic and Visual Creation and Cosmogony in some Spanish Bibles," 100.
11 Scholem (1995), 27.
12 Sitbon (2005), 99–100. Sitbon responds to the overall assessment in the field of micrography that it is a "Jewish art form," and is only an "artistic convention." Although she is concerned particularly with scholarship in France her analysis is pertinent, wherever medieval Hebrew manuscripts comprise a significant part of a repository's collection, since any examples of micrography are presented as strictly aesthetic ornamentation, a way around the use of images. See Therese Metzger (1978), "La massore ornementale et le decor calligraphique dans les manuscrits hebreux espagnols," 85–116; Michel Garel (1978), "Un ornement propre aux manuscrits hebreux medievaux: la micrographie," 158–66; Leila Avrin(1981), *Hebrew Micrography One Thousand Years of Art in Script: The Israel Museum, Jerusalem*;

Colette Sirat (2002), *La lettre hebraïque et sa signification*. See also Dalia-Ruth Halperin (2013), *Illuminating in Micrography*.

13 Scholem (1995), 138. Scholem quotes him directly.

> [o]ne has to be careful not to move a consonant or a vowel from its position, for if he errs in reading the letter commanding a certain member, that member may be torn away and may change its place or alter its nature immediately and be transformed into a different shape so that in consequence that person may become a cripple.

14 Moshe Idel (2007), "Jacques Derrida and Kabbalistic Sources," 113.
15 Luria's theory of *tzimtzum* posits that God retracts into the self in order for the space of creation to become visible. In that moment God sends out from the self the *sferot* who emanate creation through the letters themselves. As the Idel quote suggests earlier, if God exists within the letters of Torah, then, when God recedes, the letters extend into the cosmos, writing existence along the way. See Scholem (1995), 260.
16 Achituv and Utterback adopt a micrographer's lens for depicting images, objects, and the body itself, as composed of letters. The playful optimism of the piece lets viewers interact with letters, so that each movement reveals a cascade of letters tracing the body's outline. "Lost Communities" is a radical departure from that playful optimism. As the letters float untethered into the darkness, until they extinguish, viewers sense the finality of the damage, the significance of their abandonment of the universe.
17 The *siddur* prints at the end of each line of prayer, a treble clef, because in Judaism, the animate Hebrew letters sing: their music derives from Divine Being itself. During each service, readers reaffirm this belief.
18 See Jean Améry (1980), "At the Mind's Limits," 7. See also Kitty Millet (2012), "Jean Améry's Loss of Transcendence." Améry, born Hans Mayer, in Austria, survives Auschwitz, among other camps. In his definitive text, *At the Mind's Limits,* Améry focuses on how the faculties absorb the experience of the death camp. One of his examples demonstrates why poetry no longer has any affect for him when for all of his life prior to internment, it held the greatest influence. As I show in my analysis of his work, Améry recognizes how transcendence is a "luxury" that threatens to debilitate the inmate to the extent that survival would no longer have any cognitive value.
19 See Kitty Millet (2009), "Elie Wiesel's Night and Dying in the Present Tense," 175.
20 Wiesel (2006), *Night*, 34.
21 See Scholem (1995), 13.
22 Scholem (1995), ibid.
23 Scholem (1995), 137.
24 David Biale (1985), "Gershom Scholem's Ten Unhistorical Aphorisms on Kabbalah: Text and Commentary," 83. Biale reproduces *Satz 7*, in which Scholem declares the "doctrine of emanation" to be kabbalah's "real misfortune" because kabbalists preoccupy themselves with "structures of beings" rather than "Universal Essence."
25 Jean Améry (1980), "At the Mind's Limits," 6. Qtd in Kitty Millet (2012), "Contemplating Jean Améry's Loss of Transcendence," 22. Améry recognizes that the Hölderlin text no longer triggers transcendence in him; implicitly, the poem has become a golem text of empty statements.
26 Améry (1980), 7.
27 See Liliane Atlan (1985), *Theatre Pieces: An Anthology*, 91.
28 Atlan (1985), ibid.

29 Atlan (1985), ibid.
30 Atlan (1985), 143.
31 Atlan (1985), 155.
32 Harry Mulisch (1996), *The Discovery of Heaven*.
33 Mulisch (1996), 682.
34 Mulisch (1996), 718–21.
35 Mulisch (1996), 719.
36 Mulisch (1996), 720.
37 Mulisch (1996), 721.
38 Mulisch (1996), ibid.
39 Mulisch (1996), ibid.
40 Mulisch (1996), ibid.
41 Mulisch (1996), 682.
42 Mulisch (1996), 728.
43 Mulisch (1996), 728–9.
44 As noted earlier, In his 1923 letter to Franz Rosenzweig, Scholem ponders the implications of using Hebrew's Israel national language, to depict the profane, the mundane rather than the sacred. He implies that Jews have created a bridge over the abyss, akin to the actions of Jacob Frank. Quoted in Jacques Derrida (2013), "Eyes of Language," 191–2.

Chapter 9

1 Paul Celan (1980), *Paul Celan. Poems*, 191.
2 Anne Carson (2009), *The Economy of the Unlost: Reading Simonides of Keos with Paul Celan*, 114.
3 Celan's most recent translator, Pierre Joris, describes the transformation in Celan's writing and refers to it as "the *Wende*" or "Turn," a term Celan uses as well. Pierre Joris (2005), *Paul Celan Selections*, 24. See also Joris's "Introduction" in Celan (2020), *Breathturn*, 12.
4 Carson (2009), 115. Carson translates both titles somewhat differently; I have opted to use Pierre Joris' translation. Joris identifies "Todesfuge" as written in 1947. He catalogues the poem eventually as part of four books published between 1952 and 1963, specifically, Paul Celan (1952), *Mohn und Gedächtnis*. See Pierre Joris (2020), "Introduction," XX.
5 Carson (2009), ibid.
6 Carson (2009), ibid. She echoes Felman's observation in the next paragraph in that Carson grounds Celan's shift from an "aestheticism" associated with lyric poetry in the decision that he must not become "a master."
7 Biale, David (1985), "Gershom Scholem's Ten Unhistorical Aphorisms on Kabbalah: Text and Commentary," 83. Carson's observation though underscores the real tension in Celan's work between the inappropriate almost obscene need to force aesthetic experience to address these experiences and the overwhelming fear that all that is left is as Améry notes, "objective statement."
8 Shoshana Felman (1991), "Education and Crisis," 36.
9 Felman (1991), ibid.

10 In other words, it was exactly the opposite of how Rolf Hochhuth and Theodor Adorno understood it. Pierre Joris points out that the poem is first published in 1947 in Romania by a friend of Celan's and it was this publication that triggers Celan's popularity in the German-speaking world. His observation doubly articulates then an aspect of Felman's analysis: Celan's readers would have been the morally compromised collaborators, perpetrators, and onlookers of Celan's victimization. Hoping to force them to *read* him, to *see* their victims, then, he exhibits "Death Fugue." To some extent, he tries to use lyric to move his readers into the "concentrationary universe" he has been forced to inhabit.
11 Felman (1991), 35. Felstiner gives a more detailed account of Celan's response to Adorno's condemnation of lyric in relation to his own work.
12 Felman (1991), 34–5.
13 Carson echoes the claim when she references Celan's "turn away" from a "stage of himself that no longer suffices."
14 See "Cultural Criticism and Society" (1949) in Adorno (1982), *Prisms*, 34. John Felstiner notes additionally the anger Celan feels over Adorno's condemnation of "Todesfuge"; Felstiner (1995), "Etching and Alchemy" (1963–5). *Paul Celan: Poet, Survivor, Jew.*, 225.
15 As I show, Celan is invested in a name, and does abandon sense, but his poetic project does not stop with the meaninglessness of it all.
16 Pierre Joris (2005), *Paul Celan Selections*, 24.
17 I reedit Celan's quote purposely because of his inital hope to use lyric to exhibit before a reader' Jewish victimization under the Nazis. In his investment in lyric, he attempts to restore to the Nazis' Jewish victims their "songs."
18 Paul Celan (2020), "Death Fugue," 43.
19 Celan (2020), 45. At this early point in Celan's oeuvre, he wants to freeze these two positions, mapping them "explicitly." Hence "solidify" points to this desire.
20 Celan (2020), ibid.
21 Celan (2020), ibid.
22 Charlotte Delbo makes a similar claim in "The Tulip" in which as her work detail walks from Auschwitz to an unnamed place, the women see a "house with muslin curtains," with a chimney, and a tulip on the sill. The women for the rest of their march can't stop thinking about it; the image of the tulip plunges them into a reverie that continues back in the barracks until they discover that the house belongs to the SS commandant of the fisheries and in that moment, "they despise themselves," for having remembered the Beautiful, for remembering their homes. Delbo suggests that they hated themselves for hoping to be restored to the world outside the camps. See Charlotte Delbo (2014), *Auschwitz and After*, 59.
23 Jean Améry makes this very point. See Millet (2012), 21–37.
24 "Todesfuge" prompts readers to this conclusion. Celan tacks between Jewish extermination as a form of expulsion from the German master's consciousness. The poem prompts readers to this conclusion. Both Lyotard and Nancy examiine the Nazi subject's catharsis and its desired aim of purging Jews from the human genome. See Kitty Millet (2010), "Caesura, Continuity, and Myth The Stakes of Tethering the Holocaust to German Colonial Theory," 108.
25 As someone who lives through the camps, but loses everyone, Celan knows explicitly how Jewish victims were transformed into non-human entities by their persecutors. It is an experience with which survivors live continuously after their "liberation."

26 In a similar vein, Ruth Klüger describes in *Still Alive* how the mythical figure of "drunken August," living during the Great Plague, drinks each night until he passes out in a pit of corpses and every morning arises, "bright-eyed," refreshed, ready for the day. He emerges "uninfected" by their death. See Ruth Klüger (2001), *Still Alive*, 41–2.
27 John Felstiner (2001), ibid. Felstiner points out in his analysis of "Todesfuge" that Celan as a survivor speaks from a position that Adorno cannot occupy. As "a survivor and a poet," Celan is conscious of the obligation and choice he places before his readers. In fact, Felstiner suggests that Adorno, the exile, resides after the war, more on the side of the "master" than he would want to accept. Unlike Celan, Adorno doesn't actually hold one group accountable for extermination, choosing instead to hold the world responsible. The effect of this approach is the indeterminacy of the persecutor who becomes interchangeable with persecutors synchronically and diachronically. Likewise, victims become interchangeable too so that specificity is no longer necessary for understanding Nazi oppression. Adorno's stratagem subsumes Jews' general experiences as objects under a category; that is, it's an epistemological approach. Where the two, Celan and Adorno, could have intersected then should have been in the ambiguity of the "master" signifier, but Adorno cuts that possibility off, placing Celan in that subject position, but refusing to apply it to himself. Améry provides perhaps more context in his analysis of the German literary community in exile safely in the United States whose pronouncements exclude unintentionally the Nazis' Jewish victims. Jean Amery (1980), *At the Mind's Limits*, 42–3.

Pierre Joris describes the disturbing effects "the Goll Affair" had on Celan during this time. See Pierre Joris (2020), *Memory Rose into Threshold Speech: The Collected Earlier Poetry*, 454. This might be even the point of Celan's poem altogether: in the process of becoming a subject, in the process of becoming a "master," catharsis enables the subject to dispense with guilt, shame, regret, because he seeks transcendence. This subject position is unavailable to Celan the Holocaust survivor: Celan is intimately aware of it and he renounces it.
28 Felman (1991), 31.
29 Felman (1991), ibid.
30 Felman (1991), ibid.
31 In previous publications, and following Lacoue-Labarthe, and Lyotard, I have demonstrated that the Nazi subject comes into being through the physical discharge of Jewish lives. Celan recognizes then the possibility of subjects belatedly finding sublimity in the extermination of Jews.
32 I freight "receiving and transmitting" intentionally to point to Celan's perception of his poetic project. His poetics are akin to a revelation so that when the received tradition is transmitted in the way it has always been—no alteration at all due to the act of extermination—Celan enacts a "disruption" or break. This leads him certainly to the idea that revelation must take place "beyond" a human register. Consequently, he "turns" to kabbalah: he begins to permutate the letters.
33 Joris marks the practice as beginning with *Speechgrille* and becoming more pronounced with Celan's *NoOnesRose*. The common belief is that he's just trying to stop meaning and that is somewhat true, but it never ends with the stop that readers envision: Celan is always waiting for another voice to be heard on the other side of the stop, a voice silenced by meaning, and that resides "beyond humankind."
34 Felman (1991), 37.

35 Felman echoes Philippe Lacoue-Labarthe in relation to Heidegger and to the Nazi subject generally, a subject position that makes transcendence contingent on "the discharge" of Jews from human existence through the act of a physical catharsis. See my previous discussion of this thesis in Kitty Millet (2010), "Caesura, Continuity, and Myth The Stakes of Tethering the Holocaust to German Colonial Theory," 108 ff.
36 In fact, Felstiner claims that Celan's love for his mother and her love of German tradition bind him to try and make visible through *Wissenschaft's* aesthetic principles exactly what the Nazis have done in pursuit of transcendence. In this way, Celan's poetics are understood as a failed redemptive project. He knew this intimately as he gained fame for his "lyricism" that his readers used to solidify their own positions as subjects, effectively ignoring the horror underpinning their subjective liberation. In his discussion of the aftereffects of the Nazi Reich, Rafael Lemkin declared this outcome as part and parcel of the Nazis' "coordinated plan" or social project that would continue long after the war because of the steps they had taken during it. See Rafael Lemkin (1944), *Axis Rule in Occupied Europe*, XI.
37 Celan (2020), 45. Celan's pessimism is not unique among poets and writers who have survived the Holocaust.
38 This challenge informs Celan's "Meridian speech." See, Paul Celan (2011), *The Meridian. Final Version—Drafts—Materials*.
39 He's alluding here to the Jewish / Judaic belief that the Hebrew letters sing, make music, wear crowns, in their creative capacity.
40 Celan (2020), 12. While Joris notes that "his wife gives him the idea," by this time Celan is already using a kabbalist register to trigger the animation of the letters themselves. They are all he has left: they are the Being of the Hidden God.
41 Celan (2020), *Memory Rose into Threshold Speech, the Collected Earlier Poetry. A Bilingual Edition*, 339.
42 Celan (2020), xxv. Joris relies on Celan being explicit here; however, Celan's turn pushes him to code his poetry with kabbalistic content regularly as I demonstrate.
43 Esther Cameron (2014), *Western Art and Jewish Presence in the Work of Paul Celan: Roots and Ramifications of the "Meridian" Speech*, 264.
44 Cameron (2014), ibid.
45 Felstiner (1995), *Paul Celan, Poet, Survivor, Jew*, 6, 114.
46 Andre Neher's work contrasts Faust with the Maharal in order to illustrate the theological dialectic at the heart of the kabbalah. God is always searching for humankind. In his writings on transcendence, he also freights the tension between the human quest for transcendence, which always results in a Faustian wager, and the immanence of writing. See Andre Neher; Richard Neher (1946). *Transcendence and Immanence*, 3; see also Andre Neher (1987), *Faust et le Maharal de Prague*, 25–66.
47 This unarticulated aspect is part of Celan's "Meridian speech" in which he states, "the poem shows, unmistakably, a strong tendency to fall silent. 50. Ladies and Gentlemen, we write it again and again." See Paul Celan (2011), *Meridian, the Final Version-Drafts-Materials*, 32.
48 Celan (2011), "Meridian," ibid.
49 Celan (2020), *Memory Rose into Threshold Speech*, 339.
50 Normally, I would use "humankind," but it is Celan's term.
51 In Scholem (1995), *Major Trends of Jewish Mysticism*, 5. Scholem describes the Hasidic experience of kabbalah in relation to other forms of Jewish mysticism in

which the Hasid in response to a question about his experience declares that he looks at Nothing (*Nichts*). Scholem continues to explain then that the Hasid refers to God in the moniker of "Nothingness." See Gershom Scholem (1967), *Die jüdische Mystik in ihren Hauptsrömungen*, 6.
52 Paul Celan (2005), *Threadsuns*, 9
53 In the notes to his "Meridian" speech, Celan stresses that the poet engages with the "alien," the "strange," and then corrects himself to say, "the totally other," in order to "speak on the other's behalf." In his notes, "Strange" resonates with Jacob Frank's use of the term as well to signify that Celan must act against the received tradition of poetry in order to open up as Pierre Joris remarks "the word-matter itself." See David Brazil (2021), "Under the Language: A Conversation with Pierre Joris on Paul Celan." https://lareviewofbooks.org/article/under-the-language-a-conversation-with-pierre-joris-on-paul-celan/ (accessed January 20, 2021).
54 Celan (2020), *Memory Rose into Threshold Speech*, 245. Joris translates *o keiner, o niemand, o du* absolutely in the vein of Celan's thinking.
55 Celan (2020), 263.
56 Joris' translation evokes the spirit of Celan's project here even though Celan himself has yet to permutate the letters to create a new name of God, noone / NoOne. In German, Celan is really using a term we might expect to stand in for the Hidden God, or אין סוף
57 Celan (2020), 264–5.
58 There is even reason to believe that Celan invokes or imagines the Tree of Life in its kabbalist depiction of the *sferot*, enfolding all of creation, especially in light of the last poem in Book 2, in which "the tree …. stands against *the Plague*" and "Les Globes'" reference to the spheres and the *parsufim* in Book 3. In "Les Globes," Celan reveals that the *sferot* themselves are the source of this new writing "edging the abysses. All the faces' writing." See Celan (2020), 330–1.
59 Celan (2020), 284–5. The word for NoOne is again *Niemand*.
60 I differ from Joris based on the ways Celan has used *Nichts* and *Niemand*; thus I capitalize the "N" in "Nothingness."
61 I believe that Celan invokes the kabbalist register and as a result, refers to the Hasidic *En Sof, Nichts*. Thus it should not read in English as "nothingness" but rather "Nothingness."
62 Celan (2020), 286–7. Intriguingly, Celan appears to quote a phrase related to the Rhineland Hasids and *the Zohar*: to open a word is to innovate it. His psalm has now become a prayer in which he innovates his "word" in order to place it directly before God.
63 Celan (2020), 288–9. *Gemüt* has so many possible translations. While I quote Joris' translation, the force of this line really seems more amenable to "soul," so that the line should read "write the living Nothing on his soul."
64 Celan (2020), 290–1.
65 While a common epithet in biblical Hebrew, as a kabbalistic signifier, "The King" is also a signifier of the Hidden God, referenced by *Keter*, or "Crown," and the first sphere in the Tree of Life. Arthur Green observes that the epithet derives from "the relationship between *Hasiduth Ashkenaz*, or at least between works known and preserved in Ashkenazi Hasidic circles, and the authors/editors of *Sefer ha-Bahir*." In other words, "the King" as a metonym for *Keter* circulates among the Rhineland Hasids and emerging schools of kabbalists of the Middle Ages; that is, it is part of the tradition later picked up by Isaac Luria, Jacob Frank, and the Hasids in the early

modern era. Thus Celan's connection of "the King" with "Nothingness" produces for anyone familiar with kabbalah the immediate realization that he has invoked *Nichts* to be אין סוף. See Arthur Green (1997), *Keter. The Crown of God in Early Jewish Mysticism*, 121.

66 Celan (2011), ibid.
67 Celan (2020), 300-1.
68 Celan (2020), ibid.
69 Brazil (2021), ibid.
70 Celan (2020), ibid.
71 Celan's text suggests a precursor for Tokarczuk's transformation of Yente in *The Books of Jacob*.
72 Celan (2020), 306-7.
73 Celan, ibid.
74 Celan (2011), 34; 33a.
75 Celan (2020), 330-1.
76 Celan (2020), ibid.
77 Celan (2020), ibid.
78 Celan traces a *Zoharic* perspective in which the kabbalist, aware that no human is present at creation, recognizes that the Torah in its literal meaning is a human structure—not a Divine one. As Dan puts it, "humans create meaningful units of sense, but what we only really have are the sounds of the letters." Joseph Dan (2002), *The Heart and the Fountain*, 11. Thus Celan moves toward a writing beyond humankind.
79 Celan (2020), 338-9.
80 Celan (2020), 340-1.
81 Daniel Matt, ed. (2003), *Zohar*, 11-16, 1:2b-3b. In this narrative tale from the *Zohar*, all the Hebrew letters present themselves to God and God installs them within creation. Hence *Genesis* or *Bereshit* in Hebrew reflects God's choice to begin creation with "Bet." If Celan is conscious of this tradition and I believe he is because of that Hasidic background, then, the play on "Beth" and "Bet" can only be part of the discursive trigger he's attempting in inaugurate in *NoOnesRose*.
82 Hence the Maharal appears in Book III. *Memory Rose*.
83 Pierre Joris (2005), *Selections Paul Celan*, 91. Celan's "The Syllable Pain" implies that when the Nazis distort writing, language, words, syllables into the calculus of the death camp, the tattoos on their Jewish victims, they inflict so much pain that "the syllable" broke itself open and "gave itself to Your hand."
84 Pierre Joris (2000), "Introduction," 13. Joris quotes "Threadsuns," referenced initially in the volume, *Breathturn*. See Paul Celan (2006), *Breathturn*, 91.
85 Pierre Joris (2020), "Introduction," *Memory Rose*, xvi.
86 Joris (2020), ibid.
87 Felstiner (1995), 220.
88 The support for this is almost biblical: since God promises Abraham that his offspring will be as many as the grains of the sand. Moreover, sand castles or any structures build of and on sand, can be destroyed with every wave, every tide, returning to shore. If the signifier is supposed to call to mind the Jews, then, it reminds the poet metonymically of their tenuous existence.
89 Celan has entered into writing and has realized that *En Sof* or "Nothingness" has been displaced by nothingness. The key to it all resides with the absence of "the Hidden God": their dissolution and in their place, there is only nothingness.

90 Jorge Semprun makes this precipice the organizing principle of his own memoir of Buchenwald, *Literature or Life*. Jorge Semprun (1998), *Literature or Life*, 25–7.
91 While Felstiner attempts to restore the missing context external to the poem, the poem's internal register concerns me because Celan extends Jewish loss beyond something lost from Judaism.
92 Améry (1980), ibid.
93 This is a quote from David Boder, the psychologist who in 1946 travels to Europe to record the testimonies of survivors over a period of nine weeks in nine languages. His displaced persons project was the precursor to the many video archive projects today focused on Holocaust-era memories. However, as Rosen notes, Boder insisted on collecting survivors' "songs," prompting him to note the "wonder of their voices." See Alan Rosen (2010), *The Wonder of the Their Voices. The 1946 Holocaust Interviews of David Boder*, 108; 204.

Conclusion

1 Olga Tokarczuk (2022), *The Books of Jacob or: A Fantastic Journey across Seven Borders, Five Languages, and Three Major Religions, not Counting the Minor Sects*, 10.
2 Tokarczuk (2022), ibid.
3 Tokarczuk (2022), ibid.
4 Tokarczuk (2022), ibid.
5 The biblical patriarch Enoch does not die in *Genesis*, but instead ascends. With *Hekhalot-Merkavah* Jewish mysticism, as well as Jewish apocalyptic texts, he is transformed into Metatron. For an overview of Metatron and Enoch's transformation, see Joseph Dan (2002), *The Heart and the Fountain*, 61–74.
6 Tokarczuk (2022), 12.
7 Tokarczuk (2022), 10.
8 Franz Kafka (1948), *The Diaries of Franz Kafka, 1910–1913*, 122.
9 Franz Kafka (1949), *Diaries of Franz Kafka, 1914–1923*. Vol. 2, 202–3.
10 Harold Bloom (1987b), *The Strong Light of the Canonical: Kafka, Freud, and Scholem as Revisionists of Jewish Culture and Thought*, 3.
11 Franz Kafka (1949), ibid.
12 Franz Kafka (1949), *Diaries of Franz Kafka, 1914–1923*. Vol. 2, 202–3.
13 Robert Alter (1993), "Kafka as Kabbalist," 86.
14 Alter (1993), ibid.
15 Alter (1993), ibid.
16 Alter (1993), ibid. In *The Strong Light of the Canonical*, Bloom changes Scholem's three key "sets" to be instead, "Kafka, Freud, and Gershom Scholem." The shift enables him to suggest a new kabbalah, a "modernist kabbalah." Harold Bloom (1987b), *The Strong Light of the Canonical*, 77.
17 In this way, Scholem sets up his most novel thesis about Kafka, literature, and kabbalah; these sets of texts resist becoming objects of dogmatic knowledge. They resist the Law.
18 See David Suchoff (2011), *Kafka's Jewish Languages: The Hidden Openness of Tradition*, 160.
19 Alter (1993), ibid.

20 See Hannah Ginsborg, "Kant's Aesthetics and Teleology," https://plato.stanford.edu/archives/win2019/entries/kant-aesthetics/. On another note, Kafka recognizes this in his 1922 diary entry when he describes writing as an "assault from below"–profane phenomena pushing toward the sacred–and an "assault from above"–sacred phenomena expressing themselves in profane objects. See Chapter 4 in this volume.
21 Benjamin (2012), 279.
22 Benjamin (2012), 563.
23 Benjamin (2012), ibid.
24 Benjamin (2012), ibid.
25 Both essays, "Theses on the Philosophy of History," and "The Work of Art in the Age of Mechanical Reproduction" can be found in *Illuminations*; see Benjamin (1968), 217-264. Benjamin (1955), 254.
26 Benjamin (2012), 565.
27 Benjamin (2012), ibid. In the "Theological-Political Fragment," the tension between "profane" and "messianic" leads to the *mitzvah* Benjamin levies on modern subjects "to strive after such passing." See Walter Benjamin (1978), *Reflections*, 313.
28 Benjamin (1978), ibid.
29 Benjamin (1978), 565.
30 Benjamin (1978), 564-5.
31 Walter Benjamin (1968), "Some Reflections on Kafka," 144-5.
32 See Max Brod (1937), *Werke*, 942.
33 Walter Benjamin (1969), "The Work of Art in the Age of Mechanical Reproduction," 218. Walter Benjamin (1989), "Das Kunstwerk im Zeitalter seiner technischen Reproduzierbarkeit," *Nachträge, Siebter Band, Erster Teil*, 350-384. See also, Benjamin (1969), 254.
34 See Miriam Brattu Hansen (2008), "Benjamin's Aura," 336-75.
35 Hannah Arendt, ed. (1969), "Introduction," 12-13.
36 Gershom Scholem (2018), *Greetings from Angelus. Poems*, 38-41. The poem was written in 1921.
37 Scholem (2018), 40. "Ich habe keinen Sinn." The German is a bit more direct than the published translation. Thus "I have no sense," the poem's last line, plays off the first stanza's "I am an angelman." Scholem points to the different ontologies between human and spiritual beings.
38 Scholem (2018), ibid.
39 Hannah Arendt (1968), "Introduction," 3; 13.
40 Arendt (1968), 3. While she quotes Hofmansthal, the real issue is the confirmation of Benjamin's "inimitability" among several discrete readers.
41 Arendt (1968), ibid.
42 Arendt (1968), ibid.
43 Scholem (1995), *Major Trends of Jewish Mysticism*, 10.
44 Arendt (1968), 4.
45 Walter Benjamin (1978), "Theological-Political Fragment," 312.
46 Benjamini (1978), ibid.
47 Jacob Taubes makes the claim as well in "Walter Benjamin—A Modern Marcionite?" See Jacob Taubes (2016), "Walter Benjamin—A Modern Marcionite? Scholem's Benjamin Interpretation Reexamined," 164.
48 Harold Bloom (1987b), 63.

49 Gershom Scholem (1965), *On the Kabbalah and Its Symbolism,* 121.
50 Scholem (1965), ibid.
51 Bloom (1987b), 67.
52 Bloom (1987b), 71.
53 Scholem (1995), 129.
54 Robert Alter (1993), "Kafka as Kabbalist," 87.

Bibliography

Primary Literatures

Ansky, S. (1926). *The Dybbuk. A Play in Four Acts*. Trans. Henry G. Alsberg and Winifred Katzin. New York: Boni and Liveright.
Borges, Jorge Luis (1974). "El Aleph." *Obras Completas*. Buenos Aires: Emecé Editores.
Borges, Jorge Luis (1978). *The Aleph and Other Stories, 1933–1969*. Trans. Norman Thomas di Giovanni. New York: Dutton.
Celan, Paul (1980). *Paul Celan: Poems*. Trans. Michael Hamburger. New York: Perseus.
Celan, Paul (2000). *Threadsuns*. Trans. Pierre Joris. Los Angeles: Sun and Moon Press.
Celan, Paul (2001). "Todesfuge." *Selected Poems and Prose of Paul Celan*. Trans. John Felstiner. New York: Norton.
Celan, Paul (2006). *Breathturns*. Trans. Pierre Joris. Kobenhavn and Los Angeles: Green Integer.
Celan, Paul (2011). *The Meridian: Final Version—Drafts—Materials*. Ed. Bernhard Böschenstein and Heino Schmull, trans. Pierre Joris. Stanford, CA: Stanford UP.
Celan, Paul (2020). *Memory Rose into Threshold Speech*. Trans. Pierre Joris. New York: Farrar, Strauss, Giroux.
Dalley, Stephanie, trans. (1989). *Myths of Mesoptamia: Creation, the Flood, Gilgamesh and Others*. Oxford: Oxford UP.
Goethe, Johann Wolfgang von (1963). *Goethe's Faust: The Original German and a New Translation and Introduction by Walter Kaufmann*. Ed. and trans. Walter Kaufmann. New York: Anchor Books.
Heine, Heinrich (1852). *Melodien, Romanzero, Bd 3*. Hamburg: Hoffmann und Campe.
Heine, Heinrich (2008). *Rabbi of Bacharach*. New York: Mondial Press.
Heine, Heinrich (1847). *La Legende du Docteur Jean Faust*. Paris: Gerdes Editeur.
Heine, Heinrich (1910), *Heinrich Heine's Memoirs from His Works, Letters and Conversations*. Ed. Gustav Karpeles. Tr. Gilbert Cannan. London: Heinemann.
Heine, Heinrich (1851). *Der Doktor Faust: Ein Tanzpoem nebst kuriosen Berichten über Teufel, Hexen und Dichtkunst*. Hamburg: Hoffman u. Campe.
Heine, Heinrich (1890). *Sämtliche Werke*. Vol. 4. Ed. Ernst Elster. Leipzig: Bibliographisches Institut.
Heine, Heinrich (1952). *Doktor Faust: A Dance Poem*. Ed. and trans. Basil Ashmore. London: Peter Nevill, Ltd.
Kafka, Franz (1935), *Der Prozess*. Berlin: I.S. Fischer Verlag.
Kafka, Franz (1948–9). *Tagebücher, 1910–1923*. Ed. Max Brod. New York: Schocken Books.
Kafka, Franz (1956). *The Trial*. Trans. Willa and Edwin Muir. New York: Knopf.
Kafka, Franz (1992). *The Castle*. Trans. Willa and Edwin Muir. New York: Knopf.
Kafka, Franz (1993). *Nachgelassen Schriften u. Fragmente*. Berlin: I. S. Fischer Verlag.
Kafka, Franz (1948). "Before the Law." *Penal Colony, Stories and Short Pieces*. Trans. Willa and Edwin Muir. New York: Schocken Books.

Kafka, Franz (1948). "The Judgment." *Penal Colony, Stories and Short Pieces*. Trans. Willa and Edwin Muir. New York: Schocken Books.

Kafka, Franz (1948). "The Penal Colony." *Penal Colony, Stories and Short Pieces*. Trans. Willa and Edwin Muir. New York: Schocken Books.

Kafka, Franz (1948). "Imperial Messenger." *Penal Colony, Stories and Short Pieces*. Trans. Willa and Edwin Muir. New York: Schocken Books.

Klüger, Ruth (1994). *Weiter Leben. Eine Jugend*. München: Deutsche Taschenbuch Verlag.

Klüger, Ruth (2001). *Still Alive*. New York: Feminist Press at the City University of New York.

Lispector, Elisa (1945). *No Exílio*. Rio de Janeiro, Brazil: Editora Pongetti.

Lispector, Elisa (1971). *In Exile*. Rio de Janeiro, Brazil: Ebrasa.

Mulisch, Harry (1996). *Discovery of Heaven*. New York: Viking Penguin.

Mulisch, Harry (2017). *Die Ontdemming von Hemel*. Nederlands: Bezige Bij b.v., Uitgeverij De.

Schulz, Bruno (1958). *Street of Crocodiles*. New York: Penguin.

Schulz, Bruno (1977). *Sanatorium under the Sign of the Hourglass*. New York: Houghton Mifflin.

Schulz, Bruno (1989), *Opowiadania Wybór Esejów I Listow*, Ed. Barbara Antioniuk. Wroclaw: Zakład Narodowy im. Ossolińskich.

Schulz, Bruno (1998). *Opowiadania, wybór esejów i listów*. Lvov: Zakład Narodowy im. Ossolińskic.

Schulz, Bruno (2014). *Sklepy cynamonowe: Sanatorium pod Klepsydra*. Kęty. Poland: Wydawnictwo Marek Derewiecki.

Schulz, Bruno (2018). *Collected Stories*. Trans. Madeline G. Levine. Evanston, IL: Northwestern UP.

Semprun, Jorge (1998), *Literature or Life*. Tr. Linda Cloverdale. New York: Penguin.

Stein, Benjamin (2014). *Das Alphabet des Rabbi Löw*. Berlin: Verbrecher Verlag.

Stollman, Aryeh Lev (2003). "The Adornment of Days." *The Dialogues of Time and Entropy*. New York: Riverhead Books.

Tokarczuk, Olga (2022). *The Books of Jacob: A Fantastic Journey across Seven Borders, Five Languages, and Three Major Religions …*. Trans. Jennifer Croft. New York: Riverhead Books.

Von Sacher-Masoch, Leopold (1886). *Sabbathai Zewy: Die Judith von Bialopol*. Berlin: R. Jacobsthal.

Von Sacher-Masoch, Leopold (2017). "Sabbatai Zevi." *Sabbatian Heresies. Writings on Mysticism, Messianism, and the Origins of Jewish Modernity*. Ed. Pavel Maciewski, trans. Alexander van der Haven. Waltham, MA: Brandeis UP.

Wiesel, Elie (2006), *Night*. Tr. Marion Wiesel. New York: Hill and Wang.

Secondary Criticism

On Kabbalah and Jewish Mysticism

Alter, Robert (1987). "Scholem and Sabbatianism." *Modern Critical Views: Gershom Scholem*. Ed. Harold Bloom. New York: Chelsea House Publishers.

Baeck, Samuel (1877). "*Aufgefundene Aktenstücke zur Geschichte der Frankisten in Offenbach*." *Monatsschrift für Geschichte und Wissenschaft des Judentums*. Vol. 26. Heft 4. Dresden: Rudolf Kuntz, 411–20.
Baumgarten, Jean (2018). *La Legende de Yosef della Reina, activiste messianique*. Paris: L'Eclats.
Berenbaum, M. and F. Skolnik, eds. (2007). "Pardes" *Encyclopaedia Judaica*. 2nd edn. Vol. 15. Detroit, MI: Macmillan Reference USA, 632. https://link.gale.com/apps/doc/CX2587515409/GVRL?u=sfsu_main&sid=bookmark-GVRL&xid=ea5ea9cc (accessed Feb 09, 2022).
Biale, David (1985). "Gershom Scholem's Ten Unhistorical Aphorisms on Kabbalah: Text and Commentary." *Modern Judaism* 5 (1): 67–93.
Biale, David (2010). *Not in the Heavens: The Tradition of Jewish Secular Thought*. Princeton, NJ: Princeton UP.
Biale, David (2018). *Gershom Scholem: Master of the Kabbalah*. New Haven: Yale UP.
Bloom, Harold (2002). *Genius: A Mosaic of One Hundred Exemplary Creative Minds*. New York: Warner Books.
Bloom, Harold (1975). *Kabbalah and Criticism*. New York: Continuum Press.
Bloom, Harold, ed. (1987a). *Gershom Scholem: Modern Critical Views*. New York: Chelsea House Publishers.
Bloom, Harold (1987b). *The Strong Light of the Canonical: Kafka, Freud, and Scholem as Revisionists of Jewish Culture and Thought*. New York: The City College Papers.
Buber, Martin (1958). *Tales of the Hasidim*. Trans. Olga Marx. New York: Schocken Books.
Dan, Joseph (2002). *The Heart and the Fountain*. Oxford: Oxford UP.
Dan, Joseph (2006). *Kabbalah: A Very Short Introduction*. Oxford: Oxford UP.
Fine, Lawrence (2003). *Physician of the Soul, Healer of the Cosmos: Isaac Luria and His Kabbalistic Fellowship*. Stanford: Stanford UP.
Fine, Lawrence, ed. (1995). *Essential Papers on Kabbalah*. New York and London: New York University Press.
Dynner, Glenn, ed. (2011). *Holy Dissent: Jewish and Christian Mystics in Eastern Europe*. Detroit, MI: Wayne State University Press.
Gottstein, Alon Goshen (1995). "Four Entered Paradise Revisited." *Harvard Theological Review* 88 (1): 69–133.
Gottstein, Alon Goshen (2000). *The Sinner and the Amnesiac*. Stanford, CA: Stanford UP.
Green, Arthur (1997). *Keter: The Crown of God in Early Jewish Mysticism*. Princeton, NJ: Princeton UP.
Idel, Moshe (1981), "The Concept of the Torah in Hekhalot Literature and Kabbalah" (Heb). *Jerusalem Studies in Jewish Thought*, 23–84.
Idel, Moshe (1988). *The Mystical Experience in Abraham Abulafia*. New York: SUNY Press.
Idel Moshe (1990), Golem. *Jewish Magical and Mystical Traditions on the Artificial Anthropoid*, Albany: SUNY Press. 9–27.
Idel, Moshe (1998). *Messianic Mystics*. New Haven and London: Yale UP.
Idel, Moshe (2002). *Absorbing Perfections: Kabbalah and Interpretation*. New Haven: Yale UP.
Idel, Moshe (2007), "Arnaldo Momigliano and Gershom Scholem on Jewish History and Tradition". *Momigliano and Antiquarianism: Foundations of the Modern Cultural Sciences*, Toronto: University of Toronto Press, pp. 312–333. https://doi.org/10.3138/9781442684591-013

Kaniel, Ruth Kara-Ivanov (2022). *Birth in Kabbalah and Psychoanalysis*. Berlin: De Gruyter.

Maciejko, Pawel (2010), "Frankism." Yivo Encyclopedia online. https://yivoencyclopedia.org/article.aspx/frankism

Maciejko, Pawel (2010). "Sabbatian Charlatans: The First Jewish Cosmopolitans." *European Review of History – Revue europeénne d'histoire*, Vol 17, no. 3, (June), 361–378. *on Mysticism, Messianism, and the Origins of Jewish Modernity*. Trans. Alexander van der Haven. Waltham, MA: Brandeis UP.

Magid, Shaul (2003). *Hasidism on the Margin: Reconciliation, Antinomianism, Messianism in Izbica/Radzin Hasidism*. Madison, WI: University of Wisconsin Press.

Magid, Shaul (2021). "Gershom Scholem." *The Stanford Encyclopedia of Philosophy*. Ed. Edward N. Zalta. https://plato.stanford.edu/archives/fall2021/entries/scholem/.

Matt, Daniel (2003). *The Zohar, Vol 1*. Ed. and trans. Daniel C. Matt. Stanford: Stanford UP.

Robert Alter (1991), *Necessary Angels. Tradition and Modernity in Kafka, Benjamin, and Scholem*. Cambridge, MA: Harvard UP.

Scholem, Gershom (1965). *Jewish Gnosticism, Merkabah Mysticism, and Talmudic Tradition*. New York: Jewish Theological Seminary of America.

Scholem, Gershom (1969). *On Kabbalah and Its Symbolism*. New York: Schocken Books.

Scholem, Gershom (1974). *Kabbalah: A Definitive History of the Evolution, Ideas, Leading Figures and Extraordinary Influence of Jewish Mysticism*. Jerusalem, Israel: Keter Publishing House Jerusalem Ltd.

Scholem, Gershom (1993). *Die jüdische Mystik in ihren Hauptströmungen*. Frankfurt am Main: Surhkamp.

Scholem, Gershom (1995). *Major Trends in Jewish Mysticism*. New York: Schocken Books.

Scholem, Gershom (2019). *Poetica: Schriften zur Literatur, Übersetzungen, Gedichte*. Berlin: Jüdischer Verlag im Surhkamp Verlag.

Schuchard, Marsha Keith (2011). "From Poland to London: Sabbatean Influences on the Mystical Underworld of Zinzendorf, Swedenborg, and Blake." *Holy Dissent: Jewish and Christian Mystics in Eastern Europe*. Ed. Glenn Dynner. Detroit, MI: Wayne State UP.

Schwartz, Howard (2006). *Tree of Souls: The Mythology of Judaism*. Oxford: Oxford UP.

Seeskin, Kenneth (2012). *Jewish Messianic Thoughts in an Age of Despair*. Cambridge: Cambridge UP.

Taubes, Jacob (1982). "The Price of Messianism." *Journal of Jewish Studies* 33 (1–2): 595–600.

Taubes, Jacob (2016a). "Seminar Notes on Walter Benjamin's 'Theses on the Philosophy of History'." *Walter Benjamin and Theology*. Ed. Colby Dickinson and Stéphane Symons. New York: Fordham UP, 179–214.

Taubes, Jacob (2016b). "Walter Benjamin—A Modern Marcionite? Scholem's Benjamin Interpretation Reexamined." *Walter Benjamin and Theology*. Ed. Colby Dickinson and Stéphane Symons. New York: Fordham UP, 164–78.

Valabregue, Sandra (2016). "Philosophy, Heresy, and Kabbalah's Counter-Theology." *Harvard Theological Review* 109 (2): 233–56.

Weiss, Tzahi (2005). *Cutting the Shoots: The Worship of Shekinah in the World of Early Kabbalistic Literature*. Jerusalem: Magnes Press.

Weiss, Tzahi (2009). "On the Matter of Language: The Creation of the World of Letters and Jacques Lacan's Perception of Letters as Real." *The Journal of Jewish Thought and Philosophy* 17 (1): 101–15. DOI: 10.1163/147728509X448993.

Wolfson, Elliot (1989). "La hermenéutica de la experiencia visionaria: revelación e interpretación en el *Zohar*." Trans. Margarita León. *Acta Poetica* 9 (1–2): 117–43.
Wolfson, Elliot (1994). *Through a Speculum That Shines: Vision and Imagination in Medieval Jewish Mysticism*. Princeton, NJ: Princeton UP.
Wolfson, Elliot (1995). *Circle in the Square: Studies in the Use of Gender in Kabbalistic Symbolism*. Albany: SUNY Press.
Wolfson, Elliot (2005a). "The Body in the Text: A Kabbalistic Theory of Embodiment." *The Jewish Quarterly Review* 95 (3): 479–500.
Wolfson, Elliot (2005b). *Language, Eros, Being: Kabbalistic Hermeneutics and Poetic Imagination*. New York: Fordham UP.
Wolosky, Shira (1986). "Paul Celan's Linguistic Mysticism." *Studies in Twentieth Century Literature* 10 (2): article 4 (np).
Wolosky, Shira (2007). "Gershom Scholem's Linguistic Theory." *Jerusalem Studies in Jewish Thought: Gershom Scholem: In Memoriam (1897–1982)* 2 (21): 165–205.

On Sabbatianism and Messianic Movements

Biale, David (1982). "Masochism and Philosemitism: The Strange Case of Leopold von Sacher-Masoch." *Journal of Contemporary History* 17 (2): 305–23.
Baumgarten, Jean (2018). *La légende de Yosef della Reina, activiste messianique: Trois versions traduites de l'hébreu et du Yiddish*. Paris: Editions de l'Eclat.
Carlebach, Elisheva (2000). "Review of *Jakob Frank, der Messias aus dem Ghetto* by Klaus Samuel Davidowicz." *Shofar* Special Issue: Philip Roth 19 (1): 163–6.
Carlebach, Elisheva (2001). "The Sabbatian Posture of German Jewry." *Jerusalem Studies in Jewish Thought* 16–17: 1–29.
Davidowicz, Klaus Samuel (1998). *Jakob Frank, der Messias aus dem Ghetto*. New York: Peter Lang.
Goldmark, Josephine (1930). *Pilgrims of '48: One Man's Part in the Austrian Revolution of 1848 and a Family Migration to America*. New Haven, CT: Yale UP.
Graetz, Heinrich (1868). *Frank und die Frankisten. eine Sekten-Geschichte aus der letzten Hälfte des vorigen Jahrhunderts*. Breslau: Schlettersche Buchhandlung.
Idel, Moshe (2011). *Saturn's Jews: On the Witches' Sabbat and Sabbateanism*. New York: Continuum.
Kraushar, Alexander (1895). *Frank I Frankisci Polscy, 1726–1816*. Vols. 1 and 2. Krakow: Skł. gł.u G. Gebethnera i spółki.
Kraushar, Alexandr (2001). *Jacob Frank: The End of the Sabbatian Heresy*. Ed. and trans. Herbert Levy. Lanham, New York, Oxford: University Press of America.
Lenowitz, Harris, trans. (1981). "An Introduction to the 'Sayings' of Jacob Frank." *Proceedings of the World Congress of Jewish Studies* 8 (1): 93–8.
Lenowitz, Harris (1998). *The Jewish Messiahs: From Galilee to Crown Heights*. Oxford and New York: Oxford U P.
Maciejko, Pawel (2011). *The Mixed Multitude: Jacob Frank and the Frankist Movement, 1755–1816*. Philadelphia: University of Pennsylvania Press.
Maciejko, Pawel (2017). *Sabbatian Heresy: Writings on Mysticism, Messianism, and the Origins of Jewish Modernity*. Waltham, MA: Brandeis UP.
Muller, Jerry Z. (2022). *Professor of Apocalypse: The Many Lives of Jacob Taubes*. Princeton, NJ: Princeton UP.

Rappaport-Albert, Ada and Cesar Merchan Hamann (2007). "Something for the Female Sex." *Jerusalem Studies in Jewish Thought: Gershom Scholem: In Memoriam (1897–1982)* 2 (21): 77–135.
Scholem, Gershom (1962). "Ein verschollener jüdischer Mystiker der Aufklärungszeit: E. J. Hirschfeld." *Leo Baeck Institute* 7: 247–79.
Scholem, Gershom (1971). *The Messianic Idea in Judaism*. New York: Schocken Books.
Scholem, Gershom (1973). *Sabbatai Zevi: The Mystical Messiah, 1626–1676*. Princeton, NJ: Princeton UP.
Scholem, Gershom (1975). "A Frankist Document from Prague." *Salo W. Baron Jubilee*. Vol. 2. Jerusalem/New York & London: American Academy for Jewish Research/Columbia UP, 787–814.
Scholem, Gershom (1981). *Du Frankisme au Jacobinisme. La vie de Moses Dobrushka, alias Franz Thomas von Schonfeld alias Junius Frey*. Dublin, Ireland: Omnia-Veritas Publishing.
Sisman, Cengiz (2015). *The Burden of Silence: Shabbatai Zvi and the Evolution of the Ottoman-Turkish Dönmes*. Oxford: Oxford UP.
Taberner, Stuart (2021). "Redemption through Sin: Benjamin Stein's Das Alphabet des Rabbi Löw and the Heretical Dynamism of Contemporary German Jewish Literature and Identity." *The Modern Language Review* 116 (3): 462–84.
Taubes, Jacob (2009). *Occidental Eschatology*. Ed. and trans. David Ratmoko. Stanford, CA: Stanford UP.
Žáček, Vaclav (1938). "Zwei Beiträge zur Geschichte des Frankismus in den böhemischen Ländern." *Jahrbuch der Gesellschaft für Geschichte der Juden in der Cechoslovakischen Republik*. Ed. Samuel Steinherz, trans. Anton Blaschka. Prague: Neunter Jahrgang and Taussig und Taussig Verlagsbuchhandlung in Prag.

On Jewish History

Arendt, Hannah (2008), "Jewish History Revised," *The Jewish Writings*. Eds. Jerome Kohn; John H. Feldman. New York: Schocken Books, 303–311.
Dubnow, S. M. (1916). *History of the Jews in Russia and Poland from the Earliest Times to the Present Day*. Trans. I. Friedlaender. Philadelphia, PA: Jewish Publication Society.
Eisenstein-Barzilay, Isaac (1956). "The Ideology of the Berlin Haskalah." *Proceedings of the American Academy for Jewish Research* 25: 1–37.
Engel, Amir (2017), Gershom Scholem: An Intellectual Biography. Chicago: University of Chicago Press.
Feiner, Schmuel (2011). *The Origins of Jewish Secularization in Eighteenth-Century Europe*. Philadelphia: University of Pennsylvania Press.
Feiner, Schmuel (2002). *Haskalah and History: The Emergence of a Modern Jewish Historical Consciousness*. Oxford and Portland: Littman Library of Jewish Civilization.
Flatto, Sharon (2010). *The Kabbalistic Culture of Eighteenth-Century Prague: Ezekiel Landau and His Contemporaries*. Oxford and Portland, OR: Littman Library of Jewish Civilization.
Graetz, Heinrich (1892). "From the Chmielnicki Persecution of the Jews in Poland (1648 C. E.) to the Period of Emancipation in Central Europe (c. 1870 C. E.)." *History of the Jews*. Vol. V. Ed. and trans. Bella Löwy. London: David Nutt & Strand.
Graetz, Heinrich (1860). *Geschichte der Juden von den ältesten Zeiten bis auf die Gegenwart: aus den Quellen neu bearbeitet, Band 11*. Magdeburg: Druch u. Verlag von Albert Goldenberg & Co.

Goshen-Gottstein, Alon (2000). *The Sinner and the Amnesiac: The Rabbinic Invention of Elisha Ben Abuya and Eleazar Ben Arach*. Contraversions: Jews and Other Differences. Stanford: Stanford UP.

Gross, Rachel (2021). *Beyond the Synagogue: Jewish Nostalgia as Religious Practice*. New York: NYU Press.

Halperin, Dalia-Ruth (2013). *Illuminating in Micrography: The Catalan Micrography Maḥzor—MS. Heb. 8 6527 in the National Library of Israel*. Leiden and Boston: Brill.

Katz, Jacob (1984). "German Culture and the Jews." *Commentary* 77 (2): 54–9.

Keivel, Hillel (2000). *Languages of Community: Jewish Experience in the Czech Lands*. Berkeley: University of California Press.

Keren, Michael (1993). "The 'Prague Circle' and the Challenge of Nationalism." *History of European Ideas* 16 (1–3): 3–9.

Kohler, George (2019). *Kabbalah Research in the Wissenschaft des Judentums (1820–1880): The Foundation of an Academic Discipline*. Berlin, Boston: De Gruyter Oldenbourg.

Myers, David and Alexander Kaye, eds. (2013). *The Faith of Fallen Jews: Yosef Hayim Yerushalmi and the Writing of Jewish History*. Waltham, MA: Brandeis UP.

Saperstein, Marc, ed. (1992). *Essential Papers on Messianic Movements and Personalities in Jewish History*. New York: NYU Press.

Scholem, Gershom (2007). *The Diaries of Gershom Scholem, 1913–1919*. Cambridge, MA: Harvard UP.

Sorkin, David (1990). *The Transformation of German Jewry, 1780–1840*. Oxford: Oxford UP.

Weltsch, Robert (1970). *Max Brod and His Age*. New York: Leo Baeck Institute.

Yerushalmi, Yosef Hayim (1982). *Zakhor. Jewish History and Jewish Memory*. Seattle, WA: University of Washington Press.

On Literature and Culture

Achituv, Romy (2007). "Lost Communities." Ghetto Fighters House Museum, Galilee, Israel. http://m-a-p.net/yizkor/Yizkor_Hall.htm.

Aizenberg, Edna (1984). *The Aleph Weaver: Biblical, Kabbalistic, Judaic Elements in Borges*. Potomac, MD: Scripta Humanistica.

Aizenberg, Edna (1997). *Borges, el Tejedor del Aleph y otros ensayos: del Hebraismo al Poscolonialismo*. Frankfurt and Madrid: Iberoamericana Editorial Vervuert.

Alazraki, Jaime (1988). *Borges and the Kabbalah*. Cambridge and New York: Cambridge UP.

Allert, Beate (2014). "Heine's Doctor Faust, a Dance Poem." *Faust Adaptations from Marlowe to Aboudoma and Markland*. Ed. Lorna Fitzsimmons. West Lafayette, IN: Purdue UP.

Alter, Robert (1969). *After the Tradition. Essays on Modern Jewish Writing*. New York: Dutton.

Alter, Robert (1977). *Defenses of the Imagination. Jewish Writers and Modern Historical Crisis*. Philadelphia, PA: The Jewish Publication Society of America.

Alter, Robert (1991), *Necessary Angels. Tradition and Modernity in Kafka, Benjamin, and Scholem*. Cambridge, MA: Harvard UP.

Alter, Robert (1993). "Kafka as Kabbalist." *Salmagundi* 98 (99): 86–99.

Althaus, Hans Peter (2010). *Kleines Lexikon deutscher Wörter jiddischer Herkunft*. Munich, Germany: Beck.

Atlan, Liliane (1985). "The Messiahs." *Theatre Pieces: An Anthology by Liliane Atlan*. Ed. and trans. Feitlowitz Marguerite. Greenwood, FL: Penkeville Publishing Company.

Bahr, Ehrhard (2014). "The Chapbook of Doctor Faust as Source and Model." *Faust Adaptations from Marlowe to Aboudoma and Markland*. Ed. Lorna Fitzsimmons. West Lafayette, IN: Purdue UP.

Balint, Benjamin (2023). *Bruno Schulz: An Artist, a Murder, and the Hijacking of History*. New York: Norton.

Beck, Evelyn Torton (1971). *Kafka and the Yiddish Theatre: Its Impact on His Work*. Madison, Milwaukee, and London: University of Wisconsin Press.

Berner, Virginia Gutierrez (2010). "Mystical Laws: Borges and Kabbalah." *CR: The New Centennial Review* 9 (3): 137–64.

Bielik-Robson, Agata (n.d.). "Life on Margins. Bruno Schulz and the Hassidic Kabbalah." Unpublished essay.

Bloom, Harold (1997), *Anatomy of Influence. A Theory of Poetry*, Oxford: Oxford UP.

Brazil, David (2021). "Under the Language: A Conversation with Pierre Joris on Paul Celan." *LA Review of Books*. https://lareviewofbooks.org/article/under-the-language-a-conversation-with-pierre-joris-on-paul-celan/ January 20, 2021.

Brod, Max (1957). *Heine: The Artist in Revolt*. Trans. Joseph Witriol. London: Valentine, Mitchell.

Brod, Max (1937), *Franz Kafka*. New York: Schocken Books.

Bruce, Iris (2007). *Kafka and Cultural Zionism*. Madison, WI: University of Wisconsin Press.

Cameron, Esther (2014). *Western Art and Jewish Presence in the Work of Paul Celan*. Lanham, MD: Lexington Books.

Carson, Anne (2009). *The Economy of the Unlost: Reading Simonides of Keos with Paul Celan*. Princeton, NJ: Princeton UP.

Chan, Mary (1979). "Drolls, Drolleries and Mid-Seventeenth Century Music in England." *Royal Association Research Chronicle* 15: 117–72.

Charles, Ron (2022). "Olga Tokarczuk's 'The Books of Jacob' is finally here. Now we know why the Nobel judges were so awestruck." Review. *The Washington Post*. 2/1/22.

Cook, Roger F. (1998). *By the Rivers of Babylon: Heinrich Heine's Late Songs and Reflections*. Detroit, MI: Wayne State UP.

Cook, Roger F., ed. (2002). *A Companion to the Works of Heinrich Heine*. Rochester, NY: Camden House.

Corkhill, Alan (2012). "The Faustian Contest with the Authority of the Word." *Goethe's Faust and Cultural Memory: Comparatist Interfaces*. Ed. Lorna Fitzsimmons. Cranberry: Lehigh UP.

Deleuze, Gilles; Felix Guattari (1986), *Kafka, Toward a Minor Literature*. Minneapolis, MN: University of Minnesota Press.

Derrida, Jacques (1992). *Acts of Literature*. Ed. Derek Attridge. New York and London: Routledge.

Feitlowitz, Marguerite (1985). "Translator's Note." *Theatre Pieces: An Anthology by Liliane Atlan*. Trans. Marguerite Feitlowitz. Greenwood, FL: Penkeville Publishing Company.

Felman, Shoshana (1985). "Education and Crisis or the Vicissitudes of Teaching." *Testimony: Crises of Witnessing in Literature, Psychoanalysis, and History*. London and New York: Routledge, 1–57.

Felstiner, John (1995). *Paul Celan: Poet, Survivor, Jew*. New Haven: Yale UP.

Fishburn, Evelyn (2013). "Jewish, Christian, and Gnostic Themes." *Cambridge Companion to Jorge Luis Borges*. Ed. Edwin Williamson. Cambridge, UK: Cambridge UP, 56–67.
Frye, Northrup (2002). *The Great Code: The Bible and Literature*. New York: Mariner Books.
Fuchs, Anne and Florian Krob, eds. (1999). *Ghetto Writing: Traditional and Eastern Jewry in German Jewish Literature from Heine to Hilsenrath*. Columbia, SC: Camden House.
Gebauer, G. and C. Wulf (1995). *Mimesis: Culture, Art, Society*. Berkeley: University of California Press.
Gelber, Mark H., Hans Otto Horch, eds. (1992) *The Jewish Reception of Heinrich Heine*. Tübingen: Niemayer.
Gilman, Sander (1992), "Freud Reads Heine Reads Freud," in *The Jewish Reception of Heinrich Heine*, eds. Mark H. Gelber, Hans Otto Horch, Tübingen: Niemayer.
Goetschel, Willi (2002). *A Companion to the Works of Heine*. Rochester, NY: Camden House.
Goetschel, Willi (2003). *Spinoza's Modernity: Mendelssohn, Lessing, and Heine*. Madison, WI: University of Wisconsin Press.
Goetschel, Willi (2019). *Heine and Critical Theory*. London and New York: Bloomsbury.
Gordin, Jacob (1906). *Elisha ben Avuyah drama in 4 akten*. New York: Di Internatzionale Bibliotek Ferlag Co.
Grözinger, Klaus (1994). *Kafka and Kabbalah*. New York: Continuum.
Halperin, David J., ed., trans. (2007). *Sabbatai Zevi: Testimonies to a Fallen Messiah*. Liverpool, UK: University of Liverpool Press.
Hammer, Espen, ed. (2018). *Kafka's The Trial: Philosophical Perspectives*. Oxford: Oxford UP.
Hartman, Geoffrey (2011). *The Third Pillar: Essays in Judaic Studies*. Philadelphia, PA: University of Pennsylvania Press.
Henry, Barbara (2011). *Rewriting Russia: Jacob Gordin's Yiddish Drama*. Seattle: University of Washington Press.
Heys, Alisteir (2014). *The Anatomy of Bloom: Harold Bloom and the Study of Influence and Anxiety*. New York and London: Bloomsbury.
Huberman, Ariana (2022). *Keeping the Mystery Alive: Jewish Mysticism in Latin American Cultural Production*. Boston, MA: Academic Studies Press.
Isaacson, Jóse (1987). *Borges entre los nombres y el nombre*. Buenos Aires: Fundación el Libro.
Kaplan, Beth (2007). *Finding the Jewish Shakespeare: The Life and Legacy of Jacob Gordin*. Syracuse, NY: Syracuse UP.
Kauvar (1986). "An Interview with Chaim Potok." *Contemporary Literature* 27 (3): 291–317.
Klein, Ernest (1987). *A Comprehensive Etymological Dictionary of the Hebrew Language for Readers of English*. Jerusalem: Carta Jerusalem and Haifa University.
Koropeckjy, Roman (2008). *Adam Mickiewicz: The Life of a Romantic*. Ithaca, NY: Cornell UP.
Lazarus, Emma (1881). *Poems and Ballads of Heinrich Heine to Which Is Prefixed a Biographical Sketch*. New York: R. Worthington.
Lazier, Benjamin (2012). *God Interrupted: Heresy and the European Imagination between the World Wars*. Princeton, NJ: Princeton UP.
Löwy, Michael (2005). *Fire Alarm: Reading Walter Benjamin's "On the Concept of History."* London and New York: Verso.
Millet, Kitty (2007) "An Old Family Narrative: Rethinking *Testimonio* and Gender." *Revolucionarias. Conflict and Gender in Latin American Narratives by Women*. ed. Par Kumaraswami. Vienna: Peter Lang, 63–81.

Millet, Kitty (2009). "Elie Wiesel's Night and Dying in the Present Tense." *Bloom's Literary Themes, on Death and Dying*. Ed. Harold Bloom. New York: Chelsea House.

Millet, Kitty (2018). "Our Sabbatian Future." *Gershom Scholem, Scholar and Kabbalist*. Ed. Mirjam and Noam Zadoff. Leiden: Brill.

Millet, Kitty (2018a). "Introduction." *Faultlines of Modernity*. Ed. Kitty Millet and Dorothy Figueira. New York: Bloomsbury.

Miron, Dan (2010). *From Continuity to Contiguity: Toward a New Jewish Literary Thinking*. Palo Alto, CA: Stanford UP.

Moser, Benjamin (2009). *Why This World? A Biography of Clarice Lispector*. Oxford: Oxford UP.

Moses, Stephané and Ora Wiskind-Elper (1999). "Gershom Scholem's Reading of Kafka: Literary Criticism and Kabbalah." *New German Critique* Special Issue on German Jewish Religious Thought 77: 149–67.

Neher, Andre (1987). *Faust et le Maharal de Prague. Le Mythe et le Réel*. Paris: Presses Universitaires de France.

Nesher-Wirth, Hannah (2009). *Call It English: The Languages of Jewish American Literature*. Princeton, NJ: Princeton UP.

Panas, Wladyslaw (1993). "'Mesjasz rośnie pomału ....' O pewnym wątku kabalistycznym w prozie Brunona Schulza." *Bruno Schulz in Memoriam, 1892–1992*. Ed. Małgorzata Kitowska-Łysiak. Skierniewice, Poland: Wydawnictwo Fis, 22–42.

Panas, Wladyslaw (1997). *Księga blasku. Traktat o kabale w prozie Brunona Schulza*. Lublin: Towarzystowo Naukowe Katolickiego Uniwersytetu Lubelskiego.

Panas, Wladyslaw (2001). *Bruno od Mesjasza. Rzecz o dwóch ekslibrisach oraz jednym obrazie i kilkudziesięciu rysunkach Brunona Schulza*. Lublin: Wydawnictwo UMCS.

Pérez, Rolando (2016). "Borges and Bruno Schulz on the Infinite Book of the Kabbalah." *Confluencia, Revista Hispanica de la Cultura y Literatura* 31 (2): 41–56. DOI: 10.1353/cnf.2016.0024.

Politzer, Heinz (1966). *Franz Kafka: Parable and Paradox*. Ithaca: Cornell UP.

Porter, James (2010). "Auerbach, Homer, and the Jews." *Classic and National Cultures*. Ed. Susan A. Stephens and Phiroze Vasunia, 235–57.

Porter, James, ed. (2018). *Time, History, and Literature*. Trans. Jane O. Newman. Princeton, NJ: Princeton UP.

Sammons, Jeffrey L. (1979) *Heine, a Modern Biography*. Princeton, NJ: Princeton UP.

Sammons, Jeffrey L. (1969) *Heine, the Elusive Poet*. New Haven: Yale UP.

Schonfeld, Eli (2016). "Am Ha'aretz: The Law of the Singular. Kafka's Hidden Knowledge." *Kafka and the Universal*. Ed. Arthur Cools and Vivian Liska. Berlin: DeGruyter, 107–29.

Sitbon, Suzy (2005). "Intersections between Artistic and Visual Creation and Cosmogony in some Spanish Bibles." *Iggud: Selected Essays in Jewish Studies, Vol. 3, Languages, Literatures, and Art*: 99–113.

Sosnowski, Saul (1976). *Borges y la Cábala; la búsqueda del verbo*. Buenos Aires: Hispamérica.

Steiner, George (1996), "A Note on Kafka's Trial." *No Passion Spent*. New Haven, CT: Yale UP, 239–252.

Stavans, Ilan (2016). *Borges the Jew*. Albany: SUNY Press.

Suchoff, David (2011). *Kafka's Jewish Languages: The Hidden Openness of Tradition*. Philadelphia, PA: University of Pennsylvania Press.

Tiedemann, R. (1975). "Historischer Materialismus oder politischer Messianismus? Politische Gehalt in der Geschictsphilosophie Walter Benjamins." *Materilien zu Benjamins Thesen*. *"Über den Begriff der Geschichte": Text, Varianten, Briefstellen, Interpretationen*. Ed. Peter Bulthaupt. Frankfurt, Germany: Suhrkamp.
Underhill, Karen (2015). *Bruno Schulz and Galician Jewish Modernity*. Bloomington, IN: Indiana UP.
Walzel, Oskar (1917). *Heines Tanzpoem Der Doktor Faust*. Weimar: Gesellschaft der Bibliophilen.
Weigel, Sigrid (2012). *Walter Benjamin: Images, the Creaturely, and the Holy*. Stanford, CA: Stanford UP.
Weiss, Gerhard (1966). "Die Entstehung von Heines 'Doktor Faust': ein Beispiel deutsch-englisch-französischer Freundschaft." *Heine Jahrbuch* 5: 41–57.
Wolfson, Eliott (2014). "In the Mirror of the Dream: Borges and the Poetics of the Kabbalah." *The Jewish Quarterly Review* 104 (3): 362–79.
Woods, James (2008). *How Fiction Works*. New York: Farrar, Straus & Giroux.
Zardaya, Concha (1973). "El Espejo de Federico Garcia Lorca." *Federico Garcia Lorca*. Ed. Idelfonso Manuel Gil. Madrid: Taurus.
Zylbercweig, Zalman, ed. (1931). *Leksikon fun Yidishn Teater*. Bd. 1 Nyu: Farlag Elisheva.
Zylbercweig, Zalman (1964). *Di Velt fun Yankev Gordin*. Tel Aviv: Elisheva.

On Philosophy, Critical Theory, Judaism

Adorno, Theodor (1982). *Prisms*. Trans. Samuel Weber and Shierry Weber. Cambridge: MIT Press.
Adorno, Theodor and Gershom Scholem, eds. (1994). *The Correspondence of Walter Benjamin, 1910–1940*. Trans. Manfred R. Jacobson and Evelyn M. Jacobson. Chicago and London: University of Chicago Press.
Améry, Jean (1980). *At the Mind's Limits: Contemplations by a Survivor on Auschwitz and Its Realities*. Ed. and trans. Sidney Rosenfeld and Stella P. Rosenfeld. Bloomington, IN: Indiana UP.
Bagaria, Joan (2019). "Set Theory." *The Stanford Encyclopedia of Philosophy*. Ed. Edward N. Zalta. https://plato.stanford.edu/archives/win2021/entries/set-theory/.
Benjamin, Walter (1955). *Illuminationen. Ausgewählte Schriften*. Ed. Sigfried Unseld. Frankfurt: Surhkamp Verlag.
Benjamin, Walter (1968). *Illuminations*. Ed. Hannah Arendt, trans. Harry Zohn. New York: Schocken Books.
Benjamin, Walter (1978). *Reflections*. Ed. Peter Demetz, trans. Edmund Jephcott. New York: Schocken Books.
Benjamin Walter (1989), *Nachträge, Band VII-1*.
Benjamin, Walter (1996). *Walter Benjamin: Selected Writings*. Vol. 1. Ed. Howard Eiland and Michael W. Jennings. Cambridge, MA & London: Harvard UP.
Benjamin, Walter (2012). *The Correspondence of Walter Benjamin, 1910–1940*. Ed. Gershom Scholem and Adorno Theodor. Chicago and London: University of Chicago Press.
Benjamin, Walter (2021). *Aufsätze, Essays, Vorträge. Gesammelte Schriften. Band II-2*. Ed. Gershom Scholem and Theodor Adorno. Frankfurt: Suhrkamp.
Bielik-Robson, Agata (2011). *The Saving Lie: Harold Bloom and Deconstruction*. Evanston, IL: Northwestern UP.

Bielik-Robson, Agata (2014). *Jewish Cryptotheologies of Late Modernity: Philosophical Marranos*. London and New York: Routledge.
Bielik-Robson, Agata (2018). *Another Finitude: Messianic Vitalism and Philosophy*. New York and London: Bloomsbury.
Bielik-Robson, Agata (2020). "The Void of God, or The Paradox of the Pious Atheism: From Scholem to Derrida." *European Journal for Philosophy of Religion* 12 (2): 109–32. https://doi.org/10.24204/ejpr.v12i2.3327.
Bielik-Robson, Agata (2022). *Derrida's Marrano Passover*. New York: Bloomsbury.
Bielik-Robson, Agata and Adam Lipszyc, eds. (2014). *Judaism in Contemporary Thought and Practice*. London and New York: Routledge.
Charles, M. (2018). "Secret Signals from Another World: Walter Benjamin's Theory of Innervation." *New German Critique* 45 (3): 39–72.
Charles, M. (2020). *Modernism between Benjamin and Goethe*. London: Bloomsbury.
Dahlstrom, Daniel O. (2019). "Moses Mendelssohn." *Stanford Encyclopedia of Philosophy*. Palo Alto: Stanford UP. https://plato.stanford.edu/archives/fall2019/entries/mendelssohn/
Denda, Arda (1991). "*Principia Individuationis*." *The Philosophical Quarterly* 41 (163): 212–28.
Derrida, Jacques (1978). *Writing and Difference*. Trans. Alan Bass. Chicago: University of Chicago Press.
Derrida, Jacques (2002). *Acts of Religion*. Ed. and trans. Gil Anidjar. New York and London: Routledge.
Derrida, Jacques (2018). *Before the Law: The Complete Text of Préjugés*. Trans. Sandra van Reenen and Jacques De Ville. Minneapolis, MN: University of Minnesota Press.
Freud, Sigmund (1961). *Beyond the Pleasure Principle*. New York: Liveright.
Guetta, Alessandro (2009). *Philosophy and Kabbalah: Elijah Benamozegh and the Reconciliation of Western Thought and Jewish Esotericism*. Albany, NY: SUNY Press.
Hansen, Miriam Brattu (2008). "Benjamin's Aura." *Critical Inquiry* 34 (2): 336–75.
Hammer, Reuven (2015), *Akiva Life, Legend, Legacy*. Philadelphia: JPS.
Idel, Moshe (2007). "Jacques Derrida and Kabbalistic Sources." *Judeities: Questions for Jacques Derrida*. Ed. Bettina Burgo, Joseph D. Cohen and Raphael Zagury-Orly. New York: Fordham UP, 111–30.
Lacan, Jacques (1977). *Ecrits: A Selection*. New York: Norton.
Mendelssohn, Moses (1997). *Philosophical Writings*. Trans. Daniel O. Dahlstrom. New York: Cambridge UP.
Millet, Kitty (2012). "Contemplating Jean Améry's Loss of Transcendence." *On Jean Améry: Philosophy of Catastrophe*. Ed. Magdalena Zolkos. Lanham, MD: Lexington Books.
Mittleman, Alan L. (1990). *Between Kant and Kabbalah: An Introduction to Isaac Breuer's Philosophy of Judaism*. Albany, NY: SUNY Press.
Moses, Stephané (1992). *System and Revelation: The Philosophy of Franz Rosenzweig*. Trans. Catherine Tihanyi. Detroit, WI: Wayne State UP.
Moses, Stephané (2009). *The Angel of History: Rosenzweig, Benjamin, Scholem*. Trans. Barbara Harshav. Stanford, CA: Stanford UP.
Neher, Andre (1946). *Transcendence et Immanence*. Lyon: Editions Yechouroun.
Osborne, Peter and Matthew Charles (2021). "Walter Benjamin." *The Stanford Encyclopedia of Philosophy*. Ed. Edward N. Zalta. https://plato.stanford.edu/archives/fall2021/entries/benjamin/.

Rubenstein, Jeffrey L. (1999). *Talmudic Stories: Narrative Art, Composition, and Culture.* Baltimore and London: Johns Hopkins UP.
Rubenstein, Jeffrey L. (2003). "Review of *The Sinner and the Amnesiac: The Rabbinic Invention of Elisha ben Abuya and Eleazar ben Arach.*" *AJS Review* 27 (1): 117–20.
Scholem, Gershom (1970), *Über einige Grundbegriffe des Judentums. Frankfurt*: Suhrkamp.
Scholem, Gershom (1983). *Walter Benjamin und Sein Engel. Vierzehn Aufsätze und kleine Beitrage.* Frankfurt am Main: Suhrkamp Verlag.
Scholem, Gershom and Theodor Adorno, eds. (2012). *The Correspondence of Walter Benjamin, 1910–1940.* Chicago: University of Chicago Press.
Shiffman, Lawrence (1975). *Halakhah at Qumran.* Amsterdam: Brill.
Wolfson, Eliot R. (2002). "Assaulting the Border: Kabbalistic Traces in the Margins of Derrida." *Journal of the American Academy of Religion* 70 (3): 475–514.

Index

Abraham 8–9, 27, 54, 114, 160, 163, 178 n.51, 179 n.55, 196 n.11, 236 n.90
Abulafia, Abraham 10, 20, 46, 114, 116, 132, 134, 137, 140, 143–4, 171, 186 n.36, 210 n.48, 218 n.17, 223 n.8
  "absolute object" 10, 15, 20, 31, 114, 116–17, 130–1, 138, 142, 217 n.6, 223 n.8
  Hokhmath ha-Tseruf ("combination of the letters") 129, 131, 225 n.24, 225 n.26, 228 n.79
  "the path of the Names" 223 n.8, 224 n.15
  "prophetic kabbalah" 129–30, 224 n.15
  on soul and mind 130–1
Achituv, Romy 149, 174, 229 n.6
  "Lost Communities" 20, 141–3
  "Text Rain" 142
Adam and Eve 67, 97, 100, 106, 123, 185 n.10, 210 n.48, 216 n.149, 219 n.39
Adam Kadmon 96–7, 211 n.60, 213 n.104
Adorno, Theodor 76, 152, 231 n.10, 232–3 n.27
aesthetic experience 1, 3, 10–14, 44, 46, 93, 116, 152–4, 156, 162, 164, 173, 180 n.68, 193 n.43, 198 n.36, 213 n.104
aggadah (story/sacred story) 8, 12, 16, 18, 24, 35, 50, 53–61, 67, 71–3, 82, 85, 88–9, 109–10, 114, 126, 130, 171–2, 175
  aggadot 9, 13, 16–18, 26, 34, 50, 54, 56–7, 119, 129, 168–70, 180 n.72, 181 n.83, 212 n.86
Agnon, S. Y. *Yesteryear* 78
Ahad Ha'am 78
Aher (the Other) 16, 18–19, 21, 23–4, 28, 30, 34, 50, 67, 74–5, 87–9, 109, 115, 147, 169, 217 n.11
Aizenberg, Edna 129, 223 n.6

Alazraki, Jaime 129
  Borges and the Kabbalah and Other Essays on His Fiction and Poetry 222 n.2
  "the unimaginable universe" 138
Alter, Robert 5, 7, 59, 75, 170, 208 n.15
  "Binding of Isaac" 8
  Necessary Angels 5
Améry, Jean 145, 149, 233 n.27
am ha'aretz (one who doesn't study Torah) 34, 43, 72, 74, 77–9, 84–5, 204 n.48
amhoretz (simpleton) 34, 43, 72–4, 78, 80–1, 83–5, 206 n.88, 208 n.23
  prostak 34–5, 50, 80, 91, 188 n.69, 191 n.22
"the anarchic breeze" 94, 213 n.95
anarchy/anarchism 13, 17, 40, 66–7, 101
Anderson, Benedict 7
  Imagined Communities 178 n.34
antinomianism 14, 44, 46–7, 66–7, 101, 178 n.45, 183 n.104
  materialist 195 n.70
  soft antinomianism 81
apostasy 13–14, 16, 18, 26, 28, 31, 34, 39, 48, 50–1, 54, 63, 66–9, 71–2, 74–5, 88, 92, 202 n.14, 215 n.137, 217 n.11
Arendt, Hannah 173–4, 193 n.45
Aristotle 6, 8
Asiyyah (world of making) 96–8, 103, 211 n.74
Atlan, Liliane 192 n.31
  "Jewish subconscious" 176 n.3
  "The Messiahs" 20, 145–6, 149, 174, 176 n.3
Atzilut (world of emanation) 96
Auerbach, Erich 7, 9, 12, 110, 175, 178 n.45, 178 n.52, 179 n.57
"Akedah" 7–8, 178 n.51, 179 n.55

Index

"lacunae" 179 n.52
Mimesis, the Representation of Reality in Western Literature 7–8
"aura" 56, 68, 99, 103–4, 170–2, 212 n.91

Balint, Benjamin, *Bruno Schulz, an Artist, a Murder, and the Hijacking of History* 183 n.118
Beck, Evelyn Torton 74
  Kafka and the Yiddish Theatre. Its Impact on His Work 203 n.15
Benjamin, Walter 5, 54, 68, 75, 76, 170–4, 180 n.74
  Illuminations 173, 176 n.2
  "On Mimesis" 211 n.58
Beri'ah (world of creation) 96
Biale, David 72, 77, 180 n.69, 187 n.49, 197 n.21
The Bible/Biblical 6, 8, 16, 23, 42, 56, 60, 67, 77, 84, 86, 119–20, 123, 129–30, 133, 195 n.76, 223 n.10
Bielik-Robson, Agata 5, 207 n.6, 221 n.80
  "At the Edges of the World: Diasporic Metaphysics of Bruno Schulz" 211 n.78
  Derrida's Marrano Passover 192 n.36
  "From Therapy to Redemption: Notes toward a Messianic Psychoanalysis" 207 n.6
  Jewish Cryptotheologies of Late Modernity 176 n.7
  The Saving Lie: Harold Bloom and Deconstruction 221–2 n.80
Bloom, Harold 2, 5, 75, 77, 125, 169, 173, 181 n.82, 221 n.80
  "Gnosticism" 75
  Kabbalah and Criticism 197 n.13
  "modernist kabbalah" 77, 237 n.16
  The Strong Light of the Canonical: Kafka, Freud, and Scholem as Revisionists of Jewish Culture and Thought 176 n.8, 176 n.11, 177 n.21, 183 n.109, 189 n.90, 192 n.30, 203 n.23, 221 n.79, 237 n.10
Boder, David 236 n.93

Book of Creation (Sefer Yetsirah) 20, 27, 113–14, 126–7, 129, 142, 157, 163, 186 n.36, 217 n.2, 218 n.18, 219 n.39, 222 n.86
The Books of Jacob (Tokarczuk) 16, 25–32, 167, 186 n.26, 197 n.17
  "The Book of Names" 92, 109–10, 167, 209 n.35
  Elisha Shorr (fictional character) 25, 27, 75
  Frank (fictional character) 26–37
  Nahman (fictional character) 27, 188 n.67
  Yente (fictional character) 17, 236–7 n.9 25–7, 167–8, 184 n.6, 185 n.9, 185 n.11, 186 n.34, 225 n.26
Borges, Jorge Luis 129–30, 132, 226 nn.58–9, 227 n.63
  "The Aleph" ("El Aleph") 20, 129, 132–40, 174, 222 n.3, 227 n.63
  Ayin/Ani 132, 137, 227 n.76
  Borges (fictional character) 132–40, 227 n.63, 227 n.74
  Carlos Argentino Daneri (fictional character) 20, 132–40, 225 n.48, 226 n.50, 226 n.54, 227 n.67
  "En Soph" 132
  inconcibible 138–9
  "literary universe" 129, 132
  "Una Vindicacion de la Cábala" 222 n.2
  "the unimaginable universe" 138
Brod, Max 170
  Franz Kafka 184 n.120
  Heine. The Artist in Revolt 196 n.1
  Werke 238 n.32
Bruce, Iris, *Kafka and Cultural Zionism* 76
Buber, Martin, *Tales of the Hasidim* 81

Cameron, Esther 157
Cantor, Georg, *Mengenlehre* 228 n.89
Carson, Anne 151–2, 155–6, 231 n.4
Catholicism 191 n.18
Celan, Paul 174, 229 n.7, 231 n.10, 233 n.33, 236 n.80
  "A la Point Acérée" 161

"All the faces writing" (*Aller Gesichte Schrift*) 162
"Benedicta" 160
"Death Fugue" 21, 151–6, 158, 164–5, 231 n.10
"Les Globes" 162
Memory Rose into Threshold Speech: the Collected Earlier Poetry 233 n.27
living "Nothing" 162, 166
"Meridian speech" 234 n.48
"No More Sand Art" 21, 151–2, 156, 163–4, 166
NoOnesRose (*Niemandsrose*) 157–60, 163–4, 233 n.34, 236 n.83
"Psalm" 159–60, 185 n.10
"Radix, Matrix" 160
The Sand from the Urns 151–2
"The Syllable Pain" 236 n.85
"Todesfuge" 152–6, 165, 231 n.4, 232 n.24, 232 n.27
"charlatan" 16, 45, 102, 185 n.13, 194 n.51
Christians/Christianity 4, 18, 27, 30–1, 40–1, 45, 49, 53, 60, 62–3, 167, 178 n.48, 190 n.1, 194 n.49
Cinnamon Shops (Schulz) 91, 106, 108, 113, 118, 126–7, 216 n.154
  Adela (fictional character) 92, 94, 99, 104–6, 220 n.42
  dynamic innovations 106
  Father (Jacob) (fictional character) 91–5, 98–107, 109, 113–15, 127, 168, 222 n.84
  Paulina (fictional character) 99–101, 105
  Polda (fictional character) 99–100, 105
  "A Treatise on Mannequins or the Second Book of Genesis" 125
  "Treatise on the Second Book of Genesis" 19, 91, 101, 103
"cultural Zionism" 76

Dan, Joseph 1, 10, 111, 131
Darstellung/darstellen as exhibition 1, 58, 88, 170, 176 n.10
Delbo, Charlotte, *Auschwitz and After* 232 n.22
Derrida, Jacques 5, 192 n.34, 225 n.25
diaspora 28, 48, 218 n.16

Divine Being 8–9, 12, 21, 28, 60, 64–5, 67, 96–7, 114–15, 130, 136–7, 142–4, 147, 149, 159, 166, 174, 183 n.101, 216 n.149, 218 n.16, 224 n.21, 229 n.7
Divine Cosmic Stream 15, 143
Divine creation 27–8, 61
Divine Light 17, 55, 114, 130, 144, 210 n.50
Divine Self 143
Divine Speech 132
Divine writing 97, 136, 143, 146–7, 186 n.34, 205 n.69, 222 n.2
Dubrushka, Moses 49, 193 n.44, 194 n.65

ecstasy 14, 20, 46, 81, 93, 102, 108, 115–16, 121, 147, 174, 208 n.17, 217–18 n.11
Eden 44, 54, 56, 58, 79, 97, 105, 123, 189 n.87, 197 n.15, 226 n.50
Edom 27, 36, 49–50, 186 n.26, 194 n.66
Eibeschütz, Jonathan 190 n.1
Ein-Sof/Eyn Sof/En Sof/En Soph (Nothingness) (אֵין-סוֹף) 96–7, 132, 137, 139–40, 144, 158, 160, 217 n.6, 225 n.32, 235 n.63, 236 n.91. *See also* nothingness
emanation(s) 20, 28, 32, 41–2, 58–9, 62, 84–5, 96, 114, 118–19, 134, 137–8, 143, 146, 162, 199 n.55, 217 n.7
emancipation 17–18, 47–8, 51, 69, 81, 86, 101, 202 n.11
Engel, Amir, *Gershom Scholem: An Intellectual Biography* 182 n.99
Enlightenment 7, 11, 17, 39–41, 43–4, 47, 53, 68
The Epic of Gilgamesh 6
epistemology 5, 10, 12–14, 58–60, 63, 92, 94, 98, 110, 115–16, 119, 139, 173, 180 n.70, 180 n.72, 220 n.39, 224 n.21
esoteric/esotericism 2, 16, 41, 173
evil/devil 14, 34, 49, 55, 64–7, 92, 95–7, 125, 210 n.43, 211 n.69

Feitlowitz, Marguerite 176 n.3
Felman, Shoshana 152–3, 155–6, 231 n.6

Felstiner, John 157, 164, 231 n.11, 232 n.27, 233 n.37
Fine, Lawrence 205 n.68
Finkelstein, Norman, *The Ritual of New Creation. Jewish Tradition and Contemporary Literature* 179 n.62
Fishburn, Evelyn 226 n.30, 227 n.78
Fleckeles, Eleazar 48
"four worlds" 96–7
Frankism 13, 17–19, 28, 31, 33, 36, 39, 43–51, 63, 71, 74–5, 85, 91–2, 167, 182 n.92, 190 n.2, 193 n.39, 193 nn.43–4, 211 n.58
  "enlightened innovation" 46
  and Esau 27–8, 36, 185 n.24, 186 n.26
  Frankists 2, 14, 16–18, 28, 31, 33–5, 39, 41, 43–5, 47–9, 51, 62–3, 67–8, 73, 77, 80, 85, 92, 106, 109, 189 n.84, 191 n.18, 194 n.53, 216 n.147
  Frank, Jacob 13, 16–19, 23, 26–37, 39–41, 43–51, 62, 68, 72, 80, 89, 91–5, 98–107, 168, 175, 185 n.24, 189 nn.79–80
  "Demiurge" 75, 101–4, 106, 215 nn.124–5
  Sayings and Teachings of the Lord 13, 193 n.43
Frei, Junius. *See* Dubrushka, Moses
Freud, Sigmund 5, 199 n.54, 209 n.39
  "death drive" 204 n.32, 221 n.80

galut 78, 115
Genesis 106, 125, 133, 195 n.70, 210 n.50, 224 n.17, 236 n.83, 237 n.5
The Gentiles 26, 44, 74
German Idealism 18, 43, 47, 193 n.39
ghetto 5, 11, 35, 47, 49–50, 53, 55–8, 62, 68, 141, 175, 180 n.69, 197 n.21
gilgul 76, 78–9, 81, 86, 212 n.81
Ginsberg, Asher Zvi Hirsch. *See* Ahad Ha'am
Gnostic/Gnosticism 20, 23, 74–5, 91, 101, 149, 207 n.6, 209 n.33
Goethe 54, 64, 67–8, 156, 196 n.8
golem(s) 4, 19, 26, 92–3, 101–2, 105–6, 121, 126, 129, 162, 168, 177 n.15, 185 nn.9–10, 215 n.144, 216 n.147, 216 n.149

Gordin, Jacob, "Elisha ben Abuya" 16, 18, 23, 71–2, 169, 183 n.112, 203 n.15
  Akiva 71, 78, 88–9, 110, 123, 138
  ben Avuya 71–4, 202 n.14
  Eliezer 71–2
  Elishe 72–5, 201 n.1, 202 n.7
  "the incomprehensible Law" 187 n.44
  Meyer (Meir) 73
Grözinger, Klaus 74–5, 78–9, 81–3, 86
  Kafka and Kabbalah 192 n.25, 203 n.20
Guyer, Paul 177 n.31

halakhah/halakhic (law) 1, 12–16, 18–19, 24, 27, 30, 34–5, 37, 40, 41–2, 45, 49–50, 53, 55–60, 71, 73, 75–6, 81, 86, 93–4, 171, 212 n.78, 213 n.95
Hammer, Reuven, *Akiva Life, Legend, Legacy* 188 n.71
Hasidei Ashkenaz group 208 n.16, 235 n.67
Hasid/Hasidic/Hasidism 2, 14, 27, 34, 41, 51, 75–7, 81, 83, 85, 92–3, 157, 195 n.74, 204 n.45, 204 n.53, 206 n.101, 234 n.53
Hasiduth 92–3, 208 n.16, 208 n.21
Haskalah (Jewish Enlightenment) 13, 24, 44–6, 49, 51, 72–3, 195 n.73
The Heart and the Fountain 176 n.4, 191 n.23, 192 n.34, 199 n.56, 225 n.27, 236 n.80, 237 n.5
Hebrew Bible 9, 142, 169
Hegel, Georg Wilhelm Friedrich 18, 44, 178 n.45
Heine, Heinrich 18, 49, 53–64, 67–9, 99, 109, 123, 174, 196 n.1, 196 n.7
  Doktor Faust, A Dance Poem 53, 63–5, 69
  Faust 2, 18, 53, 63–8, 72, 99, 109, 155, 165, 175
  Mephistophela 64–7
  Exodus 60
  "faith" 56–7
  Halevi 53–8, 60–4, 68, 99, 174, 197 n.13, 198 n.32, 199 n.54
  Jehudah 54–6, 58–9, 63, 68–9

"Jehudah ben Halevi" 18, 53–63, 69, 109
Le Legende du Jean Faust 200 n.82
"Old-Chaldean squared-off letters" 54, 59, 61
"pillar of fire" 60, 63
"mystical Enlightenment" 62
The Power of Hell (*Der Höllenzwang*) 200 n.78
Romanzero 53–4, 62, 196 n.7
heretical kabbalah 13–21, 23, 26–7, 29–30, 32–3, 36–7, 39–40, 43, 45–7, 49–51, 53–4, 62, 68–9, 71, 74, 77, 80, 87–9, 91, 93–5, 98–9, 101–3, 105–7, 109, 123–4, 146, 148, 181 n.75, 181 n.77, 209 n.39. *See also* orthodox kabbalah/orthodoxy
heretics of innovation 17–18, 29, 33, 43, 46–9, 51
The Hidden God 8–9, 21, 115, 137, 143–4, 158–60, 179 n.57, 218 n.16, 228 n.89, 235 n.67
historical experience 1, 6, 13, 31
Hölderlin, Friedrich 230 n.25
"Half-Life" 145
Holocaust 1, 141, 148, 151–3, 155, 158, 163–4, 167, 192 n.31
Homer, *The Odyssey* 7–8
Eurykleia 7–8

Idel, Moshe
Absorbing Perfections. Kabbalah and Interpretation 179 n.55
The Mystical Experience in Abraham Abulafia 183 n.107
immanence 17, 30, 58–60, 62–4, 68–9, 88, 95, 99, 100–1, 106, 109, 113, 117–18, 143, 153, 157, 173–4
"incorporeal supernal lights" 96–7, 211 n.65
"inimitability" 21, 169–70, 172–4, 238 n.40
innovations 13, 15–18, 21, 29, 31, 33–4, 36, 39–44, 46–50, 55, 57, 59, 63–5, 67, 92–3, 99, 103, 106, 129, 156, 158, 169–70, 191 n.22, 192 n.31, 197 n.19, 208 n.15, 216 n.154
Isaacson, Jose 222 n.2

Jewish Mysticism 10, 15, 23, 40–1, 50, 71, 74, 126, 176 n.14, 179 n.57, 180 n.69, 234 n.53
Joris, Pierre 157–8, 163–4, 231 n.4, 231 n.10, 234 n.41
Judaic/Judaism 1, 3–4, 8, 10–13, 23–4, 26, 29, 32, 34, 36, 39–41, 43–5, 47, 50–1, 53–8, 61–2, 69, 71–2, 74–6, 78, 91, 94, 110, 143, 168, 180 n.70, 180 n.72
as epistemology 10, 12–14, 58, 92
"normative Judaism" 2, 18
Scholem on 209 n.37, 213 n.95

Kafka, Franz 5, 12, 14, 18, 21, 49, 105, 107–8, 126, 169–72, 181 n.76, 237 n.20
"Before the Law" 18–19, 75–89, 123, 169, 203 n.27, 206 n.99
"man from the country" 19, 76–86, 108–9, 146, 206 n.99, 208 n.23
"breakdown" 87–8, 169
"The Four who went to Pardes" 19, 23, 28, 71, 110, 169, 203 n.20, 206 nn.98–9
"interpretation" 87–8
"modernist kabbalah" 77
"pursuit" 88
The Trial 76, 83, 86, 203 n.27
"stereotypical obedience" 76, 81
Yiddishkeit 71–5
Kant, Immanuel 11, 18, 44, 46–7, 50, 62, 178 n.45, 180 n.74, 211 n.69
"subjective universalism" 219 n.23
kavvanah (intention) 33, 41–2, 80, 164
kelipot/kelipah 95–7, 99, 103, 171, 183 n.101, 202 n.3, 212 n.78, 224 n.23
kenoma 9, 175
Klüger, Ruth, *Still Alive* 232 n.26

Lacoue-Labarthe, Philippe 233 n.36
Lemkin, Rafael 234 n.37
Lenowitz, Harris 35–7, 188 n.67, 188 n.69, 189 n.80, 190 n.6

letter phenomenology 3–4, 15, 17, 19–20, 106, 109, 132, 140, 143, 164, 176 n.9
Levine, Madeline G. 126, 218 n.16
Leznai, Anna 188 n.64
liberation 1–2, 7, 13, 16–18, 28, 34–5, 44–50, 53, 57–60, 63–4, 68, 72–4, 81, 87, 97–8, 102, 109, 113, 122, 130, 147, 169, 174–5, 232 n.25
  cognitive 44, 46, 50
  imagined 44, 50, 189 n.79
  political 7, 44, 193 n.44
  subjective 44, 48–9, 63, 145
"lights" 97, 99
Lispector, Elisa, *No Exilio* 7
literary messiahs 167–8
literary prophets 169–75
literary representation 3, 7, 9
"living intuition" 11, 169–70, 173, 217 n.6, 228 n.84
Löwy, Isaac 71–2, 74–5, 86
  "pun" 203 n.17
Luria, Isaac 5, 13, 23, 36, 64, 76, 83, 91–2, 95–6, 114, 143, 146, 160, 174, 182 n.86, 183 n.101
  exile 91
  on "lights" 97, 99
  "transmigration of the soul" 76, 78–9, 126
"luster" 55, 57–60

Maciejko, Pawel 31–2, 35, 40–1, 44, 49, 187 n.54
  "Frankism" 190 n.8
  The Prophecies of Isaiah 193 n.43
  Sabbatian Heresy 181 n.75
Magid, Shaul 85, 204 n.53
  "soft antinomianism" 81
Markowski, Michal Pawel 210 n.43
Marranism 5, 192 n.36
masa duma 28–9, 188 n.69
materialization 13, 18–19, 29, 31, 65, 68, 83, 89, 93, 96–7, 110, 172–3, 175, 201 n.89
Matt, Daniel 42
  "Righteous One—Vitality of the Worlds" 42

matter 15–19, 25–6, 43, 51, 93–9, 101, 103–4, 108, 124, 131, 138, 147, 167–8, 185 n.10, 186 n.34, 215 n.123, 215 n.144
messiah 2, 13–14, 16, 20, 26–8, 30, 33, 35, 37, 39–40, 47, 50, 62–3, 89, 145, 175
  heretic 167
  literary 167–8
messianic/messianism 3–4, 13–18, 21, 23–4, 27, 37, 39–40, 42, 44, 46–51, 62, 69, 72, 75, 89, 108–9, 168–9, 171, 173–5, 195 n.73, 198 n.22, 213 n.95
  heretical 72
  infinite 87
  messianic apocalypticism 213 n.95
  messianic materialism 15, 17, 37, 39, 94, 170
  optimistic 172
metamorphosis 14, 21, 25–6, 32, 65–6, 72, 75, 78–9, 101, 105, 109, 113, 127, 136, 167, 186 n.34, 188 n.67, 194 n.65, 205 n.69
metaphysics 4, 10–14, 39, 47, 91, 170, 173, 179 n.63, 187 n.49, 188 n.67, 217 n.6
Metatron 4, 60, 168, 220 n.57, 237 n.5
metempsychosis (transmigration) 78–9, 98, 109, 126, 167, 211 n.77, 212 n.79, 212 n.81
Mickiewicz, Adam 49, 194 n.55
midrash 8, 44, 223 n.6
mimesis/mimetic 1, 3–4, 6–10, 16–17, 35, 37, 53–4, 56, 59, 61, 63, 66–7, 72, 93, 102–3, 106, 109, 116, 136, 151, 154, 156–8, 163, 179 n.55
  mimetic representation 1, 3, 6–7, 10, 35, 56, 103, 155–6, 168
mitzvah (duty) 29, 172, 238 n.27
modernity 2–5, 10–11, 13–14, 18–19, 21, 24, 41, 51, 72, 74–5, 77, 89, 170, 172, 204 n.43
Moses 27, 29–30, 32, 42, 54, 60, 79, 86, 147, 199 n.53. *See also* Torah
Mulisch, Harry, *The Discovery of Heaven* 20, 145–9, 174

mystical experience 24, 74, 93, 170–1
mysticism 1, 4–5, 23, 41. *See also* Jewish Mysticism

The Name 110–11
"the name of God" 74, 89, 92, 110, 122, 131, 138, 140, 142, 145, 158, 160, 186 n.36, 223 n.8, 228 n.83, 235 n.58
nefilim (fallen) 36, 189 n.87
Neuerung (innovation) 41, 63
"new creation" 10, 15, 19, 59, 104, 123, 126–7, 225 n.26
new kabbalah 5, 11, 14, 45, 50, 89, 237 n.16. *See also* old kabbalah
Nigleh/Nistar 217 n.5, 217 n.10 (Ch 6)
nihilism 13, 76, 88, 105, 175, 198 n.36, 221 n.80, 225 n.26
nothingness 14–15, 87, 94–5, 106, 117, 143–5, 151, 160, 164–5, 172, 217 n.6, 235 n.63, 236 n.91. *See also* Ein-Sof/Eyn Sof/En Sof/En Soph (Nothingness) (אֵין-סוֹף)
"novel intuition" 5, 11–12, 24, 41, 43, 58, 139, 168, 173, 180 n.70, 221 n.80

"object of contemplation" 50, 117
"object of knowledge" 11–12, 169, 173, 180 n.70, 181 n.83, 198 n.38, 218 n.18
old kabbalah 36, 51, 96, 187 n.45. *See also* new kabbalah
ontology 3, 5, 7–9, 18, 21, 24, 27, 32, 47, 54–6, 58, 62–3, 66, 89, 115–16, 137, 147, 159–60, 175, 189 n.87
  human 8–9, 27, 62, 130, 149, 175
  literary 4, 9, 21, 109
  poetic 60, 157
  sacred 15, 173
orthodox kabbalah/orthodoxy 13–15, 20–1, 29, 39–40, 45, 53–4, 63, 73–4, 77, 84, 86, 96–7, 103, 106, 123, 195 n.74, 210 n.48. *See also* heretical kabbalah
"other path" 14, 34, 36, 46, 75, 97, 217 n.11
"the other side" (*sitra ara*) 13, 16–17, 24, 35–6, 55, 80, 85–6, 91–3, 97–8, 124, 127

Panas, Wladyslaw 210 n.43
  Księga blasku. Traktat o kabale w prozie Brunona Schulza 207 n.6
paradise 14–16, 19, 23, 27, 36, 44, 47, 50, 56, 66–7, 73, 75, 85–6, 91, 97–8, 110, 123–4, 144, 148, 172, 214 n.104
Pardes 23–4, 28, 34, 58, 67, 71, 74, 87–8, 110, 184 n.7, 206 n.85
  Akiva 23–4, 34
  ben Abuya/Aher 16, 19, 21, 23–4, 28, 30, 35, 47, 50, 66–7, 72, 74–5, 87–9, 109, 115, 147, 169, 175, 187 n.44, 195 n.70, 217–18 n.11
  ben Azzai 23, 30
  ben Zoma 23, 30
  "The Four who went to Pardes" 16, 18–9, 23, 28–9, 47, 71, 110, 169, 179 n.54, 179 n.56, 203 n.20, 212 n.98
PaRDeS 56, 79–81, 83–4, 87–9, 110, 123, 138, 147, 174, 206 n.99, 228 n.82
  d'rash 79, 110, 184 n.7
  peshat/pshat 79, 110, 184 n.7, 220 n.39
  remez 79, 110, 184 n.7
  sod (secret) 40, 79–80, 110, 115, 124, 184 n.7
"people of the Land" 77–8
Pérez, Rolando 218 n.18
persecution 2, 7, 17–18, 28, 31, 35, 48, 51, 72, 189 n.79, 200 n.75, 202 n.11
pleroma 8–9, 77, 114, 134, 140, 165, 175, 179 n.56
poetry/*poesie* 18–19, 21, 49, 53, 56–64, 67–9, 95, 98–9, 104, 109, 153, 155–8, 164–5, 174–5, 197 n.15, 201 n.89, 210 n.45
Potok, Chaim 196 n.2
  Baal Shem Tov 81
Prague Circle 18, 39–40, 43–8, 50, 190 n.1, 190 n.8, 193 n.43
principia individuationis (principles of individuation) 29, 44
principium individuationis (principle of individuation) 99, 101
profane 1, 15–17, 40, 43, 48, 50, 88–9, 91, 93–4, 116–17, 120, 170–1, 173–5, 198 n.22, 237 n.20

"prophetic ecstasy" 130, 132, 175, 223 n.8
"prophetic kabbalah" 129–30, 224 n.15
prostak (simpleton) 34–5, 50, 80, 91, 188 n.69, 191 n.22

rabbis/rabbinic 11, 13, 27, 31, 33–4, 40, 43–5, 47–9, 57, 72–3, 75, 86, 157, 160, 166, 189 n.85, 206 n.101
"radical emancipation" 17, 95. *See also* emancipation
redemption 1, 3, 5, 9, 11, 13–21, 23, 27–8, 31–7, 39, 45–51, 56–7, 63, 67–9, 74–5, 80, 83, 85–6, 91–2, 95, 103, 106, 108–9, 143, 145, 153, 160, 163–4, 171–2, 175, 186 n.26
repetition 87, 106, 126, 129, 138, 144, 147, 154, 162, 168–9, 171–2, 220 n.42, 223 n.5
reshimu (residue) 97–8, 114, 170, 172, 183 n.101
revelation 8–9, 12, 15, 18–20, 23, 27, 30, 33, 35, 39–41, 44, 46–7, 49, 54–5, 57–8, 62–4, 68, 72, 80–1, 86–9, 91, 98, 103–4, 106–7, 110–11, 114–15, 117–18, 120–2, 124, 134–5, 138–40, 146–7, 149, 157, 165, 169, 171, 174, 224 n.22
new revelations 13, 35, 39, 42, 50, 86, 110, 170
Rhineland Hasids 41, 92–3, 102–3, 157, 199 n.55, 208 n.16, 225 n.25, 235 n.64
Rosenzweig, Franz 2, 192 n.34, 225 n.25

Sabbatian/Sabbatianism 5, 13–14, 25, 27, 31–3, 36, 39, 43–8, 51, 62, 77, 81, 85, 109, 189 n.85, 190 n.1, 191 n.21, 193 n.43, 194 n.57. *See also* Zvi, Shabbatai
sacred texts 2, 8, 33, 40–3, 80, 93, 118, 223 n.6
salvation 30, 35, 75
Sammons, Jeffrey L. 53–4, 59, 62, 198 n.30
Sanatorium under the Sign of the Hourglass (Schulz) 19, 113, 210 n.46
"The Age of Genius" 117, 122

"the Authentic" 121–2, 124
"The Book" 19–20, 113–23, 126–7, 217 n.2
"Authentic Nothingness" 127
"cluster of melodies" 125–7, 144
"immensity of the transcendent" 113–16
Josef (fictional character) 19–20, 113–15, 121–7
"Loneliness" 20, 126
nieskończonych 125–6
"pulsing light" 124–5
Scholem, Gershom 1, 4–5, 10, 12–13, 15, 41–2, 46–7, 49, 51, 55, 59, 75, 77–9, 81, 83, 86–7, 92–4, 96–7, 139, 144, 169–74, 177 n.16, 179 n.63, 180 n.67, 180 n.70, 180 n.74
on Abulafia's "absolute objects" 131
"The Adornment of Days" 182 n.99
Alchemy and Kabbalah 196 n.8
on attributes of four basic worlds 96
"dogmatic object of knowledge" 11–12, 14, 24, 58, 77, 139, 170–1, 173, 180 n.70, 217 n.6
on *Hasiduth* 92–3
human existence and dimension of Divine 131
"The Idea of the Golem" 185 n.10
on Judaism 209 n.37, 213 n.95
languages 181 n.83
"light of the canonical" 169
Major Trends of Jewish Mysticism 5, 11, 234 n.53
Tikkunei Ha-Zohar 210 n.51
on transcendence 24
"structures of beings" 5, 37, 42, 63, 93, 100–1, 144, 152–3, 160, 215 n.123, 230 n.24
Schonfeld, Eli 77–8, 83
Schuchard, Marsha Keith 196 n.7
Schulz, Bruno 98–9, 102–6, 116–17, 126, 129, 168, 174–5, 179 n.62, 188 n.74, 213 n.101
about human existence 126
Cinnamon Shops (*see Cinnamon Shops* (Schulz))
on human interiority 126

"interminable stories" 20, 125–7, 145, 165, 174, 210 n.46
Sanatorium under the Sign of the Hourglass (*see Sanatorium under the Sign of the Hourglass* (Schulz))
Schulz's use of *Book of Creation* (*Sefer Yetsirah*) (*see Book of Creation* (*Sefer Yetsirah*))
"unfinished stories" 54, 104–5, 125–7, 144–5, 165, 174, 210 n.46, 222 n.84
secular Jew 11, 43, 45, 49, 72, 78, 85–6, 209 n.33
secular kabbalah 1–2, 18, 51, 53, 55, 63, 69, 170–1, 173–4
secular literature 4, 15, 63, 182 n.90
secular texts 1–2, 5, 10, 14, 46–8, 57, 175, 202 n.12
Semprun, Jorge, *Literature or Life* 236 n.92
sensus communis 44, 61, 81, 117–18, 138, 189 n.79, 195 n.73, 227 n.77
sferot/sfera 5, 42, 55, 79, 145, 148, 162, 188 n.64, 192 n.31, 214 n.110, 215 n.129, 223 n.8, 225 n.24, 227 n.72, 230 n.15, 235 n.60
sefira tiferet 79
sefirot 15, 57, 96–7, 137, 145, 223 n.8
sin 14, 17, 28–31, 33, 36, 46, 50, 53, 67, 72, 94, 97–8, 195 n.70, 197 n.15, 202 n.3, 204 n.53
Sinnlichkeit ("the sensual world") 44, 154–6, 158, 165, 182 n.91
soul 10, 26, 31, 33, 55, 60–3, 66, 78–9, 91, 107, 109, 114, 120, 123, 126, 130–1, 137, 144, 157, 160, 162, 185 n.11, 199 n.50, 210 n.48, 211 n.77, 223 n.8, 224 n.11, 225 n.34, 235 n.65
spirit(s) 33, 48, 56–8, 61–3, 68, 95, 98, 101–4, 160, 168
spiritual/spiritualism 4, 53, 68, 96–7, 109, 172, 196 n.7, 198 n.38, 203 n.15
Steiner, George 2, 76
subjective experience 2, 47, 49, 58, 60, 63
subjective universalism 219 n.23
sublimity 2, 14, 46, 56, 60–2, 93, 144, 233 n.32
Suchoff, David 76–7
"*sui generis*" 173
supernal lights 97, 124, 213 n.102, 219 n.18

Talmud/Talmudic 3, 8, 13, 16, 23–4, 26, 28, 34, 48, 50, 55–6, 58, 71–5, 77–8, 110, 118, 184 n.5, 187 n.49, 198 n.26, 202 n.4
tanna/tannaim 23–4, 28, 34, 78, 110, 169, 187 n.49, 202 n.14
Taubes, Jacob 188 n.59
"inwardness/outwardness" 178 n.45
tehiru ("void") 15, 21, 36, 95, 97–8, 98, 124, 146, 164–5, 173–4, 183 n.101, 210 n.48, 212 n.78
tikkun/tikkunim (repair) 14, 23, 32–3, 35, 37, 47, 68, 97, 120, 146–7, 160, 162, 166, 168, 171, 174, 183 n.118
time and space 3, 12–13, 15, 19–20, 24, 30, 46, 59, 111, 113, 116, 121–2, 130–1, 136–7, 149, 155, 210 n.48
Tokarczuk, Olga 17, 167–8, 174, 213 n.101
The Books of Jacob (*see The Books of Jacob* (Tokarczuk))
Torah 8, 12–13, 27, 29, 31, 34, 36, 42, 50–1, 54, 56, 58, 68, 72–3, 77–8, 80–1, 83, 85–6, 91–3, 98–9, 106, 109–10, 114, 130, 142, 174, 182 n.86, 219–20 n.39
"bridegroom of the Torah" 33
"halls of Torah" 82–3, 88
"letter of the Torah" 93
Torah of *Atzilut* 27–30, 32–3, 83, 182 n.86
Torah of *Beriah* 27–30, 34
"Torah of the World of Emanations" 27–8
transcendence 1–2, 5–6, 8–9, 12, 14–15, 19, 24, 33, 46–7, 49–51, 57–60, 63–9, 72, 88, 91–4, 100–1, 104–5, 108, 110, 114–15, 117, 129, 134, 154–6, 165, 169, 174, 233 n.36
transcendental flow (*shefa*) 130, 137, 143, 229 n.7

transgression 1, 3, 13–14, 17, 24–6, 28, 31, 49–50, 62, 66, 74, 92, 94–5, 97–8, 102, 106, 122, 134, 215 n.125
"Tree of Life" 55, 79, 162, 192 n.31, 202 n.3
tsaddik/tzaddik 42
tzimtzum/tsimtsum 64, 95–6, 114–15, 124, 143, 183 n.101

Utterback, Camille, "Text Rain" 142

Valabregue, Sandra 23
  "Philosophy, Heresy, and Kabbalah's Counter-Theology" 184 n.5
"void". *See tehiru* ("void")
von Geldern, Simon 53
von Hönigsberg, Low Enoch 39, 43, 45–8, 190 n.5, 191 n.15, 192 n.37, 193 nn.38–9, 194 n.59
von Schoenfeld, Thomas. *See* Dubrushka, Moses

Wehle, Gottfried 48, 50, 194 n.49, 202 n.11
Wehle, Jonas Beer 18, 37, 39–40, 43–51, 73
Wienewska, Celina (*Sanatorium*) 125–6
Wiesel, Elie 143–4, 149
Wissenschaft des Judentums project 10–11, 47, 156, 179 n.65, 195 n.69, 195 n.74, 233 n.37

Wolfson, Elliot 227 n.83
word of God 33, 132
"work of creation" ("*ma'aseh bereshit*") 12, 181 n.83
works of art 1, 3, 12, 19, 29, 65, 68, 88, 91, 93, 101, 104, 106–7, 154, 170, 172
"write one's own Torah" 12, 29, 43
"Written Torah" 29, 79

Yezirah (world of formation) 96

Žáček, Vaclav 39–40, 43–5, 190 n.5, 191 n.21, 192 n.37, 193 n.38
Zardaya, Concha 66, 201 n.89
Zionism 87, 187 n.49
The Zohar/Zoharist 2, 20, 29, 36, 41–3, 55–7, 71, 93, 95–6, 114, 118, 129, 132, 137, 146, 157, 163, 169–70, 180 n.67, 181 n.84, 183 n.118, 192 n.26, 199 n.44, 218 n.18
The Book of Radiance (*prawdiziwa ksiega blasku*) 183 n.118
Zunz, Leopold 47, 179 n.65, 191 n.15
Zvi, Shabbatai 13, 16, 23, 26, 32–3, 40, 45, 62, 72, 143, 182 n.91, 202 n.7

www.ingramcontent.com/pod-product-compliance
Lightning Source LLC
Chambersburg PA
CBHW070026010526
44117CB00011B/1730